M000035878

Mormon Lives

Mormon Lives

A Year in the Elkton Ward

Susan Buhler Taber

University of Illinois Press
Urbana and Chicago

Publication of this work was supported in part by a grant
from the Lilly Endowment.

© 1993 by the Board of Trustees of the University of Illinois
Manufactured in the United States of America
C 5 4 3 2 1

This book is printed on acid-free paper.

Library of Congress Cataloging-in-Publication Data

Taber, Susan Buhler, 1947–
    Mormon Lives : a year in the Elkton Ward / Susan
Buhler Taber.
        p. cm.
    ISBN 0-252-01966-0 (alk. paper)
    1. Church of Jesus Christ of Latter-Day Saints. Elkton
Ward.   2. Elkton Region (Md.)—Religious life and customs.
I. Title.
BX8615.M3T33 1993
289.3'75238—dc20   92-15573
                                                  CIP

Contents

Acknowledgments

I express deep appreciation to the other members of the Record Year Committee for their work in gathering these materials and for their encouragement and friendship. Elena Larsen, Blane Parker, and Roy Queenan of the committee took the photographs. The photographs are courtesy of Brigham Young University Special Collections and Manuscripts. I thank Richard and Claudia Bushman for creating and sustaining the Record Year project and my family who tolerated (as Robert Taber, age four, said in 1988) my "many days" and nights engaged in this project. I would like to thank the Lilly Endowment and the Family and Community History Center of Brigham Young University for their financial support of this project. Thanks go to those who read the manuscript and offered suggestions for its improvement: Claudia and Richard Bushman, Nancy Harward, Sylvia Mabey, Kristina Martin, Julie Ridge, Jan Shipps, Charlotte Sheehan, John Sillito, Linda Sillitoe, and Douglass Taber. Most of all I thank the members of the Elkton Ward who shared their lives so freely and candidly.

Introduction

This book is an outgrowth of a larger project conducted
within the Elkton Ward of the Church of Jesus Christ of Latter-day Saints.
Richard Bushman, the bishop of the Elkton Ward and a professor of history
at the University of Delaware, and his wife, Claudia, a historian and executive
director of the Delaware Heritage Commission, had long wanted to make a collection of materials relating to the functioning of a ward, the basic ecclesiastical
and social unit of the LDS Church, as a resource for historians of the future.
Bishop Bushman had obtained permission from the church hierarchy to conduct the project over a one-year period—as an unofficial church project and as
long as working on it didn't cause members of the committee to neglect regular
church callings. He selected church members to form the Elkton Ward Record
Year Committee, which would be responsible for the organization.

As we met monthly throughout the spring we decided to collect various types
of materials. Claudia Bushman took on what we called "Scenes." She assigned
a member of the committee to write a description of every special event that
took place during the year as well as of the routine events, such as choir practice, sacrament meeting, and Sunday school classes. Lee Anderson and Richard
Bushman designed a survey of attitudes and beliefs that all members could fill
out and return anonymously. Wayne Larsen was in charge of statistical analy-
ses. Elena Larsen, ward historian, was in charge of collecting and preserving all
the records that would be assembled. She tried to collect every piece of paper
that was handed out each week—announcement sheets, class handouts, invitations to ward activities. She also tape-recorded two sacrament meetings each
month. In addition she and Roy Queenan photographed as many events as
possible.

Lynne Whitney volunteered to interview Cloyd Mullins, who was the president of the congregation when it was the Elkton Branch. She also asked ward
members to keep journals of their church activities during the year and to
submit them as part of the record. Douglas Ridge was called to be the ward

clerk and to keep minutes of all sacrament and priesthood meetings as well as minutes of the bishopric and ward leadership meetings.

Henry Tingey, the Sunday school president, and Julie Ridge provided invaluable advice and help in many of our projects. Henry Tingey allowed the committee to take over the adult Sunday school class once a month to lead discussions on various topics pertaining to church issues. In these classes the adult members of the ward were asked to write a response (anonymously) to questions such as "What is an active member?" "Is there room for individual flexibility in response to church teachings?" or "What should be the purpose of our ward?" A member of the committee collected the written responses and then led a discussion about the topic.

The committee also decided that we should obtain oral histories from as many of the ward members as were willing to be interviewed, and I agreed to make up a set of questions to be used. The interview sessions were subsequently designed so that ward members would talk about their public and private lives, both within and outside the church. The four-page questionnaire served as a guide but we felt free to depart from it to pursue interesting avenues. Most interviews lasted two hours, though some were four or five hours in length and a few took eight hours.

We asked questions pertaining to eight areas of interest. First, we asked individuals to relate how they came to be members of the Elkton Ward, which included why they lived in the geographical area as well as how they came to be members of the church.

The second group of questions was related to the individuals' backgrounds. We asked about the families in which they had been children, the occupations of their parents, the schools they attended, their experiences as members of other churches, and how they met their spouses.

The third section included questions about working life: occupation, school, and volunteer work. The questions invited people to describe how they chose their occupations, how they learned to do their work, and how they felt about their occupations.

The fourth section asked about church work. We asked people to describe their present and past church callings, including missionary service, and to reflect on the effect of church service both on their personal life and on their relationships with family, friends, neighbors, and co-workers.

The fifth section of the interview dealt with personal and family life in the context of the LDS Church. We asked things such as how the individuals' present families different from their families of birth, how and when they decided to have children, and their aspirations for their own children.

In the sixth section we asked the subjects to describe the impact, if any, of various church practices and beliefs on their lives. We also asked questions such as "How are your beliefs different from your parents' beliefs?" and "Which doctrines or practices of the church have been difficult for you to accept?"

The seventh section asked individuals to describe people or ideas that had been influential in their lives. One question in this section asked if the person could identify a turning point in his or her life. Another asked the individual to describe an occasion when a prayer had been answered.

The last section was called "A Witness of a Changing Time." We asked individuals to identify the greatest advances or inventions during their lifetimes and to identify changes in the church that had occurred during their lives. We also asked them what they thought the role of the church should be in society and the world.

Jean Bingham conducted half the interviews and also suggested that we produce a yearbook. Elena Larsen and Anne Mace created and printed a yearbook in 1986. Diane Day Howard and Debora Ennis joined us after the year was officially over, but helped us finish collecting interviews, survey information, and other materials.

Although some of us had specific assignments for certain aspects of the Record Year, we all worked together on many of the projects. We all wrote Scenes and we each took a turn leading the Sunday school discussion. Although Jean Bingham and I conducted most of the interviews, Claudia Bushman, Lynne Whitney, and Debora Ennis also helped. Lynne Whitney, Elena Larsen, Ellen Lilley, Deborah Johnston, and I transcribed the interviews from tape recordings to computer disks. Henry Tingey and Wayne Larsen helped us learn to use computers and to transfer our files from one system to another. Richard Bushman kept a confidential bishop's journal, and other members of the ward also kept and turned in journals.

The Record Year was from September 1, 1984, to August 31, 1985. We completed the survey in October 1985 and the interviewing by March 1986. All the tapes were transcribed by August 1986. In August 1989 all the gathered materials were deposited in the archives at Brigham Young University, to be made available to scholars after twenty-five years.

During one of the committee's monthly meetings, Richard Bushman suggested that we should not limit our mission to depositing our records in an archive but that we should write a book based on our materials. The committee discussed what might be included in such a book and decided that it should be written for a wider audience than the Elkton Ward. In March 1985 Richard Bushman asked me to think about how a book could be organized from our materials. I suggested that it could be organized around the events that occurred during the Record Year. Each chapter would describe one or more events as a context for the profiles of individuals who were involved in those events. About a week after the meeting at which I presented this idea, Richard Bushman asked me if I would write the book, and I agreed to do so.

This book is partially an attempt to place the information obtained during the Record Year in a larger context and to share our stories with the rest of the world. The Scenes written by members of the Record Year Committee served as source material for the narrative backgrounds of many of the chapters. Jean Bingham wrote a description of Primary that I included in her oral history. I also included part of Claudia Bushman's description of the brass ensemble and part of Julie Ridge's discussion of her duties as Relief Society president in their oral histories.

My personal journal of my activities during the year was useful in helping me establish the chronology of events. I also had access to the results of the survey and the written responses to the Sunday school discussions. These helped me keep the ward members and their beliefs in perspective.

The oral histories that appear in this book were derived from the transcripts of the interviews. After reading the interviews, I indexed them by topic. As I began to write the book, I made a list of events that could be included in the story of the year and selected individuals who were associated with those events, either because of their participation in them or because of their discussion of topics directly related to the events. From the transcript of each interview I selected passages that I thought evoked the individual's personal voice, described his or her role in the ward organization and experiences in the Elkton Ward or other wards, or expressed beliefs or opinions that seemed central to the person's identity as a Mormon.

The order of the material as it appears in each oral history is not always identical to the order in which it was stated in the interview. That is, I sometimes selected material relevant to a topic from several places within the interview and grouped those selections together in one section. Though I have altered the interviews for punctuation, grammar, and clarity I have not indicated these changes. In this way the flow of the personal narratives is not interrupted but the integrity of the material is retained.

This book is primarily an attempt to portray what it is like to be a member of the Church of Jesus Christ of Latter-day Saints at a particular place and time. The Elkton Ward extends from Red Mill Road in Newark, Delaware, thirty miles west to the Susquehanna River and from the Pennsylvania state line to Blackbird Creek, thirty miles south. Its boundaries include a large automobile assembly plant, Du Pont company research laboratories, the University of Delaware, an Avon plant, and other factories and businesses as well. The members vary in their backgrounds, educational levels, income, and occupations. Most of them, however, are converts. At the time of the Record Year two-thirds of the active participants were not born into member families, though nearly all of these came from a religious background. Members of the ward were strikingly youthful. Half the members were between twenty-six and forty years old. Only 8 percent were over fifty but 28 percent were between six and fifteen. The ward was primarily composed of people born in the area. Fifty-six percent of the members grew up in Pennsylvania, New Jersey, Delaware, or Maryland. Only 11 percent were born in Utah or Idaho.

These characteristics make the Elkton Ward different from most wards, especially those in Utah and other western states, where ward populations tend to be more homogeneous. This portrait of the Elkton Ward provides an opportunity to see a wide range of belief in Mormonism and to see the religion as a larger cultural movement. It also offers a window on the American society in which the members and their neighbors live.

A typical week for a Mormon family in the Elkton Ward begins with attendance at the three-hour block of meetings held each Sunday morning from 9:30 to 12:30. Some members of the family may have arrived at church at 7:00 or 8:00 to participate in bishopric, ward welfare committee, priesthood executive committee, or ward correlation council meeting. Other members participate in choir practice, which begins at 8:30. The ward joins together for sacrament meeting, the LDS worship service, which is followed by separate meetings for children, teenagers, and adults.

Either on Sunday afternoon or Monday evening families are expected to hold family home evening. Families decide on the format of these meetings, which may include coordination of the family calendar for the week, assignment of chores, discussion of issues of family behavior, a spiritual lesson, or a recreational activity. Monday evenings are reserved by church policy for these meetings, but many members hold the meetings on Sunday because school or community events often conflict with family time on Mondays.

The family's church activities during the rest of the week depend on the ages and interests of the family members. Weekly activities for the teenagers are held on Wednesday nights. Boy Scouts meet at the church on Wednesday nights, and Cub Scouts meet on Tuesday afternoons or evenings at the leaders' homes. High school students living in or near Newark may attend seminary, a scripture study class that meets daily from 6:00 to 6:45 A.M. before school. During the fall and winter interested teens and adults practice basketball one evening and on Saturday mornings.

Some activities follow a monthly schedule. Women meet one Wednesday evening a month for a dinner and homemaking meeting. Both men and women go out once or twice a month for several hours in order to visit the families to which they are assigned as home teachers or visiting teachers, respectively. Firesides for the young people are held at least one Sunday evening each month. Activities for all the youth of the Wilmington Stake, which covers the entire Delmarva Peninsula, are held about once a month. These include dances, recreational events, service projects, and religious activities. Social activities for just the adults of the ward or for the entire ward occur about once a month. These include dinners sponsored by various organizations, picnics, holiday parties, and programs.

During the Record Year some ward members spent several Saturdays involved in fund-raising activities. These included cutting and delivering firewood and making Easter eggs from fondant. Twice during the year the ward members filled eight-hour shifts at a cannery in New Jersey. Other activities involved some members in intense activity for several weeks at a time. September's luau and December's road show required weeks of rehearsals and involved many ward members.

To portray what it is like to be Mormon, I have chosen to use the oral histories as the substance of this book. The format of the interview was the perfect vehicle for uncovering the lives of these people because speaking about themselves comes naturally to them through their activities in the church. Verbalization of beliefs and experiences is encouraged of all members. Not only is one Sunday a month set aside for them to stand and extemporaneously bear witness of their beliefs but members, rather than clergy, offer all the prayers and give all the prepared speeches during sacrament meeting. Additionally, most active members attend or teach two or more classes each week in which discussion is encouraged. Accustomed as they are to discussing their beliefs, Mormons often slip into standard patterns of expression. At some point in each interview, however, we struck gold—when the individual clearly expressed thoughts, opinions, experiences, and beliefs from his or her unique perspective. As members candidly recounted their struggles, their victories, and their disappointments in the church and in life there was often pain and confusion, but also nobility and courage.

Each profile in this book, then, attempts to capture the personal voice of its subject. Because Mormonism is a religion of community as well as of personal belief, the book also attempts to show the interactions among the members of the Elkton Ward and their effects upon each other. The profiles in each chapter have been included not only for what they reveal about the individuals but also for the institutional or formal roles of those individuals within the Elkton Ward. Latter-day Saint wards are kept small so that each participating adult member may have an official calling, or responsibility, in the church organization. These callings include the bishopric, presidencies of various organizations, teachers of children and adults, recreation leaders, secretaries, clerks, and librarians. Members, thus, relate to each other not only informally through friendship, neighborliness, or proximity but also through being called upon to work with each other in various ways. Each of the chapters that follow portrays a blend of personal and private experience with members' formal roles and experiences within the ward structure.

Another reason for incorporating multiple centers of consciousness in the book is to accommodate the wide variety of opinions and beliefs held by this community of Mormons. Although many Mormons accept the authority of the church in matters of diet, dress, and sexual behavior, willingly pay 10 percent of their income in tithing, and believe in following the counsel of the prophet, Mormon belief and activity in the church requires the working out of a dialectic between two of the religion's fundamental principles—free agency and obedience to authority. For example, the length, format, frequency, and content of weekly church meetings are prescribed by church headquarters in Salt Lake City. At the same time, all the work of the Elkton Ward is carried out by individuals who accept the responsibility for the calling and report only to the bishop or to their organization's president. Members have widely varying opinions on how much they can or should rely on God to plan the size and timing of their families, to make financial decisions, or to decide how much time they should spend on church work. Other differences of opinion include the inerrancy of scripture, creationism versus evolution, and the role of women in the church and in society. By allowing members of the ward, including myself, to speak in their own voices, I have tried to portray how members confront and resolve this dialectic.

Much of this confrontation and resolution involved a process of self-definition and redefinition, especially for converts. For some, accepting the Word of Wisdom and giving up smoking, tea, coffee, or alcohol was central to that redefinition. Others found that they had to find a way to accommodate policies or doctrines that were personally repugnant to them, such as the church's former policy that black men could not hold the priesthood. Many of the profiles, thus, whether of lifelong members or converts, describe various ways of defining oneself as a Mormon, of becoming Mormon.

Belief and activity in the church are two other ways in which members define themselves as Mormons. Often the two are thought of as being perfectly correlated, but we found this was not always true. There were a number of members who expressed strong belief in the doctrines of the church and in its claim to be the "only true church on the face of the earth" who did not participate at all in the weekly activities. There were others who, while active participants in the congregation, felt that their views diverged from "acceptable" Mormon belief. Further, we found that only about 35 percent of the baptized members actively participate. The best predictor of activity is whether or not the member is married—regardless of the spouse's membership. Activity in the Elkton Ward seems to be less appealing to single members, at least partially because family-related activities play such a major role.

Partly because only male members are ordained to the priesthood and because the church leaders counsel women to stay at home with their children, the role of women was seen by many members to be problematic. Some ward members felt that other members blithely disregarded church teachings while others frankly looked forward to the day when women would be given priesthood authority. The inequity that most seemed to bother women was the policy that allowed men whose spouses were not members of the church to receive their endowments in the temple but did not allow women in similar situations to do so, even if their husbands did not object. This policy was changed by the first presidency of the church in 1986.

Many members also had to confront the acceptance of black members of the church. Many told of their pleasure when the change of policy to give black men the priesthood was announced, but one person felt that the change in policy was a denial of an eternal theological stance. A former Elders' Quorum president told of chastising some members of the ward for telling racist jokes, and some of the youth did not welcome black teenagers. This is probably at least partially due to leftover sentiments from slavery. Delaware and Maryland, which make up the major section of the Elkton Ward, were slave states; as recently as the 1950s it was impossible for a black person to use a public restroom or obtain a drink of water in downtown Newark, Delaware.

I believe much of the candor in the life stories presented here is because the material was gathered by an insider rather than an outside observer. Although my views of the LDS Church and the Elkton Ward are colored by my experience as a member, the views of any researcher are colored by experience. I have, as an adult, belonged to nine different wards in Utah, California, New Jersey, New York City, Wisconsin, and Tennessee before coming to the Elkton Ward. Also, coming to know and appreciate members of many other churches in various parts of the country has given me a certain breadth of perspective and insight into my own church. I also had a sense of where the difficulties and strengths were likely to be found in Mormon experience.

Despite my role and that of the other interviewers as insiders, some member of the church chose to have pseudonyms rather than have their names published. Those whose names are pseudonyms are Lynne Whitney and her husband and children, Bill, Elizabeth, Stephen, Jane, and John; Robert and Linda Hansen; Carol Beatty and her family; Richard King; and Barbara Bowes. Only two members refused to be interviewed.

A number of ward members do not appear in this book; there was not room for everyone. It was also impossible to include many experiences I personally found fascinating. These I leave to the historians of the future. I hope that this book gives a sense of what it was like to be a Mormon in 1985.

Fast and Testimony Meeting

1

The Elkton Ward meetinghouse is caught between residential and industrial Elkton, Maryland. The white frame church on the corner of Elkton Boulevard and William Street faces an empty lot, beyond which are a state highway and the Four Corners Bar and Grill. On the other side of the gravel parking lot are railroad tracks and a trucking company. Across Elkton Boulevard and behind the church property there are small frame houses, some with neatly kept flower gardens in the front yards. Next to the church the former parsonage (known as "the little house") has been pressed into service for library and classroom space.

On September 2, 1984, the Elkton Ward, like every other ward in the church, held fast and testimony meeting. On the first Sunday of each month members are expected to come to church fasting and to give to the bishop a fast offering equal to at least the cost of two meals. Bishop Richard Bushman began the meeting by making announcements, which were followed by an opening hymn and an opening prayer. Then William Meekins IV, almost two months old, was carried to the front of the chapel to receive the collective blessing of his family and his church. Four generations of his family live in the wards comprising the Wilmington Stake. His great-grandfather, both grandfathers, three great-uncles, two longtime friends of the family, and his father gathered in a circle and supported the baby on their outstretched hands as William Meekins, Jr., the paternal grandfather, prayed. After giving the baby his name, his grandfather blessed him to live a good life, follow the commandments, be faithful in the church, and be married in the temple.

After the congregation partook of bread and water in similitude of the Last Supper, Bishop Bushman stood at the pulpit to bear his testimony. On other Sundays prepared sermons or talks are delivered by ward members, but on this Sunday members are to speak spontaneously as moved by the Holy Ghost. The bishop reminded the congregation that this Sunday was the beginning of the

Record Year project. "I hope that this project will be a blessing to our ward. Many records will be kept. There are marvelous things which happen in the lives of our members every day. To lose such accounts would be a terrible tragedy. These records should be written to help those in the future understand us and our times."

He then invited the members of the congregation to stand and bear their testimonies. A few minutes later Wayne Morris strode to the front. He expressed his conviction that the Record Year would be a benefit to him and to the other members of the ward.

"No longer will I be just a cipher in the records of the church," he said, "but my life will be recorded for the benefit of posterity. Wayne Morris will be known as a member of the Elkton Ward."

Wayne Larsen came forward next. He said he appreciated the help he had received from the ward members since moving into the area five months earlier and that he had enjoyed cutting firewood from Henry Tingey's property for the Boy Scouts' fund-raising project the day before. He concluded his remarks by bearing his testimony that the scriptures are true.

At 10:40, the scheduled end of the meeting, Edna Young rushed to the front of the chapel. Her remarks indicated the complexity of family relationships within the congregation. She congratulated her twelve-year-old nephew, Aaron McVicker, who had been sustained that morning to be ordained a deacon. Then she said how proud she was of her daughter and son-in-law, Debbie and Billy Meekins, for their decision to have their baby blessed that day. Finally, Edna spoke of her love for the church, "the single guiding force in her life," and of her pride in being part of the large family present that day.

After Edna sat down Bishop Bushman announced the closing hymn and benediction. Then parents took their young children downstairs to Primary before returning to the chapel for Sunday school class. The teenagers went to their classes in the little house. The Meekins, Young, and Harding families gathered on the front steps for a family portrait.

The fast and testimony meeting offered an opportunity for people to give their own testimonies and for others to hear the complexity of faith encompassed by the ward. At this time members could gain strength from each other and from the sharing of unities and differences. The beginning of the Record Year marked a time for members of the Elkton Ward to reconsider their ties to the church. It was a time of reflection for them, a time to reevaluate their beliefs and their commitments. Members would be able to see the importance of the church in their lives from a new perspective.

Wayne Morris, 34

Wayne Morris joined the church six years ago, two years after marrying his wife, Sharon. The father of five children, ages one to sixteen, he is the presi-

dent of the Elkton Ward's Young Men's organization, which plans and oversees the activities of the boys ages twelve to eighteen.

I was baptized into the old New Castle Ward, but the area we live in was assigned to the newly formed Elkton Ward. There is a strong spirit in Elkton. I've grown to know quite a few people and I consider them some of my closest friends.

One thing that made me feel comfortable with the church and made me develop a testimony of the gospel was that anyone and everyone can be forgiven. I had felt that I was kind of left out—along with a lot of other people. I felt that once you had done things wrong you could never be completely straight again. I always pictured in my mind that ministers and pastors, who had never, ever had their hands dirty, never committed any of these sins, were the only ones who would be able to go to heaven. It was a real comfort to me to know that the bishop and the people giving talks in sacrament meeting or teaching classes are just like me. They work every day, supporting themselves. What they stood up and said, they said because they believed it—not because someone was paying them.

The expectations for each and every member are obtainable. Keeping the Sabbath day holy, following the Word of Wisdom, and magnifying your calling are things that you have to make an effort to do every day. Honoring your father and mother or not coveting your neighbor's possessions aren't any less meaningful, but not drinking coffee is a lot more tangible. You can measure your growth in the gospel and your faithfulness by it.

It was very easy to see why alcohol is bad for you. Drugs I didn't have any problem putting behind me, but when I was told that I couldn't have any iced tea, whatsoever, that was devastating. I consumed up to a gallon of iced tea a day. We even had special ways of making it. I prayed about it as the missionaries suggested, but I wasn't praying in the right way. The answer kept coming to me that I should leave it behind, but I didn't want to hear it. I didn't stop completely, but I did cut down. Then I just decided, "Either do it right or don't do it at all." It was difficult. Then I asked the Lord to help me put it behind me, and he did. My mom had made a ten-gallon bucket of iced tea for a Fourth of July picnic. My habit was to walk in and drink down at least one or two glasses before I walked around to greet everyone. Mothers don't miss anything, and she asked me if there was something wrong with the tea. I told her, "Oh, no."

She said, "Well, you're not drinking much of it."

And I told her, "No. There's a lot of caffeine in it." I wasn't ready to tell her that I was converting myself to a gospel principle that I didn't think she understood. They weren't too happy about my sister's joining the Catholic Church and they were no more thrilled about the LDS Church.

Much to my surprise she responded with, "Oh, that's great!" I immediately closed my eyes and said a little thank you to Heavenly Father for helping me.

My senior year of high school I went to school until noon and went to work at a gas station for the rest of the afternoon. A customer told me that Du Pont Chambers Works in New Jersey was looking for lab technicians. I had had some chemistry and did well in math so I went over to the Chambers Works as soon as I could. I was told that there were no lab jobs available, but they did have laborer jobs. I told them that I was willing to do any sort of work. I was getting married as soon as I graduated.

I started in July of 1968 shoveling dye in the azo area. For the past twelve years I've been working at the waste water treatment facility. I feel that there's a great future in this area. In dyes you could come up with a terrific idea but no one was willing to listen to anything new because dye making had been done for so many years. Some of the older fellows had fathers and even grandfathers who had done it. In the field I'm in now even people who are not very receptive to other people's thoughts are willing to listen to suggestions. We need to clean up the pollution we have created. I do like the idea of being in an area that is somewhat unexplored. We jokingly refer to it as the frontiers of science. Although I'm in a restricted and menial job, I'm proud to be making a necessary contribution.

My first wife's parents and mine said we were too young to be married. They were absolutely right. We were both spoiled rotten brats. Needless to say, it didn't work out. I developed an "I don't care" attitude. Sometimes I just literally did nothing that I should. I was constantly partying and carrying on. I was amazed that the world just continued to go right on. I met Sharon while dabbling in all these different things. She was one of the greatest positive influences on me.

Even then, I still had a bad attitude. One night when returning home after a college exam I stopped at a buddy's house and partook of some of the more vile things of life. In an incapacitated state I totaled our automobile in Elkton. I have very little recollection of the six miles between turning at one intersection and the accident. I ran into the back of a Pinto and drove it into the car parked in front of it, which drove that car into the one in front of it, totaling all four automobiles. Needless to say, the impact was definitely significant.

Shortly after the accident I developed a mental image of the Lord, himself, in all his power and his ultimate ability, just almost reaching down with an almighty hand and shaking me with a force that's inconceivable. The Lord said, "You've gone far enough down this path. This can be your destination or you can turn and try to find your way back to the right path."

One month after Sharon and I were married, my children Craig and Amy were turned over to us. Craig was eight and Amy was four at the time. One of the things I admire about Sharon is her love and dedication to the children. I don't believe if you were to see all our children together that you could tell which two are her adopted children.

The most satisfying thing I've ever done is to be sealed in the temple to my wife and children and to have a child be born in the covenant. I have aspirations for each and every one of my children to return to Heavenly Father, for them to be able to reach whatever goals they have. If they all were to go on missions, that would be great. My aspirations will be fulfilled if they keep themselves within the boundaries of the gospel. To think that when I've experienced what life has in store for me that I'll be able to return to our Heavenly Father with a promise of being able to be with my wife and children again is a very comforting thought. Our concern and feeling and love for one another are not restricted by the frailty of human life.

The most enjoyable of any church calling I have had is being Young Men's president. I'm directly associated with the young men, and with the young women also, at joint activities, temple trips, and firesides. It is very, very rewarding to observe the terrific testimonies that some of these youth possess. Sometimes they don't even realize it themselves.

I've watched one boy since the time he became a deacon until he left at age eighteen to go off to college. It was unfortunate that people focused too much on his normal teenage reactions—teasing the girls, disturbing the sacrament, and whatnot. I found it very rewarding to observe his phenomenal spirit. Both his parents are atheists and told him that the gospel was just a bunch of baloney, that he was wasting his time. His mother literally would come into his bedroom at 5:00 A.M. as he readied himself to go to early morning seminary. She would tell him to go on back to bed. She'd have his favorite breakfast ready for him in another hour or so. He would turn around and say, "No, that's okay, Mom. I want to go."

We try to do as we're taught in the church—put family first. In order to put family first, you have to first consider the gospel and what the Lord wants you to do. I've often heard it said, and I've heard myself say it, "Well, we can't pay our tithing right now because the littlest one needs shoes and somebody else needs . . . I believe in tithing and want to pay it, but I put family first."

That's an excuse. Satan tricks us into convincing ourselves that we're doing right when we're actually not. In order to put family first you have to obey the commandments and laws of the gospel. My wife and I and all of my family are exercising a great deal of faith. It was difficult to accept the principle of tithing—taking 10 percent of what we were used to living on and giving it to the church—but it was even more difficult to accomplish it. We were literally borrowing money to pay tithing. We would pay our tithing as soon as the check came in, but instead of realizing the need for changing our life-style, we would then buy some of our "wants." When a "need" came up, tithing and our "wants" had chewed up all our means, and we would borrow for the "need." It was easy at that point to justify—Oh, we're only borrowing for the "need." But we were really borrowing to pay for tithing, too.

Things got worse and worse until we made a disastrous choice. We decided to forgo our terrific blessing of being able to attend the temple. We kidded ourselves into thinking that we were going to dedicate ourselves to pulling in the belt and take all the money that we would have paid on tithing and apply it to the debts. As it turned out, we ended up going further into debt.

After a year of not having one moment of good feeling toward what we were doing, constantly feeling that we were getting further and further away from where we wanted to be, we finally sat down in a family council and made a firm commitment. The gospel is such a plain program, so filled with simplicity, that anybody can follow it and achieve it if they will not mix it all up with different interpretations. It might be difficult to achieve, but it's not intricate and confusing. We're promised a whole great big list of promises if we pay our tithing. I'm not anticipating a new car or a bag of money falling out of the windows of heaven, yet I do feel much more comfortable kneeling down and saying to the Lord, "Lord, I'm paying a full tithe. I'm doing all that I understand I should be doing, won't you help me?" I've been teaching my children to have a strong belief that he will help us. That certainty comes from doing what you're supposed to be doing.

Wayne Larsen, 46

Wayne Larsen moved from Utah, where he had been teaching at Brigham Young University, to work as a statistician for the Du Pont company. Only three of the five Larsen children moved with the family. Tara attends BYU, and Kirk stayed in Utah to finish high school. Wayne Larsen also works in the Young Men's organization, with the fourteen- and fifteen-year-old boys in the Teachers' Quorum.

Church was an extremely large part of our life. The branch met in our home in Waynesboro, Virginia. My dad was a counselor to the district president and then district president for twenty-eight years, almost right up until he died. Everything revolved around church. Every little gain—a new family moving in or a new convert—was a joy. There were never more than three LDS members in our high school. Most people praise the mission field experience. I was drained by church activity. We were constantly trying to keep the program going. My dad probably thrived on it. He was very shy and his church positions made him a polished public speaker. He did things he probably would not have done in a Utah ward.

I was in the Sunday school superintendency when I was a teenager and was essentially the superintendent when the superintendent went inactive. I spoke freely in church as a kid. I did feel I didn't have anybody to talk to about the church. I had close friends, but for some reason we almost never talked about the church. I never smoked or drank or swore—I almost couldn't do those things. I didn't dare. When I dated a girl five or six times, Dad got very worried and wanted me to date an LDS girl who lived ninety miles away. They were afraid I was going to marry out of the church. I knew I was going to college in six months and there was nothing to worry about.

I went to BYU where all my brothers and sisters went. I loved the four years there and got a degree in statistics. I stayed in Salt Lake after graduating because I didn't want to go back to the mission field single. I met and married Elena while I was working for Hercules. Four months later we came back to Virginia for graduate school. At Virginia Tech we were in a struggling branch.

After four years in graduate school, I took a job at Bell Labs. I stayed there for eight years except for one year I took a leave of absence to teach at BYU. I always say I got my degree at Virginia Tech and my education at Bell Labs. That's where I started to learn what statistics were for. I am a data analyst. I look at data from all angles and try to understand what it is trying to say—from ranking basketball or football teams to understanding paint experiments.

We got restless and Elena wanted to get back West. I was kind of overwhelmed by the largeness of Bell Labs—the remoteness of what we were doing. A little research firm in Provo made me an offer. That's the one professional mistake I've made. They didn't need a high-class statistician. Howard Nielson, who had found that job for me, helped me get on at BYU where I taught until we came here.

I worked on the Book of Mormon wordprint study for a lot of years and concentrated on it for about two years steady. We tried to use the concept of statistical linguistics to see whether one person wrote the Book of Mormon or not. The conclusion is overwhelming that one person did not write it. The different wordprints correspond to the purported authors. An even stronger conclusion is that Joseph Smith did not write it. His writings do not have at all the same unconscious pattern that the Book of Mormon has. When we did it we didn't think anyone would be interested. We were overwhelmed by the press attention.

I grew up on Du Pont—my dad worked for them. I even had an offer from this group twenty years ago, and I knew some members of the group very well. I was not averse to the idea of living closer to my family after nine years in the West. I like the job very much. We knew we didn't want to go to church in Valley Forge, so I called Bishop Bushman before we made a bid on our home to make sure we were within the Elkton Ward boundaries. He was wrong; we weren't. We apparently changed the boundaries unofficially. President Rice, the stake president, is trying to make it official.

The Elkton Ward is not quite as strong as the Waynesboro Ward, where I grew up, is now, but it's lots stronger than the Waynesboro Ward was when I was growing up. It's a growing ward, suboptimal in strength, but not a struggling branch. I like the mildly international flavor we have away from Utah. As a kid in Virginia, I hated singing "Utah We Love Thee" in church. That doesn't seem to happen in the Elkton Ward.

For some reason working with young people in Mutual is difficult. I think I like them too much. I get too intense. The church now places less emphasis on the programs, but I think the church has gone in the wrong direction of trying to make too much out of our callings. We try to create too many supermen. I think we try to browbeat people to do things. When I was a stake missionary in New Jersey, we had a family who was coming along well. They told us one night they didn't want to go any further. They said, "We see how active you are, and that's not for us." I silently agreed with them. I let my companion do all the talking that night because I couldn't disagree. I felt I was burned out. These eastern wards, mission field wards, are like that.

I've always lived the Word of Wisdom. I think I'd be an alcoholic if I drank. I'm very glad that I don't. I'm glad the church doesn't preach the Word of Wisdom like it used to. Judging people by surface things is detrimental. I think we've matured as a church on that score. Growing up, the gospel and the church were absolutely the same; the church was a set of rules and a bunch of programs. I think of the gospel and the church as being somewhat separate. When the church programs help us get the internal spiritual growth, they're great. When they don't, they're not great. I don't think the concepts of repentance and forgiveness were ever taught in my home. We were supposed to live the standards, but we never grappled with what to do if we hadn't followed them. I'd never even faced repentance. We all deviate in fairly serious ways, but some are just not as overt as others.

I think the church has grown a little less afraid of science. I don't think we ever need to be afraid. Bishop Bushman was telling me two weeks ago about some new studies that show that the Ph.D.'s are the most active members of the church. There is a correlation between education and activity instead of the other way around. I went through a long period of intellectual probing. I'm not against intellectual probing, but it's not the real way to truth.

When I gave a forum at BYU on the Book of Mormon wordprint study, I struggled with all sorts of emotional problems. Speaking in front of ten thousand people wasn't easy, and I was struggling with an issue unrelated to the talk. I asked my home teacher to give me a priesthood blessing and we both fasted. He gave a beautiful blessing. I had hoped to get word on the other issue as well, but I hadn't mentioned it because I wanted it to be true inspiration, not the power of suggestion. I came home, lay down, and listened to church music while Elena cooked supper. I was overcome by a strong spirit—the best feeling I've ever had. I was told very gently that the other problem was none of my business. Everything was okay. That was a great night. Experiences like that don't fade.

Edna Young, 38

The roots of Edna Young's family reach back to the early settlement of New Castle County. Through her paternal grandmother, Rebecca Talley, Edna is descended from William Talley, who came to America in the seventeenth century. The Tally Ho Lodge presently stands on what was once Talley farmland in Talleyville, north of Wilmington on U.S. 202. Edna, her mother, and two sisters joined the church in 1956.

I wasn't home the day that my mother opened the door to two missionaries. I was definitely not attracted to the church, I'm sorry to say. I was eleven years old and wanted to be with my neighborhood and school friends at the local Methodist church. I was in the choir and went to membership classes. I gave my mother a terrible time because I did not want to go to this unusual church, which was meeting at the Odd Fellows building of all places.

I had never been underwater before I was baptized. Because I was so panicked and trying to balance myself, my toe kept coming up out of the water. They'd say, "You have to go down again," and I'd cry. I had to go down three times. Then, in high school, the majority of my friends were from the church. The church's teachings have been the main force in my life.

My parents' divorce was very hard for my mother. As the oldest daughter, I had a lot of responsibility. I didn't feel like socializing in high school. I was very good in English, spelling, and grammar. After ninth grade I switched from college prep to business. I knew that as soon as I got out of school I would go to work because it was financially necessary. My mother had excellent secretarial skills and she helped me practice shorthand. Years later when I asked my father for money for books for a nine-week course he said, "Well, you should have told me that you wanted to go to college. I would have paid for it."

I met Tom on a double date and we've been married twenty-one years. I was seventeen when we got married in the mayor's office. My marriage is the single most satisfying thing in my life. I don't have a best friend other than him, and I don't think that he does either. I've always felt that your spouse comes first and your children come second.

We had a baby a year after we were married. We were still teenagers ourselves, so there was a lot of growing up to do. Since my husband was laid off periodically, I had to supplement the income. When I went to work when the children were small I always had guilt feelings. I would come home and do the wash and cry; give them a bath and cry. At that time, too, the church was much more against mothers working than maybe they are now. I definitely had a reason to work. I wished that I had more time to spend with my family, but there wasn't any way I could do that. At church other women would kind of look down on me for working. They used to ask, "Are you *still* working?"

I could never find a good answer to that until after the children were older and I had decided in my own mind that I would continue to work. I came up with the answer: "I will continue to work until I retire." That shocked a lot of people.

Tommy was born when Debbie was three. If he had been a girl, we probably would have had at least one more. We were lucky to have one of each. Money was not ever flowing and we thought that we could not educate, support, and spend time with any more children. Now that they are grown, once in a while I say I wish I had a larger family. That's hindsight again.

I have worked in hospitals, banks, law offices, large companies, small companies. I didn't have a career years ago. I had jobs here and there. I quit several jobs on my lunch hour. Now I'm an executive secretary to one of the vice-presidents at Columbia Gas. He is the nicest man that I have ever worked for. Before I took this job, I was working part-time in a law office. I needed a pension plan if I was going to work until I retired and I needed medical benefits for when Tom was laid off. I had to take a cut in pay, but in the long run it worked out because today I have tripled my starting pay.

My husband came into the bedroom one day when Tommy was a baby and found me down on my knees. You didn't see that too often—especially in those years. I had tears in my eyes. He kept on saying, "What's the matter with you? What's the matter?" I was saying my prayers that he would be baptized and that we could go to church together. He didn't attend any church and I knew if he came to know the members of the church and made friends in the church he would feel as close to it as I did. Sometime shortly after that he decided he did not want his son to grow up on the streets in the city. He started taking the missionary discussions with our neighbors. They quit, but Tom was baptized.

It's hard for me to get through a whole day without saying something about the church to somebody who's not a member of the church. I automatically talk about what I'm doing that night or that week, though I'm not necessarily inviting people to come out. Arlene Courtney lived next door to me when we were first married—our first house. One day, years later, she said, "Why is it that you never invited me to go to Relief Society with you?" She started going and was baptized.

A big part of the Word of Wisdom for Tom and me is going into physical fitness. We feel that there are a lot of overweight Mormons, and we feel that getting proper exercise and not overeating are also part of the Word of Wisdom. Maybe I don't overeat because I'm not such a great cook. At one time I did quite a bit of jogging. When I was jogging—this might sound sacrilegious—but when I absolutely thought I could not go another step I used to repeat the words to "I Stand All Amazed" or "There Is a Green Hill Far Away" to myself.

Tithing has always been easy for me. There have been times way back when I didn't pay tithing. One tithing settlement years and years ago, Bishop O'Day got out the record and said, "Something must be wrong here. This can't be right."

He went to call the clerk and I said, "Wait a minute. What's wrong?"

He said, "Well, this has all zeros all across here. This can't be right." We had not given one penny for the whole year.

I said, "No, no. That's right."

He said, "Well, what are you doing here, then?"

I said, "I want to start the new year out right and this year we want to start paying tithing." He laughed and laughed. We have been paying tithing for quite a while now. One year, Tom was laid off for fourteen months straight. We paid tithing the whole time and we were able to save more money in the bank during that one year than all the previous years that we had been married. I guess we watched the pennies.

Going to church was best when the children were Primary age. When they were teenagers they gave me a hard time about going to church. "Why do we have to do this? Why do we have to do that?" It was better in the younger years when they didn't ask so many questions. I've had trouble raising teenagers. I do enjoy working with them as long as they are not my own. I have trouble exercising the authority that I should, maybe because I feel like one of them sometimes. I think their music has a wonderful beat and I like to dance to it. I feel like they're friends sometimes. It's hard to be a disciplinarian and to be your children's friend at the same time.

When I was the Young Women's president it was kind of like a one-man band. I had no counselors, no secretary, and no teachers. I got to know the girls very well. Now I am a Sunday school teacher of the fourteen- and fifteen-year-olds. I enjoy working with the youth. I guess it keeps me young. I feel I have to show them that I'm on their side and interested in their daily life. I usually start off by asking them about the latest football games or dances or whatever they've done the past week. Once I get their respect and they realize that I'm interested in them, then they're more well behaved.

I was known for never attending a church meeting on a Saturday because that was the day when we went to the park or something like that. I was reprimanded by someone for not attending a Saturday meeting, but I told them that the church says that your family comes first. Some of the people who reprimanded me have since divorced and left the church, so I feel glad I held to my priorities.

My daughter married a member of the church, but at the time of their marriage they were both inactive. They were not married in the temple, but at the stake center. We were all surprised that they even chose to have the baby blessed in the Elkton Ward. I hope that she and her husband will become reactivated.

I would like Tommy to go on a mission. He says that he only wants to be "ordinary people," which is a joke that we have in this family. He just wants to go to work every day and earn a living for his family. I would have liked him to do better in school, but I don't know what more I could have done to get him to study. He's strong in other areas. He has a lot of friends. He has no trouble meeting people, meeting strangers. He tells people what he thinks and cannot be easily talked into anything. He's clean-cut, no drugs or anything like that.

I can't say that raising children was that satisfying although I definitely feel that not having them would have been a real loss to me. A big part of my life has been devoted to the children and I have a lot of experiences to look back on—a lot of fun and a lot of hard times. I don't see myself having the empty nest syndrome. I plan to go back to school to take more business courses, possibly get a degree. Maybe I'll get out of the secretarial field and more into business management. Now that I'm a grandmother, I foresee a lot of babysitting. I enjoy having the baby around whenever he comes.

The Relief Society's
2 | Opening Social

Friday, September 13, I spent the afternoon cooking Hawaiian Chicken for the Relief Society Opening Social. The social is a holdover from when Relief Society met on weekday mornings from October through May instead of every Sunday throughout the year. At 7:15, after leaving my chicken in the kitchen of the little house (the church's wiring is inadequate for the oven), my husband and I joined others who were waiting to enter the basement cultural hall, a large room under the chapel in which Primary is held on Sundays. Tonight it had been transformed into a modest version of an island paradise. The support poles were disguised as palm trees surrounded by shell-strewn sand and with paper fish swimming around. Paper lanterns were hung over the lights, and baskets and other ethnic items covered the paneled walls. Loud Hawaiian music dominated the room.

The tables were laden with food contributed by nearly every woman in the ward. The hors d'oeuvre table held fried shrimp, marinated fish, chicken livers with water chestnuts and bacon, and large fish-shaped tuna pates with cucumber scales and olive eyes. The main course was chicken, pork tenderloin, rice, and sweet potatoes. For dessert there was a choice of pineapple smoke and a coconut confection.

After dinner we went upstairs to a transformed chapel. The podium had been removed from the raised platform in the front of the chapel to make a stage with a draped curtain and a large Aloha sign. Flowers, plants, birds, and fish had transformed the room into a vivid site of ethnic pageantry. The bishop apparently had permitted such a use of the chapel on the grounds that it is really a multiuse area.

The program began with a processional. Ingrid Adams, the organizer, her two sons, who were dressed only in flowered pants, and seven teenage girls bore gifts to the front of the chapel. An impressive hula was followed by dances from three cultures—Hawaiian, Maori, and Tahitian. It was evident that Ingrid had taught the girls well. There were long pauses between the numbers as the girls hurried into new costumes or fell off the stage in the dark.

At the end of the program a fortunate few were coaxed onto the stage for a quick lesson in the "pineapple," the "spaghetti," and other hip-wagging steps. After a big Aloha and closing prayer—the Mormon synthesis—we collected our washed dishes and props and went home.

Ingrid Adams, 30

Ingrid Adams and her family left Java in 1957 because of the revolution. After four years in the Netherlands, they moved to Los Angeles, California, under the sponsorship of the Royal Netherlands Embassy. Her father worked as a legal counselor for business executives and bought a restaurant for Ingrid's mother where Ingrid "slaved many hours." While working there, she met her husband, John. They were married when she was seventeen and he twenty-seven. John's work for the Du Pont company took them first to Long Island, New York, and then to Delaware. Although they live in Landenburg, Pennsylvania, they attend the Elkton Ward, which is much closer to their home than any of the wards in Pennsylvania. During the thirteen years of her marriage, Ingrid has become the mother of five children, aged five months to eleven years.

You know, the church stresses talent in our cultural arts and that's why we have these road shows all the time, variety shows. I feel that if I weren't around to teach these girls and women what I know, who would they learn it from? As far as the Tahitian and the Polynesian dancing, that comes from my ancestry. At three years old I was dancing around the room and I was making little dance steps on my own.

Being fourth in a family of eight meant my older brothers and sisters came first. My sister had her ice-skating lessons and my other sister had her swimming lessons. When I was about ten years old, I wanted to take dancing lessons, but the money was not there. I said, "By darn if I can't have dancing lessons, I'll learn on my own." I would watch through the window or just be there until they kicked me out, and I would read. If I read it in a book, I thought, "Well, I can do this." When I did get a chance to have a professional teacher, I said, "I don't have credentials to show you. All I want is a chance. Let me show you what I can do." Dancing is just a talent that Heavenly Father gave me. I was probably a dancer with the angels in the preexistence.

I did get my talent for music from my father, who sang with a Dutch choir, a men's choir. I knew as a child what sounded good and I knew whether I was flat or sharp. It was just common sense to me. I've never taken any voice lessons. I can't read music.

I was once asked to sing "God Be With You" by the stake R.S. president for stake conference. I said, "I will sing it on the agreement that I will sing it the way I have felt it."

She said, "You can do whatever you want with it." When I sang it there wasn't an eye that was dry. I felt the Spirit just overwhelming me. She came up and said that she knew in her heart that I must have sung with the angels in the preexistence. I think that somewhere along the line I have.

After I met John, I couldn't have cared less about high school. I was madly in love, and I was ditching school. I'll kill my kids if they do what I did then. I was starting to get D's and F's. The only one to blame is myself.

When we got married, I planned to become a professional dancer and singer. I've sung as the lead singer in lots of bands. Even when I married my husband, I was still setting goals for that. I did not think that I was going to become a Mormon. I thought Mormons were as kooky as you could get, but I did know that I was going to have lots of children. I've danced professionally off-Broadway. I was the lead dancer with the Pride of Samoa. Every time I had a child it set me back two years. I have just turned thirty. Some of the dancers that I've danced with are now dancing on Broadway. They did not get married. They did not have children. That is where they chose to go. I'll kill them next time I see them.

I would like to get back into choreography. That is still a goal that I have. We all have talents that Heavenly Father gives us and they are there for a reason. I'm not going to let it just stay barren. I feel that I constantly have to set goals, long term and short term.

My husband, who was raised as a Mormon, said, "We've got to have the missionaries come and give you the lessons."

I said, "Fine." The first batch came and I got rid of them. The second batch came and it seemed like one set a year. I went through seven sets of missionaries. I had been raised as a Jehovah's Witness. What finally changed my mind— I was pregnant with my third child and miscarried in my third month. It overwhelmed me emotionally and it made me think. I had a husband and two children, whom I loved dearly, but I had lost someone that I had never known and it devastated me. I just wanted to make sure that I would have my husband and two kids for eternity. I fasted for two and a half days and told John that I was joining the church for his Christmas present.

I became a member in California a month or two before we moved to Long Island, New York. We were there for about four years. My husband and I were separated for five months. I grew up very fast from the little girl that he had married. My parents were sending me money to come home. The Spirit just told me, "No, this is temporary. You will get beyond this, and this is where you need to be." I was twenty-four or twenty-five when I became aware that the church was the most important thing.

When we were in Salt Lake City about a month ago, we went to the Visitor's Center where I learned (I did not know this—the seven years that I have been a member) that even though the dead have been baptized by proxy, that they still have a choice of accepting or rejecting it. I've yet to have the experience of being baptized for the dead. John has. It's my own fault. I just need to get my motor in gear.

I think it's harder being a Mormon in the Elkton Ward. In California we came from a very prominent ward—the money was there for everything that we did, whether it was road shows or variety shows. We could walk to the chapel because we all lived in a mile radius of each other. It was the same on Long Island. When there's no budget to work with you have to scrape for it. I think it takes sheer dedication being in the Elkton Ward. That's what makes it the best ward we've ever been in.

When we were house hunting here in Pennsylvania we looked at seventy-two homes. Finally we found this house and we made an offer for it. I said, "If it is meant for us to be in that home, we will get that house no matter what."

John said, "What are you going to do about it?"

And I said, "What are you going to do about it? I'm not the only one that prays in this family. Just because you don't have the priesthood doesn't mean that Heavenly Father won't listen to you."

At the real estate office the Spirit overwhelmed me to go and pray. I walked up to the bathroom and I was there for a good ten or fifteen minutes. I prayed and waited for an answer. I came out of the bathroom and I said, "I was praying and I got my answer." It was five thousand dollars more than our top dollar.

John said, "You're crazy. We can't do that."

"I have prayed and that was my answer that we are to offer this amount."

John said, "Honey, I'm going to go on your prayer. I hope that you were hearing on the right radio wavelength." As it turned out, we got the extra five thousand from the sale of our house on Long Island, and we got the house.

Right now I'm a cultural arts specialist for the church, and they don't have me doing a lot. I'll do the road show, that's true. The luau was a wonderful thing and the girls had a chance to do something they had never done before. I do believe that callings are of God. When they pray about who should do it, the names just come up.

The first time I had this calling was about three years ago for about six months. Then they put me in as homemaking leader, thinking that I would be just as good there. I hated that calling. I took it because I felt an obligation and I was not any good at it. I said to John, "I know this is not where I'm supposed to be." So I politely asked to be released, which I was. Then there was nothing for a while. When they called me back to cultural arts, I didn't hesitate.

I told John the other day that I feel like I have a calling waiting for me, and I know that I am not going to receive that calling because I have not been to the temple. I have not done my temple work. I haven't had my patriarchal blessing. I feel that I am going to be the Relief Society president.

John said, "Oh, Ingrid, come on. You don't want to be Relief Society president. You know how much work that is."

But I love people. I don't care if they are the meanest people you will ever meet, I believe that all people are good. I have the desire to be like Eliza Snow. I got to play her in the musical *Zion* last year. I want to be a perfect person though I'm not. I want to be able to control my temper better. I want to be able to be at church every week. Now I can't because my children are so sick all the time. There's something about being a Relief Society president that is something that I am striving for. I know that it's going to be more work than I can handle now. But I want to be a good person. I think that is even more important than being a choreographer or being a fantastic singer.

❈   ❈   ❈

Being president of the Relief Society is considered by many to be the top women's job in a ward. The organization began in Nauvoo, Illinois, when some of the women decided to form an organization to do good works for the poor and to contribute to building the Nauvoo Temple. When they showed their proposed by-laws and constitution to Joseph Smith, he said that he had something better for them—an organization "after the manner of the priesthood." Although at one time owning its own meeting halls, hospitals, and social welfare agencies, Relief Society is now most noticeably another Sunday meeting for women. Relief Society for the women and priesthood meeting for the men are held during the last fifty minutes of each Sunday's three-hour block of meetings. Women who teach Primary or Young Women's classes cannot attend the Sunday meetings, but they can attend the monthly homemaking meeting, which is held on a weeknight.

Overseeing the meetings is only a small part of the duties of the Relief Society president. Her two counselors help plan the meetings and work with the teachers, but the president's responsibilities include administering visiting teaching and working with the bishop in obtaining assistance for families in need. Every woman who lives in the ward is to be visited by a pair of visiting teachers once a month. Visiting teachers are asked to report to her any cases of need, and she asks the women of the ward to provide assistance to others who are sick, have new babies, or other pressing needs.

Deborah Johnston, 31

Deborah Johnston moved to the Elkton Ward from Sacramento, California, in 1981 when her husband was transferred to Delaware by the Du Pont company. Originally from West Virginia, Deborah grew up in Cumberland, Maryland, where her father served as president of a small branch of the church for many years. She has been president of the Relief Society for nearly two years, and has three children who are eight, six, and four years old. She also takes care of two other children.

I was excited about moving here from California because I was going to be able to see my parents and the kids were going to get to know their grandparents and my part of the family. The home that we happened to find was in the Elkton Branch. I told Gary, "I grew up in a branch. It doesn't make any difference to me. They might not have a full program because there aren't as many people, but I turned out fine."

I joined Gary here the week after the branch became a ward. Moving in, I didn't realize that everybody had to learn to know each other. I thought I was the outsider. I found that Elkton Ward was made up of people who had moved here from other places and who had had to make it home. There is a very small group that has been here for a long time.

We lived in Keyser, West Virginia, when my dad was made president of a branch that met in Cumberland, Maryland. Because my dad spent more time at church than he did at home or even at work, we moved to Cumberland, Maryland. I loved the song "Put Your Shoulder to the Wheel" when I was a child. We had to make and sell doughnuts to earn money to build a church. That song always reminds me of the pioneers—that you've just got to keep going—and it brings back what I did as a child. I felt I was a pioneer, too.

I wanted to go to BYU because there were only one or two kids in my whole high school who were LDS. Gary and I were in the same branch at BYU. That he was there every Sunday and passed the sacrament impressed me. My major was microbiology, and I wanted to minor in computers. I wanted to work as a lab technician in a hospital, and I knew that they used computers a lot for the testing. But they informed me that if you major in microbiology you have to minor in chemistry. I found that difficult. I liked organic chemistry, but I had to take microbiology twice. I got an A the second time around. I was in classes with all the pre-med students. I'd finished at the top of my class in high school, but I found BYU a challenge. I was in with a lot of very smart people. I always thought that I would finish college, but Gary and I were married the summer after he graduated. I had finished two and a half years.

I was always determined to marry in the temple. Growing up in the branch, I saw a lot of part-member families, and I knew that I wanted to be married in the temple to someone who was active in the church. I still feel it would be better not to be married at all than to marry someone who is not active in the church. My life now is what was my dream: living in a nice home, in a suburb with a yard, having children, and having my husband go off to work at a day job.

I enjoy making my house clean and presentable, but being Relief Society president conflicts with it. I used to like to sew, but I don't anymore because with the kids and interruptions, it's just a frustration. I've found that I do enjoy handwork, counted cross-stitch and things like that.

I like working with my kids. I worked a lot with Tia. She wanted to read. I took time to do that. We used to go to the park all the time. We used to go to the library for story time and I used to sit and read stories. I don't do much of that anymore. Other things have taken over. This morning I spent three hours talking to one of the new members. The bishop asked me to find out what her problems are. I brought along the tape recorder and while I talked with her my three children and Terri's two sat on the front steps listening to stories.

This last year I've been babysitting and I enjoy it. I'm babysitting Terri Owen's children. I like it because it makes me be stricter as a mother. My own kids kind of wiggle into my heart. "Oh, Mom, I don't want to do that" or "I'm not hungry." When I've got other kids here, everybody sits down for lunch and everybody eats it. I'm better organized. I think I'm a better mother. I take time to do things with the children because I have these extra kids with me in my home.

I want to go back to school not too far in the future. I don't want to go back into microbiology. I've learned from my church callings that I like organizing and I like working with figures and bookkeeping. I'll probably eventually get a job of some sort, but I decided it was important for a mom to be home, even with high school kids. As time goes on and things get harder to pay for, I don't know if my opinion will change. I would never leave my kids with a babysitter.

I still feel like perhaps I'd want another child, but with Shane I was almost bedridden the nine months—with two other little children running around. I was on heavy medication, and I worried if Shane would come out all right. I didn't realize what it was doing to my husband. He thought I was going to die. I feel the pressure to have children, and I struggle with personal revelation. There are times I think I want another child. I don't know if those feelings are mine or if they're promptings from the Spirit. I don't know if it's pressure—thinking other people have ten kids and I've got three.

The spiritual part of being Relief Society president I find difficult. I'm not experienced enough to have all the wisdom and answers for everybody, but I do enjoy trying to make the organization more functional, to have better socials, better visiting teaching. When the bishop asked me what one thing I wanted to learn from being Relief Society president, I said it was to have a love for the sisters. I'm not one to go up and put my arm around somebody, not that I don't think about it, but some people can do that more naturally. Working with people who have problems has made me more understanding. I can see other people's point of view, but when you start understanding everybody's opinion, you sometimes forget where the line is, where the iron rod is. Sometimes I feel wishy-washy.

Besides organizing and doing things better, my personal goal is to be more compassionate, to be as the Savior is, to learn what charity is. Lately I realized I had a problem with turning the other cheek. Sometimes I get riled when things go wrong and I want people to know how I feel. Maybe that's what the Lord meant about turning the other cheek. You don't always have to get your two cents' worth in. You don't have to have the last word.

Our ward building has an impact on the running of the ward. I used to be a lot more organized, but the library is in the other building and we don't have a Relief Society closet—we share one downstairs with the janitor. I think maybe the Elkton Ward is a little more laid back, more relaxed about things. Those of us who like to see things cut and dried and organized have had to stand back and take a look at why we're doing the things we're doing. It's not just paperwork; we're working with people. I've been learning not to take on running this church like a business. We have to work more closely with each other because we don't have a set system and the equipment that makes it run smoothly. I think we're a little bit more casual.

Some of that has to do with having been a branch. The branch never had supervisors and districts for visiting teaching. The Relief Society president called all the visiting teachers. Now it's bigger and it's more organized. Some people say, "Well, it was never done that way before. So why do it?" It's hard to fight against that. We don't have 20 sisters in the ward; we have 150. You can't keep track just by calling them all up every week. I feel I'm just now getting things changed to the way Relief Society should be. I find it hard to have to think of everything that needs to be done to make it organized.

Visiting teaching was easier in California because people were closer together. We went visiting teaching whether or not they wanted us to come. Even if we couldn't get in and we just said hi at the door, we always got 100 percent. I hear so many times, "Well, I've got a bad route" or "They're difficult" or "They don't want to see me." There are women in "spiritual rags" just like the prophet said. They should have the privilege of wearing the robes that we have. We need to go into those homes and we need to make the effort. Sure it's discouraging that they don't want to accept it, but I don't think we should take that personally. Doing what the Lord wants us to do should be satisfaction enough.

Would you ask the Lord, "Do you want me to keep going to visit these people?" Yes, he does. They're his children. They deserve the knowledge of the gospel. They need that influence, whether they accept it or not. Before I was Relief Society president I always did it because I was asked to do it and it was my duty, but now I see the the purpose.

I truly believe the basic responsibility of our salvation is our own. I hear so many people say, "Well, Relief Society is not fulfilling my needs." We're not there to fulfill every need. We're there to teach you how to fulfill your needs.

We're there to teach you that you can go out and become an educator or you can write poetry. A lot of people have the misconception that the programs of the church should be their whole life.

If we burn out, if it's not a happy way of life, if after ten years of serving you don't want to come to church anymore, that's not the way it should be. I don't know what the answer is because, well, I feel the pressure. I don't get to do everything I want to do, but we have to realize that the gospel is what's true. It's the gospel! That's why people join the church.

Clara Burke, 39

Clara Burke is the Relief Society secretary. She and her husband joined the church seven years ago. Their two sons, Andy and John, are eight and ten years old.

When my father died of cancer, I started having questions. How could the God I knew and trusted do this to my father? After Daddy died, I had great difficulty praying. When I talked to the minister, whom I had known for years, about it, he said, "When you have just lost somebody, it is a very bad time. What you need is psychiatric help."

I went home and I thought, "Something is wrong. If that's his answer to me, something is wrong." We started looking at that time—not for another religion—but for a better minister. Some Latter-day Saint TV commercials and a pull-out from the *Reader's Digest* led us to look into the church. The first pull-out told about family home evening and marriage for eternity. That was a big attraction. I liked how the close family was all tied up with the church. Matt ultimately reached Dan Harding in a roundabout way at work, and Dan brought us pamphlets and talked to us. We said, "Let us think it over." The next day the missionaries came. Dan sent them.

We had the most terrific missionary who ever lived, Sister Black. We still correspond. I don't know that we would be members if it wasn't for her. She started my testimony by sharing hers with me. I pushed Matt in the beginning when I saw that television commercial, but he was ready for baptism much earlier than I was. I got scared. It hit me that this is a lifetime thing. If it weren't for Sister Black when I hit that snag, I wouldn't be a member, let alone have a testimony.

We struggled with the Word of Wisdom before we became members. Once we decided that we wanted the gospel in our lives, we had to see if we could do it. We took two months to try to live like members before we consented to baptism.

Matt and I and the boys set some family goals in family home evening. One of them is to try to keep the Sabbath more holy. When we read Pa's description of the Sabbath in *Little House in the Big Woods,* my boys sat there flabbergasted. Our goal to do better came from that book. We have our family home evening on Sundays so my mother can participate. Sometimes I read in my diary about when the missionaries came to us. On Sunday evenings we sit down and do journal writing with the boys. It was easy before the boys could write. They'd draw a picture, then they'd tell us about the picture and we'd write it on the back for them. That spurred Matt on, but now the boys write their own.

When we were in the New Castle Ward I was a new member, so I was just content to sit in the background. The Elkton Ward gets you out. It's an open and friendly ward. Being Relief Society secretary is the first calling I've had that was not in the Primary. I enjoyed working with little ones—when they're two years old learning everything and so open for new experiences, they're special. I'm just getting started as Relief Society secretary. The Relief Society president needs somebody who can be right there on top of things. Every calling gives you more confidence. If you can't do it when you start, you can learn. Before you're released, you're doing it.

There was never a time we didn't want children and we never had any. We decided to take in foster children because we couldn't get on an adoption list. We ended up adopting the first two foster children, although we lost them at one point. Their parents had abused them, and when we found out that they were going back to their paternal grandparents after we had had them for two years, we were very upset.

We went to Bishop Dorner and asked if he could give them a blessing for protection. Andy was almost five, and we'd had them since he was three. He gave John, who was younger, a blessing for protection. He gave Andy the most beautiful blessing. He said, "Some day, you're going to find your way back into the church." I still think that's the only reason we got them back.

They went to the grandparents on a six-month trial basis. They stayed for four and a half months. We were then in the process of adopting a baby girl. The social worker called and said, "The two boys are coming back into foster care. They have to be placed with somebody. If you take them, you can't adopt the baby girl. You can't have an adopted child and a foster child in your home. Do you want time to think about this?"

I said, "No. If they're coming back into foster care, they have to come to us. They can't go to anybody else." Then I thought, "What am I saying? My husband's not even here, and I'm giving away his daughter." When he came home I said, "The boys are coming back into care. We can get them; however, we have to give up the girl. What do you want to do?"

He said, "When are they coming back?"

I said, "We can go up right now." That was hard because we didn't even know if they were going to be free for adoption. They were foster kids, but they had already moved so much. They were sad little birds. Andy will be eleven soon and John is eight. They'll both be going into the priesthood soon.

I just want my boys to be happy. As they grow up, we see the struggles that they have. Andy has some brain damage and a learning disability. It would make me extremely happy if I could ever see him happy. If I could do what I wanted to do, I'd make sure there isn't a child in the world who is abused.

A Change in the Bishopric

3

Everyone's ears pricked up as Bishop Bushman announced at the beginning of sacrament meeting that Thomas Robinson of the Wilmington Stake High Council would conduct some business. This meant that one of the leaders of the ward was to be released from his calling and someone else would be called in his place. Most changes in callings are made by the bishopric. The bishop and his counselors, the ward clerks, and the ward mission leader are called by the presidency of the Wilmington Stake, to which the Elkton Ward belongs.

Thomas Robinson, a member of the Elkton Ward, is one of the twelve high priests who make up the stake high council. His duties on the high council include auditing the financial records of the five wards and four branches that belong to the stake and serving as an adviser to the single adult organizations in the stake. Whatever business he was to transact today had been a closely guarded secret—known only to the three members of the bishopric, the high council, the stake presidency, and the individuals who were being released from or called to positions.

Thomas Robinson announced that the stake presidency wished to release Bishop Bushman's counselors, Kenneth McVicker and Rufus Lanier, as well as Gary Johnston, the ward mission leader, and Cloyd Mullins, the assistant ward mission leader. As her husband asked the congregation to sustain Rufus Lanier as first counselor to Bishop Bushman, Gary Johnston as second counselor, and Cloyd Mullins as the ward mission leader, Joey Robinson suddenly understood why she had been released from the ward's Relief Society presidency a few weeks earlier. Today's changes would result in a major reshuffling of ward leadership positions. Because Gary Johnston was to be a member of the bishopric, Deborah Johnston would no longer serve as Relief Society president; she and her two counselors would be released.

When Bishop Bushman returned to the pulpit to conduct the ward business, he released the Young Men's president, Wayne Morris, and asked the ward to sustain his former counselor, Kenneth McVicker, as the Young Men's president.

These changes in ward leadership resulted in major changes in the other ward organizations, especially the Relief Society and Primary. Because almost every active adult member of the ward has a calling, there is not a pool of unemployed talent. As vacancies occur in organizations, members have to be released from other positions to fill the vacancies. This of course creates more vacancies to be filled.

New wards and branches of the church are created not only to decrease the distances members have to travel to meetings but to keep wards from becoming so large that there are more members than callings. The roots of the Elkton Ward go back to December 1976 when the few members of the New Castle Ward who lived in Maryland began holding sacrament meeting in Cloyd Mullins's living room. In 1978 the Elkton Branch was formed from territory taken from the New Castle Ward: everything south of the Chesapeake and Delaware Canal in Delaware as well as Cecil County, Maryland. The branch grew both from the baptism of converts and from the addition of more territory from the New Castle Ward. In September 1981 the Wilmington and New Castle wards and the Elkton Branch were restructured to form three wards: Wilmington, Wilmington West, and Elkton.

Before the Elkton Ward could be organized, a meeting place that could accommodate the various meetings and activities of a ward had to be found. Since 1978 the Elkton Branch had met on Sundays in historic Holly Hall in Elkton, but the building was not large enough and was not available during the week. While visiting someone in the hospital, Cloyd Mullins, the branch president, heard of a congregation that was building a new church and wanted to sell its old one. The stake presidency began negotiations to purchase the building. Then the stake presidency and high council began to work on drawing the boundary lines that would create the three new wards. They also selected a member of the future Elkton Ward to be the bishop and sent his name to the First Presidency at church headquarters in Salt Lake City for approval. Because the negotiations and plans were lengthy and time consuming, the members were aware that the wards would be reorganized, but neither the proposed boundaries nor the name of the bishop were matters of common discussion until the boundaries were announced in the New Castle Ward priesthood meeting the last Sunday of September 1981. That evening, in the last meeting of the New Castle Ward, Stake President Johnson asked the members to approve the organization of the three wards and to sustain Richard Bushman as the bishop of the Elkton Ward.

The Robinsons became members of the Elkton branch by annexation. Cloyd Mullins and Lynne Whitney are two of the original members of the sacrament meeting group and of the Elkton branch. Their responsibilities in a struggling branch transformed their lives.

Thomas Robinson, 36

When Thomas Robinson and his family returned to Delaware from Germany in 1973, they belonged to the New Castle Ward, which was then part of the Philadelphia Stake. Thomas served as president of the Philadelphia Stake Mission, and when the Wilmington Stake, including parts of New Jersey and Maryland as well as Delaware, was organized on December 8, 1974, he was called to be mission president of the new stake. At the same time, he was mission leader of the New Castle Ward.

In 1968 I went down to the Navy Recruiter and joined the Intelligence Corps of the navy. We had a great time overseas. We got to go to Amsterdam, Copenhagen, London, Rome, Venice, Paris, Florence, and the Riviera. I guess the greatest thing that happened to us during our three and a half years in Europe was joining the church.

Joey, my wife, worked for the U.S. Army in the accounting office and one lady with whom she worked was LDS. She invited us over to her apartment. The second time we went, two gentlemen with short haircuts and white shirts and ties who spoke fluent German were there. That in itself intrigued us. They said they sold life insurance. If anyone inquired about what I did, I had to turn in their names for an investigation. When they came by our house three days later, I knew who they were. They came in and said again, "We sell life insurance."

I said, "What kind of life insurance do you sell?"

"Eternal life insurance."

I said, "Is that right? Now that's a different approach than I've ever heard from missionaries."

"Oh, you know we're missionaries?"

Then I told them their mission president's name and I said, "You have 176 missionaries in Germany."

They said, "No, we only have 172."

I said, "That's wrong. Four more came in two days ago." They gave us the discussions and six weeks later we were baptized in the city's indoor swimming pool.

We were ready for it. Joey was an Episcopalian and I was a Methodist, but we didn't involve ourselves in our religions. We had come up with a Robinson religion, I suppose. We already knew many of the principles they presented. At the time we got married, Joey and I had asked the rector if we were going to be married just for time. He had said, "Well, those are the words we use, but of course, we don't know what comes after death." We couldn't get any answers.

When the missionaries flipped the chart over and started talking about eternal marriage, that was it—preexistence, earth life, and afterlife—like a light bulb coming on. We were baptized April 17, 1971. There were fifty-three people in our branch and fifty-three were active. When we came back to the United States in 1973 we were flabbergasted to see 24 or 25 percent home teaching and 34 percent activity.

Our first Sunday in the New Castle Ward they sang "America the Beautiful." Joey and I stood up and we belted it out. The bishop smiled. Afterwards the bishop walked off the stand and said, "We haven't met, but my name is Bishop O'Day."

I said, "We're glad to meet you. You're the first bishop we've ever met."

When President Johnson, at that time a counselor in the stake presidency, interviewed me, I said, "Have you ever been in a military branch? We attended a conference in Berchtesgaden, Germany, in the Bavarian Alps for all the LDS members in Europe, Turkey, and Northern Africa. They brought over Brother Hinckley, President Tanner, Brother Benson. There were 612 of us who had never been in such a large group of Saints. The Spirit was so strong that it could push the walls out. To come back to the States and find 138 duds sitting on pews is just amazing. Somebody has got to light some fire under these people." They made me a seventy, ward mission leader, and stake mission president all on one hand raise.

As I was about to go out the front door one night, my wife yelled down to me from the living room, "I hate you. I hate the church. And I hate you going out as much as you do." That was the low point. I was going out with the missionaries twice a week, plus home teaching. I didn't understand why Joey couldn't understand. "I'm doing all these things for the church. Why are you upset?"

"What do you mean, why am I upset?" She was sitting home with a six-year-old, a four-year-old, a two-year-old, and a two-month-old. Of course she was upset. Slowly, with her help, I began to understand that the church is going to keep rolling forward with or without me. It might have a small dip in the program but it is going to keep on going. At first I didn't understand that I was doing something wrong by spending too much time in the service of the church.

When Bishop Cross sat me down and said, "You know, you're tearing your marriage apart," I took it on faith. "Okay, you're the bishop. You've lived longer in the church and you've been a part of marriage longer."

When the Wilmington Stake was organized, President Johnson became stake president and I was the stake mission president. I can remember President Johnson once saying at the beginning of our monthly personal priesthood interview, "How many times have you been out this week, Brother Robinson?"

My counselors were on either side of me and his counselors were on either side of him. I said, "This is the fourth night I've been out this week."

He said, "It's time for the closing prayer." We had a closing prayer and we went home. That made an impact on me. As a high councillor, I have counseled Elders' Quorum presidents that if they're out of their homes more than three nights a week, they're out too much.

I've come to realize that keeping myself strong and fed with scriptures comes first. Then comes taking care of my wife and building that relationship. Then, of course, come my children and my home teaching families. When I was Elders' Quorum president, first was being president; first was home teaching and taking care of the families; first was helping the home teachers who weren't doing their job. That's all well and good, but it's got to come after my wife and kids.

The thing I enjoy the most about being on the high council is the fellowship with the other brethren. I had been Elders' Quorum president for almost five years. After having that calling for such a long time, I knew all the families and was very involved in those relationships. On the high council, I'm not involved with people that way, but I have become close to the eleven other brethren and to the stake presidency. I'm not a macho man by any means, but my children have said, "Dad, we have never seen you cry except in the last few years." In my other callings I had received some spiritual promptings, but not as much as I have on the high council. I have feelings that I never felt before. The courts are the most difficult. We see individuals feel what they've done and try to express it. As they do, not only the emotions but I guess the true repentance that they feel are very hard to witness. Lately one of our own members on the high council was excommunicated. Arden Engebretsen and I just cried our eyes out. The greatest part of it is when the returning missionaries report on their experiences. They're just so full of "Let's go out and change the world. Let's do it right."

I was the ward mission leader when Steve Cherry became a member of the church and I was his home teacher when he was burned in the fire. Bishop Cross and I went up to give Steve a blessing. They said there was a good chance he would die, but the bishop blessed him not only that he would live but that every part of his body would be made whole. Today, he's grown new skin on his hands, skin on his face. He and Bonita had a child! When that blessing was given, I said to myself, "I know he gave it through the priesthood and I know we laid our hands on his head," but I strictly took that one on faith.

The church has brought things out in me which I hadn't pictured as being me. Before, when people asked for my views or thoughts, if I didn't think they were acceptable, I probably would go with the crowd. Now, not to sound conceited, it makes no difference what the neighbors think. All that matters is that we know what we're doing is right.

For instance: One day Joey noticed there was something floating on the top of our swimming pool. When I got home from work she said there was a cat floating in the water. I went over and got the neighbor because it was his cat.

Now at this time I was the ward mission leader and there was a lot of anti-Mormon feeling. I went with the missionaries to some rallies which we ended up leaving because people were burning temple garments. The minister of a church about two miles down the road from us would send me tapes and say, "This is what we think of the church. Respond."

Bishop Cross would say, "Tell me what your response is before you send it." I'd give a tape to the bishop and he'd say, "Okay, send it." This neighbor was a member of that church and when he found that his cat was drowned in our swimming pool, he thought that we had done it intentionally as an animal sacrifice. When this happened there were some very hard feelings. There aren't as many now because I've helped him and he's helped me.

Something else you have to understand is I was a home teacher to a lady who had a dog that the SPCA wouldn't even take away. The whole house was infested. I said to her, "You have to get rid of it."

She said, "Well, the SPCA won't come and get it from me. I have to put it out on the street and I won't do that."

I said, "Well, you bring it by my house and I'll take care of it."

We have a hedgerow behind us, beyond which is a three-hundred-acre farm. She brought the dog by. I took the dog back—I'd already dug a hole—tied it to a tree; it stepped into the hole and I shot it with a shotgun. Of course, this was after she had left. This neighbor had seen me do it. Well, he looked at that as being a sacrifice. The other thing is I hunt geese and various other animals. I clean them myself and my family eats them. When I get home at night, I drive my car to my garden where I've already dug trenches and I clean geese in the light from the headlights. Adding all these things up, plus the cat in the swimming pool . . .

In family home evening Dawn said, "Dad, the neighbor kids are calling us 'devil's children.'"

Aaron said, "Yeah, and they're going to sic their dog on us." The kids felt bad that I did those things.

I told them everything that I was doing, none of which was wrong. "When people call you 'devil's workers,' and it's confusing to you," I said, "when you're in that kind of a state, you get down and you have a prayer." In her prayers that night Dawn asked to know how she should cope with it next time.

Sometime thereafter she said she'd been called a devil's worker again. Right then she felt not that it was good she be called that, but good that she have the opportunity for someone to face her and say, "Do you know what you stand for? Or are you just standing on sand?" It made Dawn much stronger. The only advice we gave our children was to pray about it. We continually reassured them that they were not devil's workers.

There are some times when even though individuals are given callings with the keys and responsibilities of those callings, they don't act by virtue of the calling that they have. Instead of the church being run by the Spirit, sometimes it's run by men. I was Elders' Quorum president when Elkton became a ward and there were at that time a number of people who were investigating the church who were black and we had no black members in the ward. The revelation had been received but there were a number of jokes being told within the quorum that were literally off-color. Right in church! I literally chastised the quorum for doing that. I wasn't going to put up with it. As a quorum president it was my responsibility to counsel them not to do those things. It's just like when someone is considered by the high council for a calling and right away someone brings up, "Well, you know that individual doesn't pay income tax." They don't get a call in the church. If people continue to do these things after they've been counseled, they get released. We don't wait any longer for them to grow when it's detrimental to the other members.

Josephine (Joey) Robinson, 35

Joey Robinson is a native of Wilmington, Delaware. When she was in high school, she stood next to her future husband in the chorus. She is the mother of four children, ages twelve, ten, eight, and six. After being released from the presidency of the Relief Society, she was called as a Cub Scout leader.

When I was told I would be released, a strange feeling came over me, "Why am I being released and nobody else is?" I knew Linda Peer had started her business and couldn't give much time to Relief Society. I thought, "Now wait a minute, am I being fired or am I being promoted?" I had to think about the job I'd done. I know I didn't do everything, but I did all that I could do, so I have to feel okay about that. I feel that the callings I've received have been from the Lord, and I'll do a lot of things for him that I won't do for anybody else. I liked being a counselor in the Relief Society presidency because I gained a real appreciation of sisterhood. I never had a real sister. I have a very strong permeating feeling of sisterhood that I didn't have when I began.

Tom knew that Gary Johnston was going to be called to the bishopric and that all of us would be released. Because I was the first, I got the "What's going on here?" feelings.

My first church calling was Sunday school pianist. Of course I didn't know how any of the hymns were supposed to sound. I hadn't taken piano lessons since I was about fourteen. There was a particular week that I practiced and practiced and I just couldn't get it. I started crying and banging on the piano. Finally, I just asked the Lord to help me. I learned from that that the Lord never said, "Do everything." He said, "Do all you can do."

Six years ago when they changed the boundaries and put us into the Elkton Branch, I panicked because I had said so many times to Cloyd Mullins who was the branch president, "I don't understand why you don't have a Primary. You should have a real Primary. Boy, if I was there, you'd have one." I was asked to be Primary president the first week.

I came to a crossroad in my life as far as organizing my church time and my family time when I was Primary president. I was doing all these wonderful things. We were starting a newsletter for the kids. Half the time the teachers weren't there so I had to teach and then I had to play the piano because the music person wasn't there. So one day I went in to see Cloyd Mullins. I walked up to the chalkboard and I drew a line right down like this—Zzzzzip. A little tiny side of the board was on one side, and then all the rest was on the other. I said, "Do you know what that is?"

He said, "What?"

I said, "See that big area right there?"

He said, "Yeah."

I said, "That's all the time I spend on Primary. All the time I spend. All the time!" I said, "See that little area right there?"

He said, "Yeah."

I said, "That's the time I have left for myself and my family. I want to be released. I cannot keep doing it."

You know what he said? "Nobody asked you to."

All of a sudden it came to me. I was this great big locomotive chugging down the track of righteousness right to self-destruction. They were righteous things and they were good, but my life wasn't balanced. From then on there were several people who probably thought I was going to become the devil's advocate because they'd ask me to do something and I'd say, "Sorry." We wiped out the newsletter. We wiped out everything we didn't need and started over with what we had to have.

At this time, I was spending a great deal of time on losing weight. It dominated my brain. I've never been little. By the time I was up to 255 pounds, everything was just too hard. I would ask Tom, "Would you go get me a glass of soda," and I'd sit. One day I determined that I want to be here to see my grandchildren, my great-grandchildren. I was killing myself. Tom never complained—never made any hints at all. All he did say was he felt that we were cutting our time together short. After I lost twenty pounds I took a picture to put on my refrigerator and nobody now can believe that it was me. It took me a while, but I lost about a hundred pounds. It took a tremendous amount of self-discipline. I noticed—it's not something I can stand up in Relief Society and say—that I was much more receptive and spiritual after doing it. The discipline in dieting is only a jump towards disciplining yourself in something else.

One day after we joined the church I was in the PX looking at dresses with my friends from church and they said, "Oh, but you can't wear that one with garments."

I didn't say anything, but I went to the next one and I said, "Isn't this one cute?"

It was another sleeveless one and they said, "Oh yeah, but you couldn't wear that because of garments." It went on and on.

Finally, I said, "What are you talking about?" It was a shock to me that someone would dictate to me what I could wear. I had a long discussion with the missionaries on that. I said, "Okay, if I have a testimony of the church, I don't have a testimony of part of it, and if the church is true and right, then the things that come from it are true and right." I'm still not sure I totally understand, but I understand it enough to accept it.

Since we came to New Castle, from day one, Tom's always been in leadership positions. That was a very big change. We had always done everything together. All of a sudden having him out in the evenings and me sitting home and "supporting" was a whole new thing. One night it came to a head. He was standing down on the landing and I was standing up in the living room. I said, "I can't take this anymore. I can't live with you and I can't live without you, but if something doesn't change, I'm going home."

I can't put my finger right on what happened, but in family home evening he'd say, "I'm going to go home teaching Thursday night, is that okay?" He started planning and keeping a calender. It wasn't "Oh, yeah! I have to go out tonight." I did not like that being sprung on me because I might have had a rotten day. It was very difficult to have to choose between wanting him home because I needed him or him going and doing what he had to do. That was too hard to decide. So, instead, I'd get mad.

Tom and I never had had hard, hard times. I remember hearing people say, "I can't go out visiting teaching because I don't have the money for gas." I'd think, "A dollar for gas, come on." Then boom. Du Pont merged two departments and Tom was out the back door because he was low man on the totem pole. He couldn't find a job right away so he worked for the National Guard and made several hundred dollars less a month than what we needed. We'd just moved into a new house. I gained an appreciation for the fact that some people don't have a dollar for gas, some people don't have a dollar to put food on the table. It's been a long time coming out of the big hole that we were in. We were literally afraid that we were going to lose the house. I think the reason that we didn't is because we did pay our tithing. That's another lesson in self-control.

If I went to work, the money I would make would never compensate for what I save by being home. Yesterday I made a skirt. I started at one o'clock and finished at three o'clock and it might have cost me two dollars. The day before that I made a pair of pants. That material was a dollar a yard and it was 35 percent wool. I get a great kick out of going into the store and finding six great big Italian rolls on sale for a quarter. I feel like I've achieved something. I enjoy making my home a bit of heaven. I enjoy being there when the kids leave, kissing them and hugging them, and seeing their little bodies walk over to the bus stop and their little heads going by in the window of the bus. There's not much that I don't like about it. I don't even mind doing the wash and doing the dishes.

Being a teenager is probably one of the most traumatic things that ever happened to me. I keep that in mind with Dawn, who will be thirteen in April. I read a lot of Bible story books and I thought I wanted to be a minister. Then all of a sudden I went totally in the opposite direction. My parents had taught me that I should do things because that's what good little girls did. I couldn't see why I couldn't make a choice. That's the way I approached being a teenager. I did things because it was what I wanted to do. Just the reasons, "Well, good little girls don't do that" or "That's just the right thing to do" all of a sudden weren't enough.

That's where I hope that I have an edge with Dawn because we're talking eternity and eternal consequences, soul-binding consequences, not just the consequences I was ever given.

Lynne Whitney, 47

Lynne Whitney and her four children were members of the Elkton Branch from its beginning. The Whitney family moved to Delaware in 1966 from Salt Lake City when Bill Whitney was transferred by Hercules. They lived in northern Delaware before moving to a house in Elkton, just across the state line. An accomplished pianist, Lynne accompanies the choir, plays the organ for sacrament meeting, and teaches Primary. She works as an administrative assistant at the University of Delaware.

I was an active churchgoer until I was about nineteen or twenty, then I just didn't want anything to do with it anymore. After we moved out here I realized I had to start taking the children to church. I couldn't not let them go. Of course, you know the minute you show your face inside the church they give you a calling.

Nan Johnson, the stake president's wife, knew my family and invited us over one evening for pie and ice cream. I started going to Relief Society, a little bit. My neighbor, Genevieve Richards, used to pick me up. But I didn't entirely like it. I used to get kind of hostile feelings.

Then one day somebody came over and asked me to be the Primary chorister. I had done that when I was in high school, so I said, "Well, yes, I guess I can do that." But I didn't always come. I always had excuses why I wasn't there. I was just a reprobate. Then I stopped going for a long time. It took quite a few years for me to get back in. I had some bad habits and I didn't want to change them. I didn't want to cause any conflict in the home. I was afraid of getting totally back into the church again.

Then I became converted overnight. I was born again. It's been that way ever since. I had come to a point in my life where everything was a shambles. There wasn't anything that was going right. That's when I became converted because I had to rely totally on the Lord. He helped me get through it and has continued to bless our family. I think I'll never be able to live my life good enough to pay back what he's done for me.

My husband has been irritated many times because I've been away from him and not been here. But I think we've been married long enough that that doesn't matter anymore. I have to be able to do other things, just the same as he has other things that he does in his life. I choose church work and I also choose to sing. We've matured enough that if it's a problem, it's not a problem for very long. But in the beginning it was a problem. Every time I went to church, he'd say, "Oh, oh, I know it. I just know you're going to get back into that church. I just know it." Well, he was right.

We adopted Elizabeth in March of 1966 and Stephen in the summer of 1967. All of a sudden I was up at night feeding a baby and washing diapers. I had had no preparation at all. They were both wonderful little babies. I thought Elizabeth was exceptionally smart. She was talking before she was a year old. Stephen was very mechanically inclined even when a baby. His favorite toys were the vacuum cleaner and our coffee percolator. My parents came out to visit when we lived in North Wilmington. We were standing outside waiting for the airport limousine to pick them up when my father said, "Wait a minute. There's something I have to do before we leave. I want you all to go back in the house."

He said, "Lynne, come sit over here. I feel strongly that I must give you a blessing."

This made my mother a little uneasy. I could hear her feeling inside, "Oh, John, we don't have time to do this now."

He blessed me that I would someday have natural children, and then as soon as he was through, the limousine came and they were gone. It didn't leave my mind, but I'm not sure that I had a great deal of faith that it would happen. I was very busy with the two children that I had. A year later I got pregnant. I called my father when I found out and I acknowledged to him that I knew I was pregnant because of his blessing. I think that was the beginning of a lot of things for me.

I was thrilled with Jane, but I didn't feel any different about her than the others. I was just thrilled to death to have the experience of being pregnant after ten years of marriage. We thought, "Well, this is a nice little family." Elizabeth was three, Stephen was two, and Jane was a little baby. Then a year later I got pregnant again and had John. We had an instant family.

One day Bishop Cross announced that Cloyd Mullins was going to start holding sacrament meeting in his home for those members of the New Castle

Ward who lived in Maryland. I took the four children to sacrament meeting at his house. Usually the only people there were the missionaries, Cloyd and his two sons, the Lilley family, and Jerry Able, who lived near Rising Sun. Guest speakers came from New Castle and we'd sing to a tape-recorded accompaniment. The children enjoyed sacrament meeting because it was very short. We went to New Castle Ward in the morning for Sunday school, then to Cloyd's in the afternoon for sacrament meeting. We weren't a branch, just experimenting to see if it was possible.

Then the Cherrys were baptized and the Nielsens moved into the area. We moved down to Cloyd's basement. It was freezing cold in there. When we became a independent branch, we started meeting in Holly Hall. The people from below the C and D Canal—the Crowes, the McVickers, the Pierces—were included then.

We had junior Sunday school, Sunday school, and sacrament meeting. The Young Men and Young Women went to the New Castle Ward for their meetings. We had Primary, but then we had to stop because we didn't have enough people to staff everything. Having home Primary didn't work out. We had a good junior Sunday school, but we just couldn't do any more. Everybody was loaded with jobs. I helped with the singing in junior Sunday school, then I'd run in and do the singing in Sunday school or play the piano. I taught a Sunday school class and a Primary class during the week and helped in Relief Society. It was too much! Plus I was teaching a Relief Society class in the New Castle Ward during the week for working women.

When we moved into the building we have now, we only filled up a couple of benches. We began to have Primary again in Marcia Nielsen's home. Finally one day the Bushmans came to church and I couldn't figure out why they were there. They announced that he was our new bishop and we've been a ward ever since.

I try not to disagree with anything at church because I used to disagree so much. I think if I started doing that again I would be *damned*. I would never come out of that. I just don't allow myself to get upset about comments or remarks.

When we had to stop having Primary in the branch, I felt very bad. I bore my testimony and said, "We just have to find a way to have it. We'll find a way and we'll do it."

Then another woman got up and said, "I'm sorry that we're not going to have Primary, but when President Mullins says we're not going to have Primary, that means we're not going to have Primary."

One of my sisters who's not very active in the church was visiting. When we got home she said, "Lynne, didn't that upset you that she said that? That was like saying, 'You shouldn't have said what you said.'"

I said, "No, that didn't upset me." But I think some people feel if a member of the priesthood says something, that's IT, that's the final word. I think women have a right to express their ideas even though maybe in the end the priesthood will have the final word.

Cloyd Mullins, 48

Cloyd Mullins, the first president of the Elkton Branch, was born in Paines-ville, West Virginia, in 1936, where his father was a coal miner and Cloyd was one of thirteen children. During World War II the family moved to Elkton, where Cloyd met his wife, Ann Watson, in high school. She was baptized in 1958, and Cloyd joined the church in November 1966.

We moved to Maryland probably in 1943, maybe '42. I was between six and eight years old. We lived in the Elkton area in a government project that was called Hollingsworth Manor. You had to be a veteran or in the service to get one of those houses. Dad was here about two months, then he came back home and all of us moved into Maryland.

Just a few days before we left the farm, we went to visit all our relatives. We were moving five hundred miles from home. Mom had never been away in her life. My dad loaded all the furniture up on a sled. Then they stored it at my sister's house. The next morning as we were coming up the road different neighbors came out and talked to us. They were all crying. You'd think we were going to a funeral. This was just a great adventure for all of us little kids. We came up past Luther Horn's place where his wife Sara Margaret stood on the porch. A long ways off you could see her wiping the tears with her handker-chief. We went on up past my brother-in-law and sister's place, but she wouldn't come out on the porch to say good-bye to us. She told us later on she'd rather have seen Mom carried to the funeral home than see her leave like that.

In Maryland, I guess everybody thought they died and went to heaven be-cause we had central heat; we had running water; we had electricity; we cooked on gas. We didn't have to bring wood in at night; we didn't have to do anything. All we had to do was just mow a little lawn.

I met my wife, Ann Watson, at school. We started dating real serious in Janu-ary and we got married in July. She was seventeen and I was nineteen. Three days after we came back from our honeymoon to the Eastern Shore, we went to Illinois and I got a job out there.

Chuckie was born the following year. About that time the elders from the church came around during the day. When I came in from work, my wife said some gentlemen from a church had stopped by to see her and they were going to come back that evening. That evening we just sat around and talked a little bit. The next visit they taught us the first discussion. After the second discus-sion I told them I wasn't interested in the church and didn't want to take any more discussions. They asked me if I minded if my wife continued on. I told them, "No. That was her freedom." So she took the lessons and then she was baptized at the Great Lakes Naval Academy. She must have been nineteen. I went to her baptism. I didn't want to go, but I thought a lot of her. I loved her and I never tried to keep her from doing things she wanted to do. I sat as far as I could in the back.

She couldn't drive at that time, so I would drive her to church. They had rented a little building right beside a park in Waukegan. I drove up in front of that little old shabby building and there were five or six men and some women standing on the porch. I went on home and I said to myself, "Boy she's got herself into some mess." It wasn't very long until they started meeting in a town thirteen miles away from Waukegan. I used to drive her over there. It was too far for me to come back home so I would sit out in the parking lot and hold Chuckie and take care of him for a couple of hours until she came out.

She never talked to me about the church to pressure me, and I wouldn't listen to her anyway. I had my own habits and I liked to drink a little bit. She set a good example and I was proud that she was raising the children in the manner that she was. She believed in going to church; she believed in no drinking, no smoking, no drinking coffee—just different things that I was taught we shouldn't do but our parents did them. I just never would listen to it. I just couldn't accept Joseph Smith as a prophet. I couldn't accept polygamy.

We moved back to Easton, Maryland, from Waukegan in '59, and she was to go to church in Salisbury, seventy miles from home. She would go once in a while, but I never went with her. The home teachers would drive seventy miles each way to visit her. My wife and they made an agreement that a certain week of the month she would be home on Thursday. When I came in from work, sometimes they would be there. I could see their car way off across the fields, so I'd just go back down to the horse barn until they left and then I'd go home. Some nights I'd be at the house and I'd happen to remember that it was that Thursday they were to show up, so I'd invite my wife uptown for a sundae or something like that. We'd come back and there would be a note pinned on the screen. "Your home teachers were here. Sorry we missed you. Maybe we'll catch you the next time."

She'd say, "Oh my goodness, we missed the home teachers."

Then we moved to Elkton and she started going to church more frequently because Wilmington was about twenty miles away. If anybody came to my house who I thought was from the church, I'd just back out the lane and wait until the car with Delaware tags had left.

Then she became ill. She had a heart stoppage and we thought we were going to lose her. The attacks kept getting closer together. They called me to come because they didn't think she was going to make it. When I was in the lounge— just any minute I expected them to come out and say she'd passed away—I said a serious prayer (I'd only said three or four in my life). I promised that if she came out of the hospital I wouldn't drink anymore, I wouldn't smoke, I wouldn't drink coffee, and I would start going to church with her regularly. That was on the twenty-seventh of June, 1964. Her brother offered me a beer. I refused that beer and I never touched another drink after that. That was the only promise that I kept of those I made.

We only had insurance to cover part of the hospital bills. We were just making ends meet. I had a beautiful '58 Chevy Impala, red with white top. It was one of the nicest looking cars around. I asked Dr. Lane what his bill was. He figured it up. I said, "Well, I don't have any money at all. I appreciate all you've done for my wife. The only thing I have is a nice car. I know it won't cover the bill, but I'll sign it over to you. That's all I can do."

He said, "No, don't do that. You're going to need your car. You'll pay it somehow. Don't worry about it. Let that be your last problem."

I decided that I would work two jobs until I got that bill paid. It wasn't very long until I had the bills paid off. As soon as I got them paid off, I said, "I'm not going to quit. I'm going to work and I'm going to make a down payment for a home."

I was working at Chrysler from 3:30 or 4:00 in the evening until around 11:30 or 12:00 at night. I was working from 8:00 until 2:30 on construction work. Then on the weekends I was working security guard. I wasn't doing anything, just coming home, going to bed, and getting up. I can just remember so clearly how I stepped from the parking lot up to the curb right at the guard gate at Chrysler, and I asked myself, "What in the world am I working for?" I was just exhausted. I started talking to a Baptist boy at work about religion, just to see what he believed in.

My sister had married a Catholic boy and converted to the Catholic Church. When she and her husband saw I was interested, my brother-in-law's uncle started telling me what they believed in. I believed in their doctrine a little more than other doctrines I heard of.

My wife never talked to me much about church at that time. She was expecting Danny. I would ask her questions. She wouldn't answer me as much as I thought she should. One day as we were leaving my brother-in-law's house, I said, "How about your religion?"

She said, "You're going to have to make your own decision of what religion you want to join. You can't join my religion because of me. You've got to search out yourself and see which one you want and which one you can live." She had on a green spring coat, kind of checkered. It just seemed that things were clear to me.

Maybe the next day—this Baptist boy was still talking to me—I went over to get some material out of a big wire basket. While I was picking that stuff out of that wire basket, it seemed like I was all by myself in that little corner. There

was a forklift going down with one of those wire baskets on the end and I just
flipped those cigarettes out of my pocket and tossed them in that basket as it
went past. I walked back over to Joe. "Joe, I've decided what church I'm going
to join."

He said, "Which one's that?"

"I'm joining the Mormon church."

"Do you know they don't smoke; they don't drink coffee?"

"Yeah."

"Well, when are you going to quit smoking?"

I said, "I just quit about five minutes ago." I don't remember when I smoked
my last one, but I remember when I threw my pack away. I went home and told
my wife I was going to join the church.

I can remember my baptism day very plain because we were all great hunters
—my dad, my brothers, my brothers-in-law. My baptism was on the first day of
rabbit season. My sisters and brothers and some cousins were going to see me
baptized—my father and mother, too. When I went into my brother-in-law's to
pick up my sister, there sat all the rabbit hunters. I was all dressed up, and they
asked, "Where are you going? Aren't you going hunting today?"

My brother-in-law said, "He's going to be baptized today."

They were all sitting there drinking beer. One of them said, "There's nothing
wrong with that." We went on to church. The hunters went rabbit hunting.

All of my family was crying when I was baptized. Sister Arnold came up to
me and said, "I never saw so many tears in my life. It was more like a funeral
than a baptism."

I didn't accept the priesthood for over a year because I didn't feel that I was
worthy. I was just going to church, going to priesthood meeting, sitting there,
and that was it. One day, the teacher read out of the scriptures that a person
who doesn't do his duty in the church is—I forget the word—but anyway it
was shirking his duty and he wasn't looked upon with favor by the Lord. After
he got finished talking we sang "Put Your Shoulder to the Wheel." I accepted
the priesthood right after that. Within a week or two I was ordained a deacon
in the Aaronic priesthood. From there on the church just kept meaning a little
more to me. I kept growing stronger.

We went to the temple in '71. Even though my wife had wanted to go to the
temple I don't think she ever thought we would because it was so far away. I
was working seven days a week, ten hours a day most of the time because the
coker had burned at Getty Oil. I told Ann, "When this is over with we're going
to take us a vacation out West." She didn't believe that we were going out West
until I started preparing a month before we left. I had a little shell camper on
the truck. I fixed the boot and put air conditioning in it because of her health.
I heard it was real hot out there. When I put the air conditioner in the truck, I
think that's when she knew that we were going.

When we left, she said, "Which temple are we going to be sealed in?"

I said, "The first one we come to." We were sealed in the Manti Temple, in Utah.

When she became ill, she knew she wasn't going to make it like she had before. She accepted that. She never complained. She said, "I don't want you to pity me or do anything for me that you didn't do before. I want you to be just as natural as you can around me. I don't want you driving me to the hospital for my treatments every day. I don't want you missing work because of me." I wish I had missed work. I wish I had just gone ahead and done what I felt like I should have been doing instead of trying to please her by doing what she wanted.

If I hadn't been a member of the church and hadn't had the gospel after she died, it's hard to tell what I would have done. I probably would have neglected my family. I'd have probably got worse in drinking because I've never found anyone that I wanted to live with since her. She passed away in July of '76. We started holding sacrament meetings at my house here in December of '76. I was feeling that I was cheated. We were happy together. I felt she was taken away right in the middle of my life where we could have started enjoying our lives. I had a better paying job; we had our house settled down; we were making the mortgage payments.

One day Brother Ridge was giving a talk here in our meeting and he read from the Old Testament where God says, "My thoughts are greater than your thoughts. My ways are greater than your ways. My reasons are greater than yours." When Brother Ridge read that passage I kind of accepted her death a little more. A good while after that, I was sitting on the bed feeling sorry for myself. I remembered when I made the promise that I would quit drinking, I had asked the Lord if he would only spare her until Chuckie was out of high school. I never remembered that part of the prayer until then. I think Chuckie was nineteen at the time; he just finished high school. If I had known that prayer was going to come true, I would have asked for until she was sixty or eighty.

When she passed away the responsibility of my family was on me. I had to do what she expected me to do. Danny was only nine years old. I couldn't neglect him.

Being branch president was an experience. When it was first presented to me, I started to say no. Now that it's behind me, I'm glad I said yes. I feel good about that calling. A lot of people think that was the hardest calling that I'll ever have, but I don't think I've had a calling that was easier—even though we had hardships and people who were burdened with their callings, trying to find meeting houses, all the meetings I had to go to, the sacrifices that Danny did for me. He would go with me in the morning, stay from seven o'clock until two or three in the evening. He never complained. I think the Spirit was there with him to comfort him. The members in the branch were strong people and they were the ones that did the work in the branch.

I remember the first day we had our meeting here at the house. Lynne Whitney and her children showed up. I was wondering if anybody would show up. I didn't even know how to say the sacrament prayer. I didn't know how to start it off.

I think the Lord expects us to know this. I don't think any of us pay much attention. We have the true gospel, and I think we should practice what we preach a little more. We get on our children for not doing their chores. The Savior has given us responsibilities: home teaching, go to sacrament meetings, priesthood meetings, visit the sick, family prayers, morning prayers. I'm sure he looks down on us and he thinks probably the same as we think about our children. "Why do I have to keep telling you to do those things?"

I was over at my sister's house after Ann had passed away. They asked me, "Do you think that you and Ann are going to be husband and wife in the hereafter?"

I said, "There's not a doubt in my mind. We're going to be married as we are right here."

So my brother-in-law said, "How about me and Lexie?"

I said, "Well, you're going to get just what you believe and what you want. Now how were you married? 'Death do you part.' Ann and I were sealed for time and eternity. There you go. You don't want to be married for time and eternity or you would do it." There are a lot of people who want what we want, but they don't believe what we teach.

I can understand these people. If I had been baptized when Ann was I don't think I could have been the branch president. I wouldn't have understood people like I do. The Lord's been good to me. He's given me a lot of experience and I still had the opportunity to join the church. I can understand the wife who belongs to the church and the husband who doesn't. I can accept that husband's ways and his beliefs because I was there once. I can understand what the wife goes through because my wife went through it. I can accept that he doesn't join the church because he hasn't been converted yet. I have hopes that these brethren will be, because I was. The wives are setting the example for them as my wife set it for me.

My wife's friends would come here and they would tell her the problems they were going to see the bishop about. They talked just as freely in front of me. After they left, I would tell her, "There's no need of going to see the bishop. I can tell them it's their fault right here."

She would laugh and say, "Boy you would make a good bishop." But when I became the branch president, it was a whole lot different. It's easy to tell a person what the problem is because they know their problem. But the idea is to try to help them solve their problem in such a way that if they're wrong, you're not condemning them. You want to try to help them to understand, to try to help themselves, and to go at things a little brighter.

When my wife moved into Elkton, to our knowledge, she was the only Mormon in the Elkton area. I've often thought just how proud she would be if she were here now and could see the activity that there is in Elkton.

4 | The Primary Program

Of all the organizations in the Elkton Ward, the Primary has the largest staff. Each week about eighty-five children, ages three to eleven, attend Primary. The children spend half the one hundred minutes of Primary in one of eleven classes and half in group worship. The format and the lesson materials are provided by the General Primary Board in Salt Lake City.

The Elkton Ward Primary presidency, Virginia Lund, Jean Bingham, and Colleen Pierce, make sure that the classes are staffed with teachers, plan and conduct "sharing time" and closing exercises each week, and organize several activity days for the children during the year. During September Colleen Pierce, the second counselor, was the "Rover," free to help teachers or troubleshoot during class time. Jean Bingham, the first counselor, presented the sharing time activity. Using a picture of a young boy, she dressed him in the "whole armor of God" while eliciting the children's comments about the principles represented by the armor—truth, righteousness, and faith.

Singing time was led by Julie Ridge, who spent her allotted twenty minutes reviewing the songs the children had learned for the Primary sacrament meeting presentation, which would begin intensive rehearsals soon. Virginia Lund conducted the closing exercises. Two of the Stars (age four) gave talks on honesty, one with help from her mother. Virginia Lund told a flannelboard story about a lazy bluebird who sold all his feathers for a few worms. After a closing song and prayer, the Blazers (eleven-year-old boys) ushered the children out of the room, row by row.

On October 21, the day of the presentation, sacrament meeting began ten minutes late. Five of our children sat with their Primary classes. My husband and I sat on the other side of the chapel with just our one-year-old, Robert, with us. Other family groups were similarly reduced. The service proceeded through the opening hymn and prayer, business, and sacrament service more reverently than usual—even though all the children were seated away from their parents' control. After the sacrament table was carried to the side of the chapel, the program began.

Andrew Ridge, ten years old, played the part of a twelve-year-old boy who was graduating from Primary. During the course of the interview he told the bishop, played by Gary Johnston, what he had learned about the gospel and where he had learned it.

His first recollection was of a Star class in Primary. The four-year-old Stars with their teacher, Thelma Roberts, came to the platform. Because of her vision problem, Thelma had to memorize all her lines. Some of the children forgot theirs, and so made up new ones. Ingrid Adams showed her baby to the Star class and told them how special her baby was and how much she loved him.

Next Andrew recalled lessons learned in family home evening. Lee and Sheila Anderson with their children, Bronwyn and Pearce, were Andrew's "family." "Dad" conducted a lesson on the importance of putting on the whole armor of God. During the discussion the family members placed the words *Truth Righteousness, Preparation,* and *Faith* on a posting chart. Park Adams portrayed Daniel beside a very active stuffed lion, which was powered by Colleen Pierce. Then Andy Burke as David faced a very tall Goliath, played by Jonathan Lund.

Virginia Lund, 31

Virginia Lund has been the Primary president for a year and a half, during which time she has had four different first counselors. She grew up in New Jersey and New York and joined the church at the age of seventeen. She and her husband, Jonathan, have been married for ten years and have four children, ranging from nine years to nine months old.

When I was about fourteen I started being dissatisfied with my church. I didn't feel a lot of the things they taught us were right. What bothered me most was the idea that everyone who died without hearing of Christ would go to hell, including babies. I thought, "I'll read the New Testament. I'll do whatever Jesus said would be the right way." But I discovered that without other people, it was an empty way to practice religion.

Then I began going to other churches. I loved the Presbyterian church because of its minister. When he left, I discovered that the church could have a completely different philosophy with a different minister. I decided the church I was looking for had to be the same no matter who the minister is. I heard about a boy who was a Mormon. I went up to him and said, "Would you tell me about your church?"

When he took me there, I was so impressed with how friendly everybody was. I'd like to think I joined because I had a testimony, but would I have had a testimony if I hadn't had such a warm reception? I was having a lot of problems getting along with my father. Home was such an emotionally upsetting place, but the difference at my friend's house was almost like hell and heaven. The atmosphere helped me to be receptive.

The church was in Plattsburgh, about an hour away. As this boy and I drove back and forth, he would tell me about the gospel. It felt like the car was full of light and warmth. Everything that he said seemed so true. It was just so logical. Every time I have doubts about the church's truthfulness, I have to remember a youth conference I went to in Vermont when I had been investigating the church for some time. At the fast and testimony meeting I was overcome with a feeling of warmth and burning. When I stood up to bear my testimony that feeling was so strong that I felt like Moses when he saw the Lord. I felt like my legs were going to give way, but there was energy inside that was sustaining me. There seemed to be a golden glow in the room. Whenever I have a strong answer to prayer, I always have a sensation of light. Even though I have my little doubts or hard trials regarding the gospel, there is no way that I can deny that experience.

I wasn't happy at Ithaca College. I didn't know enough about the church. People would come up to me and say, "Did you know Mormons don't believe in dancing?"

And I would say, "Oh, they don't?" Then I wouldn't dance until I had found out for sure if we believed in dancing. I was always hearing things and never knowing what the church really believed. I decided to attend Brigham Young University even though my parents didn't want me to.

At BYU the leaders would say things such as, "You shouldn't put off having a family just because you are going to school." I look back now and realize that we could have waited a while. Jon went to school for a long time. He was going to school after Betsy, our second child, was born. Just because you wait a year doesn't mean you are putting off your family. I have to wonder if I hadn't been so eager to follow the brethren, whether my husband wouldn't have had so many problems with depression early in our marriage. I wonder how many people don't finish school because they are trying hard to do what they should and then don't have the resources to finish because they are saddled with a family. When I taught Mutual, I was told you are not to use any kind of birth control except abstinence and to teach this to the girls. I don't think people have a right to tell others how to use birth control. If you are stopping the birth of children, you are stopping the birth of children, and I don't think that the method makes a difference.

It's not realistic today, with all the demands that women have on their time, unless you are a very talented person in handling children, to have a large family. Four children is a big family. Families with five or six children are almost always families that are about twenty years older than mine. It is wrong to make people feel guilty if they don't have a big family. I have read that if you curtail the birth of children, you will reap disappointment by and by. I think when leaders speak like that, we have to remember they are speaking in generalities and each of us has to pray about it. I have heard people say, "The Lord won't send you any more than you can handle." But I see women with ruined bodies or women who cannot have any more children because they had them so fast.

When I lived in Utah, we all were told to go to the International Women's Year Convention and vote a certain way. We all did it just like sheep. I am a little ashamed of that now. We should have studied the issues on our own and voted the way that we thought was right. We don't want to be represented as being blind followers because in everything else we are not. In conferences general authorities say we must pray and gain a testimony about what we have heard. I am a little ashamed that we did not do that.

Before Matthew was born I did the very best I could in all my classes; I was carrying an A average. He was born right after Thanksgiving. I stayed home for a week and took him right into class with me, bundled in about five blankets because I didn't have a snowsuit for him. I unwrapped Matthew and laid him down in his infant seat. When the teacher started talking, Matthew woke up. The teacher apologized for waking him up. Where else but Brigham Young University?

When he started to cry in another class, I was embarrassed because I felt like I was disturbing the whole class. I got right up, picked up Matt and my books, and rushed out. To my embarrassment I heard someone following me down the hall. A boy from the class said the teacher wanted me to come back. My face was scarlet red when I went in, but the teacher told me that I didn't have to leave. He had nine children and his wife couldn't have any more. He missed the sound of a newborn baby and I could bring Matthew to class any time. I graduated with a degree in elementary education and a child.

Jon never did get his degree. He just couldn't handle going to school and working at the same time. He got a job with a computer firm. He went from making four thousand dollars a year to making eight thousand dollars, and we thought we were in big times. Six months later they raised him to fifteen thousand dollars. Within a year we thought we were so rich that we went out and bought an old house that needed a lot of work in Payson. Then Jon's company started to have problems. Even though they said Jon was one of their most important people and that they wouldn't let him go, we started thinking we should look for a new job. We decided that if we were going to have to move to Salt Lake, we should just move home. My dad was sure I would marry somebody from the West and never come home again, but I married another New Yorker.

We moved here, when Kristy was a month old, with a lot of faith. We prayed about it and felt good about moving. Within two weeks Jon was working. That was a blessing of tithing, one of those so great that there isn't room to receive it. We have had some neat blessings because we had paid our tithing. When my mother died, Dad said he would pay for our tickets to come to Mom's funeral. Although he did, neither of us worked for two weeks and that meant we didn't have money to buy food. I prayed and told Heavenly Father, "We have been paying our tithing. I don't have enough money to buy food. Please help me to know what to do." I got up, put on my coat, opened the door to go to school, and there on the front step was a big, huge turkey. The Lord must have whispered in someone's ear. Some people might have said that was a coincidence, but it was a blessing to me.

I remember a list I made when I was twelve of all the things I was never going to do to my children. I'd never say, "If you don't stop crying, I'll give you something to cry about" or "How many times have I told you" to a child who can't count to four. It's amazing the expressions that come out of your mouth. I always loved children and thought being a mother would be one big game. I thought when I told my children to go to bed that they would run into their beds just the way the children I babysat did. Or when I said, "It's time to clean up. Let's see who gets done first," that they would always think it was fun.

Last year when I was pregnant with Eric (I realize being pregnant makes you feel emotional, anyway), when my children started to cry, I had such a feeling of panic. I went to a therapist, finally, because I thought, "I'm thirty. Obviously I can't fix this myself or I would have by now." It was very helpful. I have learned to differentiate between their feelings and my feelings, but it is still hard for me to take care of someone who has lost control.

I have had four first counselors in the year and a half I have been Primary president. My counselors right now, Jean Bingham and Colleen Pierce, are a source of satisfaction to me. They are very supportive and very efficient. When we decide something, I know that it is going to be done. It is a terrific feeling to pray about something and then to have the answer confirmed. I told the bishop when he took Lynne Whitney, the Blazer leader, to be a counselor in the Relief Society, that I don't care who he takes now that I have Jean and Colleen because I finally feel like we are a team. I see the Lord's hand in these callings. Jean couldn't have been called when I was called to be president because she wasn't in the ward. I always wanted to have Julie Ridge lead the music, but she was teaching seminary. Finally, after a year and a half, she could do the music and she did a terrific job. We felt that she might be good as an inservice leader. Every time I went to pray about it, I would think, "Wait, I am not quite sure that this is right." I don't like to pray about something until I feel good about it. I just didn't get that feeling. Then she was called to be the Relief Society president. To me that was a testimony. That is where Heavenly Father wanted her.

She could fill in for a little while in the music, but he knew that it wouldn't be right for her to start doing all the inservice work because he had her in mind for another purpose. The Lord couldn't tell me the whole master plan. Now I see all the pieces of the puzzle, but during that time I could just see a piece that had fallen out.

The responsibility is heavy because no matter how much I do, there is always something more that I could be doing. I know that at least 50 percent of the ward could be doing a better job than I am. For a while I felt funny about Colleen. She is so efficient. After my operation it was hard for me to sit back and see Colleen carrying the whole load. I tend to think if I want to get up and go, I can get up and go. She was doing such a good job that I felt she would know that I wasn't doing all that I could be doing. I think everything should be perfect and because it isn't, I feel I am not doing a good job. Since Colleen has apologized for making a few mistakes, I have realized that she is not perfect either.

The first thing you learn as a president is that if you want something done the way you want it done, you have to do it yourself. The second is that maybe the way you want it done is not the way it has to be done. The third is that it is very difficult to let other people do it the way they want to do it.

One of my biggest weaknesses is that I find it is easier to help other people's children than to help my own. It is this way with the four children I babysit before and after school and at church. It is hard for me to give my children the attention that they need when there are people standing around me saying, "Sister Lund I need to talk to you." "Sister Lund, can you just sign this paper." "Sister Lund, you didn't hand in your order yet." There is my little four-year-old saying, "Mommy, I want to go home." But I have found that as I have served the Lord, I have received inspiration that has helped me with other problems in my life. For instance, a great idea for family home evening will come into my mind while I am sitting in sacrament meeting.

Any endeavor is tiring and long. Primary is a long time. I wish that they would eliminate Sunday school so that Primary could be shorter. As it is now, everyone moves into Sunday school and then into Relief Society. You could save another ten minutes if you didn't have to move. If Relief Society included a fifteen-minute scripture study time instead of having a Sunday school class, you could take half an hour off the Primary. It would make a big difference if Primary were just an hour long. I think the children would like it a lot better.

I didn't realize how negatively I was feeling about Primary, but now I can work on it and figure out how to solve it. There are things that I haven't done this year that I am feeling bad about. Doing something is easy compared to worrying about it.

Jean Bingham, 32

Jean Bingham, Virginia Lund's first counselor, moved into the Elkton Ward in June. She grew up in Baltimore and met her husband at Westminster College in Salt Lake City. Raised in the Lutheran Church, she joined the LDS Church in 1972, a month before the birth of her daughter. Jean has been an active volunteer in several pro-family political organizations.

Except for the past twelve months, I've been a Primary worker since 1973. I've seen a few changes in Primary since then. Primary on *Sunday* is the biggest change. There's much more confusion now at the start of Primary. When Primary was on a weekday after school, the children came running into the building making as much noise as was humanly possible. But we kept them outside the chapel until they were quiet. Now the children go directly from sacrament meeting to their classrooms. Being new in the ward, I'm not much help to the children. I don't know yet who they are, who their teachers are, or what classes they are in.

Fortunately, Ginny and Colleen know what they are doing. Being a counselor's a lot of fun because as long as we keep it organized it's not hard work. It's a lot of fun working with other women and getting to know them well. The little children, at least until they get to a certain age, are so trusting and they will listen and remember the things we tell them. This Primary is quite reverent—more so than some others I've worked with. Teenagers are very skeptical and think they know it all. It's nice working with little ones.

The biggest problem in Primary everywhere I've been has been staffing. It's hard to find good teachers. Once you've got them, the program runs itself. In other wards we've had teachers who just weren't interested in their classes or wouldn't show up. The children got upset because, "Why won't anybody teach us?" You always have a few discipline problems in Primary, but you can work with the children once you know them.

Before Becky was born, I took the missionary lessons. When I heard the lessons, I knew that the church had to be true. In my Lutheran elementary school, it seemed like I memorized half the Bible. There were a lot of scriptures that nobody knew what they meant. They didn't tell me in the Lutheran Church that "Other sheep have I also which are not of this fold," refers to the Nephites. "In My Father's house are many mansions" is another. In the Lutheran Church there's heaven and hell and that's it. When I heard the missionary lessons, I thought, "That's what that means!" There were a lot of things that fit together like the pieces of a puzzle.

My biggest challenge has been Becky's health. Two doctors gave up on her in Salt Lake. One of them was *the* pediatric neurologist at the University of Utah. If he couldn't cure your child, no one could. He put her in the hospital for one day of tests and said, "There's nothing we can do." They were talking about institutionalizing her. She certainly does not need to be in an institution, but she was in bad shape at that time.

She was six and she had started having grand mal seizures at three, one or two a year. Then she was okay until she was four and she started blinking. Those were petit mal seizures. With medication she was fine until she was five. Then the petit mal seizures got out of control. She was unable to talk, feed herself, take care of herself in any way. It just about did me in because I had a child who was functioning like a six-month-old baby.

The Lord works in mysterious ways, let me tell you. My mother got sick. I said, "Vern, I'm going back to stay with her for as long as she lives or until we get this problem straightened out."

He was 100 percent supportive. The only thing we disagreed about was he wanted me to fly and I said, "No, I need to drive."

He said, "I don't want you out on the highway for four days by yourself with a sick child in the back." If I couldn't have three or four days by myself out on the road with no one around me, I would have lost my mind. I'm an only child and being alone helps me get my act together. When he has a problem, he wants to talk to people. He was mad at me when I left because he said, "What if you break down?"

I said, "Well, there are truck drivers out there. They'll come along and help out."

And he said, "Oh, now I'm really worried."

I don't worry about things like that. I figure when your time's up, it's up. Becky was like a little zombie in the back of the car, didn't say a word for two thousand miles. We stopped about every two hundred miles to get gas and at every other stop I'd let her get out and go to the bathroom. I drove fourteen hours a day for three days, and it was wonderful. It was what I needed to get back in control of myself.

It turned out that my mother had cancer. She lived six months. My husband didn't want me to leave her. While I was in Baltimore, someone said, "Why don't you take Becky to Johns Hopkins? They have a seizure clinic." At Hopkins they said, "No wonder she didn't get better. They had her on the wrong medicines. Even on the rare occasions when they had her on the right medicine, they didn't have her on large enough doses to do anything. We think we can help." Even at Hopkins they didn't expect to see the change that they've seen. They expected her to have fewer seizures, but Becky can now go for weeks, even months, without any. She has already had miracles in her life. They still don't know what causes them and they usually don't with children. She has no brain damage and she's never had a head injury. That was my bad spell with my mother dying, my child not straightened out, my husband still in Utah. When Hopkins said they could help her, I said "Honey, why don't we move back here?"

He said, "I don't have any objection to that provided I can find work." He came back and applied with Marriott. The move from Utah to Maryland, as traumatic as it was, turned out to be the best thing that could have happened to us.

In 1980 I got involved with a group that was trying to make sure that Jimmy Carter's White House Conference on families wasn't taken over by anti-family groups—the pro-abortion, pro-ERA, pro-homosexuality groups. Jimmy Carter had stacked it so they would run the conference, and we were trying to undermine what they were doing. Through that I became involved with numerous local, state, and national groups. I worked for Right to Life and the Eagle Forum. Not all of it was volunteer. I later had a job in Washington, writing for a monthly publication.

I did crisis pregnancy counseling for a year, trying to talk girls out of having abortions. The name of the center was Pregnancy Center so that the people coming in didn't realize it was run by Right to Life. Most of the girls were leaning toward abortion when they came in. I think about half our clientele had already had one abortion. We'd start talking to them about why they should not have a second one in terms of physical consequences and educating them that an unborn baby is a live human being. One girl who'd had an abortion started crying and came to a realization of what she had done. Then she didn't know if God would forgive her, and we talked about that. I never talked about religion unless the other person wanted to.

The girls told me about the inhumane treatment they'd received at abortion clinics. We tried to help them get over feeling guilty about what they'd done. We'd say, "Let's go on from where you are now. Let's not make that same mistake again." There were some who were going to get an abortion no matter what you said to them, but there were enough who would stop and say, "Okay, now where can I get medical help because I don't have money?" We'd ask them what their most immediate problems would be. That they couldn't tell their parents? That they'd be kicked out? We had shelter homes where they could live. If they didn't have a doctor, we could find one who charged what they could afford to pay. Those were the easy things to deal with. Most of them had problems in straightening out their lives. They had to decide they were going to stop living the way they were. I don't know how successful we were in that. It was rewarding that we were saving some little lives.

I don't see the fact that women don't have the priesthood as a problem. I see it as a delegation of responsibility. Someone has to be home nurturing the children. Only women can have babies and nurse them. Men can certainly change diapers—at least I've been told that they can—and give a child a peanut butter sandwich, but I have a hard time picturing how a mother with a reasonable-sized family would have time to jump up and go if someone in the ward needed the bishop. Men can usually get out of work. If you're the mother of a sick child, do you want to leave your sick child to go administer to someone?

Some of the sisters worry about the fact that there are no women on a church court. When Sandra Day O'Connor was nominated to the Supreme Court all the feminists were thrilled because they wanted a "woman's interpretation of the Constitution." There's no such thing. It's the same way with the laws of the gospel. "Thou shalt not steal" applies to men and women.

About a week after we moved to Delaware, Becky started going into seizures, bad ones. There didn't seem to be any reason for it and she seemed to be getting worse. I prayed about it, but she didn't get better. Then it came to me: "Her medicine's gone bad." In the process of moving some had been left in the car for two or three days. I asked the pharmacist and he said, "Oh, no. The heat wouldn't have affected it." I felt very strongly about it so I got her a new prescription. Sure enough, three days later the seizures were gone.

I don't go seeking after signs, but when I say a prayer I expect it to be answered, if need be right then and there. I was in a large chorus which was put together for the Legacy Concert given at Constitution Hall. I got on I-95 going fifty-five miles an hour when the steering wheel started bouncing up and down. No one noticed. They were all chatting away, a group of women on their way to some place. I said a quick silent prayer. "Heavenly Father, I have to get there. We're not on our way to see a dirty movie. This is church work we're going to do, so please let us get there safely." The steering wheel stopped shaking. I thought, "Well, I know a sign when I see one."

I drove the thirty miles down and the thirty miles back. No problem. Later that afternoon my husband and I were going to a wedding. Before he got to the end of the street, the steering wheel fell off into his lap. If that had fallen into my lap at fifty-five miles an hour I know I couldn't have controlled the car.

Even this past week I've had an experience with Becky that's brought me closer to the Lord. She'd been having seizures again. I didn't get an impression of anything wrong—other than just ride it out. It was getting on my nerves and I thought, "There's got to be something I can do." I don't ask my husband to give her blessings as much as I would like him to. I'm not going to nag him about it. I decided to go to the temple and put Becky's name on the prayer roll. I went down Wednesday because Vern was home most of the day. In the temple when the brother said the prayer, I knew that everything was okay at home. In fact, he said that in the prayer, that things would be all right at home. Sure enough the next day the seizures were gone again.

I would like my prayers answered that immediately every time, and they aren't always. One of the hardest things about being a member of the church is that you know your child can be healed if it's the Lord's will. I know the Savior healed people. I know one woman touched the hem of his garment and because of her faith her illness was gone immediately. I think it's frustrating to be a member of the church and know that healings can happen but still have to go through the trial of having your child so sick. In the long run, I know Becky will be all right. If I didn't know by now that prayers are answered, I don't know what it would take to convince me.

Colleen Pierce, 29

Colleen Pierce was introduced to Robert Pierce by a mutual friend in March 1980. When they married that August, Colleen moved to Odessa, Delaware, to live with Robert and his six-year-old twins, Stacy and Randy. Since then they have had two more daughters.

After I graduated from BYU, I taught school for one year before my mission and a half a year after I came back. I think that being a parent has helped me understand children a little bit more and it has made me a better teacher. Parenthood gives me the opportunity to use a lot of my talents, to think creatively in different aspects of life. It is very diversified. I don't get into the rut I found that sometimes I did when I taught. The most difficult thing is the discipline—keeping my temper—using the right form of discipline, not being too easy or too hard.

I was raised with the fact that women stay home and take care of the family. I believe that, but it has been a struggle because I've been in the working force. The paycheck is very satisfying. It's something that says, "Yes, you did a good job." It is not as easy to find that reward at home. What reward is there in changing diapers? The challenge for me in motherhood is finding those rewards. It's hard because goals aren't as easy to set and obtain. They are longer range.

I never thought about going on a mission when I was a kid, but when I was nineteen I wanted to go. All the boys that I grew up with were going, and I had a roommate who went. When I was twenty-one I didn't want to go, but I could never get it out of my mind. When I was twenty-three the bishop asked me how I felt about going on a mission. I felt like I had been caught. The feeling I should go had never left me. I went to Hong Kong as a welfare service missionary, not a proselytizing missionary. We helped set up some of the welfare service programs in the wards. We taught English. We worked with some of the Vietnamese refugees. We also worked with the Word of Wisdom problems and health problems. We taught nonmembers the health-related discussions, sanitation and things like that, and English. I didn't teach them the gospel. But in working with the people, I realized that the church is the same—the gospel's the same no matter where you are.

After I came home from my mission, one of the teachers at my school had taught Bob and his wife the gospel. When you are a returned missionary, everybody loves setting you up on dates. I figured, "What's one more blind date? This guy is from the East. I'll never see him again. I can go out and have a good time and not worry about it too much."

Before we were married, Bob and I decided that we would try to have children right away. We felt that would bring the two sides of the family together. I think that it has, but I think it's caused other problems, too. When I came the twins were six. I didn't have to change their diapers. I didn't get to watch them learn how to walk. I haven't made them mine as much as Bonnie and Valerie are. I hope I will.

When Bonnie was just three months old, I was called to be Relief Society president. In a lot of ways it was a relief for me to get away from these new things that I wasn't yet adjusted to and to give service to other people, too. I think that experience helps me support Bob a lot better. When you are a president you feel the weight of responsibility. Knowing that, I try harder to help Bob in his calling as Elders' Quorum president. Sometimes it's not easy when he has to be gone all the time.

I feel frustrated when members of the church lack commitment: when they say they will do something and don't; when they won't say yes or no; when they don't go visiting teaching; when members don't support each other in their callings or in activities. But one of the beauties of having a calling is that it puts you into situations where you can get to know people.

We are more well-to-do than my family was, but I find myself still shopping at K-Mart. I think that Bob appreciates knowing that I won't go out and spend three times as much as necessary. One of my fears is that the kids will grow up thinking that they can have anything they want. They're starting to want all the designer things.

I want them to grow up feeling good about themselves. I want them to be active in the church and to have strong testimonies of the gospel. I'm afraid because of the world. You never know what the outside influences are. All you can do is pray for them. You can teach them, but really all you can do is pray.

I don't mean to be pious, but if my children can't turn out better than I was, then my whole life is lost. If we're not better than our parents, that's no credit to them. We didn't learn anything from them. Even though I went outside to play on Sundays when I was a kid, I don't think that means that mine should go out and play. It's hard not to alienate the kids. If they resent it too much, eventually they rebel.

My testimony is different than that of most converts. It came "line upon line, precept upon precept" through my years of going to Sunday school and Primary. After I graduated from college there was turmoil in my mind about going on a mission. One night walking up the Hill Cumorah after a pageant performance, I said to myself, "When I go home I'm not going to be active in the church. This is ridiculous. I don't want to put up with all this." All of a sudden I thought, "You're so stupid. You've had so many experiences in your life that showed you that the church is true." I haven't had any visions, just the quiet reassurance.

I think that the Lord had a hand in when I went on my mission. After the principal of my school learned I was going, he tried to get me to teach the first half of the following year. I knew if I did that, I wouldn't ever go. When I came back I taught at a different school where I met the person who introduced me to

Bob. If I had waited to go on a mission, I would never have been in the position to be introduced to Bob. In spite of my feelings about his first wife, if it hadn't been for her, he would never have been introduced to the church, because her cousin referred the missionaries to them. The Lord does look out for us and he guides our lives. I have a very strong testimony of that.

Thelma Roberts, 72

Thelma Roberts has taught the Star A class (four-year-olds) since shortly after joining the church two years ago—five years after her only daughter, Clara Burke, joined. Thelma has been a Girl Scout leader for more than thirty years.

I got married when I was eighteen, during the depression. When I was a child, I never thought I was going to go through such hard times as I went through. I went through the depression and I learned to live on very little. I didn't lean on my parents for anything. My mother said to me, "I will give you food, but never ask me to give you money. You are on your own." When we didn't have anything to eat in the house I would never let her know. I think it made a better person out of me.

When we first got married I was working in a factory. I was a cutter for men's clothes. Then I went to the laundry to work. I worked there for about ten years. My husband couldn't find work for almost ten years after we were married. Then I got it easy. My husband said if he ever got a good job I would never have to work again, and I never did.

I love my home. We never had a pretty home, but it was always paid for. We never went in debt for anything, and what I had, I loved to take care of. I'm very thankful for all the things I have. Except for my eyes, I've had good health. I just never get tired of thanking God for all I have. I look around and I think of the time when I didn't have this. I lived five years in one little room, cooked and slept and everything in one little room. If I could go through the depression, I could go through anything.

If I had it to do over again I think I would wait a little bit longer to get married. I think if I hadn't lost my eyesight, I would have gone on to college because I wanted to be a teacher. I had a scholarship to Wesley College, but my mother wouldn't let me go. I think a girl getting married right away out of school never has a chance to find out what the world is all about. You marry and you're right down to a life and you never have the opportunities that other young people have. When you fall in love, you don't think about these things until later.

God's answered so many prayers for me. He gave me Clara. That was my big prayer. I prayed for that for a long, long time. In fact, I thought he had forgotten all about me. When I resigned myself to the fact that I might never have a child, out of a clear blue sky I got a telephone call saying, "Would you be interested in a baby girl?" I got her after I was married fifteen years. That blessing turned my whole life around. I took Clara with me when I taught Sunday school, of course. She was only three when she started coming with me. The children came in the dead of winter with little spring coats, with hardly anything on. An elderly lady who had worked in an overseas mission would bring a whole lot of drunks into the church; to get a meal they had to come to Sunday school. Afterwards I would take the children up the street to the big church. We sat up in the balcony because the church was a ritzy church and most of my kids were not rich kids. We sang hymns all the way to Sunday school and all the way back. I even used to play the organ, all the hymns.

I've been in Scouting since Clara was six years old—for thirty-three years. I lived Scouts, I breathed Scouts. Going to all the workshops and going to conferences, meeting people, developed a lot of my skills in knowing how to handle people. I was a day camp director for thirty years, so I had to learn to keep peace in the camp.

When my daughter became a member of the LDS Church, I began going to activities with her in the Wilmington Stake. One day we went to Washington and she signed me up for a Book of Mormon. Some of the missionaries brought it here, but they didn't give me any kind of lessons. Then I got sick and I went to Clara's. Clara's missionaries gave me a blessing and then they started teaching me.

The missionaries always gave me scriptures to look up. They would give me a question and they'd tell me to look up the answer. I used to sit here night after night and look up the answers. It helped me a lot. Even when they went back to Utah, I still got questions in their letters.

When I joined the church, I started bubbling. I wanted everybody to know. I guess my friends got tired of hearing me talk about my religion. I did get to go to Relief Society for a couple of months. I took the Gospel Essentials class in Sunday school. As soon as that was done, they asked me to teach in Primary and to teach in the Relief Society homemaking meeting. Now the callings are like a habit. Just as a matter of course I read my scriptures and prepare my lessons ahead of time, making sure that I can remember the scriptures to teach the children. Getting up in front of people other than my Primary class makes me very nervous. I have to memorize everything and I worry.

I enjoy those little ones in Primary. I would be lost without my Scouts, too. I know it's not going to last too much longer because I'm getting older, but I do love them. I like to see how much they have absorbed over a period of time. I'd like to play the piano. I'd like to be able to sing. I lost my voice in Scouts—too many hay rides with the kids. I used to crochet a lot, but the doctor will not let me because it makes me deathly sick because I can't see it. I wish I could do the things that they do in the homemaking class. Nobody knows how much I wish, but I have to console myself with what I have. They told me when I was sixteen that eventually I would go blind. But here I am at 72 and I have a lot of blessings. I never thought I would be seeing as much as I am today. He's been with me all the way. He's been so good to let me have my eyesight as long as he's given me. I prayed hard and he has let me teach through the years. It's harder now because I'm having more trouble. I do my callings and I do whatever they ask me to do if it's within my power to do. I try not to say no to anyone because I feel that when the presidency asks us to do things it's because there are things that have to be done.

Lots of things have given me faith. Faith that someday I would be able to have a home and to have a family was a big thing in my life. He gave me a lot of faith to overcome a lot of problems that we had at home. My husband drank an awful lot. I've lived a life where I've learned a lot.

I'd like to be able to live my gospel a little better, really learn a little bit more. I want to be able to be strong enough to do the callings they ask me to do, to keep on as long as I can with my Girl Scouts. I don't want to be somebody who sits in that rocking chair and just dwindles away—especially when they have me up there with the six-year-olds doing dances and songs.

Thomas Hearne, 35

Like Thelma Roberts, Thomas Hearne is a native of Wilmington, but he has been a member of the church all his life. Every Sunday Thomas brings his five children, ages two to fifteen, to sacrament meeting and then goes downstairs to teach Primary.

Teaching Primary is my first calling, and I'm going on to my fourth year teaching Primary. It doesn't seem like it's been that long. I've taught the CTR A class (six-year-olds) for half a year, the CTR B's and now the Valiant B's (nine-year-olds). I love working with the kids. God gave us one purpose here on this earth and that's to learn. We know that when we go to Paradise, we obviously are going to have to learn something there.

I stress in our Primary class that you should be close to God. We don't have to pray at any particular time or in any particular way. If I am having a problem in anything, I will stop and ask for God's guidance and I find that it works. I teach the children that you don't necessarily have to fold your arms, kneel down, and close your eyes to pray. As long as you stop what you're doing and just relax yourself and say a short prayer, God is going to listen to you. He's there.

I think that my own children enjoy going to Primary a little bit more with me being down there. I don't think that you could ask for or find a better way to raise children, especially in today's world, than the teachings of the church. Everything fits together—the togetherness, the Word of Wisdom, the teachings against using drugs—I can't see bringing children up without it. I've seen both sides of how people live—from friends that I have had and places that I've worked. Especially working in the automotive field, you meet a lot of people who are into drugs or are just very unreligious. I realize how lucky I am to have been raised in the church.

I was born into the church and baptized at age eight by my father on a cold winter night at Valley Forge, Pennsylvania. The ward has been divided so many times since it was a branch meeting in the Odd Fellows Hall. There was a lot of contention in the Wilmington Ward due to the different educational backgrounds or job backgrounds. People in Wilmington made more money than the people who lived south of Wilmington and out in the farm areas. That's one of the reasons that I've always liked the smaller towns, like Newark, and the smaller wards. I can remember doing a lot of the work on the Wilmington chapel. I guess that was when the contention actually started because more of the working-class or middle-class people did the work and the upper-class people reaped the benefits with them.

I have always been a self-starter. My dad and I always hit head to head because I would always try to figure out a better way of doing something. If it wasn't the way he told me to do it, I was in trouble, even though I might have saved time or done it better. When I got married and out on my own it was a real burden off my shoulders. When I decided in high school to get married at the age of nineteen, my parents were very worried because we were young. We've been married sixteen years and I've enjoyed growing up with my kids.

I like to do things with my kids when I can. One Sunday Mary Lou was working—it was right after Christmas—and I took all the kids out to dinner. Quite a few people came up to us in the restaurant and complimented us on how well they behaved. I think things are a little bit more at ease with my children than I was at home. I remember vividly the fights that I had with my father and I try not to be that way with my children.

When I got out of high school I went through an apprenticeship as a printer. That worked out well until finally we went head to head over some problems and I left there. I had another job the next day. Since then I have stuck with mechanics and the automotive field. I've always enjoyed working with my hands, building things, taking things apart to see how they work. I recently became a shop foreman at Winner Ford.

Right after we got married we lived in Oak Creek Trailer Park up on the Kirkwood Highway. We lived there in a twelve-by-sixty-foot trailer when Cindy and Seth were born. I was still working at the print shop and my wife was working part-time. When Dulcy was born we were living with my mom while we built our house and we were both still working. Mandy and T. J. were born while we lived in this house and we are both still working. It's always been working to make ends meet.

The contractor put up all the walls of this house and we finished it off. We did all the painting inside and out and stained all the woodwork. I totally built the upstairs myself. We've worked hard for everything we have. I would eventually like to build a dream house someplace in the country. I'd like to have, if not a farm, at least enough room to have horses. There is a lot to be learned from the responsibility of having an animal and taking care of it.

Two years ago my brother and I started a store—Audio-Video-Computer World. I've never put my job above my family. I've always figured that jobs are not that hard to come by and families are. On the other hand, with this new business, I keep telling the kids and myself that if we make it through the hard times now with both of us working and getting the business built up, that we will reap the benefits from it. I am losing a lot of time that I would rather be with my children. I work from 7:30 in the morning to 9:00 at night. I get an hour for lunch and that's it. I have every other Saturday off. When I have a Saturday off, I do what I can with the kids and the family. We were given a boat and the kids and I get together and go out riding. That's why I'd like to be rich—so that I could spend more time with my family. I'm hoping that this year we'll start turning around.

I've always felt that as far as teaching Primary goes I should be doing a lot more. That goes back to having the time. If I could get to the point of working for myself, I probably would have more time.

Sheila Anderson, 41

Sheila Anderson knows her way around Primary. She had been teaching the three-year-old Sunbeams but agreed to take on a large and active class of nine-year-old Valiant A's in the middle of the year. Last year she was the Primary inservice leader, presenting a monthly lesson to the teachers. She and her husband, Lee, moved to Newark in 1974.

One day when we were in the eleventh grade, my best friend Mayre Rasmussen said, "I've done a terrible thing and you'll never forgive me." I wondered what she could have done. Finally, she told me she had made an appointment for me with the missionaries. I had attended church with Mayre sometimes and had gone to some of the youth activities but had not considered joining her church. I kept the appointment out of my friendship for her, and I did eventually join the church. I suppose there was a lot of peer pressure in my decision. I felt more comfortable with my Mormon friends; I liked the Mormon way of life. I liked the fact that what you did and said on Sundays was carried over to the other days of the week.

I met Lee the spring of our sophomore year at BYU. One of my teachers in the Catholic high school had said that no woman is truly educated unless she has seen some of the seven wonders of the world. I wanted to go to Greece. I wanted to work and to have a little red sports car. It was a case of the right man coming along at the wrong time. I just badgered my father about what to do, and he calmly laid out the pros and cons for me. I finally decided that maybe another right man wouldn't come along as often as some of these other opportunities would, so about Thanksgiving of our senior year we decided to get married. We were married in August 1966.

After graduation, I taught fourth through sixth grades in Seattle and at the same time went to school for a fifth year of training. We put Lee's fellowship in the bank and lived on what I made. When he had finished his coursework, we went to Europe for four months before he wrote his dissertation.

When we moved to Miami in 1970, I taught fifth grade to the children of migrant workers. Nothing in my BYU education had prepared me for that. After four years' teaching in Seattle, I considered myself to be somewhat experienced, but these children were not at all motivated by anything I did. It was sad because I had felt that this would be a growing experience for me and for the children.

The classroom was an old converted garden shed. I had students pulling broken coke bottles and mirrors out of their desks to use as weapons. I had human feces dumped on my doorstep. Parents would come to school ready to whip their children and force them to stay in school because they could not keep their jobs if their children were not in school. I made a good friend who helped me through that year and who still writes to me. LeRoy Bembry was a great big black janitor. I think the principal feared for my safety on open house night so he sent LeRoy out to my shed to look after me. Only two parents showed up, but LeRoy and I had a long talk. Talking to him gave me a perspective on the situation that I wouldn't have had otherwise.

When we moved here, I got a job at the Spruce Avenue School in the Conrad School District in Elsmere. During my interview I told the principal that I didn't think much of teachers who broke contracts because they were pregnant. Unbeknownst to myself I was pregnant at that time. When I told the principal, I said, "I intend to finish out my contract." I had eight sick days left when Bronwyn was born. She was born on a Tuesday and I was back in the classroom the following Thursday. My mother came and took care of Bronwyn so I could finish the last four weeks of school.

When Bronwyn was about fifteen months old I got very restless. I taught science part-time at the Immaculate Heart of Mary School in Wilmington for two years until Pearce was born. When Pearce was born, I had eight weeks to go on my contract. My mother came for four weeks and Lee's mother came for four. After that year I stayed home with them.

I've been on the City Development Advisory Committee for six years. That committee decides how the Housing and Urban Development funds from the federal government will be spent in the City of Newark. As an advocate of

Scouting for girls, I was a co-leader of a Brownie troop for three years. When you have children participating in programs, you have to help make those programs work.

Until I had children, I didn't have much in common with the other women in church. Having children was a very deliberate decision on our part. My working for ten years before we had children allowed us to have financial security when we started raising children. Today I don't have to work for us to enjoy a good standard of living. I contributed to it.

Having children is the glue that binds humanity. The costs of having children are greater than I realized at the onset, but I'd make the same choice again. Having children is God's greatest gift to us. I'm probably more tolerant, however, than most Mormons towards couples who choose not to have children.

I had a hard time when my young son lost his finger in an accident. As I was clinging to that child in the ambulance, I felt that my otherwise perfect life was about to be interrupted. Things had gone the way I wanted the Lord to make them go. As I was clinging to this child with blood and tears streaming down us, the feeling came over me: "This time, my love, it's not going to be your way." Ooh, that was tough. This little boy was marred and it was my fault. I had been standing there.

The bishop makes a big difference in the ward. We came in under Don O'Day, a good blue-collar, hardworking fellow with a heart as big as all outdoors. He loved you just the way you were. He had the spirit of that ward. There wasn't much letter of the law; there was just a whole lot of spirit. I wanted to be active in his ward. He was followed by Bishop Cross. I was not very active under his bishopric. He was very much the letter of the law.

We were to have a child blessed, and he wouldn't let my father participate in the blessing because he wasn't a member. I know Bishop O'Day would have made that possible. It hurt a lot. This was one time that the church had an opportunity to make strides into my parents' household. They couldn't come and see us married in the temple. I don't think I realized how hard that was for them until I became a parent. So when my daughter was born, I thought, "Maybe we can make up for something." But Bishop Cross wouldn't let Daddy stand in the circle. We could have said it didn't count, but Daddy would have thought it did.

In 1981 when we came back from a sabbatical in Norway, we knew that the Elkton Ward was going to be started. When Elkton was formed we got ourselves active. There's just no finer man than Bishop Bushman. His heart is in the right place and he accepts you as you are and works with you. I think we've all grown with him.

I was called to teach a teenage Sunday school class, which was a new experience for me. I learned a lot from those juniors and seniors, though I felt disillusioned when two of the girls got pregnant that year. It was like what I'd said had fallen on deaf ears. I had tried very hard to be open and talk about things that sometimes are neglected. Girls need to hear that there are other options besides getting right into motherhood. I feel a strong devotion to helping young girls develop their potential. I was very sad when this happened to two of our girls. I finally asked to be released.

Then they needed help in the Primary. In my Primary lesson a week ago, we talked about "He wants us to go to church on Sunday." Then the next statement was "The Lord wants us to get married and have a family." I didn't feel comfortable saying that even to small children, because not every young girl is going to be married. Not every young girl is going to have children. Do we make them feel that if they don't they're not going to be the way the church wants them to be? I said, "And he wants you to grow up and be happy."

I am big on the women's movement, but I think women have gone astray in the effort to be superwomen. You can be a mother and have wonderful little kids and a fine career. You can keep a lovely home, entertain regularly, meet your husband's needs, and be a cheerful heart. We *can* do all that, but not all at once. I had a career for a while. Now my children are older, I can go back to school. We shouldn't be so intense about trying to have it all at once. I still have maybe forty years left.

I don't want to be like the women of my mother's generation. After they raised their children, they sat down in their rocking chairs or took up golf or bridge or Meals on Wheels. Raising children takes only twenty or thirty years of your life. You still have many years in which to make a contribution. I'm using this time to prepare for that. I have so much invested in teaching that I decided to stay in education. I'm working towards a master's in education at the University of Delaware. I'd like to be a headmistress of a day school or the principal of a private school some day. I don't want to stop being useful. My husband's career gives him a great deal of satisfaction and growth. I want to have something that will do the same for me.

The church's stand on women's issues is like the issue of the blacks and the priesthood in the sixties. That was never brought up in the missionary lessons. When I found out about it later, I thought, "This certainly is contrary to everything I believe—the way I was raised, the way I understand the Bible, the way I understand God and his infinite goodness and wisdom. This is something I cannot accept."

There was a lot of discussion about it in our ward in Seattle. I think our speaking out brought the revelation later. If you want change to come, you must stay in there. It doesn't do any good to get on the outside and criticize. I feel that way about the women's issue now, and I stay in the church largely for that reason. Through my callings I can share things that I think young people need to hear. I don't doubt that the Lord makes the inspiration come when he thinks we can handle it. He's also made us free agents to bring these issues up and ask for help—ask how the prophet sees it.

The last few decades have been dynamite for women. We're going through an exciting but awkward and painful time. I'm thankful to be a part of it. I feel a strong obligation to keep this issue at the forefront of the brethren's concerns. I think the church feels very awkward with single women, with divorced women. We have to keep championing their causes.

We tend to put the church's checklist before the human soul. It's hard to be the kind of member I am. You either do it all or you become inactive. It's hard to live a middle-of-the-road participation, but it's what I feel comfortable with. I'm confident that how God and I relate is the most important thing.

I went to a Seventh-Day Adventist grammar school, a Catholic high school, a Mormon college. I come from an Episcopalian and Methodist background. My sister is a practicing Sufi. I just see things more broadly, more ecumenically. I believe that the Joseph Smith story is just as true for Mormons as the White is for the Adventists, the Calvin is for the Presbyterians, and the Luther is for the Lutherans. I can't say Joseph Smith is the only one to have had that kind of a vision. Churches are windows to the same living God for all of mankind.

The church filled a serious need up until I was about thirty. It was a limited path, but I was growing on it. About ten or twelve years ago I began to see the world in a broader perspective. I don't feel I can grow in the church anymore. You hear the same kind of lessons over and over again. Unless you keep your life among the Mormons, seeing the Mormon way, the church is not very interested in you. I have taken my beliefs out into the world, but there's been a cost. I don't feel particularly comfortable at church, having made this choice, but I feel more comfortable with myself.

Last week was soup and song Sunday in Newark, where all the different faiths came together. I wish we had participated. Members are not encouraged to share much, except through the missionary program. You can get yourself so involved in the church, you haven't time for your nonmember neighbor. We should share and not worry about whether we're going to get some more members. As women like Claudia Bushman, and, I like to think, myself, get out into the world of work, Mormonism will be exposed in more ways than it has been.

Sharon Mlodoch, 29

Sharon Mlodoch's first calling in the Elkton Ward was to teach the Blazer class of eleven-year-old boys. Boys and girls begin meeting separately at the age of ten, so that the boys' lessons can cover both Boy Scouts and preparation for the Aaronic priesthood. The religious lessons are on Sundays, and the Scouting activities on a week night. Sharon, a high school teacher in Oxford, Pennsylvania, grew up in Reading, Pennsylvania. She, her parents, and her sister joined the church during Sharon's junior year at Pennsylvania State University.

I always wanted to teach. I hoped to be married by now, but I'm not. I don't think I would be as involved with the kids at school as I am if I were married.

I was cheerleading adviser for five years. I'm student council adviser now and yearbook adviser. I'm an adviser to the junior class and to the National Honor Society. I have dealt with being alone by making a family at school. I am very close to some of my former students. If I need something done, they help me. I see kids in school who don't have a home life, who hate to go home. They can't talk to their parents; they need someplace to be. I'd rather see them involved in activities than out in the streets. I think I have a pretty strong influence on some of them.

My parents weren't going to send me to college, but Mom pushed it. She has her bachelor's degree in nursing. Dad wanted to save the money for the boys to go to school. Mom said, "She's smart. She's going to school."

Just a few years before me, my cousin Candy wanted to go to college. My aunt said, "No, girls don't go to college. Girls become secretaries," and she did. It would have been easy for my parents to say the same thing. My mom was the only girl in her family who went to college, which she did on her own. Maybe I've been in—not a liberated family or a feminist family—but one in which responsibilities were shared

College didn't prepare me at all for teaching. It did give me the math background, but it didn't prepare me to work with people. Methods class taught me what was in the Algebra I curriculum, but not how to deal with somebody who falls asleep in class or who comes in crying because she just broke up with her boyfriend.

Student teaching opened my eyes. I didn't realize the power I had just in being up in front of the classroom. The kids think you're twelve, fifteen years older than you are. It took me a little while to develop my way of handling people: the way to say "Don't do that" and the stares that teachers develop after a while. The first year was rough. By the third or fourth year the kids know you; they've heard stories about what they're allowed to do. I don't have to read them the list of what they can and cannot do.

I should say the most rewarding thing is seeing a student's eyes light up when he grasps the mathematics, but it's not. It's helping someone in an activity, helping someone with a problem he has at home, being a mentor, a friend to some of these kids. Not that I'm a shining example of everything, but I am an example to them. Going out on weekends and getting drunk at parties is standard fare for them. I let them know that's not what they should be doing.

I was a member of the branch that met at the firehall in Avondale, Pennsylvania. When they began meeting in Downingtown, I decided I might as well go to Reading with my parents. I didn't know of a closer ward until I saw an announcement of an Elkton Ward Relief Society meeting in the *Cecil Whig*. Elkton is a lot closer to where I live than Downingtown, where I probably belong. I live less than a mile from the state line, but the ward boundary is the state line.

There seems to be a larger group of people who do things in Elkton. Maybe the ones that don't do just don't come. If the Reading Ward was told they were going to make Easter eggs, they would say "That's crazy. We'll pay our assessment, but we're not going to get together and do these things." The Elkton Ward seems to be more intellectual too. Part of that is the effect of being near the University of Delaware.

It also seems to be more open to having females be a part of things, which is good for me. My old ward had budget meetings during priesthood meeting. My only contact with the priesthood was my home teacher. Was I going ask him, "What did you do at the budget meeting?" I thought it was good when we had the budget meeting with everyone. I've been disturbed by the relative unimportance given to women's ideas in a lot of wards. That still troubles me. During a Sunday school class one of the men implied that women are just chattel. I was getting madder and madder. Just before I exploded, Brother Vander-Heyden called me in to see the bishop. I thought, "Well, apparently I wasn't supposed to explode today." I think we're beginning to have a little more openness toward women. In our ward, there's a feeling that everyone should be involved in major decisions.

Most things in the church are geared toward families. People give talks about families and family home evening. That's why Relief Society and I never clicked. The lessons would be on health habits for your children or disciplining your children. I don't think there's too much emphasis on families, but they could put a little more on individuals. I'm not in the mainstream. When you're single you have to accept that in our church you're going to hear a lot about families.

I know that wherever I am I can call somebody in the church and get help. If I live the way I should I'll be taken care of. If I pay my tithing and go to church, there will be food for me if I need it. The security, a feeling of the group is a philosophy of the church. Sister Mace is my visiting teacher and Brother Larsen is my home teacher. Sister Mace is like a sister to me. When I cut myself, I called her to ask where the nearest doctor was. I'd lived here a long time, but I didn't have a doctor. She said, "Well, just go to the emergency room. Do you want me to drive you?" Brother Larsen is the contact I have with the priesthood, so he's important to me, too.

This is my first calling. In college I traveled to Reading most weekends so they couldn't call me to anything. I was a nomad for a long time. Having a calling cuts down on going home for the weekends.

There are seven boys in my Blazer class. They are almost too old for what goes on in Primary. You can't expect an eleven-year-old boy to have a good time singing the Primary songs for half an hour. It's at the end of a very long day for them. The church says that's where they are to be, so that's where they are. When our class was responsible for the closing exercises, one of my kids wanted to give as the scripture verse "And my father dwelt in a tent."

I said, "You cannot give that scripture."

He said, "Just think of how great it would be to have the president say, 'Thank you very much for that scripture today.'"

The kids in senior Primary are eight, nine, ten, eleven. We're dealing with children who can read. Why don't we give them songbooks? Do they tell us in church, "Everybody sing without a hymn book"? How hard would it be to have fifteen books down there and just hand them out?

I was surprised by how much the kids know. I tell them things that seem almost obscure to me, and they'll say, "Oh yes, I remember that," and then tell me the whole story.

The Baptism
5 | of Three Children

Because our daughter Lisa's eighth birthday fell on a Sunday, November 18, 1984, we decided she would be baptized on that day. Children are not baptized into the church until they are eight—when they are considered able to choose between right and wrong. When I was baptized in the Salt Lake Tabernacle by my father, I was one of many children from several Salt Lake City stakes baptized that night.

In the Elkton Ward the parents organize their children's baptismal services. Because the Elkton Ward building has no baptismal font, we reserved the font and Relief Society room at the Wilmington Ward. When we learned that Danny Harding and Sean Beatty, two of Lisa's Primary classmates, were planning to be baptized on the same day, my husband, Doug, called Dan Harding, Danny's father, and arranged for a joint baptismal service.

It was a difficult time in our family life. Our three-and-a-half-year-old daughter, Abby, after a year of treatment for leukemia, had recently relapsed. I was taking her to the hospital in Wilmington nearly every day for chemotherapy and she was soon to begin a sixteen-day course of radiation treatments. On November 13 our eldest son, John, had broken both his arms at basketball practice. When Jean Harding called me the day before the baptism and asked if I would bake some cookies for a little reception at the church after the baptism, I gratefully agreed. I hadn't even thought about refreshments.

We left home at 4:15. Thirty-five minutes later, I deposited a tray of cookies in the church kitchen and hurried into the dressing room to help Lisa change into the white jumper I had borrowed from Julie Ridge that afternoon. In the dressing room I was overwhelmed with a feeling of inadequacy. Had I sufficiently prepared Lisa for this step? Was she ready to take responsibility for her own actions? Had I stressed the importance of honesty enough and given her enough experiences to practice it?

When she was dressed we went to the chapel. Because both the Hardings and Beattys have large extended families, the Relief Society room was not large enough to hold us. Jean's four brothers and sisters all live in Delaware as do her parents. Carol's two sisters, Christine Devereaux and Mary Stover, were also in the chapel with their families. I felt quite alone, unsupported by any family other than my own children, though we did manage to fill up an entire pew.

We had asked Douglas Ridge to play the piano and Julie Ridge to lead the singing. They arrived just at 5:00. Gary Johnston welcomed the assembled congregation. Lisa and her father, Danny and his father, and Sean Beatty and his uncle Don Stover, all dressed in white, sat together on the front row. After we sang "Teach Me to Walk in the Light of His Love," Danny's grandfather Bill Meekins offered the opening prayer.

After hearing a talk on baptism, we assembled in front of the baptismal font. Each child in turn was escorted into the water and baptized by immersion.

After everyone had returned to the chapel, Don O'Day, the former bishop of the New Castle Ward, spoke about the Holy Ghost. He had the children stand in front and gave each of them a red Stop sign and a green Go sign. He then explained that the Holy Ghost would let them know when to stop and when to go. A circle of men surrounded each child in turn and placed their right hands on his or her head. Each child was admonished to "receive the Holy Ghost" and given other words of blessing and counsel. Bishop Bushman then welcomed the children as full-fledged members of the Elkton Ward.

Carol Beatty, 37

Carol Beatty first came to Delaware in 1966 at the age of nineteen to live with her older sister Mary. She worked for the Du Pont company as a keypunch operator and programmer assistant, and there met her husband. Carol had been a Primary teacher until two months earlier, when her daughter Heather was born.

I'm the thirteenth of fourteen children. My father always worked at Public Works, but he still farmed. We had animals like cows, chickens, a horse. Of course my mom just stayed home with the children. My older sisters were already married and had started families of their own by the time I was born, so I can remember only six of us being home at once. I went to a two-room school for eight years.

My mom had belonged to the Mormon church since she was young, and her mother belonged. My father's mother, who lived with us, didn't want anything to do with it. So we never had any contact with the church until I was twelve years old. Finally, my mom said, "This is it. We're going to have the missionaries come." My grandmother got upset. When I was small my mom couldn't even have church materials in the house. The missionaries came and gave us the discussions, and I was baptized.

My grandmother was so outspoken. I don't know how my mom put up with it. I hate to talk about her now, but she wanted everything *her* way. Everything was a sin to her, too. We weren't allowed to have a television. My older sisters had to slip out of the house and take their makeup with them if they wanted to wear lipstick. We weren't even allowed to wear slacks. Every Sunday night my grandma would bring us all into her room and we would have devotions. She would read out of the Bible and say a prayer. My mom would let us go to Bible school during the summer. We didn't go to Sunday school that much, but we went to Bible school a lot.

When the missionaries came my father would always be in my grandmother's room. She would be in there preaching to him. As far as I know, my father never said anything against it. It just took my mom a long, long time to decide she was going to have us baptized. My mother now tells me how guilty she feels that she didn't speak up and say how she wanted things in her home. She wanted to be able to have the missionaries come and be able to teach her children about the church. She did talk to us, but if my grandmom saw a Book of Mormon lying around, she would get it and dispose of it.

I've never met anyone who can compare with my mother. I can't imagine raising fourteen children without any modern conveniences. Can you imagine doing the laundry for that many children and drawing the water out of the well? She had a wringer washing machine. It took her all day to do the laundry. She never complained. As she went about her work and raising her family, she was always happy, singing.

Even at the high school there weren't that many different subjects to learn. I took typing and business courses. There were only eighty-eight in my high school graduating class in Baxter, Tennessee.

We went to a small branch that met in the basement of a store. Then we met in a house. Thirty would be a large crowd on Sunday. Everyone was close because there were so few of us. Most of them were my relatives, my uncles and their families. Our MIA was small. We did a lot of activities, but there were only seven or eight of us in the whole MIA. After I graduated from high school, there wasn't anyplace to find a job, so I came to Delaware. I started in the mail room at Du Pont. Then they trained me to do keypunching. After two years, I decided to go back down to Tennessee and see if I could find work there.

The church was still very small. My Mom forced me to go to MIA. I was twenty years old! I was the oldest one there, but I went and took my younger nieces and Christine in my car.

I did keypunching down there for a couple of years. I dated guys outside the church. The guys that were in church were my cousins. I would probably have gone to college, but I had no one to encourage me. When Christine started high school, I buckled down on her and told her what to do because no one had told me. She had nieces and nephews her same age, so she was in all the extracurricular activities that I didn't have a chance to do. She went to college for a couple of years. Then I got the urge to wander again and I came back up here to work at Du Pont. That's where I met my husband. John and I started dating in September and we got married in June.

All I ever expected to do was get a job, get married, and have a family. That's what I've done. I'm happy with my life. I feel it's important to be home with my children. I'm able to watch them grow up and see all the different changes, hear their first word, and see their first step. It's worth the sacrifice to be able to stay home. Even though I only have Heather during the day, I am busy all the time. Heather has to be active. That's the only problem I have at church. She wants to be rocking, moving. Sitting there for three hours is hard on her.

When I was dating my husband, he went to church with me quite a bit. I thought, "Well, he'll keep going after we're married." Not long after we were married, he faded out and didn't go anymore. John has studied the missionary discussions two or three times, but something always comes up and he's never finished them.

He tells me, "I'm not going to go to church and be a hypocrite." He thinks there are many people going to church that are hypocrites. If he goes to church he wants to commit himself 100 percent and he's not ready to do that. I hope one day he will be.

Sean was sitting here the other day and he said to his little friend, "You go to church?"

The little friend said, "Yes."

Sean said, "I do too. But when I get big like my daddy I won't have to go to church."

When John came home, I said, "You should have heard your son. He said, 'When he gets big like his daddy he won't have to go to church.'"

His dad tells him, "You go to church. I went to church when I was small." My husband does support me, but he sees nothing wrong with watching television or going out to a restaurant on Sunday. It's been hard for me to do all that I should do. If he says, "Let's go visit friends up in Pennsylvania tomorrow," I'll go along just to keep from causing problems. His family doesn't keep the Sabbath day holy; his mom is always canning and freezing on Sunday. When we were first married, they would get vegetables out of the garden, but I said, "I'm not going to do that on Sunday." Now he doesn't bring me any vegetables on Sundays.

At first my husband could not understand why I was "hoarding all this food." I kept talking to him and saying, "Well, John, something could happen. You could be out of work for six months or something. We would have food to eat." He has come around. When I was working part-time I bought the wheat or the honey out of money I was making. My husband was so nice. In a small house without a basement there's no place to store things. I had things in closets and under beds, so he built a shed for me out back and put electricity in it for the winter. Now I have lots of room to store all my canned goods and everything.

When Sean was two, I said, "John I'm going to go back to work, but I'm going to pay my tithing."

He said, "Okay." The only time I felt it presented a problem was at the end of the year when John did the taxes and he'd say, "We paid that *much* to the church?" We could have used that money for something else, but I feel we've been blessed. We've never had to scrape and scrimp that much.

There's so much that I've got to work on. Sometimes I feel, "Well, because my husband doesn't belong to the church, how can I work toward having my family with me forever?" It hurts. My family's the most important thing to me, of course.

When I need the priesthood in my home, I just usually call on my home teachers or my brother-in-law, Mary's husband, Don. He blessed Sean. Now it's time for Sean to be baptized, and Heather's going to be blessed. I just depend on the bishopric and my home teachers. I always have someone I can turn to.

Sean had an accident when he was two. He had a part from the vacuum cleaner in his mouth, fell on it, and cut the back of his throat. I asked my husband if I could have someone come to the hospital to administer to him. He saw no reason for it. All I had to depend on were my own prayers. I feel sometimes that maybe I'm not as worthy. Maybe my prayers won't be answered. Everything turned out fine, but I felt so bad when my husband said no. I think if John knew how important some things are to me, it would be different.

My sisters Christine and Mary and I are all close to one another. We don't do as much together as we would like. Everyone has her own family. We're always here for one another, cry on each other's shoulder, or whatever. We have picnics and things during the summer, all of us together. I don't know what I would do without them.

My only long-range goal is that someday my husband will join the church and that we can raise our children in a loving home. I keep working toward that. I love my husband. I guess you always have a choice, but once love strikes, it's hard to think reasonably. When you're dating, you don't realize that your whole life is going to be with that person. I was so flaky and happy-go-lucky. I didn't realize how important the church would be later on in life. I did think my husband would be a member of the church by now. They promise you things, when you're dating, that sometimes don't come to pass.

It helps to know that as long as you are living righteously, everything will be okay. My mom always said, "If you just live the gospel, everything will be okay." Now that doesn't mean that you won't face trials and hardships, and maybe even lose your own life, but everything will be okay. The church seems to be just about the only thing you can depend on—it's the one sure thing. The world may change and the people may change, but the church doesn't change.

Imogene (Jean) Harding, 39

Danny Harding is Jean Harding's fourth child. He has four sisters and a younger brother. Jean's one-year-old grandson lives with the family, and Jean takes care of him while his mother works. The Hardings were members of the New Castle Ward until the Elkton Ward was organized. Jean is the Young Women's secretary and sports director, coaching basketball, volleyball, and softball teams.

My father met the missionaries at a friend's house up in Pennsylvania and he decided that this was the right church for the family. The first time the missionaries came around, we hid from them because Dad wasn't there. The second time, Dad made sure that he was there and the missionaries got in. They were invited for dinner. We kids had to sit down and listen to the lessons. Mom was out in the kitchen hiding. Eventually, she did come in and join the lessons. It took them a good six months to convince us to become members. The funny part was that my Dad didn't join at the same time we did. All Mom could see at first was that Dad had found the perfect religion: he thought he could have more than one wife. He was already remarried by the time we became members of the church. I was twelve and I joined mainly because the rest of the family did. The meetings were in the Odd Fellows Hall. A lot of our Mutual nights were spent doing odd jobs to help finish the church.

When we first came to the Elkton Ward, I was excited. I was so enthused with that little teeny church. I thought, "Boy this is great. It's almost a small town."

My kids kept saying, "Are we still Mormons, Mommy?"

I met my husband when he was on a mission, but I was only sixteen years old when he came through. My girlfriends and I had been counseled by the bishop to leave the missionaries alone. Mother used to have them over to our house for dinner almost every Sunday. That's where I met Dan, but he was a missionary, and that was it.

He went home for about three weeks after his mission, bought a new car, and came back here to work for some members at the Buy-Low gas station on the Kirkwood Highway. A girlfriend and I were going to a church luau up in Pennsylvania. She wasn't sure how to get there so she asked Dan to show us how to get up there. She told me, "You leave him alone, he's mine."

But it seemed that Dan had a liking for me. He ended up hanging around me instead of her. She never got mad, which was very nice of her. He and his friend arranged that when we stopped at the Dairy Queen, they would switch cars. On the way home Dan asked me why I didn't break up with the guy I was dating. My boyfriend had taken up drinking. I had dated him for two and a half years. Then I met Dan and married him in less than six months.

Dan was laid off indefinitely on my birthday, November 1, 1974. Everything turned around for us. Laura got quite sick that year. Terrie came down with pneumonia. We were working our way through December, trying to get some kind of Christmas together for the kids and my mom said, "Have hope. Maybe 1975 will be a better year." Well, January 5, Laura went to the hospital, so it wasn't a better year.

For a while, with the Chrysler subpay and his unemployment, we almost had what he had been bringing home every week. Then subpay ran out, and we had three kids and a house to take care of. He picked up odd jobs as a construction worker. He was out trying to make a buck anywhere he could.

I went to work for my brother-in-law in his store. Dan took care of the kids and got them off to school, then had Laura at home. He was Mommy and I became Daddy. Tempers were a little short. Dan went back on the eighteenth of July, and I quit the seventeenth. I was glad for the experience, but I was also glad to get back home. I had never missed any of the little things that Tina and Terrie had done—the first step. Dan was the one telling me, "Oh, Laura did so and so today." It hurt. It might be a dumb thing to be hurt about, but that was what upset me.

I don't want to be a working mother. If God had wanted everybody to be the same, he would have made us all unisex. I'm for equal pay for equal work, and yes, women do have a right to be in the fields of medicine and engineering and anything else that they want to go to college for. Dan and I are pretty much give and take here. There's no "You do this, you do that." When we were first married he was always there to help with the dishes. He thinks nothing of picking up a dust cloth or a dish cloth and helping out. In fact, when he was Mommy and I was Daddy, he did the wash and did the dishes and made sure the house was straightened around. It doesn't bother him one way or another. I don't hesitate to go out and work in the garden with him or even be there on a car when he's working on it.

The priesthood has helped me a lot. When Tommy was an infant, he stopped breathing a couple of times, but I knew nothing about it until my doctor poked his head in and said, "What's happening here?"

"What do you mean?" I wouldn't rest until Tommy had been given a blessing. Dan said, "Well, he's okay now. Can't we do it when he gets home?"

I said, "No, I want it done now." That is one of the times that I was very forceful with him. As soon as Tom received that blessing I was totally at ease. I knew he was fine. Sometimes it bugs me—the authority that the men have compared to what the women have. The hardest thing for me to accept sometimes is that it all depends on them. Yet there are a lot of times that the woman's shoving the guy in order to keep the religion and keep the priesthood.

I like big families. I always wanted six kids. Sure, there are things my kids do without because of being a large family, but they're getting something that's far more important than material things. I hope I can get that across to them.

I would like to be a little more together than I feel that I am. There are some people who have everything just so, and their kids come out so nice. I'm thinking of Bishop Cross's family. I'll be forever grateful to him because he set his mind to Dan and I being sealed in the temple. He just never gave up.

He talked to us a lot and explained the importance of being sealed to each other in the temple. Any time he saw us slipping in a different direction, he saw to it that we were pulled back. A lot of people think he was very gruff and didn't care for him because he ran the ward like the military. He ran a very tight ship, but there is a heart of gold underneath that firmness. In fact, he saw to it that my mother managed to get to the temple before we did so she could see us be sealed. She hadn't been able to see her other children sealed in the temple. He made sure that she progressed at a faster rate than we did.

I enjoy working with the girls. It's much easier to work with a teenager than it is to live with one. The youth programs now seem to give the kids a lot more say in what they're going to be doing. When I went, it was all structured: "This is what you'll do." Now, it's pulling more youth in. I always enjoyed going to Mutual because it was a chance to meet with my friends. For almost a year I was the only Beehive. Then my friend came in. We were quite a small ward at that time and not many of the teenagers went to Mutual.

When I taught Primary it was very hard for me to present a lesson that I felt was worth anything. I had the age group that was supposed to be prepared for baptism. I felt I wasn't preparing them. There was one little boy who was very rowdy, but after two or three months he was a totally different child. I couldn't imagine anybody not liking that kid. At the end of Primary he carried my books to my car and he'd say, "See you next week." He made a point of saying hi to me at church. That was the only thing I accomplished that year.

I was raised in a very loving household. Mom did her best to see that things stayed on an even keel. She had five kids—the eldest four and a half years older than the youngest. It is mind-boggling that she ever coped with that plus the other problems. I never remember my mother saying a harsh word about my father. We didn't have much as far as material things, but she saw to it that we had a lot of good times. There was never a time that the house wasn't jumping with half a dozen kids—not just her own. She never discouraged us from bringing our friends home. I feel that my kids have far more self confidence than I ever had as a child. Sometimes they have a little bit too much mouth. I wouldn't talk to my mother that way today, and I'm a full-grown woman. I've tried to raise my children the way I was raised because I feel that my mother did a decent job at raising five children, basically alone.

Imogene Meekins, 63

Imogene Meekins, Jean Harding's mother, joined the church in 1958 with her five children. She is also the great-grandmother of William Meekins IV, who was blessed in the Elkton Ward on September 2. On Sundays she works in the library, distributing pictures and other teaching aids to Primary and Sunday school teachers.

I came out of high school with a diploma in one hand and a marriage certificate in the other. I got divorced after we had been married thirteen years, 1953. I definitely should have waited a couple of years after marriage before starting a family. I think that I wouldn't have had the divorce if we'd gotten acquainted. We hardly knew each other. I had five little babies and no time for him. He was lonely. I was getting all the love and attention I needed from the children. He was not a husband who jumped in and helped. He wouldn't even hold the baby. He was afraid of it. Now he will, but he wouldn't then. I had three in diapers at one time—no four. When I came home with the fourth one, I still had three in diapers. I started straightening them around and got rid of a few of those didies. They all had glass bottles. I was teasing my granddaughter, Tina Harding, yesterday about Brian's having a bottle. I said, "You should be back when they had glass bottles. You took them away when they started walking. You had to, or they'd fall and break them." There was some good to the glass ones.

I went through some real trying times raising five children by myself. I didn't work because I've had asthma almost all my life. A lot of it is emotional and I was pretty well stirred up with my problems. I didn't always have enough money for heat, food, clothing. It was scratch, scratch, scratch. I would be a wreck trying to get things together so they'd have a decent Christmas. We had to close off rooms and heat just one room in the winter. My children took the wagon and went hunting for wood to put in the furnace. It's no wonder I had bad attacks of asthma. I had myself up so tight. Now I look back on it and think how in the world did I survive that?

I enjoyed my family. My children were my life. Anything they did was important to me. I was very close to my children. Now I hardly see them. They're busy in their own little worlds, but all I have to do is pick up the phone and they're here. They all moved out to the country. I raised them in a federal project. In fact, we were the last white family in our area. It was getting awfully rough—the knifings and shootings. They were in their teenage years when we moved away—nineteen, eighteen, seventeen, sixteen, and fifteen. I got after their father because he said he was going to provide a home for them. He finally bought a home in the suburbs and we lived there for five years. When the last one got married and I went to work, he sold the home and I moved to an apartment. I brag about them because I think they did real well. They all have good marriages. They're not rich, but they're comfortable. I used to tell them often that a rose could grow in a manure pile. I think they were five little roses.

They knew mother wasn't well. They tell me now that I had a military house because they knew their obligations and they did them. Sure, I spanked them when they needed it, and I loved them when they needed it. A lot of other children stayed out late at night; mine knew when it got dark to head for home. I didn't have to hunt them. They didn't smoke because they knew mother didn't like it. Even if they came in with it on their clothing, it bothered me. They couldn't sneak it. The oldest one did try, but he didn't get very far. I do believe he smoked for a while after he was married—maybe the first year—to show that Mom couldn't control him now.

When the missionaries taught the children I was not going to pay any attention, but I got curious. They started coming for meals and the first thing I knew we were all scheduled to be baptized in Philadelphia. I liked the good, clean living. I liked the missionaries. I thought, "This is the way I'd like my boys and girls to be." They were all enthusiastic about it. They've all stayed good members except one daughter who has turned Catholic. That's not a bad record.

Of my children, Jean Harding is closest to me. She's my baby and I make out real well with her. I love them all but she is the closest one. I would lean on Bill, the oldest one, if I needed to because he's a very strong person. He works for General Motors and lives down in Blackbird. His three children are all grown, and he's very active in the church. The second son, Barry, spoke in our ward recently. He's on the high council and he's a lawyer. My son out West works for a computer firm. He has four children and has lived in Sandy, Utah, for fourteen years. He went out there to go to college, fell in love with the place, and wouldn't come home. Donna has turned Catholic. She married an Italian man with great expectations of his coming into the church. He's very strong in his own church and he said both their children must be raised Catholic. Finally, she turned Catholic. She said she wanted harmony in her home, but had hesitated because she was afraid to hurt me. I think sometimes she feels uncomfortable around her brothers and sisters.

My mother was very upset when I joined the church. All she knew about Mormons was that they had many wives, and you couldn't convince her any other way. Bless her heart, she went to her grave believing that. I hope she knows different now. She would not even come to my children's weddings because she wouldn't come near the church. She went to my daughter's wedding in the Catholic church.

After the last one got married I didn't know what to do with myself. The doctor suggested I go to work, and he put in a word for me at the Delaware Division. Going to work at that age was awful. I was in my forties. I was scared, and I felt foolish being frightened. None of my co-workers could understand it. Once I got used to it, I liked it. I liked the hospital work because I knew I was helping people. I felt as though I were living for the first time in my life. I was a part of the civilization. Working made me use my mind. It wasn't just all labor. I worked in technical supply and had to learn a lot of things. We set up the equipment trays for all the procedures such as arteriograms. I had a very good boss who took pride in teaching us. If the doctor hadn't made me quit, I guess I'd still be there. He said he didn't know whether I'd make it at that time. Now my asthma has calmed down immensely. Who knows what might happen if I went back into that tension again. On the night shift I was in charge. I was quite proud of myself because I had had no confidence in myself. It scared the dickens out of me the first few times. I had to answer to all the nurses and doctors down on the floors and give them whatever they wanted. Sometimes I had to argue with them; they didn't always know what they wanted.

I wish I were still working. I worked for less than ten years, but it was a good ten years. I did a lot in that ten years. I rented an apartment. I bought all my furniture. I bought a car so I could get back and forth to work. I was doing well for a person who had never worked before. I had a lot of confidence then. God said, "You've had enough now. Sit back down." Here I am. Sometimes I wonder why I moved to this place. It's boring. There's no movement at all because most of the people here are at least seventy. The activities at the Senior Center don't appeal to me. Ninety percent of the people smoke and drink and they play cards. I haven't found anything over there yet that appeals to me. The first thing the lady next door said to me was "Do you play bridge?" Of course, let there be a bingo game and you'll see them come out of the woodwork. If there's a trip to Atlantic City, they'll hustle up there to catch the bus. My money comes too hard. I can't give it to those people down there.

I have sixteen grandchildren and two great-grandchildren, Brian and Billy IV. When he was blessed in church the whole family showed up. He's not just my great-grandson; he's Edna Young's grandson. He means a lot to her. He's her first grandchild, and he's number eighteen at my house. That's a pretty long line.

I told Edna's daughter that my own daughters had no idea that I could babysit. If I were to sit with Billy IV, I'd have to please six people—two sets of grandparents and the parents. They have made a big fuss over that baby and I can understand it. He's the first all the way around. Besides that, I did my time with five children. I didn't ask anyone to take care of them. I missed an awful lot of social life to stay home with my children. Now I'm free. If I want to get in my car and take a ride, I can do it. I'll hug the baby when I see him, but I'm not going to take care of him unless it's an emergency.

I do take care of Jeannie's. She went to youth conference last year and enjoyed it. When she got back, I said, "You get somebody else to take care of these Indians next time you go." She wants to go this year and she said, "I guess I'll have to parcel my kids out." I said, "I'll take one." It's not that they're bad. I'm just not used to it anymore. I was exhausted when I got home. I guess I slept for several days.

I went to the temple before Jeannie did. The bishop was very thoughtful. He found out that I had not been to the temple and had not seen three of my children sealed. He was determined that I was going to be there when the last one was. After seeing Jeannie, I wish I had been at the others. I just never asked what I had to do to go to the temple.

Going to the temple impresses me quite a bit. I don't get there often, but I get very tense when I'm in there. It's almost like God is watching over my shoulder to see what I'm doing. I take it very seriously. It's the only thing I can think of that gets to me. After I go through a session I calm down and feel real good, but when I'm first there I'll get my veil backwards or make a wrong move.

Don't you think a good bit of your life should revolve around church activities? If you are deep in the church, they can keep you pretty busy. I see Jeannie always running in some direction. To tell you the truth, I think they kind of leave out people like me. I'm not the only one who feels that way. Thelma Roberts, for instance, is alone like me.

Susan Taber, 37

I moved into the Elkton Ward in August 1982 when my husband began working for the University of Delaware. We married just before Douglass graduated from college fifteen years ago and have lived in California, New Jersey, New York, Wisconsin, and Tennessee.

I'm the eldest of eight children. I grew up in Salt Lake City, and my family has lived in the same ward since 1953. My youngest sister was born just five weeks before I got married, so we never lived at home at the same time. My father was the bishop of our ward for five years, beginning when I was eleven.

If I hadn't gone to Stanford I would probably still live in Utah. Going away to college seemed so glamorous, and very few from my high school went away from Utah to college. My parents were afraid I'd lose my testimony and that I would marry out of the church. At the end of a tearful, late-night session they said I could go if I got a scholarship. My little brother, David, cried the night I got the letter from Stanford because I'd be leaving home.

At Stanford, when I invited a boyfriend to go to church for a Christmas program, he said, "No, I would never go to your church because of your racist attitudes." When I started explaining why blacks couldn't hold the priesthood, those reasons did sound racist. The classes I took at the Institute of Religion helped me understand that the reasons that people gave for that policy weren't necessarily correct. I found I was more comfortable with no explanation than with any that were currently circulating. I think I was better off in the Stanford Ward and the institute than I would have been at a Utah college. I felt I either needed to adhere to the church standards or make a conscious decision to reject my religion. I couldn't drift away. The spring of my sophomore year I read the Book of Mormon again and did some serious thinking and praying. My testimony came as a feeling—that God was there to support me if I would trust in him.

I taught school for three years before we had children. I didn't expect to be dissatisfied once I quit working to raise a family. When I finished my last year of teaching, I was surprised that I had mixed feelings.

I've enjoyed the companionship of my children. I spent a lot of time with John when he was little. He was very curious and interested in things. He began reading six weeks before his second birthday, and he'd grab me by the knees and pull me down to the floor to help make words out of his blocks. It was a lot of fun to see how much he could do. I was annoyed by Lisa's forever getting into my drawers and putting on my clothes, until I realized that this eighteen-month-old person wanted to be like me. About that time, the boys began to make very chauvinistic statements such as "Girls don't go to college" or "All women do is stay home and nurse babies." Of course, that was all they'd seen me do.

When I was thirty and had four children, I thought, "If I keep having children, I'll be forty-five before I can do anything else." Having children was what I had wanted my whole life. What was wrong with me? Being home with my children wasn't enough, somehow. I don't know how I could have managed it, but I should have viewed teaching more as a lifetime career and found some way to stay involved. Since I often feel that I'm trying to do so much that I don't enjoy any of it, I wonder if I could have done this while my children were small. Because of all the work that goes into feeding, clothing, and taking the children where they have to go, I don't feel that I spend the time with them that I should. Yet the things I do for them don't give me the stimulation that I need. So I take time for myself.

Besides teaching Relief Society once a month and being the choir president, I'm the stake public communications director. I don't mind doing the stake newsletter every other month, but I detest trying to place articles in the local newspaper. I accepted the calling only because I felt I couldn't say no. I'd already said no to teaching seminary because of Abby's illness. I'm not very proud of my attitude about this calling. When Brother Engebretsen set me apart, he said in the blessing, "Your home situation will improve." I found out the next week that Abby was out of remission—there were leukemia cells in her spinal fluid. I felt like asking to be released because my time would be so consumed by taking her to her treatments. I did ditch a lot of my other responsibilities for a while, but I decided not to ditch church. I guess the core of my dislike for this calling is that the demands of being active in the church have sometimes been painful.

If going to a stake meeting didn't require three hours of travel time, it would be a lot easier to take the church in stride. It was very hard for me when Doug was the stake clerk in Nashville and was gone almost every Sunday. I had four, then five, little children. One Saturday I followed him around the backyard as he was cutting and raking the grass—just pouring out how upset I felt about our schedule and our life not together. One Sunday when he came home at 11:00 P.M. and said that the stake presidency was going to meet all day long the next Sunday, too, I got in the car, drove away, and parked for a while. I felt so guilty because I knew there were women who would give anything to have their husbands be active in the church, and I couldn't be happy.

I loved being Relief Society president in New York City because I came to love so many women. Many of them were in my situation, young mothers whose husbands were in school, but a lot of them weren't. We had people who had always lived in the Bronx, for example. I gained such an appreciation for them. I never felt I had done all I should do, but I did learn a lot about getting people to do things, following up on things.

Another calling that meant a lot to me was teaching Gospel Doctrine in Sunday school. I always felt I had to have a burning testimony of whatever I was teaching, so I did a lot of soul-searching as well as studying. Several times while preparing lessons, I thought of things I needed to repent of and I wrote letters to people asking for their forgiveness. I felt I couldn't teach the lesson unless I put certain things right in my life. I especially tried to control my tongue and not say whatever flippant thing happened to come into my head.

Sometimes we try too hard to make things fit church standards. This month's cultural refinement lesson was about a South American poet named Gabriela Mistral. When I went to the library to find out more information about her, I found the same poem that was in the lesson manual, but the manual had deleted two stanzas of the poem. The meaning of the poem was completely changed. I presented the entire poem in the lesson. It would be a richer and, ultimately, more faith-promoting discussion if we talked about our points of agreement and disagreement rather than just ignoring the parts we don't agree with.

I wonder whether I should have more children. I'm still in good shape physically, but I'm concerned about the quality of my children's lives. We've been thrown on the mercy of the church during my last three pregnancies for varying lengths of time. Right before Christina was born I had bronchitis. The Relief Society sisters kept John, Alan, and Lisa for me every day so I could stay in bed. Then I had to stay in bed for three weeks with Abby. The women in the ward kept Lisa and Christina every day, and brought in meals every night. They even packed and unpacked when we moved. I felt like such a great burden. Of course, when Robert was born the day after we learned that Abby has leukemia, we needed a lot of help. It's wonderful to have that kind of help, but I've never felt that it was the duty of other people to care for my family.

I've gained a new perspective from Abby's illness. I feel like every moment— not that I always show it since other things like clay on the carpet tend to get in the way—has great existential meaning. The events of life don't matter; it's what you make of them. Her life has given me so much joy that I will always be glad she is my child even if I don't get to see her grow up. I tell the other children, "You've got to be happy in the present because the future comes out of it. *Now* is what is important." I do have the traditional Mormon hope that no matter what happens we will be together again in the next world and that our relationship there will be built on our relationship here. Because we've gone through so much together there is a bond that will not be broken.

On the other hand, now that I know much more about what she would go through if she had another relapse, I don't want any part of that kind of suffering for her or for me or the rest of the family. I'll be very grateful if she can be spared that.

The priesthood has been very important in our lives, but I see two priesthoods. I see a family priesthood that unites a husband and wife in raising their children and I see the public one that runs the church. It's ironic that sometimes the church makes it harder for the family. I'm not saying we don't need the church.

I began participating in giving blessings to our children because sometimes it was not possible to call someone in to help administer to a child. Sometimes in the middle of the night when Doug blessed a sick baby as I held her, I felt that I was participating just as much as if I had the priesthood. When Doug read about how women used to give blessings, he asked the stake president in Nashville about it. He said, "You should do what you feel is right." I was amazed.

The first time I helped give a blessing was the day after we moved to Newark. It was a Saturday. Alan began running a high fever, and his asthma medicine was not helping him. I had to take him to the emergency room. Because we didn't know anybody, Doug and I administered to him together. Doing that made me very conscious of all the times I had not been in harmony with Doug and I resolved to do better.

I wanted to have men and women stand in the circle when Robert was given his name, but when I prayed about it, I didn't feel that I should push for it. Of course, I didn't hear the blessing Doug gave because of the noise level in the chapel. When I first heard people say, "Someday women will have the priesthood," I thought, "Hah!" Now I think it could come to pass and I wouldn't be surprised.

6 | Priesthood Meeting

On December 9, the first Sunday after our son John's twelfth birthday, Bishop Bushman called John up to the front of the chapel and asked the congregation for a sustaining vote for John to be ordained a deacon in the Aaronic priesthood. John's delight was a visible halo. As the last member of his Primary class to turn twelve, John had been impatient for this birthday. When John turns fourteen, he may be ordained a teacher, and at sixteen, a priest, but advancement is not automatic. Before presenting a young man to the congregation, the bishop interviews him to determine his willingness and worthiness. If a boy is not paying a full tithe, is cheating in school, breaking the Word of Wisdom, or having problems with chastity, he will not be ordained until he overcomes the difficulty.

The deacons' most visible duty is passing the sacrament to the congregation. Priests offer the sacramental prayers and may baptize. Men may be ordained to be elders in the Melchizedek priesthood at the age of eighteen. Men must be elders in order to serve missions, to be married in the temple, or to perform the ordinances of laying on of hands—blessing new babies, healing the sick, confirming new members in the church, or giving other blessings. Seventies serve as missionaries within the stake. When men are called to serve in bishoprics or on the stake high council, they are ordained as high priests.

After Sunday school that day, John attended his first priesthood meeting. Every Sunday, the boys and men meet together in the chapel before separating into their quorums for classes.

Bishop Bushman's counselor, Gary Johnston, began the meeting by announcing that Timothy Ridge would be baptized that afternoon and inviting the entire ward to attend. He then announced that members should contact Karel Vander-Heyden to make appointments with the bishop for tithing settlement, at which individuals declare whether or not they are full tithe-payers.

Frank Crowe, the High Priests' Group leader, and Robert Pierce, the Elders'

Quorum president, then gave their home teaching reports for the month of November. Each quorum had visited 53 percent of their assigned families during November and were encouraged to do even better during December. The Elkton Ward does not have enough home teachers to assign one to every family in the ward. Each family, or single person, in the ward is supposed to have a pair of home teachers, at least one of whom holds the Melchizedek priesthood. They visit the family each month, present a spiritual message, and help the family in time of need, such as moving, loss of work, or illness. In addition to any other callings he might have, every man who holds the priesthood is expected to serve as a home teacher to other families. Most home teaching pairs are assigned to visit four or more families per month. Even a modest home teaching route requires at least two evenings or Sunday afternoons to complete.

Richard King, 34

Richard King was baptized at the age of eight by his father and followed the normal path for young men in the church, advancing in the priesthood, serving a mission, and attending BYU. Now the father of two boys and two girls ages nine months to nine years, he is a computer systems analyst for a large bank in Wilmington, Delaware, and is the Elkton Ward financial clerk, keeping records of all donations and ward expenses. He also is a home teacher.

I grew up in Orangeburg, New York, which is about fifteen miles northwest of New York City. My family are members of the church, and I was born in the covenant. When I was seventeen I left to go to BYU. I met my wife, Ginny, there after I returned from my mission to Peru. We were two New Yorkers who just happened to be in the same college ward.

I enjoyed math and science in school and also played basketball, which was a real challenge. I was expected to play because of my height, but I did not have any talent. It took a lot of effort to improve my skill level. In college I found that I really didn't like engineering, but I did enjoy the computer class that was required for that major. I finally realized that was where I was happiest, so I switched to computers. I worked in Utah until we moved here five years ago.

I've been happier since I scaled back my expectations in life. My biggest difficulty has been a kind of energy limit that my body has placed on me, and I reach it very suddenly. Until I knew it existed, I would begin to fall apart when I reached it. I had to experiment until I found out where the limit was and how I could stay within it.

Being the ward financial clerk is a little different from many church callings because it is very exact. Once the books balance, I'm done, and I don't have to magnify my calling. I've enjoyed my clerk positions because they're well defined. Many times the changes that church callings make in our lives are not obvious to us, but I think we handle ourselves better with the public; we're a little bit more organized; we can plan better.

The priesthood is a marvelous way for the male members of the church to feel a tremendous amount of responsibility. You can point out many successes in the home teaching program, but in general, it doesn't work very well. A lot of people are lost. The catch-22 is that we are a lay church. Home teachers are untrained. They're great at fellowshipping active members. I feel very few home teachers are in a position to give legitimate help to inactive members who have problems.

A more open attitude toward the church comes from living much of your adult life in the East. It's a little bit of a challenge for my wife and me to find a life-style in which we're both comfortable. When I was growing up our family home evenings were not as structured as those of other members of the church. We do a lot of things as a family, but we do not always have a formal lesson. Occasionally, that has been a bone of contention between my wife and me.

I question everything. That doesn't mean that I always expect to find the answer. I wonder sometimes how much the culture of man has crept into the church, as opposed to pure religion. Our belief that we are the absolute true church is the greatest difference between us and other churches. Of course, many differences in doctrine result from that belief. Once you have a prophet, then you open up the whole idea of doctrines following from his teachings. We do not follow the Bible as a blueprint of how to run a church; it wasn't written with that intent.

Since the church claims to be true, it tends not to change a great deal. I think it attempts not to change the basic structure of priesthood organization—prophet, apostles, etc. They do try to adopt better ways of administration. I guess there have been some other changes, though. My father claims he can remember a time when the principle of "every member a missionary" was not emphasized in the church. The emphasis placed on missionary work has changed. I believe every member is a missionary, but sometimes members have alienated their neighbors rather than given them a positive experience with the church. Most people have to have a positive experience over a long period of time before they come into the church. I believe that missionary work is a correct principle, but I have mixed feelings about how it is applied.

My testimony is the sum of my experiences growing up. It's difficult, as President McKay once indicated, to point to a specific example and say, "Before this I did not have one and now I do."

Karel Vander-Heyden, 62

Karel Vander-Heyden became interested in the church after his only child, Astrid, joined. Born in Jakarta, Indonesia, and a veteran of World War II and the Korean War, Karel is a public accountant in Newark. As the ward executive secretary, he makes sure that families are assigned to either the Elders' or High Priests' quorums for home teaching as well as making appointments for ward members to meet with Bishop Bushman.

My father died seventeen days before I was born, so I came into the world at a very tragic moment. My father was a supervisor in the harbor of Jakarta, loading and unloading ships. In a storm, a high wire fell on the ground and he was electrocuted. He was thirty-two years old. I was the seventh child. Later on, my mother remarried and had four more children. In Indonesia high school was not compulsory; your family had to pay for it. I was the first one to finish high school from my family.

I went into the armed forces when I was seventeen. I was a noncommissioned officer at age seventeen, which I found later on was a real accomplishment. That was in 1939. In 1941 we had the war with Japan. After a very short battle with the invading forces, we surrendered—the whole country surrendered—and we were taken as prisoners of war. I was a prisoner for three and a half years.

I was sent to Burma and Thailand. We built railroads through the jungles. I was treated very badly, but I think I survived because I was young. Of course, there was no clothing left after so many years. In that environment the character of a man comes into the open. I have seen people become greedy, getting mean and evil just to survive. But I have also seen the opposite—people sacrificing themselves, their health.

At times I thought I was dying. When people had tropical wounds in their legs—big open wounds that cannot heal, there was nothing to stitch them up. Their legs had to be amputated. There was no anesthesia. In 1945 I was really, really sick and Dr. Meyer saved me. He had just a little medicine left. He gave me two shots. That pulled me out. The casualty rate from the prisoner of war camps in Germany was 10 out of 100. In the Japanese camps it was 32 out of 100. I was lucky. For one reason or another maybe God wanted me to survive.

In the meantime, we had another war, a war between brothers, the Indonesian War of Independence. When the Indonesians gained their independence, anybody holding Dutch citizenship had one year to get out or to obtain Indonesian citizenship. A lot of people who had lived for generations in Indonesia were suddenly forced to leave. My family went to the Netherlands.

I was still in the armed forces so I was automatically transferred. I went to school and became an accountant, but there were no jobs. Then war broke out in Korea. They wanted anybody without a job who had some military experience. I thought it was an opportunity at least to survive. I went to Korea for about eighteen months. That was a terrible war. I was later transferred to administrative work, but we were near the front lines. I was very careful. If they said to wear a helmet, I wore my helmet. The only time I was really afraid was when we marched through the mine fields.

When they shipped me back to the Netherlands, there was still no job. Indonesia is an easy country. It is easy to live. There is always food—an abundance of food. In the Netherlands, in the summer you have to think about the winter. In the meantime, I had married and we had a daughter, Astrid. I wanted to get out of the armed forces after so many years, but I could not get a job there in the Netherlands. I was getting old and had to start from the beginning.

Then I read an article in the paper that said President Truman had just signed a law that would allow 15,000 people to go to America! The only condition was you must be a refugee. We finally got the clearance, and they stamped my passport with the number 14,387. I was still in the service; finally they said I would be discharged April 1. We left on April 13 and arrived April 23, 1957, just seven days before the deadline.

I was in America with only one hundred dollars in my pocket. A minister from Elsmere, Delaware, was my sponsor. The women's association had rented an apartment and put some furniture in. I was thirty-four years old. I had never had a civilian job. I had been in one war after the other. My English was not adequate to get a job in an office so I got a job in a hospital kitchen. Till this day I am still able to support myself, if I have to, by cooking. There is no job that I find demeaning. Work is not boring to me. I have seen guys who cannot wait until five o'clock to get out of the office. They count the days until they can have a pension.

With a part-time job on the side, I was doing well. I think we bought a house after just one and a half years. Astrid went to kindergarten. She was picking up new words. It took my wife three or four years to adjust herself. She went to night school to learn English. The people in the Presbyterian church in Elsmere were very receptive and very friendly. We felt at ease and joined the church. A man in the Presbyterian church became president of a construction company and took me in as his office manager. I took courses at the University of Delaware. When this man made me his office manager, I began to prosper.

My upbringing was religious. Though my father was not a practicing Catholic he insisted that all the children be baptized Catholics. My mother was a Protestant. Since my high school days I always had a love for religion and a belief in Jesus Christ. Astrid was baptized a Catholic. Romkje did not object to that, but she did not want to become a Catholic herself. I felt it was important to bring the child up in a religious atmosphere. We prayed for meals but there was no personal prayer and no family prayer. Frankly, I did not know what to pray. As Catholics, we pray only what is told us—"Our Father" and the "Hail Mary."

I think that I was foreordained to be the father of Astrid, my daughter who later on brought me to this church. I came here with the desire that my children would do better. I wanted to make sure that Astrid would have a good education. Astrid and I were very close. She was a good student. I think she was the first female student body president at William Penn High School. She was a cheerleader and played in the band. She went to the University of Virginia at Charlottesville for two years and then she transferred to Florida. At the University of Florida she met her husband, Peter.

Astrid sent me some pamphlets and she said, "What do you know about the Church of Jesus Christ of Latter-day Saints?" All I knew was that they were good people. They did not drink or smoke or drink coffee or tea. Her next letter said, "I'm going to be baptized next week."

I had told her before college, "You be on your own." I think I offered a prayer or something for her on that day. In my spirit I was in agreement with what she did. In the summer Peter and Astrid came. I talked to Peter about the church. It was impressive. My church had become too liberal for me.

Peter promised me they would not be married until Astrid finished college. After they went back to school, another letter came. They were getting married in the temple. Then Astrid sent two missionaries to tell us about temples. My wife was enthusiastic and she wanted to know about it. I became more and more interested.

When we went to Florida to visit his parents, the word came out that nobody could attend the wedding in the temple in Washington. His mother hit the ceiling. That was an evening not to forget. He was the only son, Astrid the only daughter. Astrid had to explain what is the big deal. She explained that it is for eternity. They asked Astrid what the requirements were and she told us you have no sex before marriage. I thought, "This religion must be good, a better religion than most." Then his parents asked me to go to the bishop in Wilmington and ask if there could be a wedding in the church if Peter and Astrid went to the temple later on. His mother wanted a big wedding with everybody attending the ceremony.

I called Bishop Cross and made an appointment. I said, "Can't you have the ceremony in the church? You see, in Europe you are married by the judge or the mayor and after that you go to the church of your choice. The civil ceremony is the legal marriage, not the church marriage." He said, no, that cannot be. He sent Bishop O'Day to the house to explain it, and I think, to patch things up a little. From what he said, I thought, "This is a church that goes on principles rather than for the accommodation of certain people." I was glad that Astrid had found something that was meaningful to her.

The wedding was in Washington. Romkje and I went to the temple. We sat in the hall; Astrid was inside getting married. We went back to Wilmington for the reception.

During the year I saw maybe twenty-eight missionaries. I started to read and ask questions. Finally, about three months after the wedding, I asked one of the elders to baptize me. I think he was a little shocked. I said, "There is only one condition. My wife is leaving for Europe on Wednesday. I have to be baptized before she goes."

Tuesday, the day I was baptized, was the day I lost my job. They noticed that I was seeking for another religion. It was a closed corporation; we were friends. Anyway, something happened in the office so I was out and another man was out also. I will not say it was because I was joining the church, but I think it had some impact. So I was cooking again, seven days a week.

Before I was a Mormon, I had always thought about tithing. It was easy to put ten dollars in the plate, but I realized that 10 percent is the law, and I felt uneasy about it. The day that the elder asked me if I had any problems with the Word of Wisdom, I said, "I will have no problems" though I drank at that time and drank tea and coffee. Then he explained about tithing. I said, "No, I don't believe I will have problems with tithing."

When I was baptized I was overpowered. To the elder it was just a ceremonial action. Before I went to the waters I prayed and I fasted for eighteen hours. I felt good in spirit. Since I had gone to this church and that church, my wife thought that it would last two or three months and then I'd be okay. After the baptism I said, "There will be no more coffee and no more tea for me. I'm not allowed to drink it."

She said, "You'll never make it." She did not expect this. Our marriage is not ideal, but it is workable as long as I keep my religion to myself and I accommodate her. When I was not a member of the church we used to go out on Sunday, for dinner or to the beach. Now of course she knows I'm not going. But on Mother's Day, I'll take her out for dinner or whatever. We'll see friends on Sunday. She cannot understand why I wake up at five o'clock to be at church at seven o'clock and stay the whole day. She calls it a working day—going to church with a briefcase!

Through these years, we have moved a little apart. There is not that intimate relationship. I miss having a wife who is very intimate in a spiritual sense: to pray with her in the morning or to pray with her in the evening.

I do not believe that this little Elkton building is conducive to spiritual enhancement, but I am more at ease here in the Elkton Ward than in the old New Castle Ward. Maybe it is because I have been a member of the church longer and know more people. Before I was executive secretary to the bishop, I was an assistant stake clerk, another staff position. I served a very brief time as a Sunday school teacher when the branch met in Holly Hall. It wasn't a good experience. I didn't have any experience, the Sunday school president had no experience, and the facilities were poor. It was discouraging, but I later noticed that I had been picked for that position because no one before me had been able to do it.

When we meet every Sunday we strengthen one another. Sometimes during the week I have no contact with Mormons. If somebody calls me to make an appointment with the bishop, I feel good to hear a voice and know it is my brother or my sister. If I could select a calling it would be in missionary work. If you gave me a choice I would pick being a stake missionary rather than being the bishop.

Six months after my baptism, I went to the bishop and asked him if I could have my patriarchal blessing. I went to the stake patriarch's home in New Jersey at eight o'clock at night while still fasting. He asked me a few questions. Then he had a little lesson about the sons of Jacob. Then he said, "We will have a prayer." I prayed and then he prayed. Then he gave me a blessing. It said things that I hadn't told him about. It struck me. Later on I learned that the blessing is what Heavenly Father wants you to know through the mouth of this patriarch. Mine is very specific—outlining what I should do and what I should not do. This patriarchal blessing is so dear to me. Being dark, I thought maybe I was from the lineage of Manassah, but my blessing said I was from the lineage of Ephraim. Later on, when I read books about this, I found it was something special. I accept it as a gift of God. I was told that in my pre-earth life I was able to persuade certain people to accept the plan of Jesus Christ.

When I read in the paper about a young boy going out into the streets of Philadelphia giving hot drinks to homeless people, I wonder how we as a church are doing on this type of thing. I was glad that we collected some money for the Ethiopian relief. Being a good Samaritan should be emphasized more in the church. Maybe people who are born in the church don't realize that our church could do good work in this field.

The greatest gift I have had given to me through the church is the priesthood. At the time I was the Callerys' home teacher, Brother Callery asked me to go to the state hospital and give his son a blessing. I took the missionaries with me and I asked my friend, who was visiting from the Netherlands, if he wanted to go with us. He was an elder in the Dutch Reformed Church, but he didn't speak any English. One of the missionaries anointed David's head with oil and I gave him a blessing. My friend later told me, "You know, the room was dark, but when you were giving the blessing it seemed to me that a light came in and I saw that." It was very impressive to me that he told me that.

By joining this church I have prospered. I'm not rich in the material sense, but in having peace of mind. I'm rich in my heart. I have learned to love people. Before I was so indifferent, but now I have sincere love for each one of this ward. Before I die I hope for the privilege of having two things. One is to serve a mission even if I'm old, and the other is to be sealed in the temple. But I cannot control that. The only thing I can control is to be worthy to have these blessings given me.

I wish I was a Mormon long, long before I was baptized. I think I might have been able to comfort a lot of people at times. If I had had the priesthood in the prisoner of war camp, I might have stayed with somebody who was dying and comforted him. At that time everybody was just for himself, but if I had had the priesthood, maybe I would have had extra strength. In Korea, seeing people sick and wounded, I would have been able to help them.

Here I am, born in Jakarta, traveled around the world a little bit, finally came here and became a Mormon. Amazing. I have received my share of the blessings.

Robert Pierce, 35

Robert Pierce has been Elders' Quorum president for almost two years of the seven that he has belonged to the church. As Elders' Quorum president, he is not only responsible for giving home teaching assignments to the other elders but he and his counselors are to conduct regular interviews with the home teachers to encourage them in their assignments, to learn of problems that need to be brought to the attention of the bishopric, and to offer suggestions of how the home teachers or the quorum can help the families. Robert grew up in New Castle County and is a plant manager and division manager for Keysor-Century. He is the father of four children, ten-year-old twins from his first marriage and two daughters, ages three and one.

When the missionaries found me, my marriage was not going well, so I was looking for some answers—but not searching. When the sister missionaries first came I was on my way to Cincinnati for a business meeting and I told them to come back in a couple of weeks. They didn't come back. I thought Sam Pollock, who also worked for Keysor, had sent them, so I went up to him at work and said, "What happened to your sister missionaries?" I don't know why I did that, but they came back and after two or three months I was baptized.

I was divorced about a year later. My wife had joined too, but just said it was too much pressure for her to live the teachings. There were oodles of problems. It wasn't like I didn't try or she didn't try during the eight or nine years we were married, but it just definitely didn't work out.

I guess the church kept me from falling back into the same ruts that I fell into before. People in the church helped me out quite a bit. Steve Cherry and I spent two or three nights a month home teaching. It was a good jaunt from Odessa to the far side of Elkton, and we were teaching eight families at one time there. We always did 100 percent, and while we were home teaching, he was also teaching me. Ken McVicker also helped me quite a bit because he was my home teacher.

I was called to be the chairman of the Young Special Interests. It wasn't going very well because there weren't many guys coming out, but oodles of single girls. For one outing I took five of them to New York City to see *Oklahoma!* I didn't dare take one because all of a sudden she and everyone else would figure that she was "the one." Being chairman was very rewarding because I got the program up and going. We had a couple of conferences: Becoming a Better Me and Special Interest in You. At the end of the conferences there would be a testimony meeting. Most single people, twenty to thirty years old, are not going to pour their hearts out to each other, yet they did it. The last thing I did with them before I ran off to Utah to marry Colleen was go to the Hill Cumorah pageant. I had a ticket to fly home from Rochester, but they talked me into riding home with them.

I had custody of the twins, so I needed to marry someone who could relate to taking care of two five-year-olds. I wanted somebody who was already strong and who could match my faith. Then we would have that common interest that would help us conquer other problems. It's worked out very, very well.

When I came home from active duty in the Delaware National Guard in May of 1969, I went to work at Keysor in the warehouse, shipping and receiving. When September came I told my boss I was going back to school. He was pretty put out. He wasn't too sympathetic, but the plant manager offered me a part-time job in the evenings in the lab, which was great. It gave me another education. By the time I graduated six months later I had already worked in the warehouse and in the technical end of the business. Then a job opened up in the office. After I'd worked as office manager about four or five years, I was promoted to plant manager. I was the youngest plant manager the company had ever had. I was in charge of sales for the East Coast. I did the site location work and was in charge of building a plant in Toronto, and now I'm responsible for its manufacturing.

I take pride in my work. In the last three months we've conquered sales accounts that nobody's ever conquered. We've met production requirements that "couldn't be done." We have the environmentally cleanest formulations of any of the plants in the company. My biggest frustration is when people say that something can't be done and I know that it can.

As Elders' Quorum president, I feel like I am dragging people along. Is it my leadership or is it them? If they don't have a testimony of something I can't do anything about it. I guess I have to be patient, but I can't believe that they don't live up to their commitments. Sometimes I think that we are almost a church of losers. The missionaries looked at my first wife and me and said, "You're a golden couple." Listen, if we're golden, then you're in trouble. As you look around the Elkton Ward (probably an average ward), we've got 20 or 30 families out of 180 that you can count on. I look at the members and say, "These people made the same commitments that I made, which are pretty serious commitments."

The most satisfying thing is being able to help people. Steve Cherry and Ken McVicker helped me when I was getting divorced. When I look back at some of the people I've been able to help along in the Elders' Quorum, I feel gratified. Motivating the brethren to understand the importance of the things that they're supposed to be doing, such as home teaching, reading the scriptures, service projects, is hard. Everything you do for the church is volunteer. Sometimes I'd like to grab the brethren and shake them and say, "Get your act together. Tomorrow could be the last day. Are you ready for that?"

When I took over two years ago we got our home teaching rolling to 80 percent of assigned families, which is very good. This year we are cruising along and averaging about 60 percent. I guess my newness is wearing off. Steve Cherry taught me the value of home teaching. My testimony of home teaching is probably why I was called to be president. Sometimes it's a real trial, especially for Colleen. When I go home teaching I usually make a night of it. I get home about eleven o'clock so I guess I'm probably too long-winded. At least every month one family who I used to teach calls me up and kind of gives me a report and wants to know if I wouldn't come back and be their home teacher. It makes me kind of feel bad. I know I could assign myself to them. I usually assign myself to some of the more difficult families, thinking they need it. It cuts away some of the play time with the kids. When the other elders let me down, I think, "Here I am—I'm out here away from my family and these guys come off with these excuses—where's their commitment?" If I can do it—! I'm not a Utah Mormon. I'm just a Delaware convert.

David Obzansky, 31

As a counselor to Robert Pierce, one of David Obzansky's major responsibilities is to supervise and encourage home teachers to fill their assignments. A native of New Jersey, David has been a member of the church for almost three years. David and his wife, Eileen Johnston, a dentist, moved to Elkton, Maryland, when he began working for the Du Pont company in 1982.

My grandparents on the Obzansky side are from the Ukraine. My mother's family are the second generation in this country. My father, a Ukrainian, married my mother, who's an Italian. The Italian side of the family is very large and they still maintain a lot of the culture. My mother died of cancer when I was a sophomore in college. I have two sisters, one of whom died of encephalitis as a child.

I went to Immaculate Conception elementary school. I was a very poor student. In eighth grade I failed history, spelling, and some other subject and just managed to squeak out of grade school. My interests were in other areas than book learning. I was a very good little Catholic boy until I got to high school and started doing drugs and alcohol with the guys. That pretty much continued through graduate school. At Villanova University I studied for a B.S. in chemistry. I stayed on there to get a master's in chemistry. While I was waiting for Eileen to finish her dental degree I worked at Hahnaman Medical Center for a year and a half doing various research projects and published a number of papers. At Ohio State University I earned a doctorate in clinical biochemistry. There I was a good student and got all A's, some B pluses. My research adviser, Dr. Richardson, is a Latter-day Saint and bishop of his ward.

My job at Du Pont is developing the chemistry for new tests to be put onto the blood chemistry analyzer. I take a procedure from the research scale and bring it onto the market. That involves dealing with all kinds of people from Ph.D. researchers to the manufacturing types. I'll probably be doing this particular type of project for another year or so and then I'll be on another project. Du Pont's philosophy is to hire you for a career. If you're an organic chemist and they need a biochemist, you become a biochemist.

About the time we got married, we were looking for a church. We looked into the Unitarian church, then we looked into the Mormon church. We started going and felt very comfortable there. We liked the people we met. I don't think any revelation came over me during the discussions. We looked to see what kind of church we wanted to raise a family in. The Mormon church provided what we thought was a friendly atmosphere, a very practical atmosphere. It wasn't very ritualistic. I was impressed with the fact that everyone spoke and everyone taught; it wasn't just someone who was paid to give a lecture. I think we would have waited a year to be baptized but the missionaries pressured us. They only have a couple of months to do it and they want to get people in the water.

I think that the church is a tool to raise families that have a spiritual commitment. It provides a spiritual opportunity for them. Eileen and I were having some thoughts and discussions and questions about how she could combine her family with her career. Having our home and her practice in the same building was a revelation, an information-type gift to us.

Being a parent has totally changed my life. Now when I come home there's a little baby who wants attention, and he gets it for a couple of hours until he goes to bed. I don't come home and read the paper. Work on our house has slowed to a snail's pace. I used to play racquetball and squash before I had a baby and a house. I'm learning to play the dulcimer now.

In the family, the woman has the baby, carries the baby, struggles with it, nurses the baby. The only role a man has is to bless the baby. I think it's appropriate that the man has that role. It gets him involved in the family. I don't know if that's *the* reason women don't have the priesthood, and I'm not sure I understand the reason. I'm very impressed with the fact that women talk in church and they're given equal time on the podium because of some of the lessons I've learned from women. A lot of churches don't give women opportunities to talk.

In the Elkton Ward I started as membership clerk, then I became the ward clerk. I liked being membership clerk and keeping track of where everyone was. I enjoyed being ward clerk and I didn't enjoy it for the same reason: knowing everything that is going on is both a blessing and a curse. It's good to be informed, but you also hear things that you don't particularly want to hear. It's kind of cruel to expose a new member of the church to a bishopric meeting. Everyone has their dark side, but I didn't particularly want to hear what they were. The bright side is not always the side that came up in bishopric meeting.

I've been in the Elders' Quorum presidency for only a short time. As I see it my job is to keep track of the home teachers and try to put pressure on them to do their home teaching. Our record is fairly poor over the last six months or so, and I'm not sure what to do about that except to continue to put pressure on people. One thing I've found frustrating in the church is you become responsible for the success of other people's ideas that you don't necessarily support. I've figured out that when I'm not enthusiastic about someone's idea, I have to make it known that I'm not interested in that idea. I think a lot of people get into projects they don't have a commitment to. Consequently, they don't do them adequately.

Home teaching is a burden. I think we're out visiting people for statistics and not because we think we're doing any good. Some of the people don't want us to be there or don't care if we're there. We're exerting our time and effort in a place where we're probably not wanted. In a situation where we are wanted, we probably do some good. When we go to people who won't answer the door, won't make commitments, never show up to church, never do anything, I think we're wasting our time.

I don't agree with the church's hard-core missionary role. If a person wants to learn the gospel, once they know you're a Latter-day Saint they can ask. I don't believe in preaching one minute to someone who doesn't want to hear it. I don't believe in telling a Jew that he's in the incorrect faith or that he's gone astray. Our country was established for people to practice their own particular religions and I think we should allow that. We get overzealous at times in trying to dump people in the water.

Douglass Taber, 36

Douglass Taber is one of the two assistants to the High Priests' Group leader, Frank Crowe. He previously was the adviser to the Deacons' Quorum. He taught their priesthood lessons on Sunday, helped them organize their duties of passing the sacrament on Sunday, and acted as assistant scoutmaster in the Scout troop. Douglass joined the church while a college student. He teaches chemistry at the University of Delaware and is the father of six children, ages one to eleven.

I was raised to think that religion was fine for people who needed it but that there was no ultimate truth to it. I met my wife in the summer of 1968. I went to church with her. I didn't think much of it. At Christmas I visited her family and they impressed me very much, especially her mother. Her mother radiates living the gospel, the peace of the gospel.

In February as I was walking home from a date late one night, quite abruptly I knew that there was a God and that I could talk to him and that he could talk to me. One obvious question on my mind was whether this church was true or not. That answer came very quickly. "Yes, I should join this church." Another question was whether Susan was the person I should marry. It shows how young and ignorant we can be that I wasn't sure I wanted to do that. The hardest thing for me in joining the church was the blacks and the priesthood. I'd been raised to be very much devoted to the idea that black people were as good as anybody. Here was this church that practiced institutional racism. Here I was joining this church. I knew it was the right thing to do and I wanted to do it, but it was hard.

I needed my parents' permission to be baptized because I was just twenty, so I had to wait until my birthday in November. I was baptized on the fifteenth of November, 1969, and Susan and I were married that December. There was a single ward and a married ward at Stanford. There was a great gulf between the married ward and the single ward and we were now in the married ward. I was the only one in the adult Aaronic class. The instructor basically went through what would now be the new member lessons with me. It was very useful. It laid a foundation for life in the church.

At Susan's urging we inquired if we could be married in the temple before I'd been a member of the church for a full year because we were going East to graduate school. There were no temples east of Salt Lake City. I had my patriarchal blessing on the first of August and went through the temple three days later.

After my first year of graduate school I took the bus down to Fort Dix and reported for army basic training. From June until October I was training to be a clerk. You had to type five words a minute to get out of clerk school.

New York was my first experience being a pillar of the church. During our three years there I was the Deacon's Quorum adviser and scoutmaster, then the Young Men's president. We had a joint Mutual for the two wards and the Spanish branch. We took in all of Manhattan, much of the Bronx, and a piece of Queens. The way the kids came to church on Wednesday nights was that we went to get them. I'd leave the lab at about 5:00, walk down to 112th Street to borrow the Elders' Quorum president's VW bus, drive through the Bronx or out to Queens, and pick up the kids. I'd drop them off, park the bus, and get to the church by 7:00 for prayer meeting. We had Mutual from 7:30 to 8:45 and then I'd drive the route again. I'd finally get home about 11:15.

In Wisconsin I was a counselor in the Elders' Quorum. I traveled around every month having home teaching interviews with the members of the quorum. Sitting with a fellow in his house, you get to know him in a remarkable way, just by talking to him about his home teaching and about his life and trying to be a support and an encouragement. I got a vision of the place of home teaching in the church. It strengthens the families and the home teachers when they have the spiritual experience of being priests and ministering to the needs of others.

The ward in Madison was full of graduate students and postdocs—biochemistry, organic chemistry, and other works of the devil. A stake visitor, a seventy, came to speak in sacrament meeting and went on at great length about how evolution was the doctrine of the devil. The bishop, a professor of geology, did a thing that just isn't done. He got up after the stake visitor to say that all are welcome to express their opinions in the church. I think he did it to avoid having this poor visitor torn to shreds by the congregation after the meeting. I don't presume to tell the Lord how to create the earth, myself. Later, in Nashville, a friend of mine joined the church and was very concerned about evolution and things like this. I was trying to reason with him, "Look here, this is just one man's opinion. Just because he's a general authority doesn't mean it's the doctrine of the church." He was going on about the idea of the thousand year periods, the first thousand years, the second thousand years, and so on. I was about to say, "Now, look, that is a bunch of malarkey," but I felt very clearly by the Spirit not to tell him that. It said, "You don't know that, Doug."

When we first moved to the Nashville III Ward in 1975, the Nashville Stake was not quite five years old and it was pretty marginal still, just emerging. In many ways it was similar to the Elkton Ward except without the depth of church experience of Bishop Bushman. He does an enormous amount to stabilize and give leadership to the ward, both administratively and spiritually. At first I was financial clerk. I spent several months disentangling the financial records because the financial reports had been fudged every month. They had adjusted the deposit in transit to whatever was needed to make the report balance. Then I was called as a counselor in the bishopric. We had a dynamic, hard-working Elders' Quorum president. In the course of two years, with a lot of people working on it, the ward pulled together. The home teaching went from 35 or 40 percent to 75 or 80 percent. The ward paid off all its debts. Sacrament meeting attendance went up.

I tend to be an abrupt person. I was even more abrupt back then. I remember being abrupt with one of the girls. I apologized to her, but the damage had been done. I think she told her folks about it and they were offended. At ward conference the stake president told me I was to be released because of the way I'd treated people. That was a little hard to take. I knew it was right and I wanted to do better, but it was still hard. It's part of growing up in the church. I'm not sure I do a much better job now than I did then, but I still try.

I was called to be stake clerk ten days before the stake was to be divided. There was all this paperwork that nobody knew how to do. It was a very confusing week. The stake included everything from Tompkinsville, Kentucky, to Savannah, Tennessee. The stake president wanted to visit all the new wards. I disappeared every Sunday to go off and visit all these units and hold ward conferences. My four years as stake clerk was church administration at a different level. We saw the high council not as an exalted group of sages but as a bunch of guys whom we were trying to get moving. There was a great strength that came just from being in the same room with the stake presidency. I'd drive twenty-five miles to the stake center and spend every Wednesday night until eleven or twelve. A year and a half later, the stake was divided again. By then I knew how to do the paperwork.

In the fall of 1981 I increasingly felt I should focus on what I should be doing. Should I commit myself to staying on at Vanderbilt for my entire career? I read my patriarchal blessing and prayed about it and felt that it was time to look. Once I'd seen what a nice place Newark was and had begun to focus on the idea of being back in the bright lights of the East Coast, I very much wanted to come.

My studying the gospel has had more impact on the family than my callings have. I feel we need to put at least some portion of the effort we put into professional work into church work. I've made the effort to read, to try to understand. I feel keenly the necessity of having family scripture study in the morning. It's not enough for children to grow up in the church. They need to learn the gospel and feel what it is to live it.

We enjoy small children, know how to deal with them and how to get along with and teach them things. The difficult part is dealing with John, who is adolescent and has a totally different set of reactions. That is much more difficult in its own way even than dealing with Abby.

Abby is terribly ill, and has been. When it happened, we focused on what we needed to do to cope with it. The sense of grief and worry came later. When she was just sort of sniffly, we administered to her. I felt she was sick and it would take her a while to recover. I blessed her that she would recover. Two days later she was diagnosed as having leukemia. We administered to her again. I had nothing more to say. She'd been administered to and she would get better.

I take the time to pray every morning. I ask, "What could we do for Abby? What could we do for John?" By praying about things I can be much more effective. It's a very real feeling, knowing through prayer what's important to do. Life in the church, especially priesthood meeting, prepared me for family life. Priesthood meeting is very valuable in teaching you how to be a father, how to be a husband. Priesthood is the authority to act for God. What does it mean to act for God? It means you pray about things and you understand what you're supposed to do. Are men any better at that than women? Of course they're not. Why should only men have administrative positions in the church? It's convenient. Men like to belong to a club and it's a club they can belong to. Is that why there's priesthood? Is there something more eternal to it than that? I don't know, but those are questions that the feminist movement is going to lead to.

The bulk of my church calling right now is supervising home teaching. Seeing a home teacher go out and care about his families is very satisfying. Most home teachers who don't go out, don't go because they don't feel that they are being useful, that they're needed. I try to help them feel good enough about themselves that they can be a home teacher, which means feeling good enough about themselves to be a priesthood holder and a father and do all the many things they need to do. I enjoy working with people, working directly with the deacons, working directly with the home teachers. I'd much rather work at the ward level with individuals than in stake administration.

❀   ❀   ❀

After the home teaching report, the bishop discussed the ward budget. Saying he did not relish the part of Scrooge, squeezing blood out of a turnip, especially since the ward members had been very generous, he announced that it appeared the ward would end the year about three thousand dollars in the red, out of a budget of nineteen thousand dollars. After his last exhortation in October, the next week's budget donations had been more than three thousand dollars, three weeks later the figure was seven hundred dollars, and by the previous Sunday donations had fallen to sixty dollars. Because budget donations from the members of the Elkton Ward fell short of the required amount, the priesthood quorums spent several Saturdays in the fall cutting wood on Henry Tingey's property to sell for firewood. The quorum leaders had not only spent many hours cutting wood, but hours on the telephone recruiting volunteers for the project.

At the end of the bishop's budget report, the men and boys separated into their quorums for classwork. The deacons, teachers, and priests went upstairs to classrooms in the former choir loft. The high priests met in a small room at the front of the chapel, and the elders, the largest group, stayed in the chapel for their lesson.

Anthony Peer, 31

Anthony Peer has lived in the Elkton Ward for four years, first in North East, then in Chesapeake City, Maryland. Now a manager for Morton Thiokol, he was educated as an engineer and joined the church while in the navy. He and his wife, Linda, have been married for seven years and are the parents of three sons. Anthony is the instructor for the elders.

When I was stationed in California with the navy, I was trying to gain a better perspective on the type of person I could be in ten years. I went to a base chapel to have some time to myself and had a very peaceful experience. The following day I went back again. There were some men there who were holding sort of an Elders' Quorum meeting. They invited me in and gave me some literature. They introduced me to a member of the church who was on my ship. I was introduced to some young single people from the wards in the community. I joined the church because I knew the doctrine of the church was right, was true. It resonated in my soul. It scared me. I didn't join the first month. I needed to make absolutely sure that the commitments I would make were efficacious for me.

I had several long-distance romances with girls in Washington, D.C., while I was living north of Baltimore. I complained to my brother who was a member of the Perry Hall Ward that there weren't any women in the church my age with similar interests. I'd been traveling two hours for dates, falling asleep on the way home.

My brother said, "There is a new gal in the Towson Ward. She's about your age and has similar interests. She's attractive and she has a nice personality. And," he said, "I have a picture of her that I took at a Young Adults outing."

I said, "Well maybe you can introduce me to her at church." I made strategic arrangements to be around when one of her meetings let out. My brother introduced us on cue.

Two weeks after we were married and had expended all our funds on the reception, I lost my job. We had no income for five weeks. When you're a professional, it takes a while to go through the cycle of getting another position. Linda became pregnant and was very, very ill. It worked out well because I got a job at Maryland Cup, which was only three blocks away. I had been working in Philadelphia and Salisbury.

I've had some positive home teaching experiences and I've had a lot of negative home teaching experiences. I haven't had more than two active families to home teach in the seven years since I've been married. I always have inactive members and have to go far to see them because we live so far out. Real home teaching is to be a support to the patriarch in the home, but in most inactive families there's a real absence of patriarchal strength. One might recognize it as a real challenge and opportunity to develop that strength, to give water to the desert, so to speak, but it's very discouraging.

Ten years ago a lot of the priesthood responsibility was exercised by the bishopric, but since that time the church leadership has taught us the importance of personal priesthood leadership for the family. The Elders' Quorum presidency is a vital part of bringing a dynamic realization of the gospel to the members. That change is more major even than that of admitting black men to the priesthood.

I'm very grateful for the priesthood. Maybe it's an oversimplification, but I would be less than a complete man without it. I can't remember what it was like not to have the priesthood. I think when men come into this world, we are prepared and eligible to receive it. The course of our life makes us worthy or unworthy when the opportunity comes, but there's always that yearning. Exercising and honoring the priesthood is very fulfilling. Without my wife, my priesthood would not be actualized. It would be impotent in a sense. Our family is very different from the one I was raised in. I know the priesthood has a lot to do with that. We have a very strong central focus from having been married in the temple.

There are all sorts of things that one would like to do: you know, vacation in Aruba or have a Ferrari. We discipline ourselves to go to the dentist, buy food, little shoes and big shoes, and a house. We try to have an appropriate family environment, and there are financial sacrifices for that. Some people might construe sacrifice as being something that you give up, as if there's some sort of negative entry in the ledger, but it's not. It's an area of our lives that we make sacred.

When my wife, Linda, worked with the Young Women's organization, I respected the growth I saw in her and the growth that she was able to stimulate in the girls. They relied very heavily in a sisterly way on their leaders. I enjoy supporting her and helping her. There are times I get frustrated with things in the world and she is an oasis for me. There are times when she is very frustrated with things, and I feel that I can be of comfort to her, too. I respect her strength as well as her need to have her own life. What I appreciate most about her is her self-worth, her sense of balance, and her ability to give.

I think the women's movement has challenged some of the nongospel concepts about women that have existed in our church. Church leaders have redefined what they think about women. Perhaps that was stimulated by the challenges from the women's movement, but it actually occurred under the normal flow of revelation through the prophet.

I don't think the church leadership gives a clear voice on the issue of family size, but the social fabric of the church puts an inordinate amount of pressure on couples to have children—often beyond their emotional and social means to adequately nurture and support their families. I've seen some families that have almost avoided taking the responsibility for family size by not controlling it.

I enjoy being the Elders' Quorum instructor. I enjoy it when I can stimulate the minds and the spirits of the brethren in the quorum. It's also very frustrating when that doesn't happen. I've been the executive secretary for three different bishops and one branch president. I've been asked, along with the counselors, to give my ideas and feelings. I've been in the Elders' Quorum presidency twice, and both those times were difficult. There were large numbers of adult prospective elders and a very small nucleus of active elders both times. Getting a program moving forward or maintaining levels of commitment was difficult. It's an in-the-trenches position and maybe I'm just not an in-the-trenches person.

I know the priesthood has helped prepare me to fill a father's role. Stake presidents and bishops are quite often men who are established in their professions. They are fathers, and of course they have demanding responsibilities as bishops and stake presidents. Yet they always seem to excel in each of those areas even though they have only the same number of hours that the rest of us do. That additional capacity must be like an athletic prowess that they've developed. I've asked them how they do it, but it's like Coca-Cola. They don't tell you the secret.

The Choir

7 | Sings the *Messiah*

During the early weeks of December, preparations for Christmas intensified. More people began to attend choir practice. Claudia Bushman, the choir director, had purchased copies of Handel's *Messiah,* which the choir had begun practicing in August. Rehearsals were exhilarating, but also depressing because all four parts were never present at the same time. Cindy Mullins often left the alto section to sing tenor with the one or two men who were attempting to learn the part. The entire alto section switched back and forth between alto and tenor. The alto section was vastly improved by the presence of Dianna Cannon and Kelly Hindley, two students who always attended choir practice because they rode to church with Claudia Bushman. Bishop Bushman began leaving priesthood executive meeting early to join the bass section.

As they struggled through "And He Shall Purify" and "His Yoke Is Easy," the altos asked Sister Bushman which of her sons would be home for Christmas. Meanwhile, Claudia, as president of the University of Delaware Women's Club, had formed an alliance with Larry Peterson, chairman of the music department. The music department had tried to have a Messiah Sing several years earlier, but only a handful of people had attended. Claudia suggested the Women's Club and the Newark Symphony Society as cosponsors of the event. Each week, she reminded the choir of the university's sing, which would be held December 16. "It will be very good practice for our own performance the following week," she said.

The afternoon of the sing, I arrived at the music building fifteen minutes early. The Robinson and McVicker families were walking into the building. In fact, streams of people were headed for the doors. Almost the entire Elkton Ward Choir was there, many of them with their children. Students and townspeople packed the room—more than 350 in all.

The ward's Christmas service was held on Sunday, December 23. When he announced the program Bishop Bushman said that when his wife, the choir director, had told him that the choir was going to learn some of the *Messiah* he had said that it couldn't be done, for many good reasons. Yet here they were, prepared to sing all the choruses from the first section, as well as the Hallelujah Chorus. The choir's ranks were augmented by Brick, Karl, and Serge Bushman, a tenor and two basses, home for the holidays, but Kelly and Dianna had gone home to Utah for the holidays. The Primary children began the program by singing "Away in a Manger" and "Lullaby to the Infant King." The *Messiah* choruses were interspersed with congregational readings from the second chapter of Luke. Cindy Mullins and Jane Whitney played the "Pastoral Symphony" on their flutes; Jean Bingham performed the soprano recitatives that precede "Glory to God"; and Joey Robinson and Jean Bingham sang "And He Shall Feed His Flock." As the congregation dispersed after the final hallelujah, Kevin O'Day, who had always complained that we didn't spend enough time rehearsing his part, enveloped Claudia Bushman in a big hug.

Although it is not traditional for LDS congregations to hold Christmas morning services, the Elkton Ward began doing so in 1983. Sheila Anderson and Claudia Bushman had discussed the idea for several months, and Claudia had proposed the idea to the bishopric. This year, for the second time, Claudia organized the program and Sheila arranged for refreshments afterwards.

By 12:17 Christmas Day children were practicing at the pianos in the chapel and Relief Society room. Claudia Bushman was rehearsing the brass ensemble. She made a sour face as they hit a wrong note. At 12:38 Bishop Bushman welcomed the seventy members who were scattered throughout the chapel. Rob McPherson gave the opening prayer. Though focused on Christmas, this program was more of a Christmas sharing than a worship service.

Virginia Lund, Jean Bingham, and Claudia Bushman sang "Still, Still, Still." Then Elder Steenstra, a full-time missionary from the Netherlands, played a Beethoven piano solo from memory. The Ridge family sang "Away in a Manger," then Bronwyn Anderson, nine years old, played "Deck the Halls" and "Silent Night" on the piano. Linda Hansen, visiting from the Wilmington Ward, accompanied her son Ben as he played "Away in a Manger" and "Jingle Bells" on the recorder. Joey and Dawn Robinson played "It Came upon the Midnight Clear" on the piano, then six women sang "Lo, How a Rose E'er Blooming." Cindy Mullins played "What Child Is This?" on the flute, Lisa Taber played "March of the Three Kings" on the piano, and Cindy Mullins and Jane Whitney played "Silent Night."

The final performance was by Benny and the Pork Chops—Ben Bushman, his father, and his brothers—who sang several spirited songs. The brass ensemble accompanied the congregation in singing Christmas carols.

P. Eugene Dean, 37

Eugene Dean began coming to choir practice in the summer of 1983 when the choir was rehearsing for Zion, a musical produced by the Wilmington Stake. A Primary teacher for the past three years, Eugene has been a member of the church for twelve years. He works for the University of Delaware security department and is the father of a sixteen-year old daughter, Mary.

Although I was born in San Pedro, California, my father was a Delaware boy. We moved back to the Newark area when I was about three years old. My family was involved in athletics. Although I couldn't participate actively in sports, my brother and I were involved in football and baseball. I went along to baseball with my brother and I was the scorekeeper. I was the chief rooter for the football team. I've been involved in fantasy baseball for four years. We play two or three games one night each week. It's rather true to life for those of us who are involved in it. We have organized a league of twenty teams and we play 122 games a season. We have a world series.

My medical condition was such that I was not expected to have a long life. I have muscular dystrophy and many of my school acquaintances passed away as we were growing up. Long-range plans didn't seem to be a possibility. Because of accessibility problems I attended a high school that was quite far from home. I was involved in plays in junior high school and in the choir. I guess I've always enjoyed attention and being in front of people. Teaching Primary or giving talks in front of the ward doesn't distress me.

I had a chance to go to the University of Delaware, but I went to the Woodrow Wilson Rehabilitation Center and took the business course, which was nine months. Time seemed critical. There was a big difference between nine months and four years. My work at the university in no way relates to any of my specialized training in bookkeeping or accounting. I supervise forty part-time people from the beginning interviews until they leave. My record keeping and other things are now done with the computer. Over the last few years I have taken some computer courses. I have made some inroads because of the computerization of the department. I take great delight in making the computer do what I want it to.

I've been the scoutmaster in an all-handicapped troop. I was the first elected president of a disability rights organization. I'm now the vice-president and the newsletter editor for an amateur radio club.

Before I met the missionaries, I had already begun using natural foods, was very much antipesticide, had given up smoking, was on the verge of giving up alcohol. What the missionaries had to say about diet and nutrition made a tremendous amount of sense to me.

I had felt that this world was in such a mess that I didn't want to be responsible for bringing children into the world where they would have to suffer. Obviously, my perspective changed once I joined the church. Being a father is the most satisfying thing in my life. Mary has been a great joy and continues to be a primary source of delight. Mary has a tremendous burden as our only child. She doesn't have a built-in playmate. Every household chore falls to her since we're in wheelchairs.

In the Elkton Ward anybody who can possibly want a calling has one. The New Castle Ward got along just fine without my doing anything. Here, I taught Primary for three years. The children were, at the same time, frustrating and a great satisfaction. When they participated either as a group or as individuals, there was a great deal of pleasure. I was frustrated by the misconduct of the other classes during sharing time because I was a strict disciplinarian. I feel closer to the members of the ward as a result of teaching the children. I taught three or four of the children in some families. I taught three Tabers, several McVickers, a couple of Crowes. Through this I feel more a part of everybody. In the New Castle Ward we didn't have much of an interaction outside of the meetings, other than with the McVickers, the Crowes, McPhersons, and Robinsons.

I missed church at most ten Sundays in three years, which is a tremendous accomplishment compared to my attendance before and since. Since I only attended about once a month before I began teaching Primary, President Mullins went out on a limb in giving me the calling. I wasn't able to go to priesthood meeting while I was in Primary, and I still feel rather alienated in that environment.

Some of the members have tremendous testimonies. They are full of conviction. I've always had a problem trying to define my testimony. I once heard someone say that your testimony should not be of programs, but the organizational structure is so unique that it would be very difficult to understand how human beings could have developed it. The rest of it is rather difficult for me. Short of a hymn that grabs me or a testimony meeting that somehow triggers the tears (of course, I've been known to cry at weddings), I can't say I have that strength of testimony as others have. I've heard that one gains a testimony through study and through covenants. Since I'm not studying and not working on that area, I shouldn't expect—which I don't.

It troubles me to hear people shift from center. We have to be careful not to adopt the teachings of men. The scriptures provide us with a blueprint. The organization of the church provides us with the material that we are to use to build our house. We can build it according to the blueprint—in which case it would be a strong house—or we can make some modifications to it—in which case we may lose a wall. I have problems trying to sort out how much credibility to give to those who have been members a long time. After all, what do I know? I'm supposed to understand these things like those who grew up with it, who went to seminary and Primary? Am I supposed to dispute them? They talk about things I don't know one way or the other. In teaching Primary I went through several lesson manuals. Now I hear the adults slant things, but I don't want to question openly what these people say.

Over the last couple of years, I guess things have seemed more significant to me. A child doesn't think much about what a song says. The older you get, the more you think about what's being said. There were some songs in *Zion* that were moving. In the finale, we sang, "How blessed the day when the lamb and the lion shall lie down together." The trumpets were blaring and the emotions were stirring. It was a powerful point in the song. And, ah, the tears were flowing—more than I could stand.

I was pleased when my parents came to see Zion. They traveled an hour to get to Smyrna. They enjoyed it tremendously. I have to thank Sister Bushman for the encouragement to get up early enough to come to choir practice. I enjoy singing with the choir and in the congregation. I get so involved with the emotion. I can't read any music. There are very few men and we are just fumbling our way along. If it weren't for Cindy Mullins' capacity to come in and sing tenor with us . . .

We were able to gather strength from members of the church during the periods of my wife's surgeries. She had priesthood blessings. That period may not have had a visible long-term effect, but the short-term effect was quite dramatic. If there is a particularly spiritual time in my life, it would have to be those three periods of surgery and recovery. I owe a tremendous debt to so many people in both the Elkton Ward and the New Castle Ward. There are people who supported my family spiritually and in the physical performance of tasks. People guided my daughter through very formative years. People lent an ear to my wife and provided solace. I'm dependent upon other people for so many things. I have very little opportunity to reciprocate. For what they've done thus far, and for what they will yet do, I'd like to thank them for their generosity and faith.

Claudia Bushman, 50

Claudia Bushman became a member of the Elkton Ward when it was organized from the western half of the New Castle Ward and the Elkton Branch. She grew up in San Francisco where her father was bishop, stake president, and patriarch. The youngest of her six children is a high school student; three are in college in Boston, one works on Wall Street, and one in London. She is well-known to LDS women throughout the United States through her essays, books, and her role as one of the founders of Exponent II, *a quarterly newspaper published by LDS women near Boston. Her considerable organizational and promotional skills have been utilized by every official church organization. She has taught classes at the University of Delaware and was one of the founders (and first president) of the Newark Historical Society. In October 1984, she began working full-time for the first time, as executive director of the Delaware Heritage Commission.*

My husband thought it was impossible that our ward could ever do the *Messiah.* It's true we don't do a professional job. If we only did the things we could do perfectly, we could never do anything at all. We never know who will show up at rehearsal. I think as a reading chorus we do extremely well. I would say that the ward choir is remarkable because there are people in it who are ambitious. They are willing to take on challenges. That makes it possible for me to dream dreams.

Music has always been one of my hobbies. I like leading the choir because there's a tangible product. It isn't like teaching a Sunday school class that is going to take place regardless. This could very easily just be nothing, so I feel like everything is a plus. It is hard because we don't have a lot of talent in our ward. We just don't have any good male voices. I know a lot of people avoid me because I've put the finger on them to come sing in the choir. It's something that you just can't do by yourself. You can give a talk by yourself. If worse comes to worst, you can even run the Relief Society yourself. With a choir you need cooperation and help from people.

The brass ensemble was born when I realized that Kenny McVicker and Rob Crowe also played the trombone, as did my son Ben. John Whitney played the trumpet as did Jennifer Cundiff, and my son Serge played the French horn. We have just added Alan Taber. We may be the only ward in the church with a brass ensemble. Brass music is specifically barred from church services as irreligious. This assumes that all brass music is hard rock, jazz, or marches, and ignores the wonderful brass church music of the past.

I think the opportunities we have in the church are wonderful. Usually we don't have qualified people to do the jobs so we do them anyway. The only camping experience I've ever had was when I went to Girl Scout camp for two weeks when I was twelve. Many years later I was president of the Young Women's organization and was responsible to organize, staff, and set up a camp. It was the first camp ever held in that stake. Where else would you get an opportunity to do that? You can draw on every tiny experience you've ever had and use it for church service.

I like the idea that great oaks grow from little acorns. Something you start small has the potential for growth. That's an inspiring idea. My mother was a marvelous person, very skillful in all that she did. I've been helped most by her musical abilities and by her imaginative response to situations. She always had ideas for doing things and I respond much the same way. Two of my sisters are magnificent musicians, but I'm a dropout from piano lessons because my mother finally threw up her hands.

The Elkton Ward seems to me to be what an average ward should be. I'm sure there are plenty of wards in the church where conformity is required. I don't think it is here because we're shorthanded. People are valued more for whatever they can contribute. On the other hand, there are people who would consider this ward a terrible failure. The tithing is low. The sacrament meeting attendance is low. Home teaching and visiting teaching are terrible. In all the areas where a ward is judged, we're very bad. What seems like success on one hand can certainly be seen as failure the other way.

I like the new meeting schedule except that I do feel a lot of the closeness and friendship are lost. For many years I lived and died for Relief Society. I would see people from church four or five times a week. Now, quite often, I don't see anybody from Sunday to Sunday. Many of the participatory things have been taken out of the meetings. There's no song practice, and discussions in Sunday school and Relief Society are sadly curtailed. You can go to church and just be talked at the whole time. It's also too bad that the children don't get together during the week as they used to do. It's not all bad. I like very much not having to drive to church twice on Sunday.

I never like to be the bishop's wife, and this is my third time. It is a job without a job description. You're supposed to be much more unfailingly calm and generous than I ever care to be. Being bishop is very demanding of Richard's time and I don't like that either. Every ward has so many people who are in impossible situations. Their problems take endless time and can never be solved. I have made a life for myself. There was nothing else to do.

I know I resented my father's heavy involvement in the church. I think that is one of the reasons that I resent my husband's. It has made the church central in our family life—certainly our children's lives revolved around it. They have responded favorably or unfavorably, depending on circumstances. I have these long memories. Every night at the dinner table it seemed to me that my father was doing church work. There were constant calls, and we'd sit there in silence. It hasn't been that way for our children. When Richard was stake president in Boston, he was just never around at all on Sunday. The children and I had some nice family outings.

I enjoyed church when I was a teenager, but I was the worst attender. We used to have wonderful times then. We'd get all dressed up, go to church, and then we would take off and go down to the beach with our boyfriends. We would take off our shoes and go wading and ride the roller coaster.

A school teacher was responsible for my going East to school. She just opened up possibilities. You have very few free decisions in your life, but one is where you go to college; the other is whom to marry.

I met my husband when I was a freshman at Wellesley College. The first night I went to sacrament meeting some of the college students went over to someone's rooms after church. The missionaries came by and one of them was Elder Bushman, who was known to the other students because he had been at Harvard for two years before his mission. He was, at that time, the second counselor to the mission president and had been told to stay away from the college kids. He says that he fell in love with me at first sight, but it was actually my credentials. He had heard that my father was a stake president. We were married in the Salt Lake Temple after my junior year.

Combining school and children has been one of the major themes of my life. I graduated in maternity clothes. I started work on my master's degree at BYU with two children and finished with three. I started my doctorate with five children and finished with six.

I went back to school to have a sense of significance in the community in which I lived. When I went to academic parties with my husband I felt I just didn't signify because I was a housewife. I doubt that I would have gone this far academically if my husband had not been in academics. I was one of the first, I think, of the housewives who was going to graduate school. I gave up fashion, creative housekeeping, and a social life. That's how I managed. One summer Dick was home with the children and I went in every day to his office and worked there for about six hours. That's when I broke the back of my dissertation.

If I had tried to stay more in the public domain even when my children were small, started school sooner, or had a part-time job, I might have graduated when there was not such a tremendous glut of Ph.D.'s on the market. Teaching course by course, I often worked as long and taught as many students as the regular faculty, but I didn't get paid as well.

I think the advantages and disadvantages of being at home with children are closely tied. The major advantage—aside from the pleasures of seeing your children grow up, which are considerable—is having the chance to schedule your own life. You have a great deal of control over what you do and when. You are seriously tied down, but it is a freedom that people who have to be in one place for eight hours do not have. The major disadvantage is that you have to recreate your life anew every day. Because you are self-directed, it's very easy to feel that what you do is not important.

There is more emphasis now on careers for girls. One of my college-age sons mostly dates governesses. He says they're more compassionate, more interesting companions than the students. I said, "Well, maybe, but to me this indicates a lack of direction, of taking your life seriously." It made me realize that I'm prejudiced against the old-fashioned idea that we take care of children and we get married and be loving and good people. I think girls have to think seriously in other directions, but I don't think they do. The bishop says that the girls he interviews are just longing to be married.

I'm not as strong a feminist as some. Unfortunately the economy has required that women go to work, and a rationale has been developed to justify working as something women want to do. I find it quite remarkable in talking with groups of students that they define freedom as working.

I think the church was badly scarred by its opposition to the women's movement. I consider myself a feminist, which I define as meaning that the talents of women should be developed for their own benefit and the benefit of society. I don't think anybody will disagree with that. It isn't a big issue with me now. I felt so strongly about it for so long that the intensity burned out. The issue has worn out for the church as well. It will come back again.

I volunteered to teach a class about Newark for the History Department at the University. I had a good time with that. I would walk the class down Cleveland Avenue and read the architecture and took them to city council meetings.

I was shocked that there was nothing available to use as source material. So when I went to parties I'd talk about how we should have a historical society.

Finally I said, "It's time to do it." I called up everybody I could think of who had shown an interest and we had an organizing meeting. I thought if we had an organization that could focus on projects, we could get a lot done—publications and things of that sort. Other people thought we ought to have big public meetings and so we did that too.

When we were planning our art exhibition called Views of Newark, Alice Gallagher suggested that we make a quilt to auction because the Newark Symphony Society had just made one, covered with treble clefs. Everyone agreed that was a good idea. Sheila Anderson found Betty Balder, a member of the Historical Society and a serious quilter, to supervise the quilt. Sheila assigned the blocks out to members of the community.

Leo Laskaris, who designed the quilt, said that we ought to have the city seal on it to balance the university seal. But the city didn't have a seal.

I said, "Let's design a seal and then take it to the city and see if we can get it adopted." Finally, we decided to put the 1758 charter in the middle of an espaliered pear tree. When the idea was presented to the city council, they adopted it as the city seal. I think it's wonderful the way you can make a difference in a town like Newark.

My work at the Delaware Heritage Commission is very much like what I did for the Newark Historical Society. It's a little frustrating to work with committees and officials. I go into a meeting with a perfectly good, well-formed idea, and it's kicked around and beat up until I can't recognize it. But I'm a good compromiser. Until December 7, 1987, my time is pretty well accounted for. My job is to keep the business of the Delaware Heritage Commission moving. Grateful as I am to have this position, I don't think I'd want to do it forever. I would be very happy to work part-time out of my house. I value my freedom more than I did.

8 | The Baptism of Lisa Welch

Sunday night, January 6, Lisa Welch was baptized. At least fifty people attended the baptismal service held in the Wilmington Ward—including the four Elkton Ward missionaries, Lisa's parents and three brothers, Connie and Don O'Day, and members of the Elkton Ward who had become acquainted with Lisa during the previous month. Lisa had been tracted out and taught by the missionaries, but Kevin O'Day baptized her. Kevin's father, Don O'Day, gave a talk on the Holy Ghost and he gave Lisa a green Go sign and a red Stop sign to remind her of the purpose of the Holy Ghost.

Elkton Ward is a ward of converts, members by choice—not birth. Seventy percent of the adult members were not born into Mormon homes; one fourth of that 70 percent joined because their parents did. The rest joined independently. The presence of such a large group of new acquaintances at Lisa Welch's baptism illustrates the emotional support that church members routinely give to new members and investigators. Perhaps this is, in part, generated by a recognition of the role that the support and encouragement of other members played in their own conversions.

Most Elkton Ward converts were young adults at the time they joined the church. All but four of the men were between sixteen and thirty; the median age of the men at baptism was twenty-seven. The median age of female converts was twenty-four. They came from a variety of religious backgrounds. Some were deeply involved in their former churches, some attended church, and others did not. Many were dissatisfied either because their ministers could not answer their theological questions or because their church could not supply the help they needed with their personal struggles. Many of the married couples who were converts were looking for a religion in which both of them could believe and that would unite them as a family.

About one-third of the Elkton Ward converts had been Catholics; most of the rest were equally divided among the Methodist, Presbyterian, Lutheran, and Baptist churches. Two had belonged to the Episcopalian church, one each to the

Nazarenes and United Brethren, and one was a Jehovah's Witness. None were non-Christian, although five had grown up in families without any religious orientation. Six had changed religions more than once.

Lisa Welch, 22

The missionaries, Elders Hubbard and Furner, had first knocked on Lisa's door in October after nine days of searching for a golden contact in the Chesapeake Bay town of Charlestown, Maryland. When these elders were transferred to other wards within the Philadelphia Mission, Elders Lee and Steenstra took their places.

I married somebody who was Catholic and went to the Catholic church, but I knew that that wasn't where I was supposed to be. I started attending a church that was a full gospel ministry, born-again Christians. Then I stayed away, not because of anything wrong with the church but because I had a miscarriage. I believed that the Lord had given me that baby. All of a sudden the baby was taken away and I blamed the Lord, thought that it was his fault. When I became pregnant again, I told the Lord many nights that if I had this second baby, I was going to go to church. Lauren was born on Wednesday and I had her in church on Sunday. She hasn't missed a Sunday at church since she was born.

My divorce was just devastating. It was hard for me to tell my family that my husband had just walked off. I had a four-week-old baby. I realized that I had to make a life for the two of us. I just couldn't imagine how I was going to go to work and bring her up the way I wanted to bring her up. I just turned to the Lord and asked him for help, and I was able to make it. I had gone back to the church in Bel Air, and it believed in tithing. I tithed any little money that I got. There were many times when I'd think, "Oh, I'd better not pay it because I've got to feed Lauren" or something like that, but I knew that I had to have faith. One thing that that church taught me was faith.

Last August I went to my mother's to take care of the horses while they were away. My cousin happened to be there also. We started taking walks every day and I asked her about the Mormon church. She gave me all the answers. I said, "Well, I don't know why I'm not a member of your church because everything you believe in is what I believe in."

In October I was questioning whether I was attending the right church. I told the Lord that I wanted him to let me know. Then the missionaries knocked on my door. I normally send anybody like that away. I said, "Are you Jehovah's Witnesses?" They said no. I said, "Well, okay. Let me get dressed."

I couldn't understand why these two young, good-looking men were here teaching everybody about the gospel when they should be having the time of their life. They told me that in the church the divorce rate was lower and that the family meant so much more. I wanted strong family ties. I wanted Lauren to have the values and truths of life.

They taught me in October, November, and December. Even though everything they taught me seemed right, my main problem was that I didn't want to give up my cigarettes. I finally told them that I would come to church. That Sunday they started calling me at 6:00 A.M. They were so diligent, kept calling back and saying, "Are you awake?"

I'd say, "No, I'm not awake, but I'm going." I knew the whole time I wasn't going. About 8:30 something prompted me and told me that I had to go. I thought, "Oh, no. I'm not ready. I'm not showered, and it starts in an hour." I flew around, got my daughter ready, and we went. Even driving there I said, "I'm not going. I'm really not going. Lord, please don't make me go there because I don't know anybody there." I got there a few minutes late. I sat down with Elder Hubbard and Elder Furner. I was sitting there and I heard the voice blessing the sacrament. I knew that voice from somewhere. I asked the missionaries, "Where is that voice coming from?"

They said, "Up front."

"Who is that voice?"

"Oh, that's Brother O'Day." Kevin O'Day was my financial planner when I was married to my husband. His office was next to my obstetrician's in Lindell Square. He saw me every month, waddling to my doctor's. I hardly knew him. We had met with him about three times, and then when I started going through the divorce, I had to call him several times because of our accounts.

When I had talked to him in June he had said, "I can't understand how you're making it."

I said, "If it weren't for my faith in the Lord, I wouldn't be making it. I know the Lord's bringing Lauren and me through this." He later told me that he decided that he was going to send the missionaries, but he never got around to it.

At the beginning of December when I sent out my Christmas cards, I only sent out twenty-three cards out of my list of one hundred because I didn't have the money. I prayed about it and asked the Lord who I was supposed to send cards to so I didn't hurt anybody's feelings. Kevin was the only one who wasn't a member of my family. After I sent it, I thought, "Boy, I bet he thinks I'm a jerk. I should never have sent him a Christmas card."

He later said that he was surprised when he got the card because he had been thinking about me. He knew that I was going through a divorce. He thought, "She'll probably never give up cigarettes. She's not a member of the church and she probably never will be."

He didn't even know I was at church that day. After sacrament meeting he was discouraged and felt that he might have lost the blessing that the Lord had promised him of having a wife and a family. He was praying and he asked the Lord to bless him soon because he was tired of waiting. I came up the aisle and tapped Kevin on the shoulder and said, "Hi, Kevin." He looked so dumbfounded that I thought, "Boy, I have all my money invested with him and he doesn't even know who I am."

Finally, he said, "Lisa." He went to the investigators' Sunday school class with me and then I went to Relief Society. After Relief Society I told him that I wasn't sure that this was where I was supposed to be, but I needed some answers. We discussed things after church for about two hours.

Sunday afternoon I started thinking about the church and everything the missionaries had taught me. I started feeling that I had to have the answer. I called the missionaries, but they weren't there. Elder Hubbard was leaving the mission Tuesday so I knew I only had until Tuesday to get the answers from somebody I knew. Finally, about 9:30 in the evening I remembered Kevin had said something in June about having his office at home. I called his house and his answering machine came on. I said, "Hi, Kevin O'Day. This is Lisa Welch. I have some questions about the church. I know you're not in."

He said back, "Hi, Lisa."

I said, "Wow, this is neat. You've got a talking machine." I thought his machine was talking to me. He brought me the Doctrine and Covenants on Monday and we talked. Tuesday evening I decided I had to make my decision. I was scared. I had so much respect for Kevin, so the church couldn't be all that wrong because he was a member. Yet, I couldn't let that influence my decision. I got into my big garden tub to read the Joseph Smith story that Kevin had given me and I cried the whole time. I knew that what I was reading was true. I lay on the the sofa right next to the telephone. When Kevin called, I was crying.

He said, "What's the matter?" I started telling him what it was, and he said he was thinking that this would happen so he'd called me. It seemed every day that week he would call me just when I had questions and he had the answers for me every time. He came by with the missionaries to teach me.

I went to the stake center with the missionaries to see the Christmas broadcast. Kevin was there with his parents. His father started questioning me, giving me a hard time. He said, "You're married. Don't you get around my son."

I said, "Well, I can't help it if I'm not divorced. I'm having a hard time tracking down my ex-husband." I said to Kevin, "Don't you ever leave me alone with your father again."

The missionaries had never talked to me about being baptized. Elder Steenstra was here by this time. When I met him I knew there was something special about him. At Christmas Elder Steenstra asked if I would be baptized and I said yes. He said, "Well, you know you have to quit smoking."

I said, "Oh, I've already quit." I'd stopped drinking coffee, too. That Tuesday when I decided that this was it, I had just prayed to the Lord and said I knew this was real and that I wanted that desire taken away from me. That I didn't have that desire anymore told me it was real, more than anything. We set up my baptism for the sixth of January.

The fifth of January, Kevin was at my house, teaching me. He felt prompted to ask me if I knew where the golden plates are. I said they were in Utah. He said, "Did somebody tell you that or did you just assume that?"

I know one of them told me that they were in the archives. I had asked if I wanted to have proof that it was real, could I have proof of it. He had said, "Yeah. Go to Utah and see it in the archives."

When Kevin told me this wasn't true, I was devastated. I thought, "Oh, no, the missionaries lied to me. If that isn't real, what else isn't real?" I called Elder Steenstra and said, "I'm not getting baptized tomorrow."

He was so shocked. He gave me the same explanation that Kevin had. I thought, "Here these two haven't even talked but they are saying the same exact thing to me." I just started crying. I knew that the Adversary was after me. I told Kevin to leave, that I was going to work this out on my own. I would let him know tomorrow if I was going to be baptized. He was trying to convince me that I was making the right decision. I said, "No, I have to know this on my own." I was going to pray to the Lord about it because I wanted to make the right decision.

Having such a sincere heart, I got my answer that evening. I went to church the next day, and then the missionaries and Kevin came home from church with me and stayed with me until I was baptized that night.

Debbie Roeder, 27

Debbie Roeder was was baptized by Bishop Don O'Day seven years ago. She has been a Relief Society, nursery, and Primary teacher.

When I was about twenty years old, I decided that I wanted to go to church. My father hadn't stepped into a church since he got married. Knowing he didn't like my grandmother's church, I asked him, "What was our grandfather?"

He said, "Well, he was Lutheran." At the Lutheran church I met a girl whose parents were Mormon. They had come to the East when there weren't many Mormons in Delaware. They had decided they weren't being accepted by the people in the ward and dropped out of the church. The more she talked down the Mormon church in our Sunday school class, the more interested I became.

I was in the Newark Free Library one day, wandering around, and I found a Book of Mormon. I said, "I'm going to check these Mormons out and see what they're all about." So I read the Book of Mormon. I read it fast, but it seemed to me that it wasn't a dishonest book. It seemed to be very spiritual and natural. I didn't see how one man could have made that all up. I thought it would take a long time to write all the stories. I hadn't prayed in years, but I prayed and I wrote to the church. I told them, "Now don't you dare send me any missionaries because I do not want to be pressured into anything."

They gave my letter to Mary Hoffman, one of the stake missionaries, and she wrote me a very nice letter and sent a copy of the Book of Mormon. I had asked a couple of questions, which she answered. I read the Book of Mormon for a while and I read the Doctrine and Covenants and Talmage's *Articles of Faith,* which I found in the library. The more I read, the more questions I had, so I wrote to Mary and she wrote to me. Once she included her telephone number and said, "If you want a ride to church to see what it's like, give me a call."

The first meeting I went to was a fast and testimony meeting. The next thing I knew I was taking discussions over at Mary's house. About the only trial I had was trying not to upset my family and to do the right thing by both the church and my family. For instance if it has rained on Saturday, but it's nice Sunday and the wash hasn't been done, my mother wants me to do the wash. My aunt died about two weeks before I was baptized. That was hard, but it helped me learn the truthfulness of the gospel. The thing that kept me going was the belief that if I do my genealogy work and if she accepts the gospel in the other world, we can be together again. I found it was a sad, but also a sweet, time. I knew I could see her again some day, that I could do things to help her have the gospel.

I was baptized March 25, 1978. I set my alarm and Mary came to get me. My mom was up and made sure I had everything. Most of the church is not as hard as I thought it would be. When I first joined the church I think it was a mixture of admiration and fear: fear that if I didn't do this I would die in condemnation. After a while it became more—it's a terrible thing to say—old hat. One day I stopped being a new member and didn't question that Joseph Smith was a prophet anymore. It was a great feeling. It only took me about two years. Six weeks after my baptism I felt, "I'm right back where I started. I don't deserve to belong to this church. I haven't changed a bit." But I like the church's attitude that you try and you keep at it. It's not going to happen overnight. Jesus isn't going to come into the middle of your living room and say, "Now you're perfected and you don't have to worry about it."

My parents have been very supportive during the past seven years. They've always helped me with my church callings. I don't drive, so they've always helped me get to church. I've tried to get them to go to church—on a holiday or something like the Christmas program—it still hasn't worked. They've grown accustomed to my going to church. If they have a question they'll ask it. I remember when we were in the New Castle Ward my mom talked to one of the members who had given me a lift home one night. He told me how impressed he was with what my mom knew about the church.

I was going to the University of Delaware at the time I joined the church. Because my brother was four years behind me, I had to zip through my four years so my parents wouldn't have to put two through at the same time. The first two years I was in cultural shock. I'm only the second person on my father's side of the family to go to college. There was no one to tell me what it was going to be like and warn me about the pitfalls. I wanted to be a medical technician and had been in the Future Nurses Association, but my math grades weren't that great. My counselor said, "We're getting down to the wire now, make a decision." So I just picked English. Now I know I should have set my goals five years in advance—decided at seventeen what I was going to be doing at twenty-two.

Liberal arts majors have a hard time finding jobs. I was unemployed for two years. It took a lot of faith to believe that someone up there actually loved me and that things were for the best. Sometimes I felt I was going to drown—that there was nothing there and it would have been better to walk out in front of a car than to be here. I got depressed.

It helped that I had some neat home teachers and other people who cared. Don O'Day was my home teacher and he came once a month and lifted my spirits and told me to keep slugging. Having church callings helped. The members didn't measure my worth by how much money I made, but by the fact that I was willing to be a member of the gospel and willing to help.

I've been working as a substitute teacher the last couple of years and I've learned that I enjoy teaching. Now I want to start working on my teaching credential, but I have to take the education classes. I think Heavenly Father helped me find out that I enjoy teaching. I guess I realized it when I'd tell my parents, "Oh, the kids did *this* today." Teachers would ask for me to come back. That was when I realized that this was the answer to my prayers about what direction my life should take.

In my family, we're still following traditional women's roles. My sister wants to be a nurse; I want to be a teacher; my mother works in a cafeteria. In the church I think it's sometimes hard because, as a woman, I want to be a mother, but I also want to have a career. It's very hard when the church says "Stay at home." I see friends of mine in the church struggling to make it, and they couldn't if both parents weren't working.

At the beginning of the year I sent out invitations to the children who should be in my Star A class. The manual suggested sending star-shaped invitations to all the children. Kathleen Bennett had never stayed in the nursery and had never stayed in the Sunbeam class. But the first day of class there she was, just because I'd taken the time to make her a little invitation. That's rewarding. I kept it up. I send little newsletters out to the kids who don't come every week. One boy, whose parents are inactive, comes with his grandparents so he can see me on Sundays. One of the boys, though, has a very negative attitude for a four-year-old. He says things like, "I don't like Heavenly Father and I'm not going to listen to you." It's pretty hard when I have thirteen kids and he's acting up.

Anne Mace, 59

Anne Mace of Rising Sun, Maryland, was baptized Easter Sunday, 1984. She has transformed the chapel's appearance by constructing four large murals, one for each season of the year, to be hung on the empty wall behind the pulpit. She and her husband live in a historic home she restored. Across the street is Mace Hardware Store, which sells Anne's flower arrangements as well as the usual building supplies and hardware.

I joined the church after thinking about it for a long time. My son has been a member for about twelve years. His wife is from Salt Lake City and he joined the church before their marriage. I didn't want to go through eternity outside their family circle because I have five beautiful grandchildren. Since Taddy is my only child, this would have left me nowhere. I started attending the church in October 1983. I was baptized Easter Sunday 1984 in Okinawa, Japan, by my son.

My mother, being a college graduate, insisted that I take an academic course, but I wanted to take a commercial course so that I would be prepared to go to work. My father died when I was fourteen, in the ninth grade. The academic course was totally useless. I worked in a chemistry lab washing bottles, then I worked in a photo lab. From there I went to a drawing board. I had to do it all myself. My sister went to nursing school and my older brother went to college, but when it came to me there was nothing left. I wanted to be an architect but they weren't issuing scholarships for girls to take architecture. I met my first husband, Jack Hickman Tweed, at Hercules Powder Company. He passed away after we had been married twenty years. Willard and I were married three years later.

I have one child, by my first husband. Taddy was the easiest child to raise that anybody can imagine. He had no health problems and he was bright and inquisitive. One time I was putting his rubber boots on him as he was sitting on the table. I had the boot in my hand, and I said, "Taddy, that's the wrong foot."

He said, "No, Mom, that's the wrong boot." He had his own way, but he never was arrogant about it.

Every time I found myself in a difficult situation I would just see how I could make the most of it. I've done a lot of things. I've built a trailer court. It had sixty units in it. That was about the time my husband got ill. Then I went to work for the Du Pont company and sold the trailer court. I worked for Du Pont for five years. I met my second husband, Willard, when I was on a work assignment. We got married on our lunch break. You have to know Willard to appreciate that because he doesn't take time off work for anything.

This place is almost like a vacation. There are a lot of people who go away for a vacation who don't have as much fun as I have here. I'm a Shaklee supervisor for one thing. I'm working on a very interesting program to introduce these nutritional products to physicians and hospitals. I think they're so superior that it is a shame that they are not in the hands of professionals. Shaklee's structure is exactly like the Mormon church's. We have something to sell of superior quality. It has a unique distribution system. It's not put on store shelves where people can select it, but it's a system that is taught to one by another. When I interest people in better health and teach them how to interest others in better health, it's just the same kind of missionary work that we have in the church. People need guidance. They need someone to guide them through this very frustrating technology. We're learning more and more about nutrition now. Somebody has to help guide us.

I like being self-employed. I often wonder how the Lord can bless people who are not self-employed because they're standing behind an employer where they have almost no opportunity to change their circumstances.

I am beginning to develop a philosophy that by prayer and meditation we can arrive at the very same place that the greatest scientists of the world are struggling to prove in a lab. I think, "Why go through all that frustration? Live a nice life. Enjoy the planet that the Lord gave us to enjoy and don't get too overwhelmed about scientific advancement." I don't mean to sell it short, though, because I enjoy lots of it myself. We have a beautiful world out there and I want Taddy's children to enjoy the butterflies, the crops and gardens, and everything in nature.

It's too bad that I had to lose my father when I was only fourteen because I was just beginning to absorb some of his creative ability. He invented a machine that punched holes in asbestos shingles. He worked with Thomas Edison on some battery work. He was always out there just a little bit ahead of everybody else. One of the joys of being in the Mormon church is that now I'm looking forward to filling in some years that I've missed. For years there was never a day that I didn't think of him. Right now, I would just give anything to have him back because of the knowledge that he had of windmills. He sold wind-powered generating systems to farms. Now that we have an energy crisis, it would be so valuable.

My father used to say, "Whatever you believe, that's what it is." Now I realize that may be closer to the truth than I ever thought. What we believe and what we do are going to determine the reward that we have. If we believe that there's nothing to this life, we're not going to get any reward. If we believe that we're limited to just a static kind of condition called heaven, that's all we're going to get, but the Mormon church offers me the opportunity to believe in eternal progression. I believed in eternal progression all the time, but I didn't know anybody taught that. I believed that when I got over there, I would go right into school and learn all the things I couldn't seem to get a handle on here.

I had a little trouble getting a testimony of the church at first. I think I was waiting for the Lord to knock me off my horse. Finally, I realized it had to be true. There was no way that Joseph Smith, a humble boy without a formal education, could ever have produced the Book of Mormon. There's no other explanation.

When the president of a Canadian company that we do business with was here, I left a tract in his bedroom, "What Mormons Think of Christ." The next morning he said, "I didn't know that Mormons believed that Christ was on this continent." We went on to discuss baptism for the dead.

When I read it to him from the scriptures I said, "What did you think that meant?"

"I didn't even know it was there." I think that epitomizes the condition of most churches today. Those things that they don't practice, they don't even look at.

I think I can accept each of the doctrines of the church as I come to know and understand them. Until I take the temple lessons I will not know the meaning of temple garments.

I'd never done any volunteer work before I joined the church. I had the impression that it was performed by women who didn't have anything else to do. Now I'm the Relief Society compassionate service leader for Cecil County. I'm the assistant homemaking leader. I also help with the flower decorations at the church. I'm a visiting teacher, and I'm attending the missionary class, which has one more week to go. I've met all the commitments there and I'm about to turn in a referral card to the missionaries. I've brought families to church. The best satisfaction will be to see some of my friends come into the church. One of my goals is to have a branch out here in Rising Sun. I have a deadline for that, August 15, 1985.

My assistant decorator calling gives me an opportunity to create things that others can enjoy. My visiting teaching gives me an opportunity to go out and learn more about the sisters. This past week we found a sister in need. This, in turn, gave me my first opportunity to do something compassionate—at least to find out what the responsibilities of that calling are.

I have brought the son of my Shaklee coordinator to church. He has read lots of anti-Mormon literature, so he's given me an opportunity to deal with people who are indoctrinated in anti-Mormon things. He had brought up the scripture in Revelation that says you cannot add anything or take anything away from the Bible. My visiting teaching partner, Bonnie Arnold, put me on to some ideas. Bonnie said, "Well, go back to Deuteronomy because it says exactly the same thing. If you take this literally, then nothing past Deuteronomy is legitimate."

Keeping the Sabbath holy is probably the hardest thing that I have to do because I have never made a clear distinction between what is work and what is breathing. I know some of the sisters think that doing the dishes is work, and I don't. I thought it was being cleanly. I guess each one of us has to solve it for ourselves, but I cannot sit idle. Often I will review my visiting teaching lesson or I'll work on a class that I'm going to teach in Relief Society. I make the activities of that day belong to the Lord. I'll have to let the Lord decide whether it's work.

Since I have nobody to share family home evening with, once a month we bring in the missionaries and Sharon Mlodoch, whom I can't reach for visiting teaching since she teaches high school. We get together and have our cottage meetings instead of family home evening. We have a great time, and it does great missionary work. Everybody gets fifteen minutes to share with the others the things they like. Somebody will show tricks on the computer and somebody else will talk about nutrition. The missionaries have their fifteen minutes, too.

Having home teachers brings the priesthood to me. My husband has sat in on their visits. I would like my husband to be in the priesthood. I think I have to recognize the long time period that is often required for conversion.

Last spring before I went to Okinawa, I was doing a big wreath for the chapel. I had anticipated that it would take a hundred dollars worth of flowers. I didn't worry too much about it, kept putting it off. The minute that Sherri wanted me to go with her mother to the Wilmington Flower Market because they needed another hundred dollars to qualify for the wholesale card, I said, "Okay, that will be the hundred dollars that I'll put into this wreath." I didn't know where I was going to get the hundred dollars. I said, "If worse comes to worst, I'll take it out of my Okinawa money." The next morning I still didn't have it. I'd prayed about it, so I went across the street to the hardware store and said to Sandy, "Give me a hundred dollars. I'll give you a check for it." She said, "I've been saving this hundred dollars for you." She had sold something that had belonged to me, so there was the hundred dollars.

One thing I like about this church is that I have never heard politics and social things discussed from the pulpit. I used to count the number of times scriptures were cited to justify a position in my former church. The last time I went was an Easter Sunday and the scriptures were not mentioned once. I was shocked. I never went back. I know this church is true and it has given me great joy to get my life back on the track. I know it will give me even more joy to help other people find the same good feelings.

Linda Crowe, 40

Linda Crowe and her husband, Frank, were baptized in 1970 as members of the New Castle Ward. Every morning at 6:00 A.M. Linda teaches early morning seminary, a religion class for high school students, in her home. Her students are her son Robert and their neighbor Kenny McVicker. She is the mother of four children, ages fifteen, thirteen, ten, and seven.

When the missionaries asked to come and teach us, I tried to get rid of them. Frank said, "Oh, let them come back. We'll hear them once and then we'll get rid of them." After the first discussion, we read the pamphlet they had given us on Joseph Smith. It just sounded so right, so true. It was almost as if we knew it right at the beginning, although we didn't realize it. The missionaries said to pray and we did. At the time we had stopped going to church because Rob was less than a year old. We put off going to church—wrestling him in our arms in church—though we had gone to church every Sunday. Since we had moved, we thought we'd look for a church closer to us. In fact, after we had some of the missionary discussions, we went to a Lutheran church right off the Kirkwood Highway—three miles from our home. The whole time that preacher spoke, I sat there and picked apart everything he said. I thought, "Well, that's not right." I had been converted already and didn't realize it.

Of course, my mother was against it. She said, "Don't get caught up in something that you shouldn't." When we were baptized we kept it very quiet. I guess I told her later. My family sort of soured against me because I joined the church. Our feelings toward them have changed as well as their feelings toward us. There have been difficult family problems, and the church sort of adds to it.

We weren't really active when we first became members. When you have little children it's hard. We thought we'd just go to Sunday school. Keith Wilhoit was keeping his eye on us, and he tried to tell us that it was a commandment of the Lord to go to sacrament meeting. That made us think maybe we'd better go. Then we'd have to stand out in the hall with the children and say, "Is this worth it?"

I would sometimes not go when Frank was at work. I didn't want to wrestle all the kids by myself. Then Frank said, "Why don't you go and I'll come after work?" He'd get in an hour's worth of the meeting or a half hour. We were progressing a little at a time.

Someone later said, "I used to see you with all your kids in church. I figured if you could do it, so could I." It's amazing how we help each other gain our testimonies.

We had been members for a few years before we got into the Elkton Branch. Of course, when we first moved out here there was no Elkton Branch, so we drove forty minutes each way to get to the New Castle Ward. We had Primary and Relief Society during the week, too. Now we have a thirty-minute drive to Elkton. It has been a hardship since we moved. The expenses are greater.

I always wanted to have a family and a husband. As a child I played with dolls and pretended all the time. I had planned to have two children. That changed, of course. The church had a lot to do with that. The church has helped me be a mother. I had no guidance in being a mother. My mother did teach me to clean and care for the home. I could never understand why my sister would never call me. She had an older family, of course. I had little kids. I always longed for a sister who would call me up and say, "How are you? How are the kids?"

Then I'd say, "Oh, I can't do this" or "I can't do that."

Then she'd be able to say, "Have you tried this? Why not try that?" I wanted someone to help me with raising my family.

One day I was folding clothes—my favorite pastime—when all of a sudden a thought shot through my head. It was that whatever my sister had to give me would not be beneficial for me. I needed to hear the experiences of my sisters in the church.

What is so great about the church is that it gives us opportunities to use our talents. If I had not been a member, I'm afraid all I would be doing is sitting around raising my family. My mother used to say, "Why, I would never leave my family. I was always home." My husband helped me understand that that was great, but that she wasn't learning or growing.

When I first had callings that took me away from the home, Frank suddenly had to plunge in to take care of the children. I know he grew closer to them because he had to change diapers and feed them. I used to feel guilty and I said to Frank, "Am I hurting my family by going out and doing these other things?"

He said, "Linda, you're not. You're growing and you're learning. Your family is not hurting." It has been a lot of sacrifice from the family to support me in my callings. I've had a lot of leadership callings, and it's been especially hard on Frank. He always supported me, but sometimes you find out later.

When I was a counselor in the stake Primary, there were a number of situations where I was touched by the Lord. As a stake leader I wanted to give the women at the meetings something informative and useful. I had wanted to make good use of their time at the stake meetings. I went to the Lord in prayer many many times before one meeting. I said, "Please Lord, answer my prayer. I want to hear you loud and clear. I don't want any little whisperings because I want to know." One day Colleen Pierce called me and we got on the subject of Primary. Suddenly she came out with what the Elkton Ward needed, and I thought, "That's it. That's what I will teach." It was loud and clear.

Frank Crowe, 42

Frank Crowe is a pharmacist and the group leader of the high priests. He and his wife have four children, fifteen, thirteen, ten, and seven.

About thirteen years ago I started working for a drugstore chain in Smyrna. Besides the paycheck, what I enjoy about my work is helping people. People come in or call me up and ask questions. Of course, some who take up the most time asking questions will not take the product that I've recommended. There are a lot of problems with the profession. I wouldn't want my children to go into it—pharmacology, maybe, but not pharmacy. My patriarchal blessing says that I will advance in my career, but I just don't see any way to advance. I do get to see other people. I don't work in an office where I see the same two or three people every day. Another pharmacy in town has a pharmacist who is born again. We get customers who come over to our store because they don't want to hear his preaching.

One hot day in July or August we saw the missionaries going down one side of the street and coming up our side of the street. They wore black suits and the sweat was profusely coming from their heads. Linda was hanging clothes and I was working on the lawn. We offered them a cold Pepsi, but they refused. Then we offered them ice water and they accepted and asked if we knew anything about Mormons. When they asked if we wanted to know about it, we said no, we weren't interested.

They came to our house and sat in the living room. When I lit up a cigarette, the fellow said, "You know this is a religious discussion; we rather that you not smoke."

I politely said, "I guess when he starts paying my mortgage he can come in my house and tell me not to smoke." But I didn't smoke any more of that cigarette. They answered questions that no one had been able to answer. Before we got married I had joined my wife's church. When the minister said, "Do you have any questions?" I said, "Just one question. Is the Godhead one person or three?" After about ten or fifteen minutes he just couldn't tell me.

I always thought when I was a child that we weren't learning the truth. Some things just didn't jibe. When the missionaries came, we weren't what you would call golden; I asked them a lot of questions. They had the answers for me. Even when we became members of the church, not everything was fully answered. I wanted to have more knowledge, but the missionaries persuaded me that I could do that as a member.

Ken McVicker was investigating at the same time. The missionaries used to bring him and Keith Wilhoit over to help answer my questions. One day Ken came over and said, "I'm going to be baptized in two weeks. How about if you come and get baptized with me?" And we did.

My relatives are not very religious. If they see someone who is going to church every week instead of visiting the relatives, who is paying tithing with the money that would buy a new car every three or four years, to them that is eccentric. We could have more material things, but as far as spiritual things and having the opportunity for eternal happiness, Linda and I have it all over our relatives. Right now I'm in my middle-age crisis time. I expected grander things temporally, but not spiritually. Because I never expected to be a member of the Lord's church.

I think the church should use its influence more than it has. It is very outspoken on moral issues, but completely silent on political issues. If the prophet were to say, "Look, my people will do such and such," I know that the church members would get behind him. Maybe the people of the world would get the wrong impression about the LDS if the prophet said something like that. I don't know how it would be done, but I think the prophet's opinion should be revealed a little more explicitly. For example, there was an article in the *Church News* that said that abortion is the most appalling thing that was confronting us today in an unloving world. Before that article came out, people were asking me, "What's your church's stand on abortion." Having the church's stand on it sooner would have helped. I could have said, "The church thinks such and such." I don't want to say anything that the church doesn't.

I'm still getting adjusted to my calling as High Priests' Group leader. We've done a lot of rescheduling and readjusting of home teaching routes. It's a nightmare, but there's the satisfaction of having done it. I don't have the time to go out and see a lot of the people. I have three nights off one week and two nights the next. One of those I spend with my family. I think the more we know about the gospel and the more we accept responsibilities in the church, the stronger are our temptations and trials. A little bit more and a little bit more is expected of you. Each calling requires something new out of you—some greater insight and something to wrestle with.

When I was a stake missionary, just before I was a made a seventy, I was going out to see the people and I had no nights left for my family. In an interview with the bishop, he said, "Are you having family home evening?"

I said, "Absolutely, every week, however, I'm not always there. I make sure Linda has it."

He said, "Well, you've got to be there. It's one of the prerequisites here. You will have to change things around and be there." Now, I'm here for family home evening. It's a time together, anyway. It gives the children a chance to read, to show their talents. Seeing the development of my children and seeing Linda's development has been very satisfying. I've seen some development in myself. We would like to see all of our children married in the temple. We hope the boys will go on missions. I would like to see them married to good people, and I want to bounce grandchildren on my knee. I want to be able to help them with their first house.

Things weren't going just right, so we thought maybe we were doing something wrong. We kept looking at our lives. We just couldn't think of any specific thing that the Lord would be chastising us for. Then we got to thinking maybe we're not doing something that we should be. I came home last night and said, "I think I know what it is. My father died a couple of years ago and I haven't done his temple work." Linda's mother died a few years ago, and she hadn't done her temple work. I'm definitely going to do my four generations now. I think that the Lord has given me an ultimatum.

A number of years ago when Linda and I went to the temple, a man came up to us and said, "Brother Crowe?" He had been at church the first day that Linda and I went to church. He said that he saw us coming in with the missionaries that day and figured, "Well, here's another couple that's going to get baptized and we'll see them for a couple of months maybe and then never again."

I said, "Fooled you."

Matthew Burke, 35

Matthew Burke and his wife, Clara, were baptized as members of the New Castle Ward in August 1978. A native of Brownsville, Pennsylvania, Matthew works on the assembly line at Chrysler. He and Clara have two sons, eight and ten. Matthew has taught Primary and is presently the Elders' Quorum secretary.

At work when I started asking questions about the Mormons, a friend of mine said, "I know a Mormon. There he goes, right there." It was Dan Harding. I had been working with him for quite a while. When I went over to talk to him about it, he said, "Well, you know we have missionaries that we send around."

I said, "Don't send any to my house now. I'm just asking to find out."

When I came home the next day my wife said, "Two sisters came today." At first I thought she meant two nuns, but she said, "No, from the Mormon church. They said they were in the area and just happened to knock on our door."

The next day at work I said to Dan, "I thought you weren't going to send the missionaries over."

He said, "Missionaries? Did they come to your house?" Innocent. I didn't talk to him for a while. I talked to some of the born-again Christians to see if they knew anything about the Mormon church.

They said, "You don't want to get involved in that church. It is bad." They gave me a book about the Mormons and Catholics.

As I read it, I said, "It can't be this bad." I knew Dan Harding wasn't that type of person. My wife got all upset because one of her best friends was a Catholic. Reading that book made me want to find out more about it. We had the missionaries back in.

When everything was all set up to move to this house, our friends fell through and we had no way of moving. When the sister missionaries found out about it, people we didn't even know, Oliver McPherson and his boys, Dan Harding, and Brother Bobby Steward, moved us from Red Mill Road down here. We hadn't even had a chance to clean the house up because the electricity had been off. There were girls and women cleaning the house up.

After we got settled, the missionaries were here all the time, not just the two teaching us, but all the missionaries in the area. The closer my wife came to it, the farther I got away from it. I couldn't take in what they were saying. I had never prayed out loud. Finally, all of a sudden it hit me. I got an overwhelming feeling that said, "This is it. It's time and this is what I want." I immediately told my wife, "I'm ready. I'm ready to be baptized right now." That scared her and she started not wanting to believe in it. We told the sisters not to come back for a week, to give us a chance to pray and think about it. Dan Harding baptized us.

When I told my parents I had joined the church, it was a long time before I heard from them. The more we've gone back to visit, the more they've accepted what we have. We talk more about it—not that they would ever be interested enough to become members. The last time we visited them, they told me that they like the way our boys are growing up and what we're doing with them. The boys just idolize them. Though we've never been a family that touched one another, I just broke down and cried last time as we were leaving. I took my mom and hugged her, and I don't think I've ever done that before.

My dad was very strict. We grew up knowing that if we did wrong, we were in trouble. It instilled the values of right and wrong very quickly, but I do have a tendency to overdo the strictness with my boys because of it. When I grew up, I wasn't given the opportunity to voice my opinion and say, "Okay, I may have done wrong, but I didn't understand." I have the same tendency with my boys. I know it's not right. Clara keeps telling me, "Think back to when you were young. You didn't like that." Since Clara hurt her leg, the boys and I have been together so much more that I've come to see that they're growing up and that they have minds of their own. The church teaches that, too, with free agency. I've come to enjoy working with my boys now that I am spending a lot more time with them.

The priesthood has influenced my life. Being able to give blessings and baptizing my boys, performing the ordinances are the greatest things that anyone can have. Going down and getting sealed in the temple and having Andy and John sealed to us was a unique experience. We found out that the date we had set for our whole family to be sealed together was a stake temple day and everybody was going to be down there. We had asked Dan Harding and Oliver McPherson to be witnesses. Somebody from every organization of the stake and the ward came in to see us sealed. When the officiator came in, the room was full. He looked around and said, "Who do we have here?" They started to tell him and he said, "You've got some pretty powerful witnesses here."

I said, "Yes, they're pretty good people." I get a great feeling every time I go to the temple. As soon as I step out of the car, the peace and the serenity just overwhelm me.

I hadn't done much singing in the choir before last year. I started when they were looking for people to be in Zion. I was just going to sing in the choir, but one thing led to another. I ended up dressed up as an old-time missionary. We had to sing "Ye Elders of Israel" up there on the stage.

I work in the paint department at Chrysler now. All I do is wipe the excess water off the carriers after the bodies are painted. One day I noticed that the bodies were coming out with blotches all over them. I got my supervisor and said, "Hey, something's not right. You'd better check it out." We found that one of the pump motors had broken down.

I was surprised when the supervisor's boss came up and shook my hand and said, "I want to thank you. You saved the day, because if you hadn't done that the whole plant would have had to shut down." Now, I'm going to have my picture in a little newspaper they put out. I've worked there almost fourteen years, and that's the first time I've ever been recognized for doing anything. I have a good record.

I don't consider myself a chauvinist. I think men and women should have had equal rights from the beginning, but I think the women have gone too far with this equal rights stuff. I've seen a lot of this where I work. The jobs over there aren't glamorous, they're physically hard. The women want the easiest jobs and to be paid the same as the men who do the hard work. Once a girl and I and one other guy were sent to the body shop. All three of us were in the welding area. It was hot and the fumes were bad. It hadn't been more than an hour when the girl started to have problems. She broke down and cried. Immediately someone said, "Oh, don't cry. Come over here. Sit down and take it easy."

I don't think anybody ever gets out of financial problems. They're just one of those stumbling blocks and trials that the Lord gives you to get through. Health, accidents, we've had our share of those too. Now that I've been a member of the church for a while, I know the only way to get through is to keep the faith and pray that things are going to work out.

I know that the priesthood, the power is there if you use it and if you have the faith that it's going to work. A few years ago my wife had an operation for an ovarian cyst. We thought she was all right, but it came back again. Having to go in again was very hard on her. We prayed and I got the feeling that things were going to be fine—it was going to be better than the first time—and that there would be a sign or something. Before I left home the day of the operation I was praying; when I walked out the door at seven o'clock in the morning there was a big peace rose in full bloom right by the front door. The sun was shining and I thought, "There's my sign. Peace, she's going to be fine." I clipped the rose and took it in to the hospital. When she came out of the surgery there was a rose for her.

I did a lot of praying in the waiting room. I had a feeling that there was going to be something that had to be answered. Not long after, the doctor came in and wanted a decision on whether or not to do a hysterectomy. I didn't even hesitate. I said, "No, we don't want that." Even though we have been told that she can never have children of her own, her patriarchal blessing says that she will have children. It doesn't say by childbirth, but it's in there. I prayed and prayed and could not get any other answer than "No, don't do that."

It never dawned on me until after I joined the church how much my life had been guided for a purpose. The death rate was very high for the cancer I had as a child. I didn't even think about it then, but Heavenly Father was saying, "It's not your time yet. We've got something else for you to do." When I was eighteen I fell five and a half stories head first. A pulley came up and hit the back of my legs. My boss was standing below, pulling the cord that sent me over head first, and I fell on him. With the heel of my left foot, I broke his foot. All I had were cuts and scrapes and bruises. He got me up and drove me three miles to the hospital. They said to him, "Well, this guy's fine, but your foot is broken." I was in the hospital for two weeks. They had to put me under anesthesia to clean me up because of all the tar and dirt.

After finding the church, I thought back over all these things. When I got my patriarchal blessing it all came together. My time hadn't come. There was still a lot of work for me to do. My patriarchal blessing says that I was always a valiant fighter and that I fought alongside the archangel in the preexistence. It says my basic job on earth is to be a father.

Cheryl Downward, 29

Cheryl Downward was baptized in September 1982 along with her friends Dawn and David Shepherd. She works at a school for the developmentally disabled. At church she has taught the Relief Society mother education class.

When I was in high school my foster mother's neighbor worked at Hill Haven Center in Odessa. Her boss had asked her if she knew anybody who was good with children to work on weekends. Since I was always good with children, my foster mother took me for an interview. I started working weekends. When I got out of school, I went to full-time. Even though I don't make a lot of money, I start to feel bad if I think about quitting. I would miss those kids. The teachers are there for six hours, but they don't have the time that we have to play with the kids and know them.

My job was chosen for me, but I chose it, too. My foster mother was strict. We weren't allowed to do a lot. She chose our clothes. We girls weren't allowed to wear blue jeans. When I was eighteen and could drive, I bought my own blue jeans. She chose where we went, what we did, our friends, who we could date, the movies we saw, everything.

My foster mom always told us that we were stupid and that we couldn't do anything. She always told us, "Just get C's. That's all you can get. Don't worry about it." She wanted us to stay home until we got married.

I don't want to have a big family. I was in one. We had fifteen or sixteen teen-agers in the house at a time. Mom didn't have time to spend with us. I think that's why everybody didn't turn out real well. All my foster brothers and sisters have continued their childhood problems. They're not doing well in relationships. I think if even a normal family is too big, you don't have time to spend with everybody. I always wanted to have four kids, but now I think two.

I have three brothers and a sister. When I was three we were taken from our parents and put in a children's home. When I was about eight, my sister and I went to a foster home. We went to another one when I was nine. When I was ten we went to our third foster home. My sister was my mother and my sister and my best friend. I'm very attached to her.

When I was a child I was insecure and very upset a lot. I was just glad to get through each day. Life's a lot better now. I've made it a lot better. When I was little I used to pray to die. I said, "Oh, just let me die. I hate it here." I woke up in the middle of the night and couldn't breathe. "No, no. I didn't mean it. I didn't mean that at all." I don't know if it was my imagination or if that was really happening. I think I'm still insecure. My job is my security. I've had it for a long time. In a way I want to quit because I'd like to make more money, but I try not to have a lot of change in my life.

There were two turning points in my life: moving up here and joining the church. When I got out of school, I did everything my foster mother had told me not to. She said, "Bad things happen after eleven o'clock at night." So I stayed out all night long, and I thought, "Oooh. I've found out what she was talking about, I think." After three years I moved up here because I thought, "This is not the kind of life I want, and I don't want to be around this kind of people." The sister of one of the girls I work with needed somebody to share an apartment. The landlords are David Shepherd's grandparents.

In 1982 I was staying with my girlfriend, Dawn, and her husband, David, because my car had broken down. We had the discussions and all three of us were baptized. The lessons answered some of my questions. I hadn't been sure that Revelation was exactly the end of the Bible.

I'm ward singles representative, stake singles secretary, and the Relief Society singles teacher. I enjoy the meetings. We have a lot of fun at family home evening, too. When they asked me to teach Relief Society, I wanted to make myself get up in front of other people. I'm afraid to talk to other people, so I make myself do it. I'm learning to be more outgoing, even to people I don't know. My family doesn't say anything about the church because they didn't want me to join, but I think they're glad. I can tell by their reaction when I tell them about the activities that they're glad I'm doing it.

I don't mind obeying the Word of Wisdom, especially with alcohol, because my parents are alcoholics. All my foster brothers' and sisters' parents were alcoholics. I started working on genealogy, but I stopped because my mother couldn't remember where her relatives were and what their names were. Alcohol makes you forget everything. I went over to see my father a few months ago and he couldn't remember who I was. He said, "Are you from the phone company?"

I said, "Jack sent me over here." He knows Jack, my brother. I always thought my parents didn't love us and that's why they let us go. I didn't understand alcoholism. I know, now, my mom loves us.

When I was in the hospital last year with appendicitis, Brother Ridge came and gave me a blessing. After I came out of the hospital last April I tried to figure out how long it would take me to pay the bill. I figured it would take about a year and a half. A family member asked me, "Shouldn't you stop paying tithing?" I paid off the hospital bill in five months because I got every bit of overtime that I was supposed to get during the summer. Not every year do I get all of it.

My life is not interesting. I go to work and Sundays I go to church. Every once in a while I do something. The dances are so few and far between, especially in the wintertime. A girl I work with said today that she gets embarrassed if she's in the laundromat on a Friday night because everybody will know that she doesn't have a date. To me, that's no big deal. It's always bothered me that girls thought they were nobody if they didn't have a date. I've been on some dates that I've wished I'd been home, that I've wished I'd been at the laundromat.

My patriarchal blessing says that I will be married someday. As each year passes, I keep thinking, "When?" I've just hit twenty-nine. Everybody says that it will happen, but that tests my faith more than anything. I don't like being single. I want to have somebody to share my life with and spend time with me. I took the temple preparation classes, but the bishop asked me to wait before I went to the temple. If I married a nonmember, it would be a place he couldn't go.

I like what the church teaches about strong families. My foster mother took us to church, but my foster father stayed home in bed. He needed it a lot more than any of us did. He was an alcoholic, too. I'd like to have my family raised in the church and all of us there every Sunday.

Cynthia Mullins, 30

Cynthia Mullins grew up in Elkton and was baptized in Germany with her husband, David, while he was in the army. They moved back to Elkton when David began working for Du Pont. They are the parents of four children, ages one to eight. Cynthia has worked in every ward organization and is now a member of the Activities Committee.

In Germany, there was not much to do in our small apartment. When we first got there, Dave worked the midnight-to-eight shift. When he came home, I was wide awake and ready to go see all the sights. There were a lot of women in the same situation, so I would go over to a friend's house to spend the day. I became very close to one in particular, Arlene. Barry and Arlene were Mormons. The many nights that Dave and Barry were working, Arlene and I talked about the church a little bit. They lived their life in a way that was contagious. I wanted to live just like they did. Everything worked their way. They got the apartment with three or four bedrooms, and their rent was cheaper than ours. They just got all the breaks. We realized that they were happier, their marriage was strong, they never fought, they had a beautiful family, which at that time consisted of them and Jennifer, who was about six months.

One day there was a knock at the door. Since I had seen missionaries before, I invited them in. I thought that Arlene had sent them to us, but she hadn't. The missionaries looked for American license tags in the parking lot and at the names on the doors to find the Americans. We had the discussions and were baptized.

I especially liked the idea of the plan of salvation. I had a lot of questions about who God was and what he was, and I couldn't get an answer. I was raised to believe that he was like the North wind, a violent wrathful God. With the Church of Jesus Christ of Latter-day Saints, everything seemed to fit in. When we had the discussions, I constantly asked questions. Dave took everything quietly, and I asked more and more questions. I was just in awe because everything seemed to fit in.

When we came home Dave went to college in Georgetown, Delaware, on the GI Bill. Dave was going to school and had a part-time job. While we were there, my sister Susan came down with her Bible to set us straight. I let the missionaries know that if the curtains were open to come on up. "I need help." If the curtains were shut, we were fine. The curtains stayed open all night. They came up and we had discussion after discussion and Susan joined the church. She has since been on a mission to Taiwan.

When we first moved to Elkton, the branch met at Brother Mullins's home. I would sit on the doorstep along with a couple of the other mothers. Everybody had two or three callings. Everybody was willing to work. The lady who lived in this house before us let them have Primary here. They all got stuck in the basement one day and couldn't get out. There was a doorknob only on the outside of the door. She called the operator and had the operator ring the upstairs and tell the people upstairs to go down and let them out of the basement.

When I moved to this house, I got teased by my neighbor, Jan, because the lady in this house drank Coke and hid it in her car so her children wouldn't find it. Jan asked me about the long undershirts. She was picking up everything negative. I just try to ignore it. I think the most important thing is to not push anything about the church, but to be a friend. Dave and Jim spend time together in their gardens. We have yard sales together every year. We exchange Christmas presents, and I think we have a wonderful relationship. Barry and Arlene weren't out pushing. We watched them and realized that they had a neat family. I wanted to live my life the way they lived theirs.

Bonnie Arnold, 63

Bonnie Arnold became a member of the Elkton Ward when a bridge between her home and the Chesapeake Ward was closed. She had been a member of the Wilmington Branch and later the New Castle Ward before moving from Newark to Conowingo, Maryland. As the ward librarian she presides over two small rooms in the little house filled with file cabinets full of pictures and shelves of lesson manuals, scriptures, filmstrips, tape recorders, a record player, a filmstrip projector, and a copier. Each week she and Imogene Meekins place the pictures each Primary teacher will need on Sunday in his or her cubby. The lesson manuals designate the needed pictures by number, so the librarians need to know only the number of the lesson to be taught that week.

I grew up in Dewey, Oklahoma, north of Tulsa—about twenty miles from the Kansas line. I was in the middle of four brothers and sisters. We lived in the country and walked three and a half miles to school. There were no school buses. Later when we moved closer to town, about twenty miles out, a family just a mile away from us had a flatbed truck. We'd walk over there and one of their boys would drive the truck to school with a whole bunch of us sitting on the back of it. Of course we didn't have electricity in the country. We didn't have bathrooms. I give thanks for permapress sometimes. My poor mother ironed with little flatirons that she had to heat on the wood stove. She'd wipe the soot off, then she'd iron somebody's white shirt. If she didn't have the soot wiped off enough, she had to take that shirt back to the scrub board and go through it all over again. There are not many things in my house that have to be ironed.

My father deserted us when the oldest sister was seventeen and the youngest sister was about a year old. My mother scrubbed floors and washed clothes and baked and cut hair and made dresses for people. She was determined that we would all get through school. She was seventy years old before she drew any old-age pension. Her great-great-grandfather was a Baptist missionary who went on the Trail of Tears from Georgia into Oklahoma. The tribe adopted him and his family. My mother's Indian land came from him, but I know there was Indian blood in that family.

When we moved to town so mother could find work to do, she wrote to a blind cousin and we lived in three rooms in her house. Mother prepared the evening meal and did her laundry in exchange for a place to live. Miss Eva, as we called her, was a Nazarene. Some of us went to church with her, though Mother went to the Baptist church and was a believer in that. She was supporting youngsters for a long period of time, but she always gave a tenth of what she had.

When they started taking young women into the military, I was old enough. I think I got mad at somebody at work one day and I went to Oklahoma City and passed the test. Part of the time I went to school. I checked parachutes in and out and made sure they were repacked. I dispatched airplanes. The job I had the longest was as supply sergeant for a men's squadron. This was way back before women libbers had ever been heard of. Before I had the job, two men did it. My assistant was a thirty-eight-year-old man who had managed a Montgomery Ward store in civilian life, and I was a loud-mouthed kid from the country.

I believe in women getting equal pay if they're doing the same job. We can't legislate ourselves to be the same. The government has become so involved in this, they've made a mess of it. Sears hired one gal up in the stock room to lift the packages. The men's attitude was terrible. They said, "We're not going to help her." There's not one of those men who moved a big box by himself. They always got another man to help them.

E. J.'s parents had moved to California during the war. When he got out of the service, he came back to Oklahoma for a visit. I had known him before although we were not in contact with each other while we were in the service. When he got a job in California, he sent for me. The children were all born while we lived in Martinez.

Two lady missionaries knocked on the door in California. Back in those days they just kept coming. Now, if you don't make a commitment they move on to someone else. I had all the lessons. I decided to run away from the missionaries. That wasn't easy. I had two small children, was expecting another, and I didn't drive. My husband was a shift worker and we lived on the edge of the community. I found myself being gone each time they were due at my house. I don't know why because I liked them and enjoyed their company. They always showed up later apologizing for being late. One day they sat at the dining room table and asked me these direct questions. I could only hedge so much. I realized, if I was honest with myself, there was only one answer. I was baptized in October 1952. I know my life's better than it could have been otherwise. In the church we have a compass pointed in the right way.

I worked at a Sears store in Walnut Creek for a couple of years because E. J. had hurt his back and was off work. I could drive then. After I joined the church, I had to learn to drive. My husband was transferred to Delaware in 1956 by Tidewater Oil. Then because Mr. Getty owned most of the stock, they changed the name to Getty. Just before he retired, Texaco bought it out.

We watched the Wilmington Branch grow into a stake. When we first moved here, we met in the Odd Fellows Hall in downtown Wilmington. We helped build the church building in Wilmington. I have a lot of hammer marks over there. I can tell you which pieces of paneling in the foyer I hammered on and the ones I polished. E. J. and I put the ceiling up in the old Relief Society room. There were a considerable number of members in Newark. As a matter of fact, we always wondered why we didn't get a branch along the line somewhere. If we had been given a branch that would have given a stronger incentive to grow and develop.

I knew Cloyd Mullins from the Wilmington Ward and the New Castle Ward. His wife was one of my very special friends. I've heard Cloyd talk about turning around if he saw a car with Delaware tags in his driveway. I've teased him, "My car used to have Delaware tags on it."

When we moved to the country in 1977, I went to the Chesapeake Ward, which is only twelve and a half miles across the river. When they changed the boundary line, my health was such that I didn't go to Elkton. When the state closed the road that I traveled, going to Chesapeake Ward was almost the same distance as going to Elkton. So I said, "Well maybe they're trying to tell me something." I've been going to Elkton ever since then. I'm sure the boundary line will be changed again. When they build the church in Newark, people over here are going to go back across the river.

Sears had given me a transfer when we moved here, but I didn't go back to work until Nantha was in college. I worked at the Prices Corners' Sears for eleven and a half years. Ten years ago I started having bad problems with asthma. They put a toxic substance on the floor at Sears one day. I worked in the Receiving Department, keeping records of incoming merchandise, where there was no ventilation. The last couple of years have been better. If Reenie hadn't been here one time I wouldn't be sitting here now. E. J. was working nights, and Reenie's husband was out of town. She brought all the kids up here from Dover. She got up in the night with the oldest youngster who happened to be sick, and she found me unconscious. She called the ambulance. I don't remember that trip to the hospital. I don't think she figured she'd ever see me again.

For ten years I haven't done too much in the church, nor at home either. The stress of not being able to keep commitments adds to the problem. They used to say that asthma was strictly a psychological problem, but now they say that the psychological problem comes from the stress of the asthma. I was grateful when they gave me the library job because if I can't make it there every Sunday, I can get back during the week to do it. It's something that someone else can handle—not like teaching a class. I don't do well in crowds, and I don't do well in the Elkton building, either. That mustiness in the basement is horrible. I'm busy at church; I'm not twiddling my thumbs.

When I first joined the church, of course, they put me in as a Primary teacher. I don't think I was cut out for that, but I did do it. Just before we moved into the Wilmington building I was a counselor in the Relief Society. The Relief Society president moved, and I woke up one night and said, "Oh no, oh no." The next time I saw the branch president, he said, "Oh yes." I was the new Relief Society president. The day that they dedicated the building there had to be a lunch at noon between the conference sessions, but the tables had not been delivered. All the Philadelphia Mission District was there. It was made the

Philadelphia Stake before the meeting was over. We had to provide lunches for all those people and we had only one big table to work with. It was like feeding the five thousand, but we did it. Some families wanted to buy seven or eight sack lunches. The next day the tables were delivered.

I had good help. There were always those that I could lean on. The Relief Society did not get any money from the ward budget, so we had to sell things and bake cookies and cakes. We delivered telephone directories. While they were raising the money for the building, the Relief Society had to pay fifty dollars a month toward the building fund. There were about forty on the roll, but we only had ten or twelve who were active. We always made our commitment.

When the other lady was president, and I was her counselor, the branch president, Mark Weed, asked us, "Do you want to go in with the priesthood to make this certain amount?" It was a greater amount, but the priesthood would be sharing it. The women said, "No. We'll do the fifty." He just about cracked up. We made our fifty dollars all the time, and the priesthood didn't make their commitment. I think it is a good thing we don't have to earn our own money now. I am surprised that the church didn't realize it sooner.

Being president of the Relief Society was difficult for me because I'm not a talented person. I don't sew; I don't cook. We met the commitment that we were supposed to meet because I had good people working with me, not because I had any talents along those lines.

One of my counselors was from Salt Lake City. Her mother or her mother-in-law visited our visiting teaching meeting, which was held on the first Tuesday of the month. The reports came in as usual. Some were supposed to visit two sisters, but hadn't found them home; some hadn't been out. She gave her testimony. She said she'd had 100 percent visiting teaching for ten or fifteen years. I asked, "How big a district?"

"Ten families."

"How big an area?"

"Oh, all on the same side of the street." It was all I could do to watch my face because some of our people were putting fifty to a hundred miles on the car to do their visiting teaching. I think sometimes in the branches the people are closer than in the wards. We had fewer members and we had a heavier load, but we got it done. We were dedicated to a cause and we followed through.

I'm not very successful at visiting teaching out here in the boondocks. Anne Mace and I were doing a beautiful job until she went back to work in the store. Some mornings when I get up I'm not breathing right and I just don't have the push to get out. We have to call our people ahead. Back when I was in Relief Society, we didn't call ahead. We'd find a lot of women at home. Sometimes we'd go out a second time depending on who it was and how far it was to travel. It's very difficult to try to make four or five appointments living out this far. Every call is a long-distance call.

President Kimball has done so many things for the families. He put the church back on the short meeting schedule on Sundays so the family can go to church together. It always bothered us a little that you either had to have two cars or you had to make arrangements for a ride. Then they've cut out some of the other meetings during the week. Relief Society and Primary are on Sunday. When Nantha went to MIA I had to take the two little ones with me because my husband was a shift worker. We had to do something during the time she was there. Then Reenie got old enough to go with her, so we were still there. Dewey went to Primary on Thursdays.

My daughter Nantha bought the old homestead in Brookside near Newark from us. After she graduated from Brigham Young, she substituted at her old high school, Christiana High School. Then she got a job at Queen Anne's High School in Centerville, Maryland. She's taught physical education there for thirteen or fourteen years. She's a gifted person in that she's able to do the things she wants to. She rides a motorcycle; she swims; she plays hockey; she plays softball. Reenie, the middle one, is the only one who has married. She has four children, and her husband is the bishop of the Dover Ward. Dewey, the youngest, has not been active in the church since before he went into the navy. He spent six years in the navy—most of it in school. I think he had twenty-three hours of sea time. He is an electronics specialist and works for a company that works for the Du Pont company.

E. J. and Dewey both have the priesthood, but they're both inactive. I know that my improved health is due to the blessings of the priesthood. There's no doubt in my mind on that. Before I had surgery to remove my thyroid gland, I made arrangements. Cloyd Mullins had told me that he was going to be our home teacher. We hadn't had a home teacher for a long time. I said, "I want to see you before I go home today. A week from Monday I have to go to the hospital, but I want a blessing today." I don't know why I was insistent on having it that day, but the next Sunday I wasn't there, after all, because I had to go in to have blood work done. I have always known that I would come through these situations all right because I did have the blessings of the priesthood. I have no fear of dying, but I'm not going to invite it. When E. J. had back surgery, back in 1960 or '61, he had a blessing. During the operation I went out to sleep in the car. I knew it was going to be all right.

After I came into the church, I particularly resented hearing members of the church say "Mormon," and never using the real name. I've noticed in recent years the church is using the full title a little more often. I think it's more effective to say the Church of Jesus Christ of Latter-day Saints or Latter-day Saints. Not long ago a man from the church up the road knocked on my door. He had some little leaflets and was out inviting people to a revival. I was canning applesauce—had some on the stove that was pretty close to being put into the jars. I said, "Well, I'll be honest with you. I'm active in the Latter-day Saints Church. I won't be coming to the revival."

Oh, he got mad and he started telling me that everybody is going to be in heaven and he didn't like people saying, "Nope, I can't go because I'm a Catholic" or whatever. He was slicing me up because I had told him that I wouldn't take his pamphlets.

I said, "I'm trying to be honest with you. If I take it, I'll only throw it in the wastebasket. Maybe you can give it to somebody else."

He kept asking me questions. I knew the answers to all of them, but I didn't want to answer them because I didn't want to add to the tension. Finally, I said, "You know, it's the only church I can think of that goes by the name of Jesus Christ."

He grabbed those papers and said, "My wife told me to be back early tonight." He didn't have an answer to the only question I had asked him.

I had said, "Why don't they go by his name?" The name is important, and we don't use it enough.

I think the one belief that causes the greatest problem for Protestants is our idea of growing up to be gods. I'm sure they just think that's heresy. Yet, it's so logical. A kitten grows up to be a cat. A puppy grows up to be a dog. A chick grows up to be a chicken. It doesn't turn into something else. The first book in the Bible says that we're made in the image of God. Where do they get the belief that you turn into something that can't even be described? I know there are things that we don't have all the answers for, but that doesn't bother me because I know that when that knowledge is needed, it will be made available to us. It will fit right in. I particularly like the words of "O My Father." There's a real message there. You don't hear much about Heavenly Mother other than there. You would think that concept would have come through in the scriptures a little more clearly because it's very logical.

Elkton Ward Relief Society president Julie Ridge (*center*), and her counselors, June McVicker and Heather Early.

Richard Bushman, bishop of the Elkton Ward, and his counselors, Rufus Lanier and Gary Johnston.

Sheila Anderson and members of her Primary Star B class sign "I love you."

Elkton Ward members dipped 4,017 fondant Easter eggs on March 2.

The men of the Elkton Ward spent several Saturdays cutting and hauling
wood to raise funds for the ward budget.

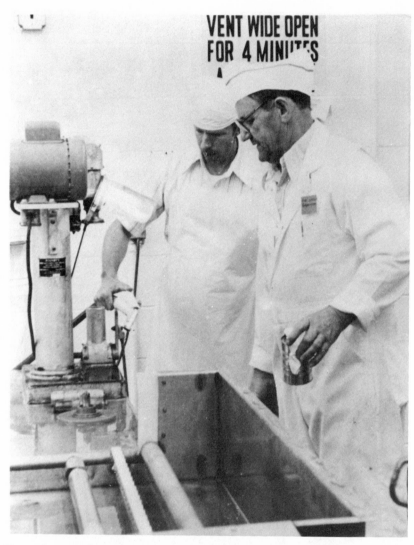

Kenneth McVicker and Oliver McPherson inspect the equipment at the church's welfare cannery.

Douglas Ridge accompanies Deborah Johnston and her helpers, Becky Harding, Christi Tatanish, Somer Parsons, and Abby Taber, as they lead the Primary children in song.

Elkton Ward Primary president Virginia Lund (*center*) and her counselors, Jean Bingham and Colleen Pierce.

The Elkton Branch and Elkton Ward met in this chapel from 1980 to 1989.

The Elkton Ward choir, accompanied by the composer, sings Harriet Pether-ick's anthem "Oh Lord I Thank Thee Now" in sacrament meeting.

Cynthia Mullins and Linda Peer apply stage makeup to Beth Ann Crowe, Emily Ridge, Shanan Larsen, and Amy Morris prior to the road show performance.

Claudia Bushman conducts a Brass Ensemble rehearsal. *From left:* Ben Bushman, Rob Crowe, Claudia Bushman, Kenny McVicker, Alan Taber.

Members of the Elkton Ward Elders' Quorum stand on the front steps of the Elkton Ward chapel. First row (*from left to right*): Thomas Mathews, Roy Queenan, Robert Pierce, Jay Petersen. Second row: Jonathan Lund, Lee Anderson, Matthew Burke, David Obzansky. Third row: Greg Bramwell, William Harrington, Blane Parker, James Rennard. Fourth row: missionaries, Grant Robison, Gene Martin, Michael Wheeler, Wayne Morris. Fifth row: Kevin O'Day, Anthony Peer, Scott Grimshaw, Thomas Hearne.

Members of the Elkton Ward Relief Society listen to a lesson. *From left*: Anne Mace, Diane Day Howard, Claudia Bushman, Elena Larsen, Susan Taber, Meg Bramwell, Terryl Owen, Diana Noren, Eileen Johnston, Shelia Lanier.

9 | A Circle of Friendship

The church is filled with activities for young people, ranging from camp to singing to basketball to Scouting. One of the favorite and most hectic special activities of the ward is the road show. Each year each ward in the stake is invited to perform a sketch based on a specific theme. This year's theme was "Remember When." The Elkton Ward script, written by Colleen Pierce, sent two teenagers, played by Beth Ann Crowe and Ben Bushman, back in time after they inadvertently started up a time machine. During their travels they witnessed the invention of the wheel and the discovery of electricity. Ingrid Adams wrote the lyrics: "An Innovative Christmas" set to "A Merry Little Christmas," "The Time Machine" set to "Yellow Submarine," and "Caves" to "King of the Road." She also created intricate dance patterns but had to spend a good deal of time simplifying them so that the troupe could execute them.

It had been difficult to find rehearsal times because of the many pressing ward activities, but finally eleven were squeezed in before the performance. Lynne Whitney played the piano, Ingrid Adams gave the dance instruction, and Jean Bingham, the director, yelled, "Face the audience! Louder! On and off stage faster!" "Faster" was important because as the date of the performance grew nearer the show seemed to be taking longer and longer. Finally the last page had to be cut to two lines to get under seventeen minutes.

All the props were ready for the show except the crucial time machine, which wasn't completed until the night before—a spectacle of flashing lights, whirring sounds, and smoke blasting out from underneath. The cast didn't get to practice with it until the morning rehearsal on the day of the show. They had only one hour to adjust their actions to the seemingly enormous space at Smyrna High School and the new props. Dedicated performers that they were, they had put aside such problems as homework, strep throat, and swollen glands so that the show could go on.

As Bishop Bushman's testimony illustrated the next morning, the show was a success in a variety of ways. They not only had managed to get through it in under seventeen minutes but they had also managed to make an impression. Bishop Bushman asserted that "all things are spiritual to the Lord. The Lord said that everything temporal can also have a spiritual dimension. Though the road show is a raucous occasion, I heard a testimony borne last night. Ken McVicker, who played Benjamin Franklin, turned to me with white paint still in his hair and said, 'I wonder if there's any other place where just anybody who wanted to perform—young people and older people—could. The road show is one of the first things about the church that impressed me.' We take it for granted but it is a marvelous thing to me that ward after ward got up and put on one of these shows.

"I was impressed last night when I saw the members up there performing together. It wasn't just a slap-dash effort. I know many of them have all sorts of difficulties and problems in their personal lives, yet something had pulled out of them a desire to have this time of fun and performance together. I want to bear testimony that God calls upon us to extricate ourselves from all of our personal problems and worries to serve others, even at times when we feel unworthy or unable to do so."

On December 23 Jean Bingham was released as a counselor in the Primary and called to be Young Women's president and Laurel adviser. She asked that Sharon Morris and Maureen Bezerra be called to serve as her counselors and as Beehive and Mia Maid advisers. The Young' Women's organization includes all girls between the ages of twelve and eighteen, organized into three classes. Beehives are twelve and thirteen years old, Mia Maids are fourteen and fifteen, and Laurels, sixteen and seventeen. When I grew up, girls advanced to the next class at the start of the school year, but girls now change classes on their birthdays, just as boys advance in the priesthood.

Not only do the Young Women leaders teach the girls on Sunday mornings during the last hour of meetings (the same time as priesthood meeting and Relief Society) but they help the girls plan and carry out Wednesday night activities. In addition, several special events were held during the first months of the new year. On the first Sunday in February Sharon Morris invited the fathers of her five Beehive girls to come to class. Each father was supposed to give a short talk of appreciation for his daughter. Wayne Larsen related an incident where he had been impressed by Shanan's generosity. His eldest daughter, Tara, had called to say that a friend was driving her home for Christmas from BYU. Not wanting her to drive so far in the winter, Wayne had suggested that Tara's friend fly with her. On learning that the friend could not afford a plane ticket, Wayne had asked his children which they preferred—to fly Tara and her friend home for Christmas and not get a VCR for Christmas or have just Tara and the VCR. Shanan unhesitatingly said that she hated for anyone not to have a place to go for Christmas and voted to fly both girls home. Luck had been with the Larsens—they had been able to do both—but Wayne was impressed by Shanan's generosity.

On February 13 the girls in all three classes and their mothers met together for their New Beginnings program. The highlight of the meeting was the girls' singing "The Circle of Friendship" by Marilyn Adams and Murray Boren together.

> Ours is a circle, a circle of friendship,
> And just like a circle, it goes on and on
> Endless, eternal, this circle of friendship;
> Enter our circle, for here you belong.
> Laughing and singing our good times together,
> And sharing the blessings sent from above.
> You and I sharing this circle of friendship,
> Join as we open our circle of love.

Jean Bingham and Sharon Morris gave talks about the purpose of the Young Women's program and encouraged the girls to make friends with each other.

Sharon Morris, 32

Sharon Morris grew up as a member of the Wilmington Branch and Ward. Two months after she married Wayne Morris, she began raising his two children, Craig and Amy. Amy, now twelve, is a member of the Beehive class. The Morrises live southwest of Newark and have five children, ranging from Craig, sixteen, to Chad, two. Sharon's brother Thomas Hearne is also a member of the Elkton Ward.

Right after I graduated from high school I got a job at the University of Delaware where I worked for eight years. When I was twenty-two I got an apartment in the downstairs of a friend's house. I felt that my youngest brothers and youngest sister needed some room of their own and that it was time for me to find out what it was like to support myself.

When everybody else went away to college, I felt like one of the lost sheep in my own ward. I just stopped going to church and became inactive for about four years. When Wayne's children, Amy and Craig, came to live with us two months after we were married, Craig was nine and Amy was five. Wayne had the basic beliefs in God and the Bible stories, but his children didn't have anything. I said, "Regardless of our feelings about church doctrine, I think that it's important that these two go to church, and I want our children taken to my church." Just because I had become inactive, I didn't feel that I had fallen away. I wanted the children to grow up hearing the lessons that we had learned. Looking back, I can see that my testimony was important to me.

I had started going again before we were married. Linda Ennis had started a young adult Relief Society, which met in a home. There were five or six of us girls. When she called me at home and said, "Look, this is what we are doing and we want you to be here" was the first time that anybody had recognized me for me. I jumped at it. We met for about a year, and I began teaching in it. Then Bishop Cross said that according to Salt Lake this was not Relief Society. We had to attend the formal organization. I had become involved enough in the church that I stayed pretty active after that.

I see girls just vanish or get into problems when they turn seventeen or eighteen. I know what it's like to fall further and further away from the church and all you've been taught. I've tried to stress to the bishop that the young men and women need a Relief Society or priesthood group that they can feel a part of. If the lessons are about marriage and children, they're lost. The boys get out of school at eighteen and don't start missions for a year. If there's not a program to keep them in, then they're gone. I'm glad for the dances and hayrides I see the Young Adults having.

I met my husband, Wayne, at a party. We enjoyed going horseback or motorcycle riding together. I didn't think that there was any question about going to bars with him because we had talked right away about the church. He would sit and talk with my dad about the church. One of the things that impressed him was that you just weren't married until "death do you part."

I had always wanted to be married on the beach. We had spent just about every weekend in the summer at my grandparents cottage. I was an outdoor person and I just could not see taking one of the biggest steps of my life inside. When I walked out on the beach, the sun was just coming up over the ocean. Over one hundred people were there, and everybody just stood there and cried because it was so beautiful.

I never gave much thought to being married in the temple. I knew that I wanted to raise my children in the church. Going to the temple wasn't a goal until after Wayne and I were married. I was totally inspired to ask the missionaries to come out to our house and start giving him the lessons. He was impressed that two young women would dedicate the most important years of their lives to the church. He worked hard to reach the goal of being married in the temple. I told him, "You're not doing this for me. These are your own blessings and I can't receive them for you." He made sure that we got to all the temple preparation classes. Seeing Wayne baptized and seeing him receive the gift of the Holy Ghost and the priesthood has strengthened my testimony. When we went though the temple, we knew that our family was going to be the most important thing in our lives. That was the icing on the cake.

When Wayne and I were sealed, Sherry was about a year and a half and Jared was six months. Craig and Amy were thirteen and ten when they were sealed to us and Sherry and Jared were old enough to remember that. Chad is the only one who was born in the covenant. I don't remember my parents talking about missions and being married in the temple when I was growing up, even though my father read to us from the Book of Mormon and we had family home evenings. My parents have spent the night here to watch the kids when we go to the temple, but getting them to go themselves is a challenge. We've tried to get them to want the blessings that we've received from going to the temple.

I want to bring my children up in the gospel. At night I sit down and write in their journals with them. I want my children to know that they have security here. I love helping them grow and learn. They share a lot of the household chores with me. Even though they may seem like menial tasks sometimes, it's helping them to grow and rounding out their education. The children work in the garden with me. They know what brussels sprouts are and how good they taste when you cook them right after you cut them off the plant. They know how to weed around the plants and what a radish leaf looks like. They've participated in canning. Working together brings us closer. I try to make everything like a game because children's interest is so short. I love that little verse that says, "Go away cobwebs and go away dustballs, I'm rocking the baby." Spending time with them as they're growing up is so much more important to me than housework. When they turn around and say, "But Mommy, you didn't read in the Book of Mormon with us today—you have to do that with us," it makes me feel so good.

I've been teaching the Beehives for four years. My daughter Amy is in my class now. I want to help the kids with the moral issues. Everything you see on television is centered around sex. They need to learn household management, too. I learned some hard lessons when I had my own apartment. I want the girls to learn how to handle a budget, how to make up a menu for the week. I tell them that if they will budget their tithing now, then when they are older and have a bigger income and more responsibilities—children and a mortgage— they will be used to budgeting their tithing.

I try to make myself aware of the environment that they're growing up in now. It is so important for them to keep up their prayers, to stay in the church. I ask them, "What kind of marriage do you want?" "Do you want marriage?" I work with the girls in the personal progress program and teach them to set their goals. If they get even one thing out of the whole lesson and take that home with them, I feel like I've done something. From what they say, I can tell they do listen to what I'm saying. Maybe it's just that twelve- and thirteen-year-olds are more susceptible and want to listen.

If I don't feel the Spirit with me when I'm trying to teach, I feel that I'm not getting across to them. I want to try to activate the girls who do not come. Maybe I come across to them as a gung-ho gospel person, but I try to let them know that I just want to help them through their difficult times. My attitude is not "This is what the Prophet says; this is what you should be doing." It is "I know what you're going through. Can I help you, share in it some way?"

My own Beehive teacher, Grace Davis, is a remarkable person. I knew as she was teaching us that she had a very special testimony. When I knew that we were going to the temple, I wanted her to be there. She and her husband have come with us both times when we had our children sealed to us. I hope that my testimony can enlighten someone the same way hers did me.

Maureen Bezerra, 30

Maureen Bezerra, the first counselor and Mia Maid adviser, was baptized a member by her husband, Julio, shortly before the birth of their first child, six years ago. The mother of two young children, Maureen is an X-ray technician. She graduated from Concord High School in Wilmington and attended the University of Delaware.

My mother died when I was nineteen. It was real rough because we all knew she was sick but she wouldn't admit it and she wouldn't go see a doctor. On top of it all, she started drinking, which wasn't good for her because half the trouble was with her liver. My dad finally convinced her to go to a doctor, but at that point it was too late. My dad seemed to survive pretty well, but he depended on us a lot. As the oldest girl at home, I was hesitant to leave my dad. I went to school, but I wasn't out on my own until I married Julio when I was twenty-four.

Julio and I went to high school together. I knew him because my girlfriends and I were always interested in sports. He was very active in sports and of course I was too. We just happened to be in the same bar one night. I turned and saw Julio sitting next to me so I started talking to him. He was exploring different churches at that time. He was baptized in August of 1978 and we were married in November. After we got married I went to church off and on with him. Eventually, I had the missionaries over and was baptized six years ago. When we were married, my husband was stationed at Fort Lewis, Washington. Then we were in Germany. The first few years were difficult because Julio was moving around in the army and then he couldn't find a job. Having faith and religion helped. I knew I could look in the Bible to find the answer to any problem.

The Elkton Ward is a lot different than the other wards I've lived in because it is smaller. I was used to servicemen's wards with a large congregation. Elkton is a little more close-knit. In servicemen's wards everybody's moving in and out. You can't get close to too many people. In Germany the whole country kept the Sabbath day. Nobody worked. The stores were closed. Everything was closed and everybody went to church. On nice days, they strolled in the park in their Sunday clothes. It's hard to feel that it's the Sabbath when people are cutting their lawns on that day.

Having a family was not one of the things I was aiming for. I said it would be nice if it happened, but I wanted to have a career. I went to the University of Delaware for two years, but was having trouble deciding what I wanted to do. A girlfriend gave me a brochure on radiography, and I thought it looked interesting. I enjoyed X-ray school. Later, I came across the aptitude test I had been given when I started college. I started laughing. The highest score I got—the thing I was best suited for—was X-ray technician. I had not remembered that.

It's important to feel that I am doing something with my life. Raising kids is a source of satisfaction for me, but doing housework, cleaning, cooking, isn't. I can see the kids grow and develop every day. I can see my accomplishments at work, too, from day to day.

If we could add a few more hours to the day, we could do all right. I rush through the day and I rush the kids. They get tired of it. They want to relax and enjoy life, too. When I was that young, I wasn't rushing around. I don't think my time is ever well balanced. When Julio didn't have a job, working seemed to overbalance family and church for me. Right now, I'm trying to give the most attention to my family and home. I think the church has finally become a little bit more understanding of the working mother. In today's world you can't make it without working. If you can, your husband is doing well, even though you may be scrimping and saving. The world could be better for my children, but I think they're tough and they're surviving.

I enjoy working with the girls in Young Women. Seeing their ideas and their innocence in life reminds me of when I was younger and going through those stages. Some of the young women seem apathetic. Sometimes they're just there because somebody made them be there. I've been trying to change those attitudes. I enjoy taking the concepts that the church teaches and trying to express them. I like to hear their responses. It's given me a lot of insight into the church's teachings.

It was hard at first for me to accept the priesthood because I was always a women's libber. Of course, there is a division of labor. The female does have the children to raise, and when something is direly wrong, the children always turn to their mom. I know Julio gets upset sometimes when they do that. But, again, when Jonathan hurt his foot, naturally the first thing he wanted was a priesthood blessing. Jonathan was sick once with a high fever and our home teacher came over and said, "I don't know why I'm here. I just know I'm supposed to be here." Of course that made my faith a lot stronger. He and Julio gave Jonathan a blessing. At the time he was delirious, but after the blessing he got a big smile on his face and went to sleep. The fever was down when he woke up.

I have a strong testimony of visiting teaching and home teaching. We've had some good ones and some who aren't. I think it's important that we be with each other—other than just at church. I've had poor visiting teachers lately. I've had good ones, but they change visiting teachers almost as fast as they do callings. I always try to be the visiting teacher that I would want to come to me. I visit two ladies who are inactive. I think my going there helps them realize that they are still a part of the church.

I always had a lot of questions, but it seemed that they were one of the mysteries. My dad studied religion when he was in college. I've always wondered if he had a period of doubt. I remember having deep thoughts when I was six or seven years old. I was always wondering who I was and where I came from. My parents would say, "Maureen, you're here." They told me that I came from heaven, but it still didn't make much sense. The church has the answers to a lot of my questions.

Faith is something you can't just take for granted. Believing something isn't the same as having faith. I have become a little stronger in my faith. I guess the day-to-day answers to prayer are the most important. My marriage was having a difficult time when Julio wasn't working and I was working strange hours. Home life wasn't good. I always got the same answer to my prayers. It was "not to nag Julio, but to love him." That was very hard to do when I could see the imperfections in his life. It was one of those times when you get the answer and you think, "Oh, come on!" It was not the answer I wanted, but it turned out to be the one that worked.

❊   ❊   ❊

Each year the young women and men go to the temple to perform baptisms as proxies for the dead. January's youth fireside, held on January 13, had as its theme the temple. That month the Priests' Quorum was in charge of planning the program and arranging for the refreshments. There was some confusion about the starting time. The speakers had been invited for 6:30, but most of the youth had arrived at 6:00. While waiting, the boys played a game in which Ben Bushman adjusted his tie, snapped his fingers, or tied his shoes and then the other boys copied the action. The speakers at the fireside were David Obzansky and Eileen Johnston, who told about their experience of being sealed in the Washington Temple the day before. They each said how wonderful it was to be sealed in the temple and what a great thing it was to know that they will be together forever.

During the following weeks Bishop Bushman interviewed the young people for their temple recommends. Youth leaders and parents encourage the young people to go on the annual excursion because they hope that visiting the temple will inspire the youth with the desire to be married there. Meeting at the ward building at 5:00 A.M., the young people and their leaders stood in a circle and prayed for safety and for an inspiring day. The girls rode with Thomas Robinson and Maureen Bezerra, and the boys rode in Stephen Cherry's van.

"It was neat to see the temple rise above the road and to think we were lucky enough to go into that beautiful place," said Shanan Larsen, thirteen. "After we saw it, we sang 'I Love to See the Temple' over and over until we arrived. They asked the adults to go do endowments so we were left alone. A temple worker explained to us the importance of what we were doing. We changed into white jumpsuits and watched each other be baptized for the dead. It was all quiet, and I felt kind of nervous, but happy that I could do it. It was very uplifting. I hope I will always be worthy to visit the House of Our Lord."

During the winter months the Elkton boys and girls also practiced and played basketball. Since the Elkton Ward has no gymnasium, all the practices had to be held at a high school, and all the games were played in Dover or Wilmington. The season began with a preseason holiday tournament on December 29 in Wilmington and ended on March 12 when the Elkton and Wilmington West boys played their final game. Had Elkton won, they would have been tied with Wilmington West for the championship and for the right to go to the regional playoffs.

Dan Harding, 42

Dan Harding, the Elkton Ward's athletic director, first came to Delaware as a missionary in 1963. After his mission he returned to the area, where he married his wife, Jean, who had joined the church as a girl along with her mother and four brothers and sisters. The father of six children, grandfather of one, Dan coaches his son's Little League team, as well as the church teams.

The basketball team worked hard all year long. They had a lot to overcome. We had a lot of individuals—guys who like to dribble the ball and like to shoot. My biggest goal was to get five boys on the court to play together as a team. We had very good spurts of that, but last night when we lost to Wilmington West was not one of them. They almost won, and I saw quite a few of them almost in tears. I told them afterwards to hold their heads high because they did a lot more than I had expected them to. Last Saturday when we played Wilmington West we came together as a team and just annihilated Wilmington West, which had been in first place. Last Saturday was the highlight. Last night's game was at nine o'clock, and there were some distractions, too. Ted Johnson pulled me away from the boys at the beginning to work out plans for the senior playoffs because there was a three-way tie. By the time I got back to the boys, the game was ready to start. I hadn't had a chance to set the mood for the game.

If you had seen the teams, both the girls and the boys, four years ago, you'd know there's been a tremendous change. We were getting beat 100–20. This year both teams won four and lost two. Since only one team goes to the regionals, we're out. If we had beaten Wilmington West last night we'd have tied for first place. Then Ted Johnson would have some more gray hair because there was no time for a playoff game between now and Saturday.

I came out here on my mission in 1963. Once I was here there was so much I wanted to see and do, but missionaries are not allowed to travel. I wanted to see the Hill Cumorah pageant and the world's fair, and I wanted to see Washington, D.C., where I had spent five months. There was no real work available at home and I wasn't a school bug. I was offered a job at a service station here, so I decided to come back. My mother cosigned for me to buy a brand new Corvair and I drove all the way across the United States. Little did I know that I would spend the next twenty years of my life here. I ran into Jeannie and got stuck.

I met Jeannie the latter part of June and we got married in December 1965. I like living out here as a member of the church because there's more of a challenge. On my mission I'd been in all these new, fresh wards—a lot of young people, a lot of activity. Back home they were all old. They were set in their ways and none of my friends were around.

I guess what's kept me coaching and working with the young people is that I enjoyed sports so much. Basketball and baseball kept me off the streets. When the high school coach came around, he saw that I could catch the balls, but I couldn't hit worth beans. I played third base and I had the best batting average because I walked more than anybody on the team. I just wouldn't swing at the ball. He had me doing a lot of bunting, which got me on base. I played intramural basketball and scrapped around with the kids in the neighborhood. I played church junior basketball for four years, same thing I'm coaching now.

I'm actually the athletic director of the ward. Since we don't have many coaches, but a lot of players, I'm the coach. With the seniors I do mostly scheduling because we work together well. There are a few ball players whose only contact with the church is playing basketball. Some are nonmembers, some have been excommunicated. It's a way of keeping in touch with them and letting them know that the church is still here.

I get to watch the young people grow up. They learn to work with others, to control their tempers and their bodies. I couldn't count all the young people I've worked with since 1974 in the New Castle Ward and the Elkton Ward. Besides coaching I've worked with some of the youth in Mutual. I've spent more time taking kids to dances at Broomall or going out on joint camping trips all over Pennsylvania and Delaware. There are other kids coming up. I work with them and watch them grow and watch them go out like little birdies out of the nest.

One boy didn't get along with his father. I said, "Well, you're going to have to stop fighting back. Try to work with him and see the other side." That kid still sends me letters, "Hi coach. How are you doing? Everything's fine out here. How's your team?"

If my children can understand the gospel is true and continue to go to church, then I think most of the battle's won. They don't have to be perfect. They don't have to be the almighty money maker just as long as they can grasp the gospel. I've seen so many kids grow up and forget about what Mom has done. If they grasp the gospel, that won't happen. I expect a family to be close and caring, but sometimes it doesn't work. Right now I'm working with Danny on his study habits. I would like to have had someone behind me like I am behind Danny. I would have had a much better knowledge of the church and the gospel and very possibly a different job than I have. If I had been a better student I would have come up with a job where I didn't have to do as much physical work. I've been blessed, but I would have liked to have been a little more intelligent.

I started at Chrysler on the assembly line in the chassis department—the underside of the car, the engine, the frame, brakes, wheels. I spent twelve or thirteen of my twenty years there in the pool. If a man didn't show up, I did his job. I learned a lot of jobs. I was a foreman for seven months in 1977, but I didn't like it because the way people do things at Chrysler is not what I think a good church member should be doing. It's a lot of cussing, a lot of not caring, and a lot of pressure. If you're a foreman you're in the middle between the company and the union. No way are you right. I went back in the pool. I had a bone spur on my right foot and the pool jobs take a lot of twisting and turning. I decided to give it up and I have a regular job on the line now. I take the starter out of the box, hook on the battery cable, put on a heat shield with a clamp, then put it in the engine and put on a nut so it will stay on. I have approximately fifty-one seconds to complete it and put it on the car. I keep quite busy, but it's not very stimulating. In the pool, I had many different jobs and I ended up being substitute foreman a lot. I've learned a lot of things, gotten to know a lot of people.

At the plant we have thirty or forty robots doing the work. All you do is stick in a card and off it goes. The only time it needs any maintenance is when the tips need to be replaced. There are two different lines and the noise is deafening—sparks flying everywhere. Automation and computers are fascinating.

Matt Burke is a product of the *Reader's Digest* inserts and me walking down an aisle. Matt was talking to another guy who said, "That guy's a Mormon. Come here." I thought, "Oh, here we go on another religious discussion." I had my lunch in my hand. I talked to him for a few minutes and I went back to my job. I was supposed to get some pamphlets on Sunday and bring them to Matt on Monday. I had this burning feeling inside that I should get those pamphlets today and get them up there. I did. I also lied. I had to overrule my promise not to send any missionaries because of the way Matt and Clara were acting. I told the missionaries not to tell Matt and Clara that I had sent them. When you see a golden person, somebody who's ready for the gospel, you don't walk away from it.

For three or four months now, we've been visiting different families to find out whether they want to have home teachers. I ran across one man who I knew on my mission. He had Hodgkin's disease or something of that sort. He told me the missionaries blessed him and the disease disappeared. I remember going in and blessing him. He has said he wants his name taken off the records of the church. We sat and talked for a good half hour as if we were buddies of old, yet he has no use for the church.

That man upstairs has been guiding me all my life. I was out on the street since I was a young kid. I've been on my own all my life. I could have been dead by now or in some sort of trouble—murder, robbery, drugs, or anything—except that I was in contact with the church all this time. It doesn't say it in the Bible, nor has a bolt of lightning put it on the wall that the Church of Jesus Christ of Latter-day Saints is true, but I have a burning faith and knowledge that it is true. I've never lost a loved one, never had to ask God, "Why did you do this?" I've never been tested. More than anything, I've been guided.

If society were to structure itself like the church—the welfare programs, the tithing, the Word of Wisdom, working with the people—it would be better. I think society could learn from us. Some people joke about our radio stations and cattle farms, but they're not reading between the lines. We're just taking care of ourselves. The structure of the church tries to build young people—teaches them to grow, how to work, how to study. I'm prejudiced as far as the church is concerned, but I feel that if you get a couple of Mormons working somewhere you can see the difference because of the way they act.

Janean Parsons, 28

Janean Parsons is the camp director for the stake Young Women's organization and is responsible for planning and running the annual girls' camp each summer. During their four-day stay, the teenage girls learn and demonstrate their knowledge of various camping skills as they advance through four ranks. Like Sharon Morris and Jean Harding, Janean Parsons spent her teenage years in the Wilmington Ward. She met her husband at BYU and they lived in Utah until moving to Delaware in 1983. Her three daughters are three, four, and five years old.

In high school I played hockey, basketball, and ran track. I like volleyball, too, but it's at the same time as hockey. Our track team went to state every year. My parents figured sports were for boys, not for girls, until I got a full scholarship to BYU. All of a sudden it was okay. Even now I play on a hockey team. I was in high school when girls' sports were first considered to be as important as the boys'. We got the first new uniforms in fifteen years. I'm not a women's libber, but I think the equality of women's sports is an important change.

At BYU Daris was my home teacher. We got engaged a month after we met and married in the Washington Temple four months after that. Life's a little more hectic than I thought it was going to be. Since we've been married we've had financial problems, a lot of medical problems with the kids. The employment situation wasn't good in Utah and Daris wanted to go back to school, so my dad said, "Come out here and you can live with us while Daris goes to school." It didn't quite work out that way.

I worked up until two weeks ago as a bookkeeper. I realized that I was only spending three hours at home with my girls. It was always, "Hurry up and eat your breakfast, we've got to go to the bank" or "Hurry up and eat your dinner so you can go to bed." I decided it was better to be at home and not have so much to do. At least the kids know they have a mother.

We play games a lot. We play Duck, Duck, Goose about ten times a day. Sometimes we read books. Now Daris is going to school, he's not home a lot, so having family home evening is a challenge. Because the kids are little, we have very short lessons and long activities. I look forward to Sundays. I think the kids dread Sunday because they know they can't go outside and play, but I look forward to it because it's different than any other day of the week.

My parents are quite upset that we're expecting a fourth child right now, but they'll get over it. The Lord won't send you any more children than you can handle financially or emotionally, so I feel I can leave it up to the Lord. This space between our youngest child and the new baby is longer than any of the others.

Jane Whitney was the only student who came to early morning seminary this year. When we talked to her and got a response that we wanted or when we could see that she was touched by the Spirit it was very rewarding. Our girls had to get up at the same time as we did because we had to go to work right after seminary. Getting them up at 5:30 in the morning to have breakfast before seminary wasn't easy for them or for us.

I always admired my advisers in the Young Women's program. They were the ones I looked up to. I enjoy working with the teenagers. Last year was my first year as stake girls' camp director. I went into it feeling apprehensive. When the girls told me what a good time they had, it was very satisfying to know that what I had planned had actually worked out.

We had one problem at camp last year. Two girls went over to a boys' camp and were gone about four hours. The priesthood leaders at camp gave me some advice, but I didn't like it. I stayed up that whole night praying. I knew no one would like the answer when I got it, but I told them, "This is the way it's going to be."

I sent one of the girls home, and the other one stayed. When I got home, the bishop of the girl called me and yelled at me and told me off. Then he called back a couple of months later and told me that this girl had written an apology to me. He said that he thought it was a turning point in her life because she had realized that maybe she couldn't do everything she wanted to do. He thought it had worked out the best for her. The other girl was inactive. If I had sent her home, we'd never have seen her again. At the time I didn't know their personal situations, but I knew I had to go by the Lord.

❀   ❀   ❀

Scouting plays a major role in the lives of the boys in the ward. This year Danny Mullins and Craig Morris both achieved the rank of Eagle, Scouting's highest level. Their joint Court of Honor was held in March. Kenneth McVicker, the Young Men's president, conducted the court. Elders Steenstra and Oldroyd gave the prayers. Rodney Hearne, Craig's grandfather, spoke about great men in American history who were Eagle Scouts and Stephen Cherry about the history of Varsity Scouting in the Elkton Ward. Roy Queenan gave the charge to the Eagle Scouts, and Gary Johnston narrated a slide show tracing the path to Eagle Scout. Danny and Craig had selected Anita, a popular disc jockey from Philadelphia, to be their invited dignitary to introduce the speakers and present the awards. All the boys seemed at first to be more excited about the appearance of Anita in her limousine and Arvie Wrang's new IROC Z than the Court of Honor. The Court of Honor was a memorable event for the Scout leaders as well as for the boys and their families.

Roy Queenan, 42

Except for a stint in the Sunday school presidency, Roy Queenan has worked with the youth of the Elkton Ward either as a Sunday school teacher or as the Varsity Scout leader. Originally from Ambler, Pennsylvania, he graduated from Lincoln University and is a representative for a pharmaceutical company. He and his wife and two sons joined the church in 1982.

My father was a farmer and a construction worker. There were twelve of us children, seven boys. Each of us had his own minifarm. One brother had a goat, someone else had a cow, and I had a lamb. My mother used to get furious because we started our chickens in the house. My mother was a domestic worker. Saturdays were very special days for us because mother worked just half a day.

My father became a mountain of a man on certain issues. We were not permitted to use profanity in the house. You would lose your teeth if you ever said "Shut up" to anyone. We were not allowed to call anyone a liar because his concept was "No man is a liar. He may not tell you what you want to hear, but he is never a liar until you prove what he has said is false."

If I forgot to slop the hogs, my father said, "Well, go slop them now."

"It's dark and I don't want to go down there." The hogs stayed a good distance from the house.

"It's your job. You will go down in the dark."

"Alone?"

"Yes." After I did it once or twice in the dark, I didn't forget. I don't think we give the kids those learning experiences today.

The major upset of my life was the death of my father when I was eighteen. When I wanted to quit school, he had come up to the campus one Sunday to talk to me. He said, "Your life will change if you stay here." After his death my mother said, "You have to stay in school because that's what your father wanted."

For the past several years I've worked with the National Alliance for Business—the Youth Motivation Task Force. We try to make underprivileged and disadvantaged youth aware of job opportunities and of the skills required for them. At the college level we try to make minority youth more aware of the professions—engineering and psychology, as well as medicine and law. Back in the fifties the only way a member of a minority group could succeed was as a teacher, a doctor, a lawyer, or a preacher. We attempt to show them that that era is gone.

Shortly after my wife and I set our wedding date in 1967, I got a draft notice. I didn't think that it was wise to get married. Calva had a brother in Vietnam; she didn't need the additional strain of having a husband there, too. After I had less than a year left, I said, "Okay, now we can get married. There's a very slim chance that I'll go to Vietnam." I went to Germany alone. She didn't want to fly and there was no bridge.

I had no desire to be an officer. When I was interviewed for a job, I said I wanted to be a cook. The sergeant said, "I think the colonel should talk to you." The colonel reviewed my test scores and said, "There's no way in the world we can allow you to be a cook. You should be an officer." We went back and forth, and he finally said, "We'll have to put you someplace where you will not cause trouble." That was the medical service corps. I became immersed in medicine. When I got out of the service I sought employment in the area of science and medicine.

Being involved in something that is beneficial to man is very satisfying to me. I get excited when we come out with a product that makes a difference. Three years ago we introduced a drug that significantly increases the life expectancy of people on dialysis. It's exciting, too, convincing someone to think the way I think. In the hospitals, though, I see and hear stories that you just wouldn't believe. When I was in the service, nothing bothered me. I was very callous. Now when I see people who die or become maimed for a life as a result of their lack of concern for themselves, I get very upset.

After completing college, I decided that I wanted to go into the ministry, which struck my in-laws very favorably. My father-in-law was the chairman of the board of a church in the African Union Methodist Conference. It just so happened that the church in Ambler needed an assistant pastor, so I went to the African Union school of religion and was the assistant pastor in Ambler. After two years I became a circuit preacher. Then my father-in-law said, "We could use you as an assistant pastor at our church." I never did actually take the assignment, but I did help the pastor whenever I had a Sunday free.

After three, three and a half years in the ministry, I became very discouraged because of what happens behind the scenes—the deals that were made by the trustees. I'll never forget the last sermon that I preached in Elkton: "There will be peace in the valley." My concluding statement was there will be peace in the valley even if I'm the only one there. I just didn't want to be a part of the aggravation that went on in the church. An apology was demanded, and I absolutely refused to apologize.

For approximately four years my wife and I could not come to an agreement as to what church we would attend. My father-in-law said, "If you just walk away from it like that, you weren't called." I said, "You're probably right." I didn't know it, but many of my beliefs were in line with Mormon doctrine, though I had never studied it. I began to study non-Christian religions. I was studying the Book of Mormon as non-Christian scripture. I was baffled because I could not find anything that was not Christian in nature. Then two young men knocked at the door and said, "Hi, we're from the Church of Jesus Christ of Latter-day Saints." When I presented this problem to them, they informed me that the Mormon church is a Christian church.

The first discussion that they gave me was the plan of salvation. After that discussion, I said, "You guys are absolutely right."

You can imagine the looks I got. "What do you mean we're absolutely right?"

I said "I know of the preexistence." I had gotten a number of whippings as a child by talking about the preexistence. In Bible Club, there was no preexistence. I did not believe in a heaven and a hell as my church defined them, the hellfire and brimstone and the streets of gold and so forth. My father-in-law had cautioned me, "Don't ever say that in church." When the missionaries talked about outer darkness and the celestial kingdom and the fact that each and every one of us has a purpose in life, I recognized them as truths. I said, "This is it. I've found what I wanted. This is the church we're supposed to join."

My wife said, "You don't really believe that."

I said, "Indeed I do. My studying the Book of Mormon and the Mormon missionaries happening by and discussing the beliefs that I was afraid to voice are circumstances too strong to be a coincidence."

My mother-in-law said, "If that's what he wants to do, let him, but you and the boys shouldn't have anything to do with that." I said, "Your mother has nothing to say about the boys. They're my children and they will be raised in this church. You're free and you're responsible. If you want to pay the consequences, go ahead." This has created a horrendous conflict within my wife. She tries to please both of us and can't. I've told the missionaries that they may not try to recruit her back into the church. She's never left the church; she's just dealing with conflict right now. The minute she says to her parents, "I am going with my family," I know everything will be totally solidified.

I do things for the church that I would not do for a friend. I would not drive my truck through the woods, hauling wood, for instance, for an everyday type friend, but I do for the church.

We've lived in Newark about twelve years. Newark has a lot of the things that we wanted as an atmosphere to raise the children in. We wanted to live in a professional or semiprofessional neighborhood. I enjoy watching my boys grow. I often think, "I hope I'm here to see their children, to meet their wives, to just see what they do with their lives." I often wonder if my father sees what his offspring are doing. We have fewer children and more material goods than I grew up with, but not the happiness that I remember as a youth. I'm not saying that my boys are not happy boys, but they cannot find anything to do. I have to dive on them and say, "Why don't you go play with your computer?" The imaginative spirit is missing. We could go sit on a tractor that didn't move and have a field day.

I enjoy working with the youth in church. I've seen enough of life that I can save the youth from a lot of heartache, if they'll listen. I believe that a fifteen-, sixteen-, seventeen-year-old can still be a good Latter-day Saint. Working with the youth in our ward has proven that to me. We've gone to concerts together. I don't think the youth need to be deprived of going to concerts because of what happens there. I think my little experiment has proven that our youth can go into that environment to enjoy the concert and not the other things that are going on.

I'm not trying to raise anyone's children, but I like it when the youth come to me to discuss their problems. I get a great deal of satisfaction when I can say, "It's obvious that you disagree with your parents, but let's look at it from a different perspective." They'll say, "Well, I don't agree, but I understand." A lot of people get the wrong impression; they think I agree with the youth. It's not so much that I agree, it's that I say to them, "If you are unwilling to look at the problem from the father's or mother's perspective, then you're being unfair."

Sometimes I would like to go to some of the parents and say, "You're creating a monster" or "Why don't you start talking to your child?" I can't do that. I don't think most of our parents are sophisticated enough to accept that their child discussed a problem with an outsider. If someone came to me and said one of my sons had talked to him instead of to me, I would be upset. That's one of the doors I try always to keep open even if they have to swing from the chandelier just to get the problem out.

Much of what I tell the youth I have to apply to myself. That has given me an opportunity to take a better look at myself. I believe that the sixteen-year-old priest is on a par with me, spiritually. The elder who is younger than I is spiritually much wiser. That's what makes it important to advance in the priesthood. I want to advance to elder and to make my first temple trip.

For my own peace of mind I needed to know about the plan of salvation. Repentance and the miracle of forgiveness are very important—especially in talking to some of the young people. Repentance is the only eraser we have in life. If we're not sincere, it comes right back up. It is very important to know that there is a mechanism by which we can cast our weakness out.

Martin Luther King was a big influence in my life. Even though he was not a Latter-day Saint, I do believe that he was a prophet. I justify that by going back into the older scriptures. Not all the prophets were from the same house and they each carried a different message. Spencer W. Kimball is the prophet, seer, and revelator of this church. Martin Luther King was a prophet like Moses and he was charged with leading the tribe to the promised land, just as Moses was. That promised land is desegregation, equal housing, equal employment, etc. When this started to come about, then Spencer Kimball had his revelation that said all males could have the priesthood. Moses led the tribe to the Promised Land, but he never went in with them. Martin Luther King led minorities to the promised land and never got in. It's very natural that Spencer Kimball's revelation followed. I don't think President Kimball was waiting for Martin Luther King to do something so that he would have this revelation; it just all occurred in its natural order.

Stephen Cherry, 36

As the first Varsity coach of the Elkton Branch, Stephen Cherry was well qualified to speak on the history of Scouting in the Elkton Ward. The youth programs were the last Elkton Branch programs to become independent of the New Castle Ward. Of the six boys who belonged to the first Elkton Varsity Scout Troop, Danny Mullins and Craig Morris are the fifth and sixth to become Eagle Scouts. Stephen and his wife, Bonita, were baptized in September 1977 shortly before the Elkton Branch was officially organized. The father of two children, Stephen has been a member of the stake high council since 1982. His duties on the high council include being the adviser to the seminary programs in the Wilmington Stake as well as first counselor in the stake Young Men's presidency.

In high school I was president of the Future Farmers of America club, and then I was state vice-president of the FFA. I went to the University of Delaware to study agriculture. After I received my associate's degree, I worked on a ranch in Texas for about a year. It was probably the best time of my single life.

The ranch had fifty thousand head of sheep, nine thousand head of cattle, and twenty-seven thousand acres. I harvested five thousand acres of wheat with the combine. I knew I would have to have a lot of money to own my own ranch, so I gave it up and came back. I worked at a gas station for a while, then I was an estimator for a contractor. I should have given as much effort to my school work as I did to not making any effort. I was a B student, but I never studied. I'm a good writer, I think, but I'm bad at grammar. When I send something out to a bishop or a Young Men's president, it bothers me because I know something's not right in that letter.

I met my wife, Bonita, when I was working at the gas station. I was working on her car, and I asked her out. Before her, I never dated anybody for more than three or four months.

I've been working on the loading docks at Avon for about seven years. A year ago Avon first approached me about going into management. I was a happy, proud, blue-collar worker, like Archie Bunker. I had always been able to speak my mind toward management. Other people looked to me to indicate how to react to a policy decision. About a year ago, I starting feeling that I needed to start using my mind rather than just my body. I have been doing that in my church responsibilities. About four months ago, I began interviews with the twelve department heads. Now I'm waiting for a position to open up.

During my interviews, I told them of my responsibilities in the church. They were impressed with the responsibilities I had in church and in the Boy Scout program. At the beginning they stressed the importance of having a four-year college degree. By the end of this three-month period, they emphasized that I need not worry about having just an associate's degree because of my church experience.

A year after I had this house built, one day while I was working in the yard, Bonita was talking to two young persons, who I thought might be insurance agents. While Bonita was talking to them, she had said, "If you're going to get Stephen interested at all, you're going to have to overcome the fact that he thinks people who go to church are hypocrites. Stress that just because you pray for something it doesn't necessarily mean you're going to get it." As we talked out on the back porch, they hit those points real quick.

We went to the New Castle Ward at first. About two and a half months after we began receiving instruction, we were told about a meeting over at Cloyd Mullins's on Sunday afternoons. I had envisioned a Bible study group sitting around talking about scriptures, but it was a full sacrament meeting with tape-recorded piano music and about twenty people.

When the missionaries said that I shouldn't smoke a pipe, I was concerned. I asked to see the bishop because I didn't want to stop smoking. It took about three weeks to get the appointment. By that time I knew we were going to join the church. The appointment was at ten o'clock. I smoked my pipe at nine. I told Bishop Cross of my concerns about that and tithing. We spoke for a while, and he asked, "Have you stopped smoking?"

I said, "Yes, Bishop, I've stopped." I haven't smoked since. We were ready. We knew the church was going to be good for us. It wasn't any problem to stop smoking. I still have my pipe in the house. Every once in a while I smell it and hold it.

The Elkton Branch was a typical struggling branch. We lost some members because of their having so many callings and responsibilities, but it tested our mettle. It made us appreciative of our responsibilities. The buck didn't stop at someone else; it stopped at us. I think the members who stayed grew from those experiences. I think a lot of those who fell away have regrets, but their pride is in their way.

As a ward, we seem to have lost that "buck stops here" attitude. A lot of the parents don't support the youth programs as they should. That's true throughout the stake. The uniqueness of the Elkton Ward is that we have a variety of people, but we're respectful of each other. We appreciate each other. I don't notice that we have cliques. I don't hear much backbiting here in Elkton. We're a good little ward as far as having basic decency towards other human beings.

I'd like to see us do ward projects, fund-raisers, instead of having budget assessments. Maybe it's an idealistic approach. I pay a full tithing and I feel good about that, but I don't like to put out extra money for the ward maintenance and not make an effort. There's effort in the Easter egg project, but it's not a total commitment.

I remember telling Bonita just before we joined the church, "I hope I never have to deal with all those young people because I wouldn't know how to handle that." I was called as Young Men's president in the Elkton Branch about a year after my baptism. The first Sunday I asked Scott McAlees and Jimmy Andrews, George's son, "What does it take to be a good adviser? I have no idea. I want you to tell me."

They said, "You have to be honest with us and care about us and get us to do things." That was my basis for my work with the Young Men. When the boundaries were changed, we had more young men. There were six deacons who were terrors. They were soon going to become teachers, and I had to teach them. I went to the Boy Scout council to see if they had any sort of program for the older boys because these six boys were losing interest in Scouting. They said there was a new program called Varsity Scouting and that our district was one of nineteen that had been selected to pilot the program. We chartered the first Varsity Scout Team in the Delmarva Council. We had to play it by ear a lot. It was a nice program because it taught delegation and gave the boys leadership opportunities. We did all kinds of things. We went to Florida. Danny Mullins, Craig Morris, Tommy Young, Bentley Stanton, and Steve Whitney became Eagle Scouts and we reactivated Arvie Wrang. Serge Bushman earned one merit badge with us, but he earned his Eagle in the New Castle Ward.

The day I was released as Young Men's president I had an eighteen-month calendar, and I was ready for an easy time because three of the boys had become Eagles and we were planning all kinds of neat things to do after that. I didn't like being called to the high council because I enjoyed working with the young men. I didn't feel that I should be on the high council. It took two years to overcome that insecurity. When President Johnson called me to it, he charged me to develop Varsity Scouting in all the wards and branches. It took three years, but this September every ward had a chartered team. About two weeks ago President Johnson told me, "We called you on the advice of the regional representative. He said that we needed someone in that position who had worked with the program and had been successful." He knew of my bitterness at being released as Young Men's president and said, "We gave up one Young Men's president, but we gained a person who has developed five Varsity coaches."

Being first counselor in the stake Young Men's presidency requires a lot of time going to wards and branches evaluating programs and building a rapport. A person on the high council goes into a ward and says, "This is what you need," but not too many bishops do it. Everything is developing this year. The bishops have called excellent seminary teachers. They've called very capable brethren to be Varsity coaches and Teachers' Quorum advisers. I'm in the same position now as I was when I propped my feet up on the table and had that eighteen-month calendar.

When I need to do something better, I'll agonize over it for two or three months, or six months, but then I master what I was trying to do. When that point comes, it's a complete change. It's happened four times since I joined the church. The first one was overcoming society and becoming LDS. The next was being branch clerk. I've been a very outspoken person, never very humble. I agonized over some of the things that I saw being done in the branch. Even though I had only been a member for a couple of months, I thought they were wrong. I just woke up one morning and became the way I felt a branch clerk was supposed to be. That humbled me and has helped me at church and home, not worrying about every little thing.

The third was agonizing over not having children. That was a four-year torment. Bonita would cry at Mother's Day and Christmas. Near the end, before we got Shiloh, I was the one who was weak and she was strong. I asked for a priesthood blessing. I had exercised all the other options. I'd only received one other blessing, right after the explosion. I knew the journey was just about ended, but I was worn out. Four months later we got word about Shiloh. I learned that blessings do come for those who work for them. I learned about the priesthood when I received a blessing after the explosion at Avon. I received miracles and the assurance of the Holy Ghost.

The fourth time was this past summer. I felt inferior to the people around me. I agonized over that for a long time. I prayed and went about my responsibilities as best I could, even though something was missing. I have never asked to be released. That's not the way out. Then I just woke up one morning without that feeling. That's when things started clicking with the institute and seminary programs.

If I had to see my Heavenly Father right now I would say I'm failing miserably in missionary work. I just don't have any desire to do it like I should. I give presentations on Varsity Scouting to civic organizations—Kiwanis, police athletic leagues, Catholic church administrators. The first thing I say is that this is an LDS-originated program. All the Delmarva Council knows that Steve Cherry's LDS. I'm spreading the word that way, but I have never given a Book of Mormon to one of my co-workers. I need to sit down and analyze it. This might be the next thing I'll break through on.

As I was growing up, I never remember anybody in our home saying "I love you." To develop a strong family and to communicate with our children is very important to me and to Bonita. We have a purpose and an eternal goal. We have family council once a week. We have a little bit of family home evening with the children, then we go into our family council meeting. We ask each other five questions. How do we feel about our family? Do we feel we have a good family? Do we do things together? Do we support one another? We give positive examples. Bonita and I feel it's very important that a family has a good strong sense of itself as a family. We rate the previous week's family self-esteem, like eighty or ninety, or whatever. Then we say, "I appreciate." Bonita says she appreciates something I did the week before and I say something that I appreciated and our children do the same thing.

We also write down what happened to the children the week before. I type it up about every three months. Most of the stuff comes from Bonita. She's teaching them to love one another and to be kind and to forgive one another. A babysitter wouldn't take the time to do that, so I'm glad my wife isn't working full-time. The job that she has, she can do right here. We're strapped, but it's worth it.

Bonita was hot on genealogy. She bought me a $9.98 book of remembrance kit. I stuck it away somewhere. She nagged me for two years to do something so I decided to write one letter and when I had nobody left to write to, I'd stop. In three years I wrote about six hundred letters. I got information from twenty-seven different relatives. This book of remembrance goes back to 1480. I wrote first to a fellow named Don Cherry, a professor at Juniata College in western Pennsylvania, and he gave me some information. I worked three years on this and I did seventy-two endowments in the temple and sixty-one sealings.

I feel that our church is a church on the offense. We score points. We are not trying to play catch-up. Thursday night Ron Adamson and I drove down to Salisbury. There are only six seminary students there. But if we hadn't, we would have been on the defensive because they would have said, "Well, you know, they didn't come." That is what keeps Steve Cherry going. Either I'm on the offense or defense with my family. Do I anticipate things or am I always trying to play catch-up? I have a little book where I write down things to follow-up. I can be anywhere when a solution to a problem comes to me.

We've escaped the turbulent sixties and the experimentations of the seventies. Our church builds leaders and this world needs leaders to help their own families. I think we're going to see (I'm surprised we haven't seen it yet) great growth in this church if we maintain our standards. We seem to attract the downtrodden a lot now. I think there's going to be a time where being a Latter-day Saint is going to be the thing to do. People are going to want to be a part of this.

Kenneth McVicker, 39

The Young Men's president, Kenneth McVicker, is responsible for the success of several overlapping programs. He is chair of the Scout troop committee, which oversees both the Boy Scouts and the Varsity Scouts. He and his counselors and the Young Women's presidency are jointly responsible for all the ward's youth activities as well as helping the youth attend activities planned by the Wilmington Stake. Kenneth often teaches the Priests' Quorum—whenever their adviser has to work on Sunday. In the fourteen years since Kenneth joined the church he has not only served as a counselor to Bishop Bushman but as Elders' Quorum president of the New Castle Ward and on the high council of the Wilmington Stake. The McVicker family became charter members of the Elkton Branch when it was organized in July 1978. An airplane inspector for the Delaware National Guard, he is the father of four children, ages seven to fourteen.

I was born in West Virginia and raised in Baltimore. My father was a steel worker and was killed at work when I was thirteen. When my father died, my mother had to work. When she remarried, I told her not to because it was too late to give my sister and me a father. My half-sister was born when I was sixteen. I had to bathe her, feed her, walk her, and put her in bed. Then I let her cry while I did my homework.

I always had one problem in school, a problem I overcame when I became a member of the church—reading. I didn't do badly in history and English literature, but I could not read out loud. I think it was because my mother smoked and drank before I was born. My father had an education and realized how important it was. He made a deal with the fifth-grade teacher. He said, "If he reads this book and passes the test, will you pass him? I will make sure that he passes the next year." I started reading on Friday night. That history book was two inches thick. I read the entire book that weekend, stopping only to eat or sleep. I passed the test. After that he monitored what I was doing.

I think the time I grew up in was as good a time as any. There weren't any wars; you didn't have to worry about gas shortages. It was exactly like *Happy Days*. Right across the road was a place like Arnold's. You walked in and the juke box was playing and the kids were dancing. They would dance before school. We had dances on Friday nights at the Teen Center. If you had alcohol there they threw you out. They had a place where you could smoke. The boys who were ahead of me in school had trouble. It seemed like the police were always nearby. Those guys were always drinking and carrying on. That group was more of a gang. They would actually fight—chains, bottles, and everything else. We weren't into that kind of stuff.

I left home when I was eighteen to go into the service. I had started going to business college at the University of Baltimore. It was too expensive and too far to drive, too difficult to find a parking place. I learned to be an airplane mechanic when I was in the air force.

Working with airplanes, I cannot afford to have bad habits. I'm able to change the habits of the other mechanics by not accepting their work. I try to do it in a way that's not nasty or critical, and they respect that. They know that my standards are whatever the engineering standards are, and that's it. I don't back down once I've made up my mind. In a couple of situations they've gone above me. I said, "Okay, you accept the safety features of this problem. Once you do that, I'm relieved of all responsibility if the airplane crashes or anything happens to it." If I had to do it over again, I would go into engineering. Sometimes I work with the engineers, and I like solving problems.

I resisted becoming a member of the church for about a year. I told June's family I would join the church when I was ready. After we were married, June had a home teacher, Keith Wilhoit. Every time I turned around, he was stopping by for a drink of water or inviting me to play basketball or something. He asked me if I wanted to take a special group of lessons—missionary discussions is what they were. I finally decided to join the church about a year after we were married.

The church is a hobby if you like your calling in the church. It's a challenge. I feel most satisfied when I help somebody solve a problem that can't be solved or help him do something that he can't do. I've had cases where people had large problems. They told me they wouldn't be home teachers. I thanked them for being honest about it. Several months later they came around and said, "I'll home teach now." They became terrific home teachers. Home teaching is one of the best things in the church. It is the part of our religion where we are forced into (though we shouldn't have to be) loving our neighbor.

The best calling I had was being priesthood leader of the Elkton Branch. Everybody in the group was dedicated to the church—in just about every way. We only had thirty-five families, and thirty-two of them were active. Even though everybody had three or four callings, it didn't seem like a problem. Everybody worked together.

There's an education in having a calling in the church. I've heard a couple of bishops who have Ph.D.'s and master's degrees say they have never learned as much anywhere as they have in the church. You learn a little bit about accounting because of financial problems. You learn about psychological problems. You get drawn into everything that's involved in life.

I picked a man to be my counselor when I was Elders' Quorum president. The stake president and the bishop didn't want him. I went over the list a hundred times and prayed about it. I didn't want anybody else. I said, "That's the answer I got. There's a reason behind it. I don't understand it all right now, but I think it's going to work out." He did a terrific job. He had never had anything in his church life that was that important, and he just answered the call.

The most satisfying thing as Young Men's president is working directly with the kids—not standing up in front of them as a leader but working with them. When I'm able to encourage them to do things and they see how good it is— that's what is satisfying. It's disheartening when they don't even try. My philosophy is no matter how hard something is, don't give up. I feel that way because I gave up a couple of times in my life when I shouldn't have.

Thomas Young, 40

Thomas Young became a member of the Elkton Branch when the boundaries were enlarged in 1980 and he was called to be the scoutmaster. His son, Tom, received his Eagle Scout in 1982 at the age of fifteen. His daughter, Debbie, son-in-law William Meekins III, and his grandson William Meekins IV are also members of the Elkton Ward. Now a member of the Sunday school presidency, Thomas supervises several Sunday school teachers.

When I first joined the church it was very difficult. It probably took four years before I got mingled in. When they first asked us to leave the New Castle Ward to go to Elkton, I just about went up the wall because all I could think about was starting over. We had to say, "If that's what you want, we'll go," but I was very uncomfortable about it.

When we changed from a branch to a ward, for some reason they released the branch president and named another person as bishop. I don't think it was fair because this branch president had made the branch grow from nothing.

I was born with a learning disability. I can't spell and I can barely read. Growing up, what was I going to do when I had to go out and work was always in the back of my mind. Reading has been a problem as I knew it would, but I never thought I would have a house this big or new cars. I have spent a lot of hours and worked a lot of double shifts to have what we have. I'd say that I have done very well considering everything.

I've spent the last couple of years trying to find a way around my reading problem. Nobody can tell by looking at me that I have a reading disability. There's something wrong with the left side of my brain. I can learn, but I can't retain. I took me years and years to find this out. I went to night school four times and brought my reading level up to the seventh-grade level. Four weeks later I was back down to fourth-grade level. I went to see a specialist for learning disabilities and I took a very expensive test. She said there's nothing that can be done at my age. If it had been caught when I was young, there was a possibility—then she said I'm the poorest case she has ever seen. When I got an answer to why I couldn't read, it wasn't the most encouraging thing, but it was an answer. I could stop searching.

I quit school in the ninth grade. I had failed twice up to then. All I can figure out is that they knew there was a problem but they didn't know what to do about it. After I failed first and second grade, they just passed me year after year until I hit the seventh grade. I ran into problems there. They tried to send me to special classes, but it was too late. I was so frustrated, I wasn't interested in learning.

I used to be a printer. I did engraving and silk-screen printing. I moved up to the photographic printing, dry transfer. We photographically put designs on a steel cylinder. Then we took them out and put them on a press. It was interesting—something I could learn by doing. It was a very technical field. I was very satisfied until I got laid off three times in a month.

I got tired of being laid off, so I went to General Motors and started there at a dollar an hour more than I was making before. It's not the most ideal place to work, but I make fairly good money for what I do there. It's boring as heck. It's the same thing day after day. It's hard to find Christian-type people there, although there are some who are very born-again Christians. I'm worried about what General Motors is going to do next. We'll be shut down for six months while they completely automate the plant. The high-tech could be a problem for me, but I've already talked to someone about that. Years ago I had a real interest in computers, which is something I know I could never work with.

Edna and I agreed when we got married that she would work. There were times when Edna didn't want to work, and she didn't. She found out that if there was no work, there was no money. I think there's been a change in the church's attitudes, but I don't think anybody's changed the basic policy of the church. A lot more women are working now than fifteen years ago. If you are going to send five or six kids to college, somebody had better work. Even a guy who has a doctor's degree is not going to make enough money to do it.

I do have quite a few hobbies. I run a lot. I've been running a race every weekend, but I'm going to stop competing. I damaged my knee pretty badly training for the Marine Corps marathon. I'm getting ready to do a one-hundred-mile cycling trip in two weeks. I also lift weights. I start work at 6:30, so I get up between 4:00 and 4:45. The bishop says I should give up some of my hobbies and do more church work!

I have problems with church callings, not because I don't want to do them but because I don't have the ability. People don't understand why I won't do certain things in church. I get tired of explaining it. I think temple work is important, but there are reasons why people can't do it. They'll give me a name that's twenty-five letters long. By the time I get through the session I still can't say it. I've had a couple of pretty embarrassing things happen to me. I didn't do something perfectly right and they said, "It's got to go through again." It took me two hours to drive down there and an hour and a half to go through this and you're telling me you're not going to accept it? Even they couldn't pronounce the name.

I think the priesthood is a very positive thing. I probably don't use it as much as I should. When Tom got his face bashed in by a neighbor boy, Debbie took him to the hospital because Edna and I were both at work. I gave him a blessing as soon as I got to the hospital. When Debbie was in a head-on collision, Rufus and I administered to her right before the doctor put forty-six stitches in between her eye and her eyebrow. I'm glad that I have it.

I'm now the first counselor in the Sunday school. If the teachers show up and do their jobs so I don't have to find substitutes, I'm satisfied. When Brother Tingey isn't there, I have to watch out for his teachers, too. The second counselor is new and doesn't know what he's doing yet. Each of us is supposed to worry about his own group of teachers, but it doesn't always work that way. The first thing I do when I walk into sacrament meeting is to look around and see who is there.

I used to have problem with home teaching, but I don't anymore. I have good families for a change. When I first joined the church, Don O'Day and I went home teaching. I never will forget one family although I never met them. They would tell us to come over, but they wouldn't answer the door. We went every month and knocked on the door. We could hear them inside, but they wouldn't answer the door. I home teach the Peterson family. Their three little children are the neatest little kids I've ever seen. When the kids are glad to see you, it's a good sign. They look like monkeys climbing all over me. It isn't being active that makes a family good to visit. It's up to them if they want to be active. It means a lot to me if they are receptive.

I like to have a persistent home teacher, which we have not had very often. We had Brother Taber for about a year. I'm not saying that I get along with Brother Taber that great, but as a home teacher he is A-1. He was there every month, with or without his partner. He was interested in every person in the family. They change home teaching too often. Once you get a family's confidence it shouldn't be broken. If the next month you have someone you don't know, you think, "Forget it. You can come if you want, but I'm not going to tell you anything."

When my daughter, Debbie, was about fifteen, she didn't want to go to church. I said, "You are going anyway." She is now, even though she is married to a Mormon, inactive. Sometimes I blame myself because I made her go to everything except seminary whether she wanted to or not. I tried for a while to make her go to seminary then I said, "This is ridiculous. I'm ruining my whole day making her go to seminary." I accept part of the blame for her having negative feelings about the church.

Tom attends church on his own. Of course, he's tough to call in the morning. It's difficult for him because there are only two other kids in his class and they don't show up half the time. The church's Scouting program has helped him a lot. I think he has learned a lot. He got his Eagle. It took a little pushing at the time. I spent eight years in Scouting so he would get that Eagle. He had two merit badges to go and just stopped. I pushed him the rest of the way through. The church has kept him out of trouble. His girlfriend says he is pure Mormon. As far as she's concerned, no other religion exists. I think Tom's pretty well set in his ways. We'll find out once he gets to boot camp. He's going into the navy in September.

You have to give kids a chance to make decisions on their own sooner or later. Tom needs to get out on his own and not have Mom and Pop to rely on every time he gets into a little jam or argument. I gave him the choice: "You can go to college, to trade school, or the military."

I'm not convinced that every young man is cut out to be a missionary at the age of nineteen. Tom won't be going on a mission. He was brought up to go on a mission, but the final decision was left up to him. I could shoot myself for the way I laid out his choices, but anyway, I did it. Now we're going to stick by his decision. I think he can do a lot of good in the navy because he has the right background.

I don't think he's prepared to be a full-time missionary. He needs a lot of growing. If he would have gone to college for a year, he probably would have been ready. But he would have worked during the day and gone to Delaware Tech at night. After a year of that I don't think he would have wanted to go on a mission. After a kid starts making money he doesn't want to do anything else.

I don't hold it against anybody, but it irks me when people stand up there and say, "This is my son. He's going on a mission." It just eats my insides out. I've had people say, "My son is going on a mission. Why isn't yours?" We wanted it to be his decision because he's the one who is going to have to go through it.

It's not easy to have your youngest child leave home when you're only forty years old. Most people our age still have small kids. Sometimes we wish we'd had more, but with the things we had to go through we feel our family size was just right. Being married from age eighteen to now is quite a feat. Of the twenty guys I hung around with in school, there's only one other who is still married.

I need something to get me up past the plateau I'm on. I don't know what it is yet. When I took up running I went from running one block to a twenty-six-mile marathon. If I do any more I'll get damaged. I've taken up cycling, but I'm limited in that, too. I would like to study psychology, but I haven't figured out a way to do it yet. I'll find it eventually.

The Ward
10 | Conference

On February 17 the regular schedule of Sunday meetings was suspended; it was the Elkton Ward Conference, the day the Wilmington Stake presidency visits the Elkton Ward, reviewing the progress of the ward during the past year and exhorting the ward members to fulfill their duties more faithfully. Ward conference day is preceded by visits from the stake Relief Society, Primary, Young Men, Young Women, and Sunday school presidencies, who evaluate the ward's organizations.

During the first hour of the church day, the stake Relief Society president addressed the women about their duties and privileges as members of the Relief Society while one counselor in the stake presidency spoke to the adult men and the other to the youth. Primary was held as usual, and Sunday school was omitted from the schedule so that sacrament meeting could be extended to two hours. The choir sang, the brass ensemble played, and the stake president, Vernon Rice, and his two counselors spoke to the congregation.

After sacrament meeting the Relief Society served lunch to the ward presidencies, bishopric, and stake presidency. The afternoon was apportioned into half-hour meetings, during which ward presidencies met with a member of the stake presidency and the bishopric. After a prayer, the stake president or counselor asked how the ward leader felt about his or her calling as well as about various aspects of his or her stewardship, such as visiting teaching, compassionate service, Sunday school attendance, the number of boys in each quorum, and efforts being made to reach those who are inactive.

"The tone of the meetings was positive and warm. The purpose seems to be as much to build up the leaders as to give them directions," said Bishop Bushman. "The meetings also give the stake president a chance to show the ward leaders what concerns him most. Usually at the end of the day, the stake presidency spends an hour reviewing the status of the ward with the bishop and offering recommendations for improvements. There was no time for this last meeting because we had to hurry to inspect a proposed building site."

The stake presidency had been looking for property in the southwest part of Newark on which the church would build a new stake center that would also serve as the Elkton Ward chapel. A representative from the church's real estate office in Indianapolis would do the actual bargaining and make the final decision. The Wilmington Stake would pay 4 percent of the expected two-million-dollar cost of the building and land; the rest would be paid by the church from tithing funds.

Although relieved to be spending the hour outside in the balmy February weather, Bishop Bushman thought that if the critique had been offered, it might have been helpful. "I am somewhat inclined to be defensive about the ward. I feel that I do the best I can with not many really strong leaders. Many times stake leaders speak as if we bishops just insisted or developed our own testimonies of the program, we would get it all done. The fact is that it requires great effort to get the simple basics accomplished. President Rice, I believe, understands this. After all, he has a whole stake that does not set records for high percentages in anything. You can only develop real strength if you begin by acknowledging the realities. On the other hand, a reminder of a shortcoming here or there can be a spur to help us make a more vigorous effort that may improve our work."

Richard Bushman, 53

Richard Bushman, like all other Mormon bishops, leads a double life. A professor of history at the University of Delaware, he has just finished a six-year term as chair of his department. In addition to making sure that all the ward's leadership and teaching positions are filled and that each member has a calling, Bishop Bushman oversees the planning and funding of all ward activities, gives counsel to members who have problems, and gives material assistance from the bishop's storehouse or from fast offering funds to members in need.

A native of Utah, Richard grew up in Portland, Oregon, earned his undergraduate and graduate degrees from Harvard, and was on the faculties of Brigham Young University and Boston University. When he moved to Newark, Delaware, in 1977, he was released as president of the Boston Stake. Bishops are asked to serve for an indefinite term, usually three to five years; this is his third calling as a bishop.

I don't think I was fleeing Boston, but when I came down here just to look, it came over me that this was where I was to come. In the kind of work I do, the University of Delaware is a national center. There is no better place for training museum people and people who do material culture. It was professionally appealing, and it was a tremendous increase in salary.

Claudia had nothing good to say about the move. I said, "Well, let's discuss it." She said, "You've already decided. Why should we discuss it?" I was trying to make it a democratic decision, but it didn't work. As she would be the first to admit, it has worked out well for everyone.

I am working on two books, one on the Book of Mormon as history and my big book on gentility and respectability. The other things take care of themselves. The kids will go to college. They'll go on missions. The Lord's been very good to us financially and I just know all of that will be taken care of. I'm as far ahead in my career as I will ever be or care to be. I have a great concern that I have stored in me books that I won't write. I feel an urgency to get them out, and I feel the end of life approaching. I'm now measuring not how far I've come, but how far I have yet to go.

My father was called to be branch president for two years in a tiny branch in Portland, Oregon, the classic situation where we had to arrive at the meeting hall a half hour early to sweep out the cigarette butts. That was five stages more primitive than Elkton is. I taught Sunday school classes at age fourteen.

When my family moved closer to the center of Portland in the middle of my sophomore year, I felt like a wallflower. Many times I ate lunch all by myself because I didn't know anybody. I wasn't miserable, but I certainly didn't have any friends at school. In the high school there were maybe ten Mormons. They were as good friends as you could have, but I didn't see them much at school. We knew each other at church.

A couple of Mormons in this high school had been quite outstanding. One had been student body president. When I was a junior, a senior (among the Mormons) came to me and said, "You know, Bushy, you've got to run for student body president. Someone has to take over the Mormon tradition." He knew that I didn't know anyone. I wasn't in any clubs. I wasn't on any sports teams. I thought it was absolutely impossible, but when he said it was "my duty," that pressed the button.

I went home and prayed about it. I thought, "Well, I will do it for the honor of God." I said nothing about it to my parents. When I came down for breakfast on the morning of my campaign speech, my mother said, "What are you doing in that suit?" There was no campaign manager, no posters. If you were funny enough when you gave your talk to the school, you got elected. I'd had experience talking in church. The previous week I had thought a lot about the talk and tried to find jokes. I remember standing in the phone booth that very morning as my dad read me some jokes to add at the last minute.

My talk was pretty funny with a nice little twist at the end. The other guys had not prepared. I got a majority in the first round because the freshmen and sophomores voted for me.

That immediately thrust me into the center of life, and the faculty became aware of me. So, when the Harvard recruiter came around they thought of me. One day I was called out of class and asked to go downstairs with two or three other kids to meet the Harvard representative. This opened up a possibility in my senior year that I'd never thought of. When I was admitted and got a scholarship, I decided, as a lark, that I would do it.

When I arrived in Cambridge, the church had never built a building in New England. There were no chapels. The firesides and Mutual were held in the mission home and next door was a big house where Sunday school and sacrament meeting were held. There were three or four of us in each Harvard class—a total of ten or twelve in the whole college, plus some MIT students, and a number of graduate students. We all played basketball and were in one-act plays together. The undergraduates got together every Sunday afternoon and talked about the scriptures. We were all gung-ho Mormons. Cambridge was not a liberal atmosphere in the way you normally think of intellectual centers being. It was far less liberal than the University of Utah campus was in the early fifties. We've always felt good about sending our kids to Boston because we have a lot of confidence in that atmosphere.

The strong intellectual challenges came from the Harvard atmosphere. I felt Harvard was not anti-Mormon, but it was antireligious. This was the time of logical positivism and Bertrand Russell's star was in the ascendant. The major religious issue for me was "Was there a God?" If I could solve that problem, then it was only the Mormon God that interested me. I always went to church. I knew the answers and I prayed and studied the scriptures. But I was always intellectually oriented, and that made it necessary for me to cope with intellectual challenges.

After my sophomore year I served a mission in New England. The call was disillusioning and disappointing because when I explained to my Harvard friends what I was planning, I had used words like *abroad*. I had known the mission president quite well before my mission because he and his wife were deeply involved in the branch. We became very close friends, lifelong friends. I learned on my mission that you don't convert by argumentation, that it's the Spirit that makes a difference.

When I came back to Harvard from the mission field there was a change in the temper of the times. The new president of Harvard was a devout man. He built up the Divinity School and brought in people, like Paul Tillich, who spoke authoritatively from a religious point of view. In my senior year I chaired an undergraduate committee that wrote a report on religion at Harvard. Though there were agnostics in the group, all were very respectful of the religious position. I didn't feel as defensive as before about believing in God.

When I went into the mission field I didn't have a testimony of the gospel. My mission president handed me the Book of Mormon and said, "If you can find another explanation of this other than the one Joseph Smith gave, come and tell me." There was no admonition to pray: just read this book. I read it and read Hugh Nibley and thought about the witnesses. Finally I came to the conviction that it was right. Spiritually, it was right.

The most difficult church assignment I have ever had, by far, was as Elders' Quorum president in the Provo Thirteenth Ward. We had to get people to work on the beet farm. I was perpetually trying to get fifteen men to turn out at five in the morning to weed beets or clean ditches. I was on the phone all Sunday evening going through that whole list of guys pleading with them. Those were the days when percentages were everything. Every month all the Elders' Quorum presidents had to sit in the stake president's office while he went down the percentages and asked us individually to account for our failures in getting our sacrament meeting attendance up. It was a style of church administration that was borrowed from industry.

I thought when I was made stake president in Boston that I was going to be subjected to the same kind of torture, but I didn't get a smidgen of that from any visiting general authorities. I enjoyed being stake president. Looking back, it seems very hard. It is demanding and draining because there is so much administrative detail. It is just incredible how much is required of the stake president, but I enjoyed it. There were many good parts. A stake president has a tremendous amount of authority in his stake to accomplish what he wants to do.

Being bishop here has been most enjoyable because I have a better idea of how the job is to be done—what doesn't have to be done as well as what does. Seeing people at church, talking to them, sensing where they are, is personally very rewarding. It's always tremendously satisfying to see someone growing in a calling, when it brings out things they didn't know were there. The most difficult part is with the people who have serious problems—in their marriage, finances, righteousness, difficulties with children. It's very hard to help in a real way. I can give them some help, find things that push them in the right direction, but people must solve their own problems.

I believe that a calling is redemptive. I see this in women who will lose patience with their children at home, but in Primary class they are marvels of patience, kindness, and understanding. Learning to act that way provides an anchor and a place to refer back to. For me, having to counsel people, having somehow to say something in difficult situations that will be useful and kindly has deeply affected my personality and character. My ideal is to treat all people all the time the way I do in my very best moments as a bishop. I would like to treat my students and colleagues that way. One of the primary reasons that the church is powerful in people's lives is that it compels them to move into a role where they have to act for God. That's true for women as well as for men. I think in that sense the priesthood is held by women, too.

There are two points of view on how this has affected my family. One is that I have abandoned my wife and family for long periods of time, putting undue stress on them, requiring my wife to be a single parent, and seeming to demonstrate that I loved the church more than my family. That's a very hard argument to counteract. It can't be done with words because I have been away so much, sometimes when they needed me. I now think that sometimes you have to slight your church work in order to be with your family.

On the other hand, I do believe that the most important thing a father can be is close to what a good bishop is. That is, someone who stands for truth and right, and yet who is loving and understanding and takes a genuine interest in the person's total well-being and growth. I don't think I could ever have done as well in my family, nearly so well, if I hadn't had these short-term practice sessions as bishop.

Claudia has educated me to feminism. I think I've become much more sensitive, simply because I've made so many mistakes and she's let me know it. Though I was not and still am not for the ERA, I would consider myself a feminist in the sense of feeling that there is much unacknowledged bias and downputting. Men are just deaf to what they're saying about women. The worst thing about the feminist movement is that there's a lot of pressure on women to get jobs. It would be a shame if women felt that they could only achieve dignity by having a full-time, paid job. We need another culture besides the corporate culture. I think the church has the capacity to say no to a reform movement and then gradually distill what is useful and good from it. It always seems to be slow in coming around, but that's what conservatism means: wait until you decide what's good. Whether this will lead to women's having more authority in the church—I will be interested to see. It may.

The priesthood means a lot to me, not in the sense of miraculous healings, but in the sense of conveying to my sons and daughters, when I bless them, what I feel about them. In acting for God, I try to act like God. I believe a great deal in ordinances. Lots of things that you think about you can dissolve with thought. When you say any word twenty times, pretty soon it sounds silly. Something that happened is much harder to reduce to rubble. In rituals like the temple ordinances and baptism God gave us something that we could hold onto. Physical ordinances where we touch and go under the water, somehow, are more real and lasting than theology.

For some reason both of our first two children grew up with the feeling that we were strict and that they had to break out of the strictness. By her late teens our daughter was inactive. When she became engaged to Charles, we immediately liked and admired him, but he was not a church member. We felt he was good for Clarissa. He had integrity. We had a difference over whether champagne would be served at the wedding. I had just been stake president. The wedding was to be in New York. If someone from the Boston Stake walked into the reception and champagne was being served, what would they think the standards of the church meant to me? Charles and Clarissa saw it as an occasion to gather around all of their friends. They both, especially Charles, had a keen sense of doing things "right" in every detail, and champagne was part of that. It wasn't just a matter of saying, "Well, look, it's our party. Can't we have sparkling something else?"

It was also a problem because Charles felt like this was Mormonism creeping into his life. We went round and round. He felt if the wedding and reception were in Delaware then his friends wouldn't be there and it wouldn't matter so much, but we couldn't find a place in Delaware that would do. The whole wedding was postponed an entire year because we couldn't solve this problem. I was angry and bitter that he would impose on me this way. Clarissa was distraught because she didn't want us to knuckle under and yet she was loyal to Charles.

Finally we decided to have the wedding at Columbia, but Claudia and I wouldn't go to the party afterwards. It would be their party, not ours. That was a horrible thing. I came down to my study one morning and prayed that God would give me the words to say that would somehow help them understand why I couldn't give way on this, words that would bring them around. But the only thing I could pray for was that I would find a way to assure my daughter that I loved her. I called her on the phone and said, "We'll have champagne at the wedding." My first-born was to be married outside the temple, and there was to be champagne at the reception, and yet I felt it was right. I was telling her that she was more important to me than champagne.

When I pray with my family I try to express how I feel about God, about the church, about them. That's where they are taught, more than in any other place. Prayer is like being in a room that's sealed tight except for one little breath hole that the oxygen comes through. You have to keep filling yourself up.

Rufus Lanier, 45

Rufus Lanier, one of Bishop Bushman's two counselors, helps him with the administrative work of the ward: making staffing decisions, issuing calls to members, planning sacrament and other meetings, and conducting the Priesthood Executive Committee, Welfare Committee, and Ward Council meetings with the presidencies of the Elkton Ward organizations. Rufus, a lifelong member of the church from North Carolina, has been Bishop Bushman's counselor since the organization of the Elkton Ward in 1981. While serving in the air force he baptized and married his wife, Shelia. A district sales manager for Chevrolet, he has lived in Delaware since 1970 and is the father of three children.

When I finished school I got a job as an accountant. I hated sitting there with a pencil and figures. I could do my job within an hour and a half. The rest of the day was boredom. I began working for Chevrolet as a distribution analyst. I do what I'm doing very well. I'm compensated and I'm recognized for it. It's very satisfying when I can do jobs that no one else has been able to do. Once in a while a dealer comes up to me and says, "Hey, thanks for the effort that you put into this thing." The bad part of it is not being promoted because of the limitations of being a Mormon. I can't lie. I won't stick a program on somebody because someone in the Chevrolet Motor Division says to. There is a conflict between my conscience as a human being as opposed to being a business person. I only have two alternatives: either live with it or go into some other profession. In eleven more years I can retire and do what I want to do. I've always wanted my own business. If I didn't have a family or the church, I would have had it. I would have been very successful because I do have the ability to walk across dead baby bodies to get where I want to. But, as Shelia said years ago, the day I ever get my business, she'll lose a husband because I would dedicate my entire time and resources to it. For that reason I have put it off, knowing that someday if I still want it, it will be there.

I've always followed the church's line in believing that a father should discuss things with the family, but I believe that the husband should make the ultimate decision, if there has to be a decision made. He should also have the stamina to live with that decision. If it's wrong, it's on his shoulders.

It is very satisfying to be thought of highly enough to be asked to hold a position in the bishopric. After everything—as low as I've been and, boy, that was pretty doggone low—for Bishop Bushman to have that confidence in me means a lot.

I've gotten to know the people of this ward, not only as a member of the bishopric, but individually. They're my friends. If I need anything I can call on them and they feel the same way. I have a very special feeling when I go to church, not because I'm sitting up front. There are people I care about and people who care about me. In the process of fulfilling a calling in the bishopric, something happens to you. You do change. Have you ever knelt and prayed with Bishop Bushman or Karel Vander-Heyden? I guess Bishop Dorner is another one. There are a few people who when they pray are actually talking with God. Sometimes when we hold bishopric meetings I truly expect to hear an answer come back. I have never considered myself to be a religious man, but exercising the priesthood through that calling is probably the most satisfying thing I've ever done.

There are an awful lot of people, both in and out of the church, who really hurt. It's satisfying to me to be able to sit down with them and talk with them, reason with them, let them know that other people have the same problems, trials, tribulations, and fears—and to at least bring them some comfort. The drawback is that it is very hard to know of certain situations, of the emotional trauma. There are so many people whose testimony, belief, and dedication are so strong, but they're constantly having family problems, financial, Word of Wisdom, inner strife, or problems in their careers. They come to you asking for some type of answer and you don't always have the solution to it. You have to tell them that that's something they'll have to work on themselves. It's even deeper than that because I think you can't tell them how to search their own minds, their own inner selves, to find the answer. You can't give them the inner feeling that you know what God is. It hurts so much. When they're talking to you, some of this hurt and anguish are transposed from them to you. I have never been able to handle it. It eats at me, and it hurts. Bishop Bushman has been doing it for years, and I respect him for it.

Shelia gets on my case because she says church takes too much time, but I don't think it takes near as much as it should. The amount of time that the bishop spends away from his family is unbelievable.

I have discussed tithing with the bishop many times. Will the 10 percent tithe always be in existence? At some point in time will the 10 percent become 5 percent? Ten percent, to the vast majority of people in the church, is a great deal of money. I've asked the bishop if more people would pay a full tithing if it were 5 percent. I know three or four people who do not hold temple recommends because they just cannot pay 10 percent. The bishop's answer to that is, "Well, when a person says he can't, that's when he needs to pay it the most." He says, "Rufus, do you think that those people who aren't paying 10 would knuckle themselves down to pay 5?"

I once had a person say, "Look, if I have to pay my way into that temple, what good is it?" I do know some very good people, whose testimony is just as strong as mine, who do not hold a temple recommend. I look at some of these people who are just scraping by and are too proud to say, "Okay, I'll pay my tithing," knowing that they'll have to get food from the church. The church says if you'll pay your tithing, we'll pay your grocery bill. The average American isn't going to do it. I would find it very difficult.

Tithing is a very strong subject in this family. Since I started paying it, we have done things and we have more than we ever did before. I'm not saying that it was the magic thing that opened the door. I'm only saying that once I did start paying it, more doors have been opened.

In our ward we have 482 members and an average attendance of 165. Periodically I'm assigned to go find certain individuals. We ask the person, "Tell me what happened. Why did you stop coming to church?" I run into: "I couldn't be a perfect Mormon, so I didn't feel as if I belonged there. I couldn't pay my tithing every month. I didn't feel as if I could take the sacrament every Sunday. I didn't agree with that gospel doctrine teacher. At times I didn't feel that I had the spirit of the Holy Ghost with me. I didn't feel I was in tune with what the home teachers were saying when they came and presented a program. When somebody called me to do something, I didn't respond with the degree of perfection that was expected. I can't walk on water for you people and I don't hear trumpets every morning. My husband and I fight like cats and dogs."

Someone called me up last week and said, "I can't give a talk in sacrament meeting because I haven't been living worthy. I don't feel I have the right to get up and address the ward."

I said, "I don't give a damn whether you've been living the church to perfection or not. I want you to get up and express your feelings on a certain subject."

There are so many people out there in the ward. Some of them would love to come back if someone would say, "Okay, so it happened. Come on back. You're going to try again. You're going to make mistakes again."

※　※　※

The statistics the stake presidency reviews with the bishopric and ward leaders come from the quarterly reports submitted by the ward clerk summarizing attendance at meetings, home teaching visits, and other measures of members' activity. The reports go to church headquarters in Salt Lake City, with a copy to the Wilmington Stake. The ward clerk compiles these reports and takes minutes of bishopric meetings, priesthood executive committee meetings, and sacrament meetings. He also supervises the work of the financial clerk, who keeps records of all donations and ward expenses, and of the membership clerk, who keeps records of all ward members. The clerks' office is a cubbyhole, with a desk and one chair, between the chapel and stairway. After the days' meetings are finished, Richard King, the financial clerk, and a member of the bishopric open the small grey donation envelopes. Members have filled out preprinted forms that indicate the amounts donated to each fund: tithing, fast offering, ward budget, or missionary fund. After counting the money, the clerk puts it in a locked bank bag, which the bishop will deposit in the bank on his way home. The financial clerk types the receipts, and the Presiding Bishop's Office in Salt Lake City sends a quarterly report of members' donations back to the ward. At the end of the year, members meet with the bishop to check the accuracy of their donation record and to state whether or not they have paid a full tithing.

Douglas Ridge, 40

Midway through sacrament meeting each Sunday, Douglas Ridge walks slowly around the chapel. Often trailed by one of his five-year-old twins, he is counting the number of people present. Besides his duties as ward clerk, Douglas Ridge shares the job of playing the organ for sacrament meeting with Lynne Whitney. Douglas grew up in Provo, Utah, and is a professor of chemistry at the University of Delaware.

There had been a few people from my high school who went to places like Cornell and Yale, but I hadn't thought much about it. I was a semifinalist for a National Merit Scholarship. In filling out all the forms, I thought, "If I'm going to win a big scholarship, it seems silly to use it at BYU. I'm going to put down Harvard." After a while I thought, "Maybe I should apply." It was past the deadline, but I wrote off. Much to my shock, not only was I admitted, but they sent me a big certificate that said I was a "Harvard National Scholar." I didn't know what to do. I made lists: strong points for Harvard and strong ones for BYU. I finally went. I got on the bus in Provo, and seventy hours later I dragged myself off the bus in Boston. Boy, was I green!

My roommate, Jeff, had also run the half-mile in high school. His father was a Baptist minister. One of Jeff's friends in the Divinity School liked to give me a bad time about being LDS. When he found out I was LDS, he said, "Near as I can tell, it's just a hodgepodge of nineteenth-century theology and middle-class American values." From the way he said it, I knew nothing could be worse. I didn't have much to say in defense. Jeff and I became fast friends. He once had me teach his Sunday school class, and he came with me a time or two. He said, "I can see why that's so appealing—all that 'brother and sister' stuff."

I felt like a hippopotamus out of water. It didn't seem possible to be LDS and part of the world at Harvard. I felt like I belonged to neither one. I did make some friends at church. One of the first people was Tony Kimball—one of those perennial graduate students. He is, the last I heard, the only unmarried bishop in the church. Tony would take us undergraduates out to dinner on Sunday. Well, we'd pay—but we all went together. That feeling of fellowship was so valuable although I was closer to Jeff and a couple of his friends than to the LDS undergraduates.

Our institute class was taught by the mission president, Truman Madsen, at 7:00 A.M. on Tuesdays. He seemed nonjudgmental, an openminded, bright, intellectual person. He talked to us in a way that made me feel like it might be possible both to go to Harvard and be LDS. Blessing the sacrament in the junior Sunday school reminded me of home. The church was a real lifeline to me at Harvard, more important to me than I think it would have been in Provo.

My parents were not sure that they wanted me to go on a mission. This was the era of baptizing by whatever means. My parents heard reports of missionaries misrepresenting themselves. "Well, you've got to be baptized to be on our basketball team." They were also concerned about the interruption of my education. I felt I wanted to go, but I was very apprehensive because my friends would all have graduated by the time I returned.

My academic adviser, Frank Westheimer, an eminent organic chemist who was Jewish, was not enthusiastic about it. He said, "So you're going to South Africa. Well, from what I've heard of the Dutch Reformed Church," (of course their doctrinal position favors apartheid) "you'd be doing those folks a favor if you persuaded them to believe in Baal."

It was difficult for me to talk to white South Africans. When they discovered I was an American, they'd say, "Now that you're here, what do you think of South Africa?" What they meant was "What do you think about apartheid?"

I learned to say, "I think it's one of the most beautiful countries I've ever been in," then talk about something else.

I remember visiting one man for the third or fourth time. We were trying to set up an appointment when his wife would be there, but we finally went to see just him. As we were giving him the Book of Mormon lesson, he stopped us and said, "I've got a problem. It looks like my wife may leave me." At that point the phone rang and he left the room. My companion and I looked at each other. I was the junior companion so I figured, "You're the boss. You decide." We just hurried through the rest of the lesson and left.

When we went back the next week, he called us to task. He said, "I'm disappointed. If your faith is something special, couldn't you have offered to help? Why did you just go on with your little sales pitch?" We tried to explain that we didn't feel qualified to help. Several weeks later we went by the house and it had cracked in the middle, which was a frequent occurrence in this mining country. It was such an incredible metaphor for what was going on. We were being lectured by someone.

I was sent to a big fair at Pietermaritzburg, Natal. We set up a display that people could walk through and had books and posters. Black people came to see the display. One man wanted to buy a big illustrated Book of Mormon, and I had to tell him it wasn't for sale. That pained me. The mission president had to hold my hand for a while afterwards. The government was very suspicious of American missionaries. We could have only a certain number in the country at any given time. We'd either try to get Canadians as missionaries or we'd send missionaries to Rhodesia when we found ourselves with more than our allotted number. I was very uncomfortable with the situation. They told us not to sell or give Books of Mormon or pamphlets to blacks.

After my mission I began to feel real unrest with regard to the church and sex and marriage. I felt I had an obligation to go to Harvard. There were no LDS girls there. I felt it was somehow the church's fault: they collected all the young women in Provo and sent all the best male youth away.

The Cal Tech years were my most difficult years as far as the church was concerned. I went to church regularly, but my commitment was more strained. At Harvard the church had been such a lifeline to me, but I didn't find that at Cal Tech. I think if I had not married a good LDS girl, my ties to the church might have disappeared. I got tied up in my work, and if I'd found some sort of satisfactory arrangement, legal or otherwise, to end my celibate days that would also have allowed me to spend all my time at chemistry—I'd have done that. All my interests were in the lab until I met Julie, who was clearly sent to Pasadena to rescue me. We had a fight at family home evening over the Negro question. I was impressed with how well she stood up for herself.

One day somebody from Delaware called up my adviser and said, "This guy's quit in the middle of the semester. We need a physical chemist starting next fall. Have you got anyone?" I came to Delaware in April for an interview. It had just rained and all the flowering trees were out. Coming from smoggy L.A., I thought I'd come to heaven. People were laid back and friendly. I called up Julie and said, "I think this is it."

I had my thesis defense at two o'clock Monday afternoon and gave my first lecture at Delaware the next morning at ten o'clock. Julie had been here a few days when our bishop, Don O'Day, knocked at the door. He wore a white shirt with the sleeves rolled up and his tie was pulled down. He sat on the floor with me and Julie sat in the chair with the baby. He stayed for about two hours. He talked about his feelings about the church, what he hoped for us, and how much he wanted to be of assistance. I was glad that he was going to be our bishop. E. J. Arnold came over the next day with some furniture from the bishop's basement in his pickup truck.

About the time I was being evaluated for promotion to tenure I was called to be a high priest. All the other high priests in the ward were either on the high council or in the bishopric. They needed a High Priests' Group leader so they called me to be both the Indian and the Chief. I remember thinking, "At least I'll never be a seventy or an Elders' Quorum president." I felt that my situation in life was not understood by those who develop programs for the church. Not only were we expected to pay tithing we were expected to pay hundreds of dollars every year for building fund and budget. Our resources, and everyone else's in the ward, were meager at most. My work involved many long hours and lots of pressure. I remember noticing that there were no scientists among the general authorities. There were no academics—except people from the church education system. Fred Somers was, in fact, my most useful role model.

Hearing on the radio, "Today in Salt Lake City, Spencer Kimball announced that blacks were going to be able to hold the priesthood," got my attention pretty quickly. I went over to the Campbells. I said, "Meredith, blacks are going to be given the priesthood." She looked at me and I looked at her. "I'm pretty sure. Turn on your radio." I went home and I remember being moved, very grateful. There was more to it than just having been proven right. A revelation had been given—not just to the prophet, but to all of us. The most important thing to me was not the content of the revelation, but the fact that we'd been given a revelation.

I think Spencer Kimball is the most significant innovator since Brigham Young. Very fundamental and important changes are occurring in the church. There are the consolidated schedule, the changes in temple garments, filling up the Quorum of Seventy, changes in the length of missionary service, changes in the church participation ratio for building chapels, an enormous number of new temples. In the last fifteen years a lot of responsibility within the ward has been transferred from the bishop to the Elders' Quorums. By themselves these aren't earthshaking. I sense that President Kimball feels an enormous urgency to do the simple things so the Saints can live their lives with the church's requiring only the time and energy that's absolutely necessary for the specific functions of the church: sharing the gospel, work for the dead, as well as perfecting the Saints. The Saints ought to work on raising children, making money in order to be self-sufficient, so that the next generation will be emotionally, economically, spiritually self-sufficient enough to take care of themselves while they are caring for others. These changes are ways of adapting everything that can be adapted to the needs of the members.

I was called to the high council shortly after the twins were born in 1980. I think President Johnson thought it would be nice to have another physical chemist around. He seemed to get quite a kick out of it when I would use scientific language to talk about ordinary things. I learned a great deal on the high council. When I visited the little branches, the leaders were so hungry for very basic kinds of information and advice. "What can we do to help our four Aaronic priesthood holders stay active in the church?" Working with them, I began to appreciate the church programs. I began to feel less cynical and less likely to carp because everything wasn't wonderful.

The Elkton Branch was just hanging out of the windows of Holly Hall. The stake president began playing with maps and drawing boundaries here and there. It was discussed at several high council meetings. Everyone agreed that Newark and Elkton should be together. People did not agree about what to do with the rest of the New Castle Ward. The hot issue was Hockessin. The people who live there are well-off and energetic, generally speaking. Most of them are transplanted from the West and work for the big corporations. The people from Wilmington Ward were worried that if they lost Hockessin, the ward just wouldn't hold together. After Newark was taken out, the New Castle Ward was just nothing. I was there when the High Council approved putting Hockessin into the New Castle Ward, over the objections of the high councillor from the Wilmington Ward.

At the close of the last meeting before I went on sabbatical I said, "President, I realize it's not on the agenda, but I think it would be great if something were installed in the men's room of the stake center that would be suitable for changing a baby's diaper on."

President Rice said, "What? Revolution!" Within a few months something was installed. With twins there were times when both of us were out there fighting with the diaper. It's awkward to change a diaper on the floor.

I went on sabbatical as much to get out from under what had been dumped on me at church and at work as for any compelling professional reasons, although I was interested in getting Julie and the kids back to Utah for a while. It was interesting to talk to my friends the Campbells who had moved to the East Bench from Delaware. They had been in Salt Lake a year before being given any assignment at all in the ward. Their ward didn't need much in the way of contributions. Budgeting two thousand dollars so their Young Men could take trips wasn't any problem.

As soon as we returned from sabbatical the bishop called us to teach early morning seminary. That was the one thing I never wanted to be—besides stake missionary or Elders' Quorum president. The two years we taught seminary were certainly the most rewarding thing I've ever done in the church. This might sound strange because two of our star students got pregnant. One got married and the other didn't but had her baby. A number of young people attended irregularly. It was a little like being a missionary again. It was something I did every day that I knew was worthwhile and enjoyed doing. We were particularly fortunate in our group of students. A core of them were remarkably devoted. I had an interesting conversation with one of my colleagues who is a committed Christian, and he knows Serge Bushman. Serge, evidently, was looked up to in the high school. When my friend discovered that Serge was coming to early morning seminary and when I described the program to him, he was absolutely astounded. He could not imagine what we could do that would get a young person to do that at 6:00 A.M.

In the last two weeks I've given three priesthood blessings. The first was to a girl whom I home teach. She was concerned about making some changes in her life—getting some education, a more productive social life. I made it a matter of prayer for a couple of days. When I laid my hands on her head, I knew what to say to her. It wasn't very dramatic, but she seemed comforted.

As I talked to my son, Andrew, about his school problems, he asked for a priesthood blessing. I didn't feel I was ready to give him a blessing. I didn't know what the issues were that should be addressed, but when I put my hands on his head, I felt I knew what I should say. I think a blessing was bestowed. The third was a woman in the ward with a very pressing family difficulty. She asked Julie to come over. Julie suggested that she might like a blessing, so I went. There wasn't time for me to prepare, but, perhaps more than either of the other times, when I put my hands on her head it was clear what I should say. The times when I feel that the Spirit is present in my life are when I'm exercising the priesthood.

My testimony isn't built on things. It is me. It's a lifetime of giving talks, saying prayers, going to church, going home teaching, going on a mission. It's a lifetime of getting on my knees and saying prayers that have been answered.

Vern Bingham, 36

Vern Bingham, the ward's membership clerk, has lived in the Elkton Ward since June 1984. When a family moves into the ward, their previous ward sends their records to church headquarters in Salt Lake City, which forwards them to the Elkton Ward. When babies are born, children baptized or confirmed, young men ordained to the priesthood, or when men or women take out their endowments in the temple or are married, the membership clerk updates the records, sends the changes to Salt Lake City, and types certificates that are signed by the bishop. Vern was born in Salt Lake City, grew up in Michigan, and attended Westminster College in Salt Lake City.

I am a training manager for the Highway Division of the Marriott Corporation, and I also run the highest volume Big Boy/Roy Rogers in the country. I train all the managers for the toll road rest areas that Marriott has acquired. My decision to move here was not based on my career. We were seeking medical help for our daughter at Johns Hopkins Hospital. Everything else just fell into its place. Sometimes I think it was meant to be. The company I worked for in Salt Lake was willing to foot the bill for us to stay back here for however long it took. I had a good career going with them. I appreciated their offer, but I wanted to take care of my problems myself.

I see a lot of similarities between the church and the Marriott Corporation. Either the church is run like Marriott or Marriott is run like the church. They're very fair. They look after their people. They believe in their employees and managers. They're interested in their quality of life. They want you to work hard, but I believe that's also a part of our church. It's structured a lot like the church. A lot of the decisions are made the same way.

I like seeing people that I have helped develop start their careers and be successful. Most of the people I train are graduates of one of the hotel/hospitality colleges. A lot of them have had summer jobs as chefs or cooks, waiters, waitresses.

My job's very demanding—not so much physically as mentally. I'm pressured for the bottom line, for making the restaurant work—ordering the food and taking care of all these people. Right now I have three female assistants. They're doing well and they will make good managers.

I work with so many young people and I see their problems with drugs. I deal with it on a daily basis. I terminate a lot of people because of it. Parents call and talk to me. It's like a disease that has spread to the point that virtually no one is untouched by it. Not all the kids are involved. I see the pressure on these kids. I never had pressure like that when I was growing up. A lot of kids don't have the education or the family support to deal with it.

I had been active in the church as a child, but I didn't stay very active. I grew back into the church after we were married. I felt something was missing on Sundays. Just getting up and having a leisurely breakfast wasn't enough. I had the honor of bringing Jean into the church. Baptizing her gave me the greatest feeling I've ever had in my life. I knew right then that it was the right thing. It was very spiritual. I don't think even Jean realizes the feelings I had then.

My first calling in the church was cubmaster. Jean was a den mother. I used to laugh at her because she always had problems with the Cub Scouts. One day she called me up at work and asked me to come home. I said, "Honey, I'm very busy and I just can't come home. What's the problem?"

She said, "Well, I'm locked out of the house and water is running in all the sinks and the bathtub."

"Why would that be?"

"We are doing papier-maché with the Cub Scouts and they've locked their den mother out of the house."

I came running home. All the drains were clogged with papier-maché. If I hadn't come home the house would have flooded. As we were mopping up I said, "Why did you ever get involved with Cub Scouts?"

She said, "It's a lot of fun, and you'd enjoy it." About three weeks later I became the cubmaster, and I did enjoy it. We took over a program that was in very bad shape, and I enjoyed putting it together. We had nine dens from the two wards that met in our building.

As membership clerk, I'm responsible for keeping accurate records for the members of the Elkton Ward. It's a hard job if you do it right. The thing I dislike the most is not always knowing the proper procedures. It's very satisfying when records show up and I can pinpoint everybody and have everybody in the right file, when everything's up to date. I have to work Sundays quite often, so I spend a lot of week nights working on my calling.

Members of the church abuse home teaching because they don't use it. The church doesn't push it as strongly as they did back when I was a kid. In the last two years I think we've been visited only twice. People at work ask me all the time about home teaching. They admire it, but as LDS people we don't take advantage of it. If we took advantage of it, a lot of people would be activated.

A year and a half ago I was the home teacher of a gentleman who had joined the church about three years earlier. Right after he joined, everybody just stopped fellowshipping him and nobody visited him at home. Just from our going and seeing him, he became active and very interested in the church again. It wasn't a social thing. It was a learning experience. He needed to know where to get more knowledge and he needed people to talk to.

People at work know that I'm a Latter-day Saint. They ask questions like, "Why do you take care of all these records. Why doesn't a church employee do that?" It gives me an opportunity to explain a little bit how the church works. The way we live is a lot different than other religions. Everything from the Word of Wisdom to reading the scriptures on a daily basis to eternal life to temple marriage is different. People ask me why the church "imposes" things on us. I do more than explain. I let them see different things. Sometimes people feel they have to drink to reach the upper echelons. I never have a problem with it. A lot of people feel that the church teaches you're going to go to hell if you drink. They don't understand that the Word of Wisdom is not only for your eternal life, but also for your life here.

A lot of people ask me about the history of the church, about polygamy and other things. Some people think it is still part of the church. I resent those polygamists for giving the church that image. Alex Joseph married one of my waitresses. She was number thirteen. When he goes on shows like Johnny Carson's, a lot of people think that he represents our church.

The Sabbath day is a very special day even though I am often not at church. Spiritually, I am there. You might think that a little hypocritical, but my first concern is to make a living for my family—especially with the illness we have. Making the best living I know how to make does require Sundays. I can't change that. My goal is to be a district manager. Then I would be able to have Sundays off or at least the flexibility to attend church.

The priesthood has meant more to me in the last ten years than it ever did. I've used it most definitely for Becky, and I hold it very dear to my heart. Becky's illness forced me to my knees because I'd done everything I knew of and it just wasn't enough. The doctors were giving up; they were suggesting an institution. I'm ashamed that it took me so long to call on Heavenly Father. Though that definitely was a trial, it was a very rewarding experience. I honestly believe that we had an answer even though it didn't come at that time. It was several years later. My daughter is always on my mind. I'm always concerned about the quality of life she will live. Who will take care of her when her father and mother are not around?

11 | Egg Day

On Saturday, March 2, a path of brown paper led from the side door of the ward building downstairs to the Primary meeting room and the basement classrooms. A neatly printed sign instructed us to wash our hands and put on plastic gloves and caps. The Elkton Ward had been transformed into a candy factory. I remembered Richard Bushman's quip, "Eating chocolate isn't against the Word of Wisdom. In our ward we encourage you to eat chocolate."

On January 13 the ward members had voted to make Easter eggs. Bishop Bushman had begun the meeting by announcing that a new ward building was in the planning stages. He next discussed the amount spent by the ward in 1984 for supplies, utilities, and its share of the stake budget and building fund, and presented a proposed budget for 1985. Members contribute between 1 and 3 percent of their annual gross income to the ward budget—in addition to their tithing and fast offerings. Because the ward had received less from budget contributions, fund-raising projects, and interest than expected during 1984, Bishop Bushman asked that each organization raise funds in addition to the profits from the Easter egg project. The Young Men and Young Women were to raise $350 each, the Relief Society, $400, and the elders and high priests, $500 each.

The bishop asked comments on the budget and proposed fund-raising activities. Douglass Taber reminded the members that selling firewood cut from Henry Tingey's property meant the men would have to spend many Saturdays out cutting and delivering wood. Cindy Mullins then proposed that the ward find another way to raise $4,000 other than the Easter egg project. She suggested a cookie booth at the Cecil County Fair.

Bishop Bushman responded, "All the other projects that have been suggested have serious difficulties. For example, there are many health problems with making and selling pizzas. There are tax difficulties in buying and selling candy bars. For some reason, selling Easter eggs that we have made is okay with the Internal Revenue Service." Beulah Somers asked how much profit could be made from each egg. He replied that the cost of the chocolate for each $1.50 egg was approximately $0.22. The fondant and labor were donated by the members.

When it was time to vote, the members voted unanimously in favor of the proposed budget. Only one person voted against making Easter eggs. The bishop then announced that Bonita Cherry would be in charge of the project and that members should start preparing their fondant—twenty batches from each family.

Debora Ennis demonstrated making fondant at the January Relief Society homemaking meeting. Although she had lived in the ward for just a few months, I learned that her husband's family had originated the Easter egg project in the Wilmington Ward twenty years before. The Elkton Branch first made Easter eggs in 1979 when thirteen branch members, with help from the New Castle Ward in dipping and boxing the eggs, made 1,902 eggs. Debora emphasized that the fondant should be cooked to 243 degrees and that it should not be kneaded smooth, as we had been told before. It should be wrapped, rock hard, in double plastic bags. Last year some of the eggs had flattened out because the fondant was too soft.

My first year in the ward I had been dismayed by Ken McVicker's dire warnings about the difficulties of making fondant, so I had gratefully agreed when Julie Ridge suggested we make it together. After our first fondant-making session her ten-year-old daughter inquired, "Mother, wasn't Sister Taber active in the church before she came to Delaware?"

"Yes, she was."

"Then why doesn't she know how to make fondant?"

This time Julie and I decided to make our fourteen triple batches, forty-two single batches, of fondant on Wednesday and Thursday of the second week of February. I arrived at Julie's at 9:15 with two toddlers, my biggest pot, the candy thermometer, and thirty dollars' worth of sugar, cream, and butter. While Julie took her five-year-old twins to nursery school and my children played downstairs with the two children Julie baby-sits, I cut up the butter and started one pot cooking.

When Julie returned, we began cooking a second pot while the first came up to temperature. By 10:30 three glass pans of fondant were cooling on the table and two more were cooking on the stove. Out of pans in which to cool the candy, we called Joey Robinson for advice. She said that Bonita Cherry had successfully used metal cake pans. As we washed metal pans, we recalled our past failures: the batch that had cooked for hours without coming to 243, those that had turned to sugar because we had beaten them when they were too warm, the batch that was so hard after recooking we had had to break it up with a hammer and soften it in the microwave.

Julie had gone to pick up her two children and to buy her ingredients when it was time to beat the first two batches. As I pushed the gooey mass back and forth, light bubbles began to form. After a few more passes with the spoon, the candy set up hard and pale gold. I began chipping and scraping it out of the pan, but where were the plastic bags? I couldn't leave Julie's house even for a minute with batches four and five boiling on the stove and four small children playing in the family room. I left the spoons planted like standards in the mountains of candy. Julie returned a few minutes later with a big box of plastic bags, an aluminum roasting pan, and two huge wooden paddles. She fixed lunch as I washed pots and started batch number seven. We tasted the first two batches—they were smooth. If our luck held, we might finish in one day.

At 3:45 Julie's children began coming home from school and hung around the kitchen eating the pan scrapings as we cooked batches thirteen and fourteen. If the pioneers ever had to make fondant, we joked, polygamy would have been a real advantage! We had accomplished far more in that day than either of us could have separately. Even with six preschoolers wandering through the kitchen, we had functioned like a well-oiled machine. Not wanting to be known as fondant experts, we agreed not to tell anyone that we had made fourteen triple batches in one day.

On Egg Day ward members, seated on both sides of several long tables on one side of the Primary room, were breaking off chunks of fondant, weighing them on small postage scales, and pushing them into plastic wrap–lined egg molds. I found a vacant seat next to Sharon Mlodoch and began. Julie, an expert dipper, went to work at the front of the room. Behind her in the kitchen Thomas Young and Rufus Lanier were melting chocolate in huge pots. Several tables on the opposite side of the room were loaded with bags of fondant. Signs above the tables said Hard and Soft. Bonita Cherry and Linda Crowe were in the kitchen mixing hard and soft batches together in a heavy-duty mixer. The center of the room was full of tables, too. Sheets of wax paper–covered cardboard, each with eight smears of chocolate on it, were spread over every available surface. Not only had Bonita and her committee covered the floors with paper, set up the tables, and prepared enough cardboard to hold four thousand eggs, but they had made four thousand flowers from royal icing and added coconut, peanut butter, or chocolate to some of the fondant.

After an hour of molding, I was asked to go learn to dip. Julie showed me how to hold the egg in my hand, smooth chocolate around it, and place it on the tray. The little girls stuck a colored flower on each egg to indicate the flavor, and the deacons and Beehive girls carried the eggs out. I thought I had the hang of it until Ben Bushman came back from Quality Control with a tray of eggs Beulah Somers had rejected because they were not completely coated. They were mine. Julie and Sharon Morris's mother showed me again how to dip. At the other end of the table Jean Bingham was demonstrating her method, laying the egg in a nest of chocolate on the marble slab and slurping the chocolate up over the top of the egg. I tried Jean's method and was more successful.

After two hours of dipping I was relieved to go upstairs for lunch. The molders were still shaping eggs; the tables in the center of the room were filled with cooling eggs. It was warm for March 2, so even with the windows open the eggs were slow to harden. Fred and Beulah Somers were inspecting the eggs and smoothing their edges. Teenagers were putting the boxes together, dropping in a few strands of Easter grass, and slipping in the color-coded eggs. In two basement rooms cartons of boxed eggs were mounting toward the ceiling.

By 6:00 4,017 eggs had been made, boxed, and crated, the rooms cleaned of all traces of chocolate, fondant, and Easter grass, the tables taken down, and the chairs arranged for Primary in the morning. On Sunday each family was asked to go downstairs and take at least 100 eggs to sell. Since Stephen Cherry was now in a management position at Avon, he could no longer sell his customary 1,000 eggs to his co-workers. The other members would have to sell more. Monday afternoon I sent my children around the neighborhood taking orders. It took us three weeks to sell and deliver 125 eggs.

Bonita Cherry, 32

Bonita Cherry, Easter egg chair, has been making Easter eggs since she joined the church in 1977. Besides overseeing the Easter egg production, she teaches a home study seminary class and is leadership trainer for the stake Relief Society. Now the mother of two children, Shiloh, three, and Joshua, two, she grew up in Newark, Delaware, and lives in Elkton.

When I was twelve I went to confirmation classes. I hadn't been baptized as an infant because my mother's church didn't believe in infant baptism, so I was baptized and made a member of the church in the same service. The preacher had more trouble with me than with anybody else. The church taught that we're predestined to go to heaven or to go to hell, to be a good person or not. I said, "Why bother if I'm already going one direction or the other." He couldn't seem to explain it.

We were married in Stephen's church, and I went there occasionally. Reverend Jordan was one preacher that I respected. The first time I went, several months after we were married, I saw the piano player say something to him in the middle of the service. He looked up and said, "Sister Cherry, is that you back there?" I said, "Yes, sir." He said, "Is Brother Cherry all right?" "Yes, sir." At least he didn't ask me where he was; he was still in bed asleep.

The sister missionaries had first come to my parents' house while canvassing and gave them the lessons. I spent a lot of time there so as not to be stuck alone in a little apartment. I heard a couple of the lessons. At dinner, they wouldn't drink iced tea. I thought, "What would it be like to put that kind of restriction on yourself? You would have no belief in yourself if you didn't stick with it."

The sisters made a mistake. I'm not saying that my parents would have been baptized; I don't think that they would have been willing to change that much, but the missionaries aimed everything at my father and practically ignored my mother. That ccoled things with my parents. I did not know until several years after we were baptized that it was my mother who had asked the missionaries to come see us. My mother said she felt it might help Stephen figure out where he was in life and what would fill his need. Stephen was working eighty or ninety hours a week. He wanted a house. He thought that if we had nice things that would take care of his hunger.

When they came tracting, Stephen was pushing fertilizer around the yard. I recognized them as missionaries and said I'd be willing to talk with them. I thought it would be good for my life, but I didn't want to do it without my husband. I remembered they didn't have a preacher and I told them to get that across because my husband had no use for preachers. I knew they believed that you shouldn't just sit down and pray for something, but that you should pray for the strength and health to achieve what you needed. That was something that my husband would have to hear very quickly. There were two or three other things. I said, "You're going to have to wait until he's finished pushing the fertilizer over this whole yard because I'll guarantee you that he will not stop." When he finished we all went to the back porch. Every time the elder made one of his points, he looked over at me and winked. It was so hard not to start laughing. After two or three visits my husband caught it. Then he went like wildfire—learning and being interested.

Before we were baptized I knelt down one night and said, "I think this will be good for my life, but is it true or is it just a good organization? How will I know?" I felt calm inside, then it came through, "You will know them by the children. You will know them by the way they treat their children." It was such a strong feeling. I thought, "That's kind of an unusual answer."

When we joined, we were part of the New Castle Ward. It was a forty-five minute drive to Sunday school, to Relief Society on Tuesday, and Primary on Thursday. We had sacrament meeting at Cloyd Mullins's in Elkton. When we became a branch they gave me the job of starting the library because I had been Primary librarian in New Castle. I was also made first counselor in the Relief Society. Of course, I didn't know a thing about what I was doing. I just did what Linda Crowe, the president, asked me to do. I also taught Primary and Sunday school for a while. One of my bedrooms was the library. I was excited to be growing.

Working in the library was a quick way to learn about the church. I learned all the temples by sight. I knew the presidents of the church by their pictures. It was a great experience. I became Primary librarian in New Castle because Thelma Moudy, without even knowing me, went to the bishop and said, "This woman belongs in the library." She was an excellent teacher. She got it through my head very strongly: "The church is true; the doctrines of the church are true, but people make mistakes. Sometimes even the leaders will be wrong. Something that they do can insult or hurt you, but that's not the church."

I love to watch the professors in the Elkton Ward work side by side with the fellows who work on the assembly line. No matter what their backgrounds are, the members don't put each other into classes. The Elkton Ward has people who have been members all of their lives and new members. Some of the new members have had very rough backgrounds, spiritually and socially, as well as financially.

Before I joined the church I was a very quiet person. When I was baptized I decided it wasn't right for me to keep my talents and abilities to myself just because I was shy and uncomfortable around people. It was a hard battle. I feel very uncomfortable on the Stake Relief Society Board. I guess it's because I sit at the table with all these women who have been members of the church for so many years and are so talented and capable. I feel so dumb. I'm the leadership trainer. Elkton Ward's leadership trainer has done it on the stake level before. She's way ahead of me.

I would like to be like Claudia Bushman. I admire her ability to organize things and her ability to decide what she's going to aim for and what she's not going to bother with. Right now I'm working very hard at my callings and at being better organized at home.

When they asked me to teach home study seminary I had to convince each of the boys to come. That was scary because I knew none of them wanted to. When I called Arvie Wrang he said, "Oh sure, I'll come." His mother later told me that he had said he absolutely wasn't going to come. I know that it was the Lord's work. It couldn't have been mine. It happened with the other boys as well. The calling is good for me because I wasn't good about reading my scriptures every day. Even though we meet just once a week, I have to read and study every day for it.

We were married for almost ten years before we had Shiloh. When no children had come after three and four and five years, I was very upset about it. The New Castle Ward had thirty-two three-year-olds plus all the other kids. When my parents came to one of the ward socials that Stephen was in charge of, my father said, "My word, we'd better get out of here. It's catching." I said, "What?" He said, "I don't see a woman in here that's not expecting or carrying a baby in her arms." There were children all over the place and I didn't have any.

Even before we went to the temple to be sealed, we had all the paperwork for adoption done. As soon as we were sealed, the waiting period began. It was a long, long wait. Mother's Day was horrendous. One year I walked out about halfway through and sat outside and cried. The next year I stayed just until the sacrament and then went out. Joey Robinson came out and talked with me. The next year I just didn't go. Stephen didn't bother to bring me a flower because he knew that would upset me.

I had never discussed my desire for children with the missionaries, but when

I was confirmed, I was told that I would have children in this lifetime. When Stephen was in the explosion, we didn't know if he was going to survive. In the middle of giving him a blessing, the bishop informed him that he was to have children, which shocked the bishop more than it did anyone else. My patriarchal blessing assured me that I would have children and I kept praying for them. I knew it would come; it was just a matter of being faithful and worthy.

When Brother Byrd was transferred to the Washington, D.C., social services, he wanted an interview with us. Stephen was not happy about having to take off a day of work just to meet this new fellow. We got stuck in traffic for an hour at the bridge over the Susquehanna and for another hour and a half in the Baltimore tunnel. By the time we got there, two hours late, we were both just a little agitated. Brother Byrd asked us how we were doing with the waiting. I said, "Terrible."

Stephen said, "Do you have a child for us?" It threw Brother Byrd off guard, and he said, "Yes, we think so." We finally got him to say that the child had already been born. It was a girl, but there were a few legal problems that had to be straightened out. This was April 3, and we didn't get her until June 3. We couldn't tell anyone. I couldn't stand for everyone to be talking about it and then have it fall through. By my birthday, May 21, I suspected that I was pregnant. I didn't let anyone else know because I was afraid the adoption would be stopped. We picked Shiloh up on Thursday. That Saturday night, they got us down to the ward through a little bit of mischief. All the men and women in the ward and my parents were there. My little girl had more dresses than you can imagine. The following Friday I went to the doctor. He said everything was fine and the baby was due January 19. We'd spent almost ten years with no children, then suddenly had two.

I make sure I take the time to sit down and play with my children—playing with them out in the backyard, squirting them with water. I enjoy sitting and rocking them. In fact, sometimes, if I've been away during the day or it's been hectic, before I got to bed I'll go in and pick one of the babies up. I give him something to drink so he doesn't get upset and just sit and rock. I nursed Josh until he was fourteen months old. I just loved that time.

I was so convinced that I was such an ugly duckling and useless. In fourth grade I thought maybe I would make it to fifth, but surely I would never pass sixth grade. It's horrible for a child to feel that way. It's important to teach my children that they are beautiful, that what they are now is very acceptable. All they have to do is try.

❀   ❀   ❀

Co-operative work has long been at the heart of the Latter-day Saint religion. Although the early experiments in cooperative agriculture and manufacturing were eventually abandoned as a means of providing the livelihood of the members, many cooperative practices still exist. In addition to the firewood project and the Easter egg project, the members also worked at the cannery to put food in the regional bishop's storehouse.

The church's welfare system of food production and bishop's storehouses was formally launched at general conference in April 1936. Since then the church has taught that members should try to be self-sufficient by storing a year's supply of food, clothing, and (where possible) fuel, and that the needy should be provided for by the collective efforts of the church. Ideally, the church's welfare system produces food and other commodities that are dispersed by the bishops. If the plan worked perfectly, people who needed the commodities would have a place to work in return. Until five years ago, the wards in the Wilmington Stake each had gardens. The tomatoes or cantaloupes they grew were sold for cash, which was donated to the Welfare Fund. Then the church built a storehouse and cannery in southern New Jersey that is stocked with food and household supplies from church production units all over the United States. If a family is in need the bishop asks the Relief Society president to order food from the storehouse for them.

The Elkton Ward put in an eight-hour shift canning pork and beans in May and another one canning corn in August. The members arrived between five and six o'clock on Friday evening. The storehouse manager instructed them to put on gloves and plastic caps. After being instructed in safety, cleanliness, and proper testing, the members went to work. Jim Rennard, Oliver McPherson, and Gene Dean, who had been previously trained as retort operators or shift supervisors, had come earlier in the afternoon to get things ready, including repairing the mechanical corn husker. In the canning room, workers with long broad knives cut the corn from the cobs. The machine that was to do that had not been repaired in time.

There were more than enough people to do the job. As the evening went by the original group of fifteen grew. There was good-natured joshing over the roar of the various machines. Near the end there was a ritualistic taking of orders for pizza. After eleven o'clock everything slowed down. The whole crew was not needed to hose down the tables and floors; a crew from Dover Ward began work at midnight.

Bishop Bushman was especially pleased by Gene Dean's leadership. "Gene had not been coming to church for two or three months, but he got a big kick out of running the shift. He grasped what was needed and kept us operating very competently."

Evelyn Mawson, 40

Unable to support herself because of serious health problems and a limited education, Evelyn Mawson works several days a week as a clerk at the storehouse as well as studying for her high school equivalency diploma. She expects that her work experience at the storehouse will help her eventually find a job at better than minimum wage.

When I was growing up, Mom and Dad worked. Very seldom was there anybody at home. I can remember taking my younger brother to school with me the first year because there was nobody home to take care of him. The teachers just sat him in the back of the room and gave him little things to do. I got married at fifteen to get out from under all the family responsibilities.

I took care of both my grandparents until they died. My grandmother died when I was thirteen. By that time I was taking the responsibility of the whole family, so she was just one more. I already had Sarah, my oldest child, when Grandpa died.

I never thought about an education being a stepping stone for a career because I thought I would get married and have a family. I'd never have to work. Boy, did I get a surprise! I'd like to try to go back to school and learn to do something else. I might even pick up on some of the things I'm doing down at the storehouse. I've found I enjoy that.

My husband divorced me. I didn't divorce him. I had a mental breakdown because I had too much with three kids and trying to hold a job and provide a home. I just couldn't manage to do it. The oldest girl had brain damage and the youngest had her own problems because she had spinal meningitis. I couldn't quite cope. I went through a year where I actually became an alcoholic. Once I got out of that, I began to realize things.

After having quite a few blackout spells and realizing that I was taking every ounce of strength and every bit of money I had and putting it in a bottle, not knowing what I was doing when I was drunk or who brought me home or what I did when I got home, I just said it wasn't worth it. I went down to detox and dried out and learned to do as they said.

I was delivering early-morning newspapers, but I had to go to the hospital for surgery. I'd been quite sick. I had a couple of heart attacks and a couple of strokes. Philis was only twelve years old at the time and I couldn't leave her alone. One of my customers was a member of the church and she put the missionaries in contact with me. They arranged for somebody to take care of Philis while I was in the hospital.

Initially, I took the discussions more or less out of curiosity. It was strange because a lot of lessons said things that I had always thought. The church brought back a lot of the beliefs I had lost over the years. It has let me know that people can be good. When I have problems with Philis, it's nice to know that I have somebody to talk to who can give me some counseling or help her out.

Because of things being the way they are, we actually depend upon what we get from the storehouse as our bread and butter. I do the clerking and the paperwork at the storehouse three days a week. When Brother Weston has me call out to Utah I find the people out there so very nice to talk to, and so helpful. The paperwork is kind of hectic. Right now we're getting ready for an audit on Wednesday. I'm finding it quite challenging doing the books and making sure that they are in order. I can see where my work at the storehouse is serving a purpose.

On Sundays I'm the assistant nursery leader. When my kids were small we were under the impression that you don't get children to sit down long enough to teach them anything. All of a sudden I find out you can! It's amazing to see how much they improve from week to week. We have lessons and teach them a game or a little song or try to get them to crayon a picture. It's very exciting to see that they can learn so much! If they cry we usually hold them. Since I've had my calling I feel like I have a responsibility to these children and it's important that I get to church. My co-workers at the storehouse are all happy and proud to find I've got a calling within the church that puts me in contact with the kids.

I enjoy the visiting teachers when they come and just plain teach a lesson. If I'm not going to church—like right now I'm not in Relief Society—at least I'm getting something. But some of them come in and they say, "You should be doing this and you should be doing that and that's why you're having all the problems you're having." I don't particularly need that. I have enough trouble. Lynne Whitney is my visiting teacher right now. I like her except sometimes I don't quite know how to take her. She's so quiet and I don't know what she's thinking. A couple of times I've told her something in confidence that she's told the bishop, and he's gotten back to me all mad and upset. I think, "Oh, why did I tell her?" But that's her job, too, I know.

Everybody keeps saying I've always been a women's libber and I say, "Not by choice." I guess I have been because I have had to support my family and I've had no help from the kids' father. I'd like to get back to school and start a career. I'd like to become more active in things at church.

Gary Johnston, 35

By March, Gary Johnston had been in the bishopric for five months. Although he also attended Ward Welfare Committee meetings, Priesthood Executive Committee meetings, and Ward Correlation Council when he was ward mission leader, being in the bishopric has changed his perspective. The Welfare Committee, composed of the bishopric, Relief Society presidency, and priesthood leaders, directs the ward's efforts in giving help to members with pressing needs and tries to help members become more self-sufficient. During the year the committee helped members find jobs, presented seminars on career development and financial management, and enlisted volunteers to work at the cannery and storehouse. The Priest-

hood Executive Committee oversees home teaching and other priesthood quorum activities, and the Correlation Council, which includes the Sunday school, Primary, and Young Men and Young Women's presidencies, coordinates the activities of the various organizations.

Raised in Bountiful, Utah, Gary Johnston was brought to Delaware two and a half years ago by the Du Pont company, where he is a marketing communications supervisor in the textiles division. He met his wife, Deborah, at BYU, and is the father of three children, ages three to nine.

When I graduated from high school I went to Weber State College in Ogden. Another fellow and I formed a little car pool. We talked a couple of the best-looking girls we knew into being in our car pool. I wasn't sure what I wanted to do, but I had to get into school. You had to make some good decisions quickly or you would end up in the jungle shooting at people.

I began to realize that there were other things in life besides being the best athlete or the most popular kid at school. How was I going to make it through the rest of life? I became very anxious when I started looking at a mission, Vietnam, higher education. The church played a role by saying, "It's life, Gary. You've got to get involved in life. You're going to have to spring out of this nice comfort zone that you've been in for the last nineteen years." I've always fallen back on the training that I got in the church—"just do your best and see what comes of it."

Because of the draft there was a quota for missionaries. There were two of us in my ward who were ready to go at the same time, so I borrowed another ward's quota. I went to Northern California. When I'd been out for a few weeks, I could think of a lot of other things I'd rather be doing. I could be cruising in Salt Lake City in a convertible instead of talking to people who didn't want anything to do with me. Some elders quit and went home. I finally realized, "I can't go home. I might as well start performing, taking advantage of what I'd been sent out to do." I was very frightened for the first four or five months.

There were probably 130 baptisms filled out in my recommend book, but I only wore my white suit of clothes a few times. All the baptizing was done by friends of the people we were teaching. I felt this was the way missionary work is supposed to go—people were talking to their friends about the gospel.

My testimony is based on my personal conviction that Jesus Christ lives. I've spent time in prayer and meditation and fasting and asking questions to come to that. My testimony is that I am a son of God and Jesus Christ has given us an opportunity to return to him and that the human race is basically good. I don't believe "the natural man is an enemy to God." I believe the natural man is a friend of God. It depends on your definition of *natural*. If I am a child of God, then my natural tendencies are to become like God, just as my children's natural tendencies are take on the attributes of their mother and me.

The summer after my mission, my ward called me to teach a Sunday school class of fourteen-year-olds. They couldn't get a teacher to take that class. The girls were worse than the boys. They tried to run me out, too. The first week or two I wanted to give up, but I finally realized that I wasn't too much different from them and that a lot of adults had probably looked at me just the way I was looking at them. I tried to figure out what I had wanted my teachers to do. I taught the Sunday school class that way. We talked about things that were happening in their lives and tried to put ourselves into the scriptures. For example, Samson was a Nazarite and was supposed to be a spiritual person. He didn't want to be that. He wanted to drive a sports car and date all the women in town and be a real carouser. Yet he had a birthright and a religious mother who had promised that he was going to be a certain type of person. He was a very handsome, virile, debonair person who took advantage of his physical appearance and just used everybody. I tried to use that situation to draw out the relationship between the kids and their parents. By the end of the summer we had a good group of young men and women who, I think, were excited about the church. Some of my attitudes had changed too.

While I was on my mission I decided to go to Brigham Young University. I felt I'd be more at ease with myself if I lived away from home. I started in accounting. Then I got bored. I couldn't stand filling out ledgers and fitting numbers into little boxes. I started studying sociology until I realized that sociologists don't make any money and people always telling you their problems could be very depressing. Then I thought advertising sounded exciting. I'd already taken the required accounting, economics, and marketing courses.

After graduation I took a job with a small company that sold computers. I threw my stereo and my clothes into the back of my car and headed for California. I called the mission home in Sacramento, and the mission president's daughter gave me the name of a friend of hers who had a vacant apartment. I slept on the floor that night, got up the next morning, and met my boss downstairs to start work—calling on accounts, totally confused, scared, and bewildered.

When I stepped out of the ivory halls of Brigham Young University, I thought I knew what I needed to know to launch a career. I was wrong. First of all, you don't get into advertising unless you know somebody or you work for free for five years. My mission had prepared me to talk a little bit and to convince someone that I had a good thing that would perform for them. I found that advertising principles—working on people's buying motives and their emotions—could be applied to selling. I became quite successful. When I had the opportunity to get into advertising, I took it.

I was working for the Du Pont company in pharmaceutical sales—pushing drugs to hospitals and doctors. They asked me to transfer to the home office for a temporary assignment in advertising and promotion. I expected to go back out as a district manager. When I took on the responsibility of promoting carpets and fibers, I changed career paths, so I'll probably be here for a while. I've just been given a new position as a supervisor. It's satisfying to work with the New York agencies and then say to the marketing manager, "This is what we're going to do for you." When it works out, he's excited and grateful that I was there. It's frustrating when I go to all that work and the program bombs. Then I'm a real bum; I don't know anything. There's constant pressure to perform well.

I don't get to spend much time with my family. I was away on business all but four nights the entire month of January. I didn't do a very good job on my church responsibilities and I didn't do a very good job with my family. The reason I go to work and the reason I attend church and accept responsibilities is so I can have my family. When I'm not able to spend any time with them, I start asking, "Why am I doing all these things?" Sometimes I let my church responsibilities slip. Am I going to spend the four hours that I have this night with my daughters talking about what they're doing at school or am I going out to a meeting or home teaching? That becomes a battle within me.

I think the line "Just give your family quality time, then you have the time to do other things" is an excuse not to spend time with your family. Your family doesn't need quality time. They just need time. My children need to know that they've got a father who can sit on the living room floor and play checkers with them or just be in the same room with them for a while. I dread the day that my daughters start being interested in boys because I know what boys are like. I just happen to be one myself. I want my children to be active in the church, but that's up to them. I hope we can teach them that way.

My one nemesis in the church is home teaching. Once I get there and spend time with the people, I'm glad I've gone. I'm working on going every month. I'll probably have to work on it the whole time I'm in the church. I'm not concerned about a home teacher's visiting my family every month. Having somebody in my home every single month to talk about the gospel isn't as valuable as knowing that if I need somebody to come over to help me administer to one of my children or just to talk with me that I've got my home teacher. If there's a crisis when I'm out of town, I know Debbie has someone she can call.

I've noticed that the church has started to treat women a little better than they did in the past. On my mission I once asked a woman to give the closing prayer in sacrament meeting. Somebody told me that women don't give prayers in sacrament meetings. That was crazy. Now the church is encouraging women to be educated. They say, "Go get educated and learn all these wonderful things." Then they say, "Stay home with the kids." The church has developed a little contradiction. The *Church News,* the *Ensign,* and the *New Era* highlight women who are successful: Congresswoman so and so is a member of the church or she's a woman with a Ph.D. who is teaching at a university and traveling all over the country. If she's been able to do all that, she has probably shunned some other responsibilities. What about the woman who went to school for two years, got married, and supported her husband through school? Now she's raising four children and keeping a happy home. She's not a congresswoman; she's not an executive in a corporation. The young women see that the people who are featured in the *Church News* are the college professors, but they're being told in church that they should be responsible mothers.

It's the same situation with young men going on missions. At the last general priesthood meeting, they had an Olympic gold medalist stand up and tell all the young men to set objectives, to be wholesome, and to live their religion. Right before that the speakers had said, "Every young man should serve a mission," and, "don't let anything stand in the way of serving a mission." Here's this young man who didn't go on a mission. He dedicated twelve years of his life to becoming an Olympic champion. Okay, now he's a stake missionary and was married in the temple, but he didn't go on a mission. A young boy sitting in the congregation might say, "I want to be a superstar like him. He didn't go on a mission, but he's here in general conference telling all of us how to plan our lives."

I enjoy associating with Bishop Bushman and Rufus Lanier and Doug Ridge and Karel Vander-Heyden. They're very spiritual. Bishop Bushman is one of the "super people." He's very successful outside the church and yet takes on a lot of responsibilities inside the church. I like trying to figure out how he does it.

My biggest frustration in the bishopric comes from trying to deal with people, getting them to accept callings and to be happy in them. I always end up as a sounding board. Sometimes I feel people are complaining about a lot of things they don't need to complain about. We all have our ups and downs with our callings, but we should do our best to accept the responsibility. Too many of the members say, "Well, I'll try it for a couple of weeks and if it doesn't work out, I'll dump it and do something else."

My attitude toward the church has changed. As the ward mission leader and especially as a missionary, I'd say to people, "This is what the Savior has done for you. This is the Book of Mormon. We have the restoration of the gospel. Here are all these wonderful things: overcoming physical death and spiritual death. If you ever have problems, the church will take care of you. If you move, the Elders' Quorum will come over and move your things. You'll have home teachers and visiting teachers come to see you. If you're ever out of food we can get food from the bishop's storehouse." I was selling them on the church.

In the bishopric, we have a ward to run. We have a lot of people to be responsible for. The gospel of Jesus Christ should not be sold to people on the basis of what the church is going to do for them. We should sell people on the fact that Jesus Christ has made an Atonement that enables us to have our sins forgiven and has given us the priesthood for the service of our fellow man. If you accept the gospel, you're accepting the responsibility to be a Christian and to serve in the name of Jesus Christ. You get to go visiting teaching. You get to go home teaching. You get to go help somebody who needs help. You will be able to show some true compassion and brotherly love for your fellow beings. Rather than saying, "The church is going to do wonderful things for you; your kids can go to Mutual and play basketball and the girls will grow up sweet and luscious in the Young Women's program," we should say, "Here's an opportunity for you to take that Christ-like feeling, magnify it, and make it grow."

12 | A Trip to the Washington Temple

Wayne and Sharon Morris knocked on our door at 5:30 A.M. Saturday, May 11. Within ten minutes the four of us were headed south on I-95; our destination was the Washington Temple, ninety miles away. At the temple by 7:30, we dressed in our white clothing and each obtained the name of a deceased person for whom we served as proxies during the 8:00 endowment session—making covenants and receiving the promise of blessings on their behalf. While Wayne and Douglass were waiting in the Celestial Room for Sharon and me at the end of the session, a temple worker asked them if we would go upstairs to help with some sealings. They agreed, so we took the elevator to the sixth floor. Another temple worker ushered us over to the group that needed additional members; it was Rufus and Shelia Lanier with Gary and Deborah Johnston. None of us had known the others were in the temple.

In the sealing room, Deborah, Sharon, and I sat in front of one of the pair of mirrors, the multiple reflections of which suggest eternity, as Rufus and Shelia were proxies for his deceased parents. After they were sealed—married for time and eternity, Rufus and two of his deceased siblings were sealed to their parents. Douglass, Gary, and Wayne acted as proxies for the children and as priesthood witnesses. Rufus had tears in his eyes, and all of us were touched by his joy at being sealed to his parents for eternity.

The church is universalist in its belief that salvation, that is, a resurrection of the physical body and ultimate redemption from hell, are freely available to all as a result of Christ's Atonement. In order to attain exaltation, however, one must, in addition to living righteously, be baptized into the church. The highest level of exaltation is reserved for those who have been endowed in the temple and sealed to a spouse. These blessings are not denied to those who have died without receiving these ordinances, for the church teaches that the dead will be taught the gospel in the spirit world and will have the opportunity to accept the ordinances that are performed by proxies in the temple.

Many temple patrons do ordinances for individuals whose names come from the church's name extraction program. Volunteers copy names and birthdates from parish registers or other primary sources, and the temple assigns patrons to serve as proxies for baptism, endowment, and sealing to parents. The church teaches that members should serve as proxies for their ancestors, and the Wilmington Stake operates three libraries—in Wilmington, Dover, and Salisbury—for genealogical research. Open three days and one evening a week, each library consists of two rooms of file cabinets and microfilm readers and a few shelves of books, and each has a microfiche copy of the card catalogue of the Salt Lake library. Any film can be ordered from Salt Lake for use in the branch libraries.

Beulah Somers, 73

Beulah Somers and her husband, Fred, direct the operations of the genealogical libraries in the Wilmington Stake. The Somers came to Newark in 1951 when Fred started teaching at the University of Delaware. At that time, Beulah says, "Newark was just a little one-horse town." Since then the town's population has grown from 6,731 to 25,515, and the university from 1,722 undergraduate and 645 graduate students to 13,806 undergraduate and 1,964 graduate students. Because many of their peers have either returned to the West or live in the Wilmington Ward, the Somerses find themselves a generation older than the other active members of the Elkton Ward. Their three grown sons live in Hawaii, Ohio, and Mexico. In addition to working in the library, Beulah takes turns with Anne Mace providing floral arrangements for the chapel, usually from her own gardens. Active in community work as well as the church, Beulah has been involved in the YWCA and was a president of the University's Women's Club. One of her projects this winter was making the appliquéd university seal in the center of the Newark Historical Society's quilt.

I grew up in Liberty, Idaho, with three brothers and four sisters. My mother's grandfather was Charles C. Rich. During the depression going to school at all was quite a struggle. There were many who didn't go to high school because they couldn't afford it. The only way to go to college was to work your way through. Working never bothered me. I think I was taught to work from the day I was born. In the depression you either worked or you starved. Sometimes I wonder if people who say they haven't the money to go to school have really tried. My parents' main ambition was that we all get college educations. Two of the children died before finishing, but we all got college educations and we all worked. My oldest sister died suddenly during my freshman year of college. That broke my mother up, and after that I had the responsibility for my six younger brothers and sisters. I went to school and took care of them, too.

I met my husband at Utah Agricultural College in Logan. We were married five years later. When I graduated in 1934 with a teaching certificate in secondary education, there was only one teaching position in my field open in the whole state of Utah. After I went to work for the government I couldn't afford to teach school. I had to have some money, and the best way to get it was to be a secretary. I worked in Salt Lake City, San Francisco, and Logan before I went to England to be married. A family in Salt Lake took me in and provided a lot of things for me; otherwise, I don't think I would have made it.

The first time I went out of the valley was when I went to San Francisco to work. It was the first time I'd worked with non-Mormon people. It changed my perspective on the world. I opened my eyes and saw that they were really human beings and they had a lot of the good things of life. So many of our members think we're so good. I just don't see how we can feel that we are so superior. We should be able to live better lives with the teachings that we have. This attitude isn't as strong now as it used to be. In some communities if you weren't a member of the church you were an outcast. As soon as you joined the church you were somebody.

I could have had a good career in what I was doing, but I wasn't interested in pursuing it further. I knew that as soon as Fred got through school we would have a family. I don't regret giving all my time to my family. I enjoyed being home. Other people couldn't understand how I could enjoy it, but I did. My children enjoyed it too; they didn't want me to work. I began teaching in the Extension Service when our youngest one was in high school. It was very satisfying to teach something that people wanted. People signed up to take dressmaking because they wanted to learn. Some of them turned out to be pretty good seamstresses.

I was the nonprofessional because I didn't have a degree in home economics. One day I met a lady at the grocery store who asked me if I was teaching the tailoring class. I told her I wasn't. She said, "I've taken it from the other teachers. But if you were teaching it, I'd take it from you because I can understand you better."

I thought, "If somebody feels that good about it, I don't have to care about what the others think." I learned to do my best and not worry about it. I got quite a bit of satisfaction from knowing that the lay person could understand my teaching.

I enjoyed teaching Primary and Sunday school more than anything else. I enjoyed relating to the children and watching them grow. When we were in graduate school at Cornell University, there weren't enough people to run a separate Sunday school and Primary. We taught the Primary lessons in Sunday school because I thought they were better. I remember going to the church offices in Salt Lake City and asking for the Primary materials. They said, "What are you teaching?"

I said, "I'm teaching Sunday school."

They said, "Why don't you have a Primary?"

"Because we don't have enough children. We don't have a place to hold it. We are just now getting a junior Sunday school." When they said they weren't allowed to give me the Primary manuals, I said, "That's fine with me. I don't have to teach those children. This is volunteer work, and if I don't have any materials I won't teach them."

They finally said, "Well, under the circumstances, we will let you have them."

I went visiting teaching all my life until the last two years. There are some good aspects of it, but I do not enjoy being visited by teachers who bring five or six children. I have had as many as eight here, running wild. The things I've had destroyed by the children of the visiting teachers! I finally laid the law down and said, "You can sit." I enjoyed all the women. I don't expect children not to make a move, but I don't feel I should have to put everything up out of reach when my visiting teachers come.

One day they came when we were having guests for dinner. I had the things to make a pie set out on the kitchen table. I shut the doors, but they don't lock. When I went back to finish, I found the cream cheese all matted up in a wad. Once, I went out after they left and found that they had taken our neighbor's woodpile and thrown it all down the hill. One of the teachers had her husband come stack it back up. I do like to visit with them and there are toys in the closet for two or three children to play with. Most visiting teachers stay too long. I used to have that trouble with one of my companions. I couldn't get her to leave.

At the genealogical library I spend most of my time keeping books and don't have much time to do research. We are there a lot of hours. We don't get many church members there, but we've met so many interesting people from the community. Most of them have done research in many places. We learn a lot from them.

One fellow came in and found exactly what he wanted in the place where we told him he might look. I've never seen anybody so jubilant in my life. He said he had looked for years. Another man who comes two or three times a week is working on Switzerland. We had a lot of work to do one Saturday so we told him he could stay to finish his work. He said, "I found it! I finally found it!" He had been looking for it for weeks and found it in that little extra bit of time. We have a very dedicated staff. Everybody's willing to pitch in to help the others out. We have a sharp crew.

Doyle Stroup, 44

Every Saturday Doyle and Rita Stroup drive from Port Deposit, Maryland, to Wilmington to work at the branch library. Doyle is a chemist at Aberdeen Proving Grounds in Maryland. A graduate of BYU, he met Rita in his home branch in Bradford, Pennsylvania. Their son, Stephen, was born in January 1985.

I still consider Bradford my home. If I had an opportunity for 80 percent of my salary, I'd move in a minute even though they get twice the snow and it's thirty degrees colder in the winter. It's pretty country and has an odor all its own—raw crude oil.

My dad died just after we got married in 1976. After my dad died my mother started working as a nurse's aide, but she's just been called on a two-year mission in the Washington Temple. We never had a whole lot. One Christmas my brother wanted an electric train. My dad never had any money until a day or two before Christmas. He went around the city of Bradford looking for an electric train. He found one in the store window the day before Christmas Eve and bought it. Christmas Eve, he found out the seller hadn't put the train into the box. He called him up at 11:30 and the guy said, "You come down tomorrow, Christmas Day, and I'll give you the train."

My dad said, "Christmas is in the morning. It isn't tomorrow afternoon." So they went and got the train at midnight. The interesting part is that my dad had paid with a check. Two days after Christmas the man was asking my dad to make the check good. My dad always made good on all his checks. He wanted his kids to have a good Christmas. He knew the guy would be after him. To a lot of people this story would probably be an embarrassment. It means a lot to me. My dad went without so we could have school clothes. A lot of times a car payment was missed because we needed food. He was willing to take his shirt off his back to give to somebody even though he didn't have a shirt to give. He never asked for anything back.

My mother was baptized in the church in 1935—before she met my father. My brother and I were blessed in the church. Mother didn't start going again until the 1960s. The Bradford Branch had some severe problems, and the membership had fallen off to almost nothing. Some of the members moved West and those who stayed behind fell out of fellowship. Outside of seeing my mother's Book of Mormon in her drawer, we had no contact with the church until 1951 or 1952 when two missionaries came to visit us. Being eleven at the time, I immediately fell in love with this big, handsome Wyoming missionary, Elder Gardner. He was about six feet four inches tall and the epitome of manhood. I begged my mother to let me be baptized. She said I had to wait another year. Meanwhile she began sending us to church. My parents didn't go, but they rounded up the four of us and somebody took us to church. Bradford was always a very small branch. It encompassed a fifty-mile radius, and the average attendance was about twenty people. The missionaries always hung around our house. They'd come for dinner. They always said that if they were out of money they could always come to the Stroup house for a meal. After my dad joined the church, things were done in accordance with the church's principles and ideals.

I like the Elkton Ward. I like it much better than our previous ward, which we didn't go to that much. Our area of the ward is kind of no man's land. Ninety-five percent of the Elkton membership lives in Elkton or north of there—

Newark, New Castle, Bear. There aren't many active members in this area. There are a lot of inactives though.

We had some very trying years in the church. When you're inactive, you feel guilty when you go to church because you feel like you don't deserve to be there. Many church members say such inconsiderate things like, "Well, I haven't seen you here for the last month and a half." I wanted just to come in quietly, get back in the groove, and then I could talk to people.

One of the most inspiring figures in the Elkton Ward is Cloyd Mullins. I liked seeing Cloyd Mullins up in front as the branch president on Sunday mornings. He is a very strong, forthright, down-to-earth person. Even though he sits in the back now, when I go in on Sunday mornings I look to see if he's there. I have a great deal of respect for his testimony and for the strength he gave to me in a time when I needed it.

The church is in the way I do things. Especially now that we have Stephen, I think a lot more about what I do. Every father probably becomes much more conscious of his own shortcomings because he doesn't want his son to be the image of him. The church is the one thing that gives me guidance as to what is right.

When I got married I looked at myself and said, "You're married and you have a wife and, hopefully, a family. They're going to depend on you." I began taking a different attitude toward my job. At that time I wanted to quit. I'd take off a few minutes early. I'd come in a few minutes late. I didn't volunteer for anything. Then I decided, "Maybe part of my problem on this job is me." It took a long time to turn it all around. It was probably five years before the supervisors began to see I was serious. Maybe I'm overdoing it. I hate to leave work. Sometimes I've just got to get one more thing done. Then I look at the clock, "Oh, Rita's going to kill me." Excuse me for being a little self-righteous, but I believe there's a lot of inspiration from the Lord involved in my work. Although I might not be the most righteous person, I believe that when I'm truly seeking to do what I think is in the best interest of my country and my organization, the Lord is helping me.

The people at the genealogy library are choice. They are well educated, attorneys, retired Ph.D.'s, etc. They're nonmembers and very respectful of the church's wishes. They speak very highly of the church because they recognize the amount of money that the church has invested in the library. Talking with them about their problems in genealogy has taught me. It's a joy to see people enjoy doing it. As the Prophet Joseph says, we can't be saved in the kingdom of our Father in heaven by ourselves. We must have our patriarchal line of authority. Genealogy also enriches my life by giving me a testimony of the indomitable spirit that some of these people must have had.

A man named Harry Diehl, a next-door neighbor to Dave Finch of the high council, is a volunteer worker at the library. He's not LDS. He thinks so highly of

the contribution the church makes to genealogy he got the Delaware Genealogical Society to donate two hundred dollars to the library. A lot of the Delaware
Genealogical Society members do research at the library.

The library is very humble in looks. In fact, one patron came in and said,
"Next week, I'm going to a real library where they have books on the wall." He
was talking about the Mennonite library up in Lancaster.

I said, "You know, sir, the material that's available to you through this library
is almost endless. You cannot even begin to comprehend the amount of material
that's available to you through this very humble facility."

He said, "I don't think it's any help to me." I felt sad that a person would walk
out not even understanding that he hadn't even scratched the tip of the iceberg.

The hardest part is getting Rita and Stephen out of the house and to Wilmington by nine o'clock. We've been working there since the library opened in
1981. We have the Saturday morning shift, which nobody else wants, but I don't
mind. If they dismissed me, I'd just volunteer to do it.

Church callings make the world very real. They make you realize your shortcomings. President Mullins called me to teach Primary a few years ago. I told
him when he called me that I had a real problem relating to children in a class.
It made me start to think, "How can I learn to do something I don't know how
to do?" I saw a great shortcoming in my life. Maybe it was helpful in preparing
for Stephen. One of my greatest goals is to have Stephen be able to tell me that
he's grateful for the way I brought him up.

The most meaningful thing about the gospel to me is that it's a gospel of
repentance. You can make some very dire and bad mistakes, but there are only
two things that I know of that can't be forgiven: one is the sin of murder and the
other is the sin against the Holy Ghost. Everything else, even unto adultery, can
be forgiven. If you're truly sorry and if you can make as much compensation to
the other party as you can and never do the thing again, you have the power
and ability to be forgiven. You can grow from there.

I'd like to go to the temple again—to qualify for a temple recommend. I'd
like to be able to meet all my spiritual, temporal, and financial obligations. I'm
probably wrong in wanting this, but I would just love to sit down and talk to
my father again. There have been so many times since I've been married that
I've been driving the car and said out loud, "Oh, Dad, if I could just get your
advice," because he was so much wiser. Maybe one day I'll get the opportunity
just to see him, talk to him and tell him that I love him.

Rita Stroup, 36

*Rita Stroup joined the church while a student at Millersville State College.
She has a degree in library science from BYU and has worked as a school librarian.*

Besides working Saturday mornings in the genealogy library, she plays the piano for Primary.

When I was a freshman in college I found a book called *The Mormon Story* at the farmers' market in Lancaster. I brought the book back to school. Then I went to the college library and the public libraries and found all the books I could on Mormonism. I wrote a paper for my freshman English class on the social aspects of Mormonism. I guess I did a good job because my professor gave me an A+++. The Spirit must have been moving me as I put the words down.

While I was at summer session, two missionaries knocked at my mother's door in Bradford, Pennsylvania, about three hundred miles away. She told them to come back when I got home several weeks later. I had some of the discussions before I went off to a Presbyterian church camp as a counselor. In my free time I read Mormon pamphlets. I compared what I learned about the church with the scriptures I already knew from the Bible. I decided that it was the answer to my prayers.

I was baptized on the nineteenth of August in Jamestown, New York, as a member of the Allegheny Branch. Back at school in Millersville, I had to take a taxi to church the first time because there was no public transportation on Sundays. Some good people in the Lancaster Ward took me to church after that. When I first joined the church, I can remember being tremulous about shaking someone's hand or having to make any kind of conversation. Doyle's father used to corner me to talk to me, but I always tried to make a beeline out of church so I wouldn't have to talk with anybody. The church later became an extended family to me, and that made me feel very comfortable. I don't have that feeling as much now.

After college and working for four years, I considered going on a mission. I used to have people come to my apartment for the discussions. For a long time after my conversion I wanted to convert the whole world. I tried to be prayerful about it and use my head. I decided to go to graduate school so I could get tenure in my job, and I wanted to be in the BYU atmosphere. I thought I could earn some money and go on my mission later.

I liked the atmosphere at BYU. Everybody was like a mother or sister—just like in church. The year after I came back we got married.

Stephen's been a real blessing in our lives. He's the answer to many prayers and also the fulfillment of a blessing that we had. I think he's going to teach us more than we'll teach him. Just a week before he was born I wrote in my journal:

"I hope he or she might grow up to find love and acceptance and that my husband and I will provide him with a temporal and spiritual education. I pray that I might somehow instill in this beautiful child the principles of righteousness that are taught in the Gospel, that I might be a worthy example. I hope the child might be healthy and strong, and of sound mind, and that he or she might ever strive to utilize his God given potential. I hope others might benefit and be enriched through our son or daughter. I have long dreamed of being blessed with a special spirit from our Heavenly Father. I hope that his spirit might feel my love. If I were able to give a blessing (although I know women don't hold the priesthood), I should like to bless him to endure to the end and return to his Father in Heaven one day. I've also prayed that he will know of the life and sacrifices of his forefathers and appreciate their earthly conditions. If I'm not able to see that their temple work is completed, I pray that he will do so." I didn't write it down, but I would like him to go on a mission if he had the desire to go.

I enjoy him, but sometimes I feel like I want to take a nap and I can't. By the end of the afternoon I'm ready for Doyle to come home and lend a hand watching Stephen. There are so many good parts to it. He's a real joy. He gets so pleased about his little accomplishments.

We began coming to Elkton before they changed the boundaries to include Port Deposit. Bonita Cherry was one of the first people we met. She invited us to a picnic at her house that first Sunday. About five months later Tom Robinson stopped by to tell us that the boundaries were changing and we would be in the Elkton Branch.

If I lived in Salt Lake, I might like to work in the genealogy library. I have a testimony of genealogy. About 95 percent of the library patrons are nonmembers. When I see nonmembers being as fervent about genealogy as I am, it increases my testimony of its importance. I think it was President Kimball who said genealogy is one of the first things we are supposed to do. Sometimes the church keeps the members so busy in other things that they don't have time for genealogy or they think it's all been done by somebody else in their family.

I can remember questioning my relatives. My grandfather was raised in Ticonderoga, New York. When we went up there, I'd wonder if any of my ancestors were buried in the cemeteries out in the countryside. A long time before I joined the church, I felt that there was a reason they wanted me to find out about them and their lives. At BYU I took a genealogy class. I didn't know much more than what I had written down from the family at that time.

After we were married, I wrangled Doyle into taking me down to the library in Silver Spring, Maryland, and he got hooked on it. We used to go to a lot of libraries—the Library of Congress and the state library in Harrisburg. We've been to a lot of courthouses and cemeteries. When I'm reading the microfilms, sometimes, a spirit takes over and I feel very close to these people. Besides finding the names and dates, I like to find out how they earned their living and a little about their trials and tribulations. I have some letters that were written in 1853 by one of my third great-grandmothers. I feel very close to her and to the people who are mentioned in them. I want to do the temple work for them myself. It's probably selfish of me not to turn the names in so someone else can do it, and I worry that I won't get it done. I don't always have a temple recommend, but I want to do the ordinance work for my direct ancestors. I feel very bad when we don't meet the expectations like paying a full tithing so we can go to the temple.

Linda Callery, 32

Linda Callery works at the genealogical library on Thursday evenings. She has also been a stake missionary and the ward single's representative. The eldest of Bernard and Betty Callery's six children, she went to high school in Delaware. She works as an aide at a nursing home and plans to go back to school for nurses' training.

Because I was brought up in the gospel, it wasn't until I was in my late teens that I got my own testimony. I always relied on my father's. I've often wondered if I would have let the missionaries in if they had knocked on my door. My parents have given me a lot more than material things and love and understanding. Even though they haven't been active in the church, they have strong testimonies.

Moving to Delaware was a big transition because the people are different. There are a lot of people in the area who are still fighting the Civil War. We never had that in New England. There is a lot of prejudice down here—not only against blacks, but against Portuguese. A Mia Maid teacher, Charlene Weed, helped me over the rough spots. She helped me gain some insights into myself. When I asked her my questions, her answers were basically along the same line as my parents', but hers seemed more objective to me because she was outside the family.

My brother in Utah and I are the only ones in the family who are active right now. When my brother's first wife divorced him, he was so hurt he left and went to Salt Lake. A short while later he married a nice girl. They have four children. I don't worry about him because he's so strong. He's getting ready to go to the temple soon. If I could only get the family here to be active. I know they have testimonies. Every Sunday that they don't go makes it a little harder. It's something that they've missed, something they could have learned. My dad said, "Well, we can't all pay our tithing—"

I said, "Well, that will come if we can just get going to church."

After high school I worked at McDonald's for a short while, then as a nurse's aide. After I was laid off from both of those jobs, I began working in a maternity shop. I worked there for eight years. I enjoyed working with the expectant mothers. They were in a nice frame of mind. Last spring I went back to working as an aide. I enjoy nursing so much that I'm going to get my RN. I'm going to try to go to the University of Delaware.

I've always been a visiting teacher, but in the last few years I've appreciated it more because it gets me more involved with other people. I see the members in a different light—at home with their families. Sometimes at church we want everyone to see how good we are. I like to see the other side, the side that's vulnerable. It strengthens me. We'll be talking about the message and all of a sudden we'll get onto other things. It helps me see I'm not the only one who has to go through things. The strong bond between the women in Relief Society comes from visiting teaching. I've had a strong testimony of the gospel, but I'm learning to have a testimony of its function.

My friends all have this undying fear that they're never going to get married. Every time they give a lesson, the first thing they bring up is marriage. I don't know if it's because we're getting older. It was never one of my fears. I know the Lord will look out for me when the time is right for this gentleman to walk into my life. If he were to walk in right now, I don't think I'd be prepared. Maybe the other girls feel threatened by the married sisters. I don't. They're examples of how I want to make my home life. When we talk about things in Relief Society that don't relate to me, I can still get ideas to think about.

Now I'm a librarian at the genealogical library on Thursdays. I help the patrons get started on their work or get an idea of what they can do. Some people come in with the idea that the LDS Church has it all done for them. There is a lot of work and time involved. It can be exciting, and it can be pretty depressing. Not only do I tell patrons about what's in the library, but if I have things at home they wish to use, I'll share with them. As I learn more about my ancestors, I find out a lot about myself, maybe why I'm like I am. With each little thing I find out, my family tree becomes more real. I guess when you do genealogy a lot of skeletons come out of the closet. If my family were perfect I would wonder if they had been tested. Were they tried? Even though some of them weren't so great, I have to give them credit for whatever they did. Maybe they learned something from it, and maybe I wouldn't be here if they hadn't done it.

My mother was about four or five when her mother died. When I went to the temple to be baptized for my grandmother, I had a very strong impression that she had already been a member of the church for a very long time. From talking to my father's family, I've noticed that when someone in the family dies, they're dead and buried. They don't want to talk about them anymore. I appreciate the fact that my own ancestors are real close. They're still alive.

I used to tell my mom and my father to come into the graveyard when we visited relatives. We all would have a prayer for the infants who were buried outside the graveyard. I used to wonder, "Well, why weren't they so holy, just because they weren't baptized?"

My mother grew up in an orphanage and had always wondered about her roots. When I started helping my father with genealogy, I wrote a letter to my mother's great-uncle. She remembered his name, Warren Staples. When the postmaster got the letter, he closed up shop (everybody was getting ready to leave early because of a snowstorm), and he made a special trip out to give the letter to the man's sister. Warren had died fifteen years earlier. When my great-aunt opened this letter, she was quite relieved because she had wondered what had happened to my mother, the daughter of her youngest sister. We started exchanging letters with the whole family.

That summer when we made a trip to New England, my mother wanted to see her mother's grave. She found her way to the graveyard, but she couldn't find the grave. All of a sudden she started to cry. She was just beginning to find out about her family, and now we couldn't find the grave. I said, "Mom, look, we'll have a prayer right away." We got down on our knees and we had a very strong prayer. We met a gentleman along the way and he told us to go to a house near the graveyard.

We told the lady there why we were there and she told us how she had said a prayer almost at the same time as we had. She was so lonely and no one cared about her. I thought, "How many prayers go up to the Lord, yet he takes time to answer each one." She told us how to find the plot, then she invited us and we had lunch and dinner with her. It turned out to be a great day.

I enjoy going to the graveyards. I like to go and stand over the graves. We'll always have a prayer, just to let that person know we're doing the very best we can. We ask the Lord to bless us to find a lot of doors that will open up. Sometimes I can almost see people reaching out with their arms, wondering if I'm in their lineage. They've been waiting so many years and it's like they're wondering if I'm going to be the one to stand over their grave. There's so much work to be done, and I wish I was related to everybody so that I could get it done.

The University Students

13

Although Newark, Delaware, is a university town, most of the local members send their children to Brigham Young University in Utah. Consequently, there are few LDS students at the University of Delaware. When we first moved to Delaware in 1982, my husband was asked to be the faculty adviser to the Latter-day Saint Student Association and I was asked to teach a class for the Institute of Religion. At universities where there are enough LDS students, the church has Institutes of Religion near the campus where students may attend classes in church history, doctrine, or social issues. Our institute met at first in our living room, then in a classroom on campus. In September 1984, Ron Adamson, the new church education instructor in the Baltimore area, began teaching the weekly class. This year there were several undergraduates who were active in the church as well as a handful of graduate students.

Angela Martinez, 19

Angela Martinez, one of four LDS sophomore girls at the University of Delaware, came to the University from Dover Air Force Base with a scholarship to study computer science. By the end of her first year, she had changed her major to international relations. As the president of the Latter-day Saint Student Association on the campus, Angela works with both the Wilmington Stake committee for singles and with Ron Adamson to plan activities for the students. This school year was difficult for Angela because one of her close friends was struck and killed in October by a drunk driver as they were walking back to the dorm together late at night.

My father has been in the air force for twenty-three years. He's a flight engineer on the C-5 transport planes. My family has lived in Dover for eight years. In high school I played field hockey and tennis. I was in the choir, the Thespians, the Spanish club, and Honor Society. I was looking for something to get myself in shape before tennis season started my senior year. Natalie Badell asked me if I wanted to play basketball on her church team. When I found out that I had to go to church once a month, that wasn't too bad. I'd been looking for a church for a long time.

The first day I went to church, a fast Sunday, it impressed me, but when basketball season ended I lost contact. One day, Natalie asked, "Would you like the missionaries to come over?"

"Okay, why not." My sister also wanted the lessons and our parents were giving us a little trouble, so Brother Victory, the basketball coach, said we could have the lessons at his house. We began on my sister's birthday, April 5, and were baptized three weeks later. When I started to read the Book of Mormon, it didn't take very long. I was ready for it. Once we talked to our mom and told her this was what we wanted to do, she gave her permission. My dad, too, because he knew there wasn't a lot he could do to stop this.

The past two summers I worked with computers on the base. I did a little bit of everything. I was in charge of all the magnetic tapes from the airplanes— recordings of the engine vibrations and other stuff on the aircraft. I processed the tapes, cleaned them, and stored them. If someone wanted to know about a certain flight, I'd pull out the tape, run it on the computer, and give him the information. I helped run a console, made deliveries, and answered the phone. Since I've changed majors, that job is no longer open to me. They have said they will find me another job on the base for this summer.

At first the computer science program was okay, but I wasn't doing as well as I thought I would be. I started looking ahead and realized that computer engi- neering wasn't what I wanted. International relations is a combination of a lot of different subjects—some history, math, Spanish, economics, anthropology, sociology, and political science. This semester I'm taking American history, microeconomics, Spanish literature, sociology, and a course about how the court system works.

I've thought of either working in Washington or New York City as some sort of liaison within the diplomatic corps, but I think once I get married I'll want to stay home and take care of my children. This field wouldn't be too hard to keep up with and eventually I could go back to it.

I'm pretty sure that I'll marry a member of the LDS Church. If you marry a nonmember, the priesthood won't be in the home. I know what it's like not to have the priesthood there. When I compare a nonmember and a member man, I can tell the difference the priesthood makes. That impresses me a lot.

I thought of going to BYU for a little while last year, but I was going to lose credits and I have few enough as it is. I like it here at Delaware. I've known my friends for almost two years now, and they all know I'm Mormon and that I don't drink or smoke. They never try to pressure me into doing something that I wouldn't want to do.

I try to get the college age members to attend the institute class. We swelled to enormous numbers in the middle of the year. It's slacking off now, but there seems to be at least a little bit of steady interest. It's a lot bigger than I expected it to be this year. We average about twelve at the class.

Institute is amazingly helpful sometimes. I come in sometimes thinking about a problem, and we start talking about it during institute class, as if by chance. For example, my friends and I were going to have to be witnesses at the trial of the man who killed a friend of mine. One Tuesday, we got a phone call from our friend's father saying that the trial wouldn't be until a month later and that her mother had had a nervous breakdown. We also heard that day that the person who hit our friend said that he didn't swerve to avoid her because if he had, he would have hit a nonexistent telephone pole.

I was very, very angry and vengeful. That day Brother Adamson started talking about forgiving and forgetting, that those who don't forgive have the greater sin. All of a sudden I thought, "Oh, my gosh, I shouldn't be feeling the way I do."

The man finally did plead guilty, twenty minutes before the start of the trial. The attorney came in and said, "Well, he pled guilty. It's over. Go home." It was a big relief.

I wasn't going to have to testify except as a rebuttal witness. My main concern was to help my friends who were going to testify. The attorney warned us the first day, "I don't know if you're going to want to sit through this. When the coroner comes you might not want to stay. He may be showing pictures." I almost left school. My parents thought I should come home and let them take care of me. My friends and I decided we had to get through this together. I talked to the dean of students a couple of times. He bent over backwards to help us.

My home teacher has helped me a lot, especially in the last six or seven months. Having scripture study with him helps me get someone else's viewpoint. By myself, sometimes I get stuck in a rut, but with someone else's input, I see new things. It's like having my own little slice of priesthood. I can go to my home teacher for help.

This year has been a real test for me. I spent a lot of time praying and reading the scriptures, trying to find something that would not necessarily make me feel better, but help me go along, and I usually always found it. That not only helped me but I was able to help my friends. It's funny because right after it happened one of my friends said to another friend of mine, "You better watch out for Angela. She may go to pieces. Take care of her and make sure she doesn't get too caught up in this." I was about the first one of us to get back on track.

Lately, the drinking and driving issue has been getting to me. I'm also bothered by the idea of having sex whenever you please. I don't see how anyone my age is prepared emotionally to handle that commitment, or noncommitment, as the case may be. A lot of my friends think about it; a lot of my friends do it.

I can't condemn them for it, but I've seen the problems that it's caused. It just doesn't seem worth it.

The church singles program is important for kids my age. Most of us are away from home. It creates an atmosphere where we can develop friendships. I think it's helped me grow in the church. Right now the singles program in the Elkton Ward has deteriorated a little. I hate to say it, but it has. We don't have family home evening as much as we used to. Rob McPherson is starting to get attached. Mostly now the activities are stakewide. In Dover, they were doing a lot of things during winter session because there were a lot of singles who weren't going to school. Transportation to stake and regional events is a problem because I don't have a car.

Sometimes it confuses my parents. "Why do you have so much to do?" I think they have the concept of church being one hour on Sundays. I'll have single adult family home evening, volleyball, and Relief Society, meetings here and meetings there. Sometimes they think it's too much. "This is going to interfere with your schoolwork."

"No, Mom, I can do it. It's okay."

Dianna Cannon, 19

Dianna Cannon grew up in Salt Lake City. The eldest of eight children, she is a descendant of early church leaders George Q. Cannon and John Taylor. As do many Salt Lake City high school graduates, she enrolled in the University of Utah. During her freshman year she and her friend Kelly Hindley applied to the National Student Exchange and they have spent their sophomore year at the University of Delaware.

When I came home one day and said, "Well, I've decided to go to Delaware to school next year," my parents were kind of taken aback. My dad did not want me to come. I have considered staying on for another year, but it's an impossibility. I'd have to pay out-of-state tuition. Delaware has such a good art history department. I love its accessibility to museums. There's nothing like that in Salt Lake.

I'd like to go to graduate school in art history or English, who knows? If I did pursue art history I think I'd probably be a professor somewhere. I'd like to have a family, too, somewhere in there. I don't think I could dedicate my life just to art history. I don't know what will happen. Maybe I'll get to the end of college and say, "I'm going to law school."

In my family you get married. If you work, it's because you have to work: your husband is in school or you're starting out and you need money. You don't try to have a career along with marriage. Most of my cousins have graduated from college, but only one cousin hasn't married. Everybody in my family has more than five children. I think that perhaps I'd have three or four, five at the most. If my work ever became more important than my family, I would have no qualms about dumping work. But unlike my mother, I don't think I could stay home. She is a very talented seamstress, and she works as a secretary at home. I like to do other things.

I want to have fewer children because you can't also have a career with that many children. I'd like to give my children more of a cultural education. You can't do things with a large family that you can with a smaller. We were so big. You can't go to the movies with ten people.

I love having little brothers and sisters because they're such a kick. Well, it's a love-hate relationship. There are times when I like being in charge. I used to feel like their second mother. I'd come home from school and I had to take care of the children because my mother had to go do something else. When you're right in the middle of being fifteen or sixteen, you become very self-centered. I played basketball and ran track. I was on the Seminary Council my senior year. I was in chorus, always, and the madrigals. We did plays every year. I had a whole bunch of home responsibilities and a whole bunch of school responsibilities that often clashed.

My first Sunday at the Elkton Ward, I found out that people wanted to get to know us. I wanted just to sit in the back, but the first Sunday we were here, I was asked to give the prayer. I was singing in the choir. I *performed* the first time I was there. Back in Utah half the people can go to church and just sit there. Here you have to be involved. The building, itself, was just entertaining. At home I walk to church. Here, I have to be driven to another *state*. I like it a lot more because I feel needed.

I haven't had a social life here. I don't know if I miss it or not. There are a lot of nice people that we go out with and do things. There's no comparison to back home. Here if you don't drink, you're kind of weird.

My father's said, "You ought to go on a mission, and I'll pay for it." I'm going to wait until I'm twenty-one to decide. My closest cousin is on a mission in Portugal right now. Another is on a mission in Switzerland. It's not a rare thing in my family for women to go. I just have other things to do! I feel like I've been on kind of a mission back here in Delaware. I might have a hard time with the mission rules. I've had more contact with missionaries here. We had Thanksgiving dinner with them.

I don't know if I differ religiously much from my parents. The things I feel differently about have religious connotations, such as premarital sex. I came home one day very upset because I'd learned that one of my girlfriends had had an abortion. I was talking to my mom about this and then my dad came in. I said, "I think that they should have taken responsibility for what they were doing and used birth control." Boy, did I say the wrong thing!

My father was so angry—and my mother! They said, "That's not taking responsibility; using birth control is avoiding responsibility." I was flabbergasted.

I said, "They were going to have sex no matter what happened. I think they should have taken the responsibility for it." I couldn't understand how they couldn't see it from my point of view. I tried to see it from their point of view and it didn't make any sense. I saw a lot of girls getting pregnant and lives just being ruined—their lives, their boyfriends' lives, the babies' lives, their parents' lives. I, as a friend, was affected.

The best way to avoid all this is not to have sex at all, but these people should have accepted the consequences. They should have realized that they would be punished by the church, but they should have used birth control instead of hurting a lot of other people. When you have a sexual relationship you should have it for other reasons than just to have a good time. It's inappropriate before marriage, but if you are going to, take responsibility.

Except for life plan and sex, my parents and I are in agreement on everything.

Since I was a kid, I wanted to be a Primary pianist. I took lessons from age six until sophomore year in high school. I practiced all the songs in the orange book, but I never got to be Primary pianist until I came here. I'm fulfilling my true calling in life! Rob McPherson said to me, "Congratulations on your exile to Primary." That's what it's like sometimes. I'm glad they called me to be a pianist, and I like working with Sister Debbie Johnston. There are nice things about this job, but in general the attitude seems to be, "We don't have anything else to do with the young singles. Let's get them involved. Stick them in Primary."

The priesthood is a definite power that I've felt at work in my life. I'd like to separate priesthood from patriarchal order, somehow. The problem is, I think, they're not separate. Priesthood is man's authority to use God's power for the betterment of everyone, and I've seen that a lot in my life. I think that's good. When it's used as a type of hierarchy it gets carried to an extreme: "Oh, my dad's the bishop" or "My dad's the stake president," as if they have more priesthood authority.

I could never understand it when they said, "Women share the priesthood with their husbands." I've never been to the temple. I don't think that's what they mean when they say "share the priesthood." For some reason, I don't think men will always hold the priesthood alone. I think women will hold the priesthood, too. There! I don't think we have to start a revolution and say, "We want the priesthood." I don't want to be part of the hierarchy, but I think that there will be duties, specific things for women to do with that priesthood. I think it's a definite power and that women have it too.

My ancestors were polygamists. When we have family reunions, you put on your name tag which wife you're from. I don't know if I believe that this is how it will be in heaven. I've often wondered if I could ever be a polygamous wife. I don't think I'd like to, but if I had to, I don't think I'd be averse to it. What bothers me most is that people say that it's going to be the celestial law. Where do they get this? Is it from Joseph Smith? It's like the patriarchal order thing. It just drives me up a wall.

I'd like to have a career in art history. I'd like to teach. I'd like to travel, meaning, I'd like to live in Europe. Since I'm learning French and German for art history, I may as well go there and learn the languages. Maybe I'll even go on a mission. It would be one way to live there. There are two sides of me that I'd like to develop. I'd like to be a more spiritual person and come to the point where I didn't have to rely so much on what I think, but more on how I feel. I'd like to be able to rely more on my spirituality than on what I think. I'd also— this is the other side of me—I'd like to own a Jaguar someday.

Denise Lanier, 19

Denise Lanier is also a sophomore at the University of Delaware and teaches a Primary class. She was also raised in the church, but in the East. She has lived in Newark since she was ten. She enrolled at the University of Delaware to study nursing, but has changed her major to languages.

College is not what I expected it to be. I thought that college people knew everything and never had any problems with math. Last year I took biology and chemistry. They didn't interest me at all. Special education was interesting, but I don't have the patience to work with that all day. I got straight A's in Spanish and Latin in high school, so I figured, "Why not give that a try." I took Spanish 101 and Italian last semester and got A's, so I added French in my third semester and I got A's there. I've finally found my niche. Sometimes I'm not too enthused about studying, but just seeing the paper come back with an A on it makes me think that I can do something right.

When I failed nursing that was a big change in my life. Everybody knew I was in nursing and asked all the time, "How are you doing?" Having to admit that I failed took a big chunk out of me. I study so much now because I never want to go through that again. I'm going to pick up a minor in business. I'm not sure if I want to go on a mission or not. All through my life I've been planning on going. It is in my patriarchal blessing that I will go sometime in my life. My main goal right now is to graduate with good grades and get a good job, working with languages. I want to travel a lot.

My father wasn't too happy when I went into languages. He wants me to go into sales, just like him. Everybody knows my father. I resented that the only way people knew me was as Rufus's daughter. It got to the point that when I was introduced as "Rufus's daughter," I'd say, "No, I'm Denise." There would be this moment of silence. My father finally started saying, "This is my daughter, Denise."

I enjoyed the Young Women's program. I enjoyed being with my Mormon friends because adolescence is one of the roughest times of life. You're making decisions. Whichever group you go with pretty much decides the rest of your life. I could have gone with the ones that party. I could have said, "Well, I may be Mormon, but I'll drink anyway." During high school I got a reputation for being a goody goody. Now I like the Word of Wisdom because it makes me different. The church has had an effect on my life. At least eight of my ten closest friends have little kids. Some are married and some aren't. If it hadn't been for the church teachings being engrained in my head all my life, I might be like them.

I was friends with a girl who came out here from Utah. Her father was on sabbatical here. I liked her, but it seemed she never had any temptations, no trials at all. Her main goal in life was to do what the church wanted her to do: get married at a young age and have children. I think the smaller a family the better. I can't see how someone can pay equal amounts of attention to nine children. A lot of rivalry can go on between the brothers and sisters. The poor mother! When I mentioned to her that I didn't want nine children, she gasped, "That's what you're expected to do!" I didn't like the way she carried the church teachings as a weapon instead of as a comfort.

She came out here just a few weeks ago to stay with one of her friends. She is my age and has been engaged two or three times. I asked her, "What was your family's reaction when you called off this last engagement?"

She said, "Well, I know some people who were saying, 'Patty, you'll never get married.'"

"Why do you have to get married now?"

"Well, I'm in the prime time. I have to get married sometime soon."

I said, "Patty, you're nineteen years old, come on. What are you going to do with your life?"

"I'll marry somebody. He'll make a nice living and I'll keep my job for a little while until I have kids, then I'll stay home with them." She was going to New York the next day and she was talking about the high-rise apartments and everything that she thought she'd see. She said, "Someone could easily put me in one of those."

That is the key difference between us. She wants somebody to put her in one of those and I want to put myself there. I'm concerned about being able to afford all the things I want for me and my children when I grow up and have a family. I want them to have as good a life as possible—not just to make do. I wonder just where our economy is going. What does it hold in store for me? As determined as I am, I hope I don't get so hard up for money that I won't care who I have to stomp over. I hope I don't end up like that.

I enjoy teaching Primary. The girls come up to me after church and say, "Hi, Sister Lanier," and tug on my arms. When I taught the little Sunbeams, they'd call across the church, "There's my teacher." But the lessons in the manuals seem to be stereotyped. I try to adjust them to the girls that I have, to meet their needs. Trying to teach things that I'm not too sure about myself is hard.

We had a lesson about the father being the head of the family. I agree that men are the main money earners. It was a little hard for me to teach that they are the head of the family and they make the decisions. I have to give my father credit. He's come a long way. He believed that the women should stay at home with the children. It bothers me when we say that men and women are created equal—they are just given two separate jobs. A father is given all these opportunities like holding the priesthood. I'm not sure I would want the responsibilities that go along with that. When my father became a member of the bishopric, he was called out of the house so much to give blessings to other people. But, suppose the father was away and one of the children was sick. Would the mother's blessing not count in God's eyes? I hope it would. Teaching Primary has made me look more into the church teachings. "What do I think about?" "How can I use this in my life?"

I remember going for a long time without praying. One night the missionaries came over and showed a filmstrip on temples. Then one of them bore his testimony of the power of prayer. He looked at me and said, "I think that you should try prayer."

I thought, "What does he know?" But then I thought, "Why not?"—besides the guy was gorgeous. That night I knelt down and prayed. It was hard at first. I didn't know what to say. I was almost apologizing, "I'm sorry I didn't talk to you for a long time." The prayer lasted a long time, just telling him the things that had happened and the way I thought my life was going to go. I went through a box of tissues. No matter how many days I go without praying (he won't be happy about it) when I do pray, he will be there just as strong as the last time I prayed.

I hate to have to say I'm sorry. It is bad enough to have to say it to my parents, but when I have to say it to my Father in heaven! There are times when the trials are tough and I think, "Why should I try anymore? Why not just give in?" Then I think, "No, I'll have to face him again in heaven." In fact, in my patriarchal blessing I was promised to be in the celestial kingdom. I think, "He gave me this much. It's the least I can do to try one more day, just to say 'No' one more time." I'm glad that being back with my Heavenly Father again is something to look forward to.

John Noren, 26

John Noren came to the University of Delaware in 1983, earned a master's degree in Chemical Engineering in June 1984, and is now in the Ph.D. program. He and his wife, Diana, had been members of the church for a year when they moved to Delaware. As a child, John had moved up and down the West Coast with his family as his father worked in various city governments.

When my parents divorced, I was at an age where I needed a very firm hand. I would live with my father until I got tired of a very firm hand. Then I would live with my mother until I got out of control. After I went to England as an exchange student, I moved down to Ventura, California, to live with my father and start junior college. I hadn't been there two months when he came home and said he had a job up in Mountain View. A couple of months later he and my stepmother were gone. I was on my own.

I stayed in Ventura for a couple of years. If I had gone directly to the university, I might have finished up quicker and my life would be further along, but I might not have finished at all. At the community college I learned very little from an academic standpoint, but I learned a lot from an emotional one. My character developed during those years. I became more independent, more self-willed. If I had locked into university life then, I could have been led off by party life and never made it out. As it was, I was in an easy atmosphere and I had quite a social life. It was nice to be only half a mile from the beach, throw the textbook down on the sand, and pretend I was studying. I didn't advance my life that much, but I sure straightened myself around.

My first year at Berkeley from the financial point of view was sheer terror. As soon as I got the opportunity to go to work for a gas company as an engineering co-op, I jumped. I went to Visalia, California, and worked in the marketing department, supposedly as a conservation consultant. If you have ever run across a conservation consultant, you'll know why I'm laughing. It was a good job. Not only did I earn enough so I could go to Berkeley without having to worry every time I opened the mailbox but I came back engaged and we were married six months later.

As my family moved around we always attended either a Methodist or a Presbyterian church. The church that I remember most is the Methodist church of Dixon, California, a nice little white chapel, very much like the Elkton chapel. I wouldn't be surprised if they had the same floor plan, a little frame church with the rector's building off to the side. In Ventura, I started to attend a church that was only two doors away. They had a good college group there. I don't know that I quite believed everything that was taught. I think they taught "Repent and be saved and nothing else matters." If you repent often enough, you're all set no matter how many times you keep messing up. It seemed to me that that was just putting a Band-Aid onto one's life and not taking an aggressive stance in living it. I guess I believed too strongly in the admonition that we are to be perfect to sit back and follow a religion like that. I feel that what we do in this life is going to have a direct and everlasting effect on what becomes of us after this life.

After we married, Diana and I looked around for a church that taught what we thought was right. Without too much looking we sort of stumbled upon the church. We listened in for two or three months before becoming too obvious. We invited the missionaries over and went through the lessons. We felt that what they were saying was what we needed to hear, and it was the way we should conduct our lives.

Obviously, we don't drink coffee or alcoholic beverages anymore, but there's more of a subtle difference. I'm more at ease with my feeling as to what God expects of me. I was missing that guidance before I joined the church. I noticed right off that people in our church tend to take the commandments more seriously. I won't say that means that we are obeying them more than other people, but we do take them seriously. We don't take the attitude that breaking them won't hurt us that much. We're serious about the prospect of living the way that God has chosen. Joining the church provided some sense of direction in how Diana and I were going to raise our family.

I came out here to go into the Catalysis Center, part of the Department of Chemical Engineering. I wanted to get a little engineering exposure, so I went into the intern program. I went to school and spent a few days a week at Du Pont in their consulting department working on absorption columns and heat exchangers. It was a good experience, but we were required to attend as many classes as the other incoming graduate students and put in 120 days at Du Pont. There were four of us. I'm one of the two who finished on time.

As for chemical engineering, I like playing with computers. I like playing with chemicals. This is a good combination of the two. I'm fascinated by the results that I get, even by the problems that I have. I've been working for the past two months on one problem that we haven't as yet solved, but I'm getting close, I think.

The most difficult thing for me to do is schedule my time. Perhaps if I had started out at the university I would have learned how from the beginning. The easy years at the community college put me into a pattern which was at first very difficult to break out of. I'm not all the way out of it yet. School demands quite a bit of time. I need to spend a lot of time here with Diana; we have a very good marriage because we spend a lot of time together. There are many opportunities in the church for growth. That's where my schedule has fallen short.

If I had foresight and could do it again, I would perhaps have stopped after my master's degree. Because I'm not good at scheduling, working would be a lot easier on me than going to school. My father was always working late hours. It was very difficult to see him and get to know him. I don't want to put in much more than a forty-hour week at work. When I worked at Dow, I put in a solid eight hours of work and when it was quitting time it was all I could do to crawl out to the car and commute home. But I enjoyed it. If I can find a university position somewhere where I can do my own thing, put in the hours, and not be under the type of pressure that people are here, I'll do that. If not, I'll be in industry.

I was a home teacher. In fact, they say I still am. Being a home teacher requires that you set aside time for something other than your family, your job, or your own activities, and that's a bit hard to do. I was fluctuating back and forth between being able to go and not being able to. When I get to know someone,

I can't show up one month and not the next. As I get my feet on the ground, that is the first thing I would like to get back into because that's a direct involvement. Not only do we see that we are helping someone, but we find joy in it.

It seems to me that one can obtain the priesthood without knowing that much about it. I won't argue qualifications. If the Lord says you're qualified to go out there and try, that's it. But it does bother me that in many cases I don't know what I'm doing, such as in giving blessings. I believe in the underlying principles of the priesthood, but I don't know what to do with it yet. I don't do that at work. I spend enough time in the library so that I know what I'm doing. I learned the hard way that you don't do it the other way around. It seems that the Lord put more trust in me than I do in myself.

I feel I can devote my life to becoming closer to God, provided I can also work and have a family. I work hard. Sometimes I take longer than people expect. Right now I'm at the stage in my research that I wanted to be last spring, but I've always succeeded to my satisfaction. I think that's because God is there to give me the strength to go on. In some cases, he's there to give me the inspiration to find my way out of a hole.

Diana Noren, 26

Diana Noren is from Nicaragua, where her father raises cattle and rice. He had attended college in Kansas where he married her mother. Each of the six children in the family was sent in turn to junior college in California. After spending several years working, Diana has returned to school. She is expecting her first child and teaches a Primary class.

We lived on a farm about twenty-eight kilometers from the nearest city. We were rarely only the six children because there are thirty-six cousins. Our cousins would always come to the farm. We always had plenty of people for two teams to play baseball or to go to the river. When we started to grow up, of course, we said the farm was no good. We wanted to live in the city. We used to tell our father, "Why don't you sell this house? Let's go to the city." I'm glad he didn't listen to us.

Seven or eight people owned all the land in our valley. Four other families lived within ten minutes of us. My parents and the neighbors bought a little bus and sent all the children to the same schools. The bus would start at six o'clock in the morning, and by seven we were in school. In the afternoon we got out at one, but we always had piano or ballet classes or sports. We wouldn't come home until about five or six. The girls' schools were run by nuns, and the boys' schools by priests.

We liked to walk out along the streets after school, eating a mango or other fruit. We used to sit on a corner, somewhere, and watch the guys. That was the big thrill. We weren't allowed to ride with them or go anywhere with them, especially if we had our school uniforms on.

I used to look forward to the big dances that we used to have. Almost every month somebody would have a party. When I turned fifteen, four hundred people came to my dance. We'd all get new formal dresses. You didn't want to wear the same dress twice. Your parents always went with you. The parents were on one side of the room, and we ended up on the other side. You knew you were being watched by your parents at all times. The club had security guards in the main entrances, exits, so we couldn't just get up and go out.

We didn't date. You couldn't go out with a boy alone. I don't know how people got married. At the dances you got to talk to the boys, but never were you alone. That kept girls out of trouble, not that there weren't girls getting in trouble. A girl knew she couldn't have too many boyfriends because if she did she would not be considered good enough to marry a "worthwhile" man.

The clubs and the dances where people looked nice—none of that exists anymore. The country club is now a military base and the social club is now government offices. They are totally run down. The swimming pool is full of algae and broken bottles, and the tennis courts are growing grass.

I'm an American citizen. We all had dual citizenship until we were twenty-one or until somebody asked us to turn over one of our passports. The plan was to come here and get educated and go back to Nicaragua. Now there's no life there. My brothers wouldn't have anything to do there. One is an architect; another is a civil engineer. The third is an agronomist; he planned to help my father with the farm. Even he couldn't go back because there's nothing to do. They're all in this country, hoping that someday they'll go back.

California was a big shock to me. I couldn't believe, first of all, that the boys and the girls were together in school, and also that different social classes of people were all mixed together. The main thing that shocked me was the way the students talked to the teachers. Some of the teachers would answer right back with a vulgarity. That was a shock. Why would the teachers let the students treat them like that?

My mother has a degree in home economics, so I thought I would study home economics, just for a year or two, and then go back to Nicaragua. We girls didn't grow up to go have careers. I thought my children would be raised the same way that I was, but even if I were in Nicaragua, now, they wouldn't have the same things I did. I'm happy, now, here in the States with John.

I didn't see anything in John that I thought my parents wouldn't like. Their requirement was that I marry somebody who was educated and not marry somebody below me, meaning, socially, or I guess intellectually. We just told them, "We're going to get married on this date next year."

My father said, "That date wouldn't be good for us because at that time I will be harvesting and couldn't come." We moved the date so my parents could attend. They liked John a lot. They couldn't say no to my marrying an American because my mother is an American. They couldn't say, "No you can't marry somebody who isn't Catholic," because my mother isn't Catholic.

When John and I got married, we decided we should have some kind of church or religion, but we didn't know where. We went to the Catholic church for four weekends. I wasn't getting anything out of it. I said, "John, we'd better try something else." We went from church to church. Then for some reason I said, "John, why don't we try the Mormon church?"

And John said, "What? The Mormon church?"

I knew some people that were Mormons. I didn't know anything about the Mormon church. From the beginning it just felt good. When we went to the Berkeley Ward for the first time we found how many Mormons lived near us. We had lived in the same apartment complex for about a year and didn't know one person until then. A lot of people that I knew from church were in the same situation that I was. My husband was always studying. Their husbands were always studying.

At the beginning when we started to talk to the missionaries, we were very proud. Then we started to think, "Let's listen to it with an open mind and see what happens." Testimony meeting bothered me at the beginning. I couldn't understand why people would tell their feelings to everybody. I like it now because a lot of times you come out of testimony meeting in a much more spiritual way.

I had always thought, "Why do only the priests have the authority to do all these things. What gives them the authority anyway?" When we learned about the priesthood, it made so much sense to me. A lot of people think it is weird that even the little kids, twelve years old, have part of the priesthood. I guess I was very ready to join the church because a lot of things that are weird to other people made so much sense to me, such as the way the church is organized. If you live in a certain area you go to a certain ward. You get to know the people and you belong somewhere. The members can't just live their own lives and be Mormons only on Sunday. There is more unity this way.

My mother never said, "You can't change your religion. You have to be Catholic." My father is very open-minded so he didn't mind at all. As a matter of fact, they had been in Utah about five years before that. They had gone to Temple Square and he knows more about the Book of Mormon than I do because he's read it all. He said, "How come you haven't read the Book of Mormon?"

When my sister Carla came to stay with us, she took an interest in the church and she was baptized about four months later. Carla and I have something that we share that doesn't exist between my other sister and me—not that I like Carla better. The church has made it so much easier for us to realize that Heavenly Father is actually real. Before, religion was something remote. It was a mystery. Now it's part of us. John and I also have the church in common. Now that we have the church, we're more alike.

The only thing difficult for me about teaching the Sunbeam class is knowing how much the children are learning. There are some that you can't reach at all. I show them a picture and talk about the lesson for about five minutes, and then they want to color. When they finish coloring, we'll talk about the lesson some more. I want them to hear the message at least once. Sometimes it's very difficult for them. There are some who remember everything I say, and exactly the way I said it. They get attached to you. If there's a substitute, they don't like it. At the beginning, I just knew for sure I couldn't do it. I'd never been around children before. Pretty soon it was fun. I'm more a part of the church now. It has more meaning to me than just going to church. I don't want to be without a calling now.

I worked at a bank as a teller and later on as a bookkeeper so I could help John through school. Now I am also going to the university, studying nutrition and dietetics. I have one or two more years, depending on whether or not I do an internship. School has been a major problem in my life the last three years, having John always in school, always involved in his work. I know he has to do it, but it has been very hard for me to accept the fact that he works that hard. I don't want him to do that all his life. If I didn't have the faith I have now and if I didn't have Heavenly Father to talk to, I don't know what would have happened in our marriage.

I think about whether or not we will be able to be a good Mormon family— have family home evening and teach our children like they say you should in the *Ensign*. I want it. I think that if we don't have that, then our family would fall apart. In the United States it is easy to have children and not even know them. I want our family to be like the church has taught us.

14 | Serge Bushman's Missionary Farewell

Sacrament meeting on June 16, Father's Day, was preceded by the usual scurrying around, small children crying, and bustle in the aisles. Gary Johnston made the announcements and commented on the success of several recent events: the Wilmington Stake girls' camp and a Friday evening canning session at the regional cannery. He thanked the four men who had organized and supervised the cannery effort—Rob and Oliver McPherson, Gene Dean, and Jim Rennard. He also announced that Kevin O'Day and Lisa Welch had been married on Thursday.

After the opening song "There Is Beauty All around when There's Love at Home," Douglas Ridge hurried from the organ to the pulpit to offer the opening prayer. The ward business included giving an official welcome as new members of the ward to Douglas Mullins, Cindy Mullins's oldest son, and Georgette DiVirgilis, an adult convert, who had both been baptized the previous Sunday. Danny Mullins and Arvie Wrang were awarded certificates of attendance at seminary.

Serge Bushman and Kirk Larsen then blessed the sacrament. Serge, who turned nineteen on May 1, was spending a few weeks at home before beginning his two-year mission for the church on July 10. The bishopric had scheduled the Bushman family to speak in sacrament meeting prior to Serge's departure. Claudia Bushman, Serge's mother, spoke of his early life. She said it was notable that Serge, who had been named for his grandfather, Serge James Lauper, was to be a missionary in Oakland, California, where his grandfather and great-uncles live.

Bishop Bushman spoke about missionary work in more general terms. Comparing the LDS Church to other, larger, missionary-minded churches, he said that we manage to field more missionaries. He also said that there is no guarantee that living a good life will make your children want to do so and expressed his happiness that Serge wanted to serve a mission. He reminded the congregation that missions are hard, and compared the experience to the vision quests that young Native Americans go on. Tracting would help Serge discover his own strength and forge him into a man who would serve the Lord mightily.

Serge and his friend, Mike Richardson, played three short pieces on their French horns; then Serge spoke. He said that he knew he needed to change his attitude in order to serve a mission. He knew many reasons why he should not go, including having hated to sell things door to door for the band. He then listed the reasons he should go, among them that his weaknesses would be changed to strengths. He said he had enjoyed working hard for the Lord with other members in the canning project and that going to the temple had shown him the great experience of eternal life, that families would live together throughout eternity. He thanked the people of the ward who had worked with him, particularly Stephen Cherry, who had "made the Young Men's program into a science."

At the end of the day's meetings, the ward members gathered in the Primary room for refreshments. A few of us helped Claudia set out potato chips, pretzels, cookies, brownies, cakes, and punch. When they were almost gone, Claudia sliced and served the leftover loaves of banana bread the Relief Society had given out as Father's Day treats.

The Ridge family happened to have reservations on the same plane that was to take Serge to Utah for his eight weeks' training in the Tongan language and missionary work. Serge and his father had been the Ridge family's home teachers for several years, and Douglas and Julie Ridge had taught Serge in early morning seminary. The Ridges gave Serge a ride from the Salt Lake airport to the Missionary Training Center in Provo. When the Ridges left him at the Missionary Training Center, five-year-old Claron Ridge wondered aloud how Serge would ever get back to Delaware alone.

Serge Bushman, 19

Serge Bushman graduated from Newark High School in 1984 where he was drum major of the marching band. The fifth of Richard and Claudia Bushman's six children, he attended Boston University for one year.

We moved to Delaware when I was about eleven and a half. I hated moving. I saw no reason to mess with bliss. My Dad is very democratic, but of course his vote was bigger than anyone else's. I was the most violently opposed. I remember crying and making up songs about how I didn't want to move to Delaware.

When we were in the New Castle Ward, most of the kids my age were in the Elkton Branch. The youth in the New Castle Ward were going their own way a little more, but the Elkton Branch had a great Scouting program and all the kids were active in the church. I got my Eagle Scout in the New Castle Ward. Most of the Eagle Scouts in our ward got their start there. Steve Cherry continued the tradition and worked hard at getting those guys to be Eagle Scouts.

I was a pretty good French horn player and that won me a lot of respect in school. Throughout high school all my friends were in the band. Delaware is a lot easier to excel in than other places, but our band is the best in the state. I played bass guitar in the jazz band and French horn in the regular band. I was the drum major my senior year. All the drum majors before me were hated and everybody thought they demanded unreasonable things. I was fascinated with the problem: how can a peer be a good leader? It's easy for teachers, but you can't demand a lot of respect from your peers. Leading the band on the field was the smallest part of it. I wasn't a very showy drum major. I think I did an okay job. I tried to set a good example. The director gave me a lot of responsibility. I did well in rehearsals. I was good at teaching and correcting people.

I did my audition tape for the McDonald's All America Band during an exam period the last day I could turn it in. Some guys had special taping gizmos and spliced all their tapes together. Mr. Ross showed me how to use the tape machine, and I just played. I was surprised that I made it. After a while I realized they didn't have much of a choice. First of all, they had to take two from Delaware. Secondly, the Newark McDonald's, about two hundred yards from Newark High School, has the most profitable drive-through in the world. Maybe that's why Newark has had more people in this band than any other high school in the country.

My parents didn't tell me to go to Boston University. They said, "You should go to Boston or Utah." My mom always said, "You can go somewhere else," then she'd silently turn away and make it obvious that she didn't want me to go anywhere else. I think they wanted me to go to Boston because there is such a great church tradition there. The student ward is one of the finest wards in the world. Everybody's strong and there are so many great examples there. My dad figured it was a good way to keep me in the church. If I'd gone to the University of North Carolina, they thought maybe I wouldn't have any friends in the church and I'd become inactive.

I'd been thinking of concentrating in Russian history, but I might go for a general history major. I'm getting more interested in Jewish history and in American history. Seeing *The Crucible* excited me about the backwardness of those Puritans. I'm also trying to decide whether I want to major in music. I've seriously considered trying to go for my doctorate. I think being a professor would be the greatest thing. I'd love to wear tweed and flood pants. My brother Brick and sister Clarissa are business tycoons. Karl's going to go to medical school, and I haven't figured out what Margaret's going to do. We've always been in the humanities, but at the last minute Clarissa and Brick bolted for the business scene.

At BU I met a lot of people like me, a lot of people who are interested in liberal arts. I had a great floor—all political science majors. We'd talk about societies, communism and socialism, and the advantages of those ideologies. I wish Americans were more aware of what's going on. We just get filtered information of the government's actions. I wish we were better educated as a people. I think the proletariat would be a lot happier if they were educated. Maybe they wouldn't be. I guess what concerns me is the unwinnable social situation. I can't think of any government that will be successful, in which everybody will be happy.

I'd like to think I've become more sensitive to people's plights. In Boston we're all students and we all have families to take care of us. Everybody in the ward was reasonably well off. In the Elkton Ward there are serious problems and things that people can't do anything about. I'd like to think that I'm more sympathetic now, although I have a long way to go. Before, I thought people made their own problems. Now I realize that people are unfortunate. A lot of things go against them.

I was talking to a guy at church yesterday, and he said, "You know, I think the church emphasizes tithing too much. They just want money." He is poor. I think maybe he's had welfare checks a couple of times. I've had some pretty miraculous things happen with tithing. It's always been true that when I paid my tithing and was broke afterwards, money just plopped into my lap somehow. Sometimes I wonder if we overemphasize tithing. Obviously, it's an important thing, but other people, I'm sure, haven't had money miraculously plop into their laps.

It was a new experience having people at school be interested in the church. People would ask, "Say, you coming back to BU next year?"

I'd say, "No."

"Well, what are you doing?"

"Well, I'm going on a mission for two years." Sometimes I could just say, "I'm going on a Mormon mission."

"Oh, you're a Mormon, tell me about it."

Or people would ask why I was dressed up. "I just went to church."

Then I'd tell people I was having a great time in church because I was. I'd come back and tell my best friend, "Boy, we had the best discussion on the hunger situation in Ethiopia."

A lot of people would say, "Oh, I want to go to your church sometime because I've had a lot of problems with religion," but I never followed through. I regret it.

People who aren't Mormons or who don't have the same values can have some pretty good arguments about why we're wrong. Sometimes my mind's a blank. Sometimes I can be convinced of the silliness of what I'm doing. Where is there any concrete evidence of anything? There are a lot of witnesses of everything, but the whole gospel is just based on faith. I tell people that you have to pray about it. They always say, "How can you go on a mission if you don't know this stuff?" I tell them I'm going because then I'll be able to know. I always say, "I have to give it a fair shake."

I saw my brother Karl at church every Sunday, and sometimes we did things. There's no one like my brother Karl. He's accomplished; he's smart. He paved the way for me. He'd tell me about his girlfriends and ask my advice. He was always encouraging me to go out on double dates with him. I'm not into the dating scene. I'm kind of mad at a lot of the girls my age in the church. I decided it's just not worth it right now for me. I might as well establish myself in the real world before I start chasing after girls.

Margaret didn't come to church as often as Karl did. She lived within walking distance, and I went over there a few times and we did things.

Achievement and accomplishment are emphasized in our family. My dad loves his work. His best friend's his wife; they're the closest business associates either of them will ever have. We get a lot of things done and a lot is expected from us. A lot of people sit on the back porch and talk about things. Instead of hanging out, we'd sing a song. We'd all sing parts. I don't feel that much pressure, though Mom certainly put pressure on me to get my Eagle Scout, she said, "You'll thank me later." I guess I do. I'm happy that she pushed me to play the French horn. I hated the horn for a long time. It was a very frustrating instrument.

Recently Brick came home with his fiancee, Harriet. He's soon to be married to her in the London Temple. I was depressed throughout their whole visit. I thought, "I'm never going to get that far." Going to the Harvard Reunion didn't help any either. I'm not sure I'm ever going to get into Harvard. I'm going to apply as a transfer student. It's not that I have to be in the best institution; it's part of the family heritage. My Mom knows all the Harvard fight songs. It shook me up to find out that Karl, who was graduating from Harvard, was thinking exactly the way I was. "Brick's got it all. He's an international business man and he's got a great wife." I realized that I shouldn't worry about what other people have done. Clarissa said, "You're just wasting your time if you're not being the best you can. If you're going to be a history professor, that's great. Be the best you can be."

I'm realizing more and more that I want to be just like my dad. He's very spiritual. In his letters he tells me his weaknesses and what he's doing to deal with them. He works very hard. Everything he does seems so honorable to me. My dad is so logical, so fair, and rational. He thinks up a good answer for everything and he can back up everything that he says.

I don't know what would be different if my dad weren't the bishop. We're not a vacation family. Unless he's in a meeting, I can talk to him whenever I want. He'll always drop what he's doing and talk to you and discuss your problems. A lot of times he's just down in his study writing a book or something. I don't mind that he's the bishop. I think my mother does sometimes. I think she wishes he would stop being so nice to a lot of people who she thinks are taxing him unfairly.

My mom is so persistent and she's so active. She kept pushing and she finally got her doctorate. How could anyone possibly do that and raise kids? There are a lot of things that seemed like they'd never happen. Who would have thought our ward could have a choir? She talked about this for so long. "Oh, wouldn't it be great to have a choir—not just for special events." Leading the ward choir is a great job for my mother. She's very good at getting people to do things and keep doing them. She never discriminates. She lets anybody sing who wants to. I think it makes her want to come every Sunday.

My parents have treated me as an adult as long as I can remember. I always had more freedom than my friends. I could stay out as late as I wanted and I wouldn't have to tell my parents where I was going. I guess that put me in a lot of situations I wouldn't have had to be in. I love the way my parents treated me. If they'd watched me more, I think I would have been more rebellious. I guess I'm turning out okay. Their main goal was that I go on a mission and be active in the church. I'm going on a mission. If I left the church at all, I'm back. The Word of Wisdom is probably the most touchy thing for teenagers these days. I used to have a problem with it, and I'd even break it every now and then. I think I've seen that it's ridiculous to even come close to breaking the Word of Wisdom. My friends know that I don't drink and they respect me for it.

I think I'm getting a better sense of the priesthood now. It's dawning on me that it's the power of the Lord on the earth. My dad's given me blessings a lot of times—mostly just to help me fall asleep when I couldn't. It was always comforting. The biggest effect the priesthood has had on me was my patriarchal blessing. My mother's father gave that to me. I read over it pretty often. It's just vague enough that I'm not sure if something is specifically meant for me. It's always a comfort, and it always makes me feel spiritual. That's a miracle in itself—that I'm moved to have a soft heart.

I think I have more of a testimony now. They always tell you that you're going on a mission to further the kingdom of the Lord and to make yourself a better person. Being the selfish person that I am, I'm looking forward to knowing the gospel, knowing the scriptures backwards and forwards.

I don't mind going away from my family. Actually, all of my cousins live in the Oakland mission, so I'll have a lot of dinner appointments. Proselytizing is what I fear. All through high school we sold submarine sandwiches for the band. I hated it because I knew people didn't want them. I feared imposing on someone else. I've been talking to a lot of people about this. You just have to develop an attitude that you believe in your product. The gospel has something that will benefit anyone you talk to. If you just use that attitude, it's probably not as bad.

I have this great itinerary planned out for myself. Of course, I'm going on a mission. When I come back I want to be diligent in school. I want to go out for crew and I want to play my horn. Actually, what I want to do in the year after I come back from my mission is make myself look good enough to transfer to Harvard.

Philip Parkinson, 20

Elkton Ward not only sends out missionaries, it is part of the mission field, specifically the Philadelphia Mission, which covers parts of New Jersey, Pennsylvania, and Maryland, as well as all of Delaware. Two pairs of missionaries, one for Elkton and one for Newark, work full-time to bring new members into the church. Philip Parkinson, of Papakura, New Zealand, is one of the Newark missionaries. Missionaries are supported financially by their families or home wards, in addition to their own savings. Missionaries rarely stay in a ward for more than six months, and are assigned to areas and companions by the mission president.

Home is a 160-acre dairy farm. After my mission I'm definitely going back to the farm. I don't have the education for anything else. I never liked school. I will work for my father and eventually buy him out. My dad was in an accident since I've been here. I've had to find a lot of faith that he would be able to return to work. He's now working part-time on the farm. I still have to have a lot of faith that he will get back to normal.

The church has done a lot to educate the people of the South Pacific— the Samoan Islands. They've taught the younger generation agriculture so they could get along. In New Zealand the church has helped the Maoris a lot, and now they feel more important as a race.

My parents joined the church about two or three years after they were married. My mother's mother was a semi-active member, and she introduced the missionaries to my parents. It took a little while for my dad to come around. After having three girls, my mother promised Heavenly Father that if he'd give her a son, she'd make sure he served a mission. I was never interested in serving a mission until my sister went on her mission to Perth, Australia. She was the one who started the fire going, so I shaped up and went back into the church.

When I was younger, knowing that I had a responsibility was important to me. I felt important because I had a duty to pass the sacrament. Having the priesthood has helped me understand a lot of the things that go on in the ward. Receiving the Melchizedek priesthood opened my eyes to the authority that God's given us. Being able to give blessings to people and having the faith to heal—Wow! I've had the opportunity to bless a few people while on my mission. It's neat to be able to let the Holy Ghost take over what you say. I don't know where I'd be without the priesthood. I guess the Young Women's program helps the girls a lot, too. They can build friendships there.

When I first came here, the hustle and bustle of city life got on my nerves. I wasn't used to always being on the go and worrying about traffic. It's quite interesting to see how people live here.

A typical day in the life of a missionary who wants to work as hard as he can would begin at 6:30. He and his companion would study the scriptures together at 7:30. 8:00 is breakfast and 8:30 is personal study. At 9:30 he's expected to be out of the apartment, proselytizing. Proselytizing can be tracting or asking the golden questions at the shopping mall. "Have you ever heard of the Mormons? Do you want to know more?" They'll visit part-member families or member families, trying to contact as many people as they can. Between 12:00 and 2:00, they'll go back to the apartment for an hour to have lunch. The afternoon is spent proselytizing and teaching discussions. At 5:00 they come back for dinner and at 6:00 they're out again proselytizing until 9:30. Then they plan the next day and retire no later than 10:30. We call them "rock missionaries."

Other missionaries like being out on a mission, like to contact people and teach discussions, but have an enjoyable mission by having their freedom. They'll look for things to do other than tracting. They'll probably go shopping at the mall and get referrals by just talking to people. They'll come back whenever they feel like it for lunch and then go back out again and teach discussions. I've known missionaries who sometimes don't wake up until 9:00, yet teach a lot of discussions and baptize. We follow a white handbook that we read through every Sunday. We're supposed to live according to the "do's and don'ts." They say the consequences of not following it are we won't have the Spirit as much and we won't do as well in the work. In a lot of cases that's true, but in some instances not.

I will work hard, but I make it fun while I'm working. Sometimes it's hard to go to bed in the evening. We're not supposed to talk on the telephone to friends or to family. When you make friends in the mission, you're not supposed to call them up in the evenings, even after 9:30, because we're supposed to spend our money wisely. I have a hard time spending my money on the things I should rather than the things I want. Not calling home was hard for the first two or three months.

The mission has a hierarchy. The mission president has two assistants. Then come the zone leaders. Within the zones are the district leaders. Most of the districts have from six to twelve missionaries. I am the district leader for four missionaries—Elder Troseth and I in Newark and the Elkton missionaries. Messages from the mission president go to the assistants, then to the zone leaders, the district leaders, then to the missionaries. The president wants it to work the other way, too. If a missionary has a problem, he tells the district leader. If it's important enough, it goes back to the president. Then the president will call and discuss it with the missionary as well. Every six to eight weeks we have a zone conference with the mission president. He also interviews every missionary once a month. There are 120 missionaries, so he visits between 10 and 20 missionaries a day.

Being stuck with someone twenty-four hours a day can get pretty tough. Sometimes I would have liked to hit my companions and tell them to get lost. I've had other companions that I'd have liked to be with for a lot longer. Sometimes I've had the opportunity to wander off by myself, and I've felt lost. I've had seven companions.

Out on my mission I've gained a personal testimony because I am in situations where I have to know whether it is right or wrong. It's easy enough to say, "My parents know that this is true and I follow them." To be able to say, "I personally know the church is true," is just fantastic. When I've wanted to know whether something was the right thing to do, I'd kneel down at night and pray: "Okay Heavenly Father, I want you to give me either the burning feeling or the stupor of thought. If it's not right, I don't want to remember it. Fine, wipe it from my mind and I won't do it." A lot of times I'll get up and not remember what I talked to him about. When he's said, "Yes," I've felt strongly that was the right decision. I know he answers prayers.

A lot of people find our concept of the Godhead hard to believe because they've been brought up otherwise. I use a scripture from the Doctrine and Covenants. I just tell them it's a scripture. "God has a body of flesh and bone as tangible as man's." Then it says that Jesus Christ has also and the Holy Ghost doesn't.

When we first tell people about the Word of Wisdom, they're shocked. It's like, "Well, forget it." Then we can talk them around to seeing how very important it is. If they're willing to give those things up, with the missionaries' help, it's a lot easier. I haven't come across anybody who hasn't accepted the principle of tithing. They feel that it's a lot nicer to pay it in secret than with everybody looking at them as they drop money into the collection plate. When we're teaching tithing, we try to have the Spirit there the strongest so the Spirit will touch them and they will commit to it. I had one investigator who was only getting $398 a month and her rent was $290. When we talked to her about it, the first thing she wanted to know was how much she needed to pay out of her paycheck before she could pay her rent. She said she'd try to pay her tithing fully.

The breaking point for a lot of people is when they see they have to change their life-style, not just their religion. Everybody that I've baptized who had a "friendshipper" has stayed active in the church. Those who did not have friendshippers didn't. One investigator depended on the missionaries a lot as friends. She called them every five or ten minutes. The missionaries who had been working with her hadn't had friendshippers. The first thing we did was get friendshippers for her. She started getting involved in the ward and now she's active in the church.

When I go home I plan to work for my father for four months, then I plan to come back again. Maybe I'll visit the East again, the areas where I worked and the friends I made. I never wanted to be married, but that's changed by being out here. The girl I'm in love with is in the United States. She's a missionary in this mission. President Flynn knows about it. Once our missions are over we'll probably get together and get to know each other a little bit better. I would get to know her family. I don't know what sort of things I have to do to marry an American. I want to live in New Zealand because that's where my family is and where I have my job. If I'm in the United States, I'll feel lost.

❀   ❀   ❀

Serving a mission is highly regarded as a training ground for future church service. Because so many of the Elkton Ward members did not grow up in the church, only about a third of the men who hold positions in the ward and just three of the women have served missions. Most members, however, indicated a strong desire for their sons to serve missions. About half would like their daughters to go on missions. Of the twenty-one members of the ward who have served missions, half served in the United States (three in the East, seven in the West). Five went to South America, one to Europe, three to Asia, one to South Africa, and one to Australia.

Robert McPherson, 25

Robert McPherson and his brother David both went to Colombia on their missions. Robert returned home in January 1984. He lives with his father and takes classes at the University of Delaware. He is the Webelos Scout leader and the single adults' leader.

When I was seventeen I went out to Ricks College. I was rebellious after my first year of college. I went way downhill for quite a while and then just before my mission I started back on the right track. I was influenced by a young lady who later joined the church.

My mission has prepared me more for life than anything else will. It's the best education I ever had. I had some bad companionships, but I survived them. It tempered me quite a bit. You learn patience on a mission. I was one of the lucky ones. I never got attacked. One of my companions drew attacks just like flies. Two or three people attacked him because he was obnoxious. He liked to brag about his karate expertise. My second companion, while traveling with one of the branch presidency, witnessed a murder in the front of the bus. There were quite a few missionaries who saw incidents of that type. We got used to having people routinely walking by with machine guns pointing into the crowd. It makes you appreciate your freedom. There were sixteen-, seventeen-, eighteen-year-old kids carrying machine guns in the military. The night before I was to come home, the National Department of Security lost my papers, so I had to stay in Colombia an extra day.

I have a letter here from one of my converts. Her husband found us and we started teaching him. Her husband was assassinated six months ago, just after I came home. She's strong in the church and is looking forward to living eternally with him. When these people are strong that makes me the happiest.

I'll read to you from my missionary journal. "Yesterday we went to do interviews. Why we went is interesting enough to relate. On Sunday when the elders called, Elder Small was in our apartment and took a message. The elders said they would call us on Sunday night or Monday to make arrangements for a baptismal interview on Tuesday. Tuesday morning I was worried because they had not called. I told my companion, Elder Burnett, to pray about it while I showered. After I prayed, I asked him how he felt. He hadn't felt one way or the other, but I told him I felt strongly we should go and the Lord would provide for us. We called them but no one answered.

"When we got there at 10:30, they were still there, even though the missionaries are supposed to be out of the house by 9:30. They were surprised to see us, and we told them that we had prayed and decided to come for the interviews. The elders told us that they had prayed about it and were despondent because they hadn't been able to contact us. The baptisms were scheduled for that day. That we got there in time to do the interviews strengthened all our testimonies concerning prayer and the divinity of the work."

My testimony is built upon the answers I've received to prayers. It's like in Doctrine and Covenants 6:22, "Verily, verily I say unto you, if you desire a further witness, cast your mind upon the night that you cried to me in your heart that you might know concerning the truth of these things. Did I not speak peace to your mind concerning the matter? What greater witness can you have than from God?" After the Lord has given you a certain number of answers to the same question, he says, "Remember when?" You can open your journal and come across experiences that bring the same witness again.

Most answers to my prayers have reinforced that I should keep going to school until I get my degree. I have to get about fifty credits of A's to bring my average up enough to be accepted in electrical engineering. It's going to be a lot of work, but I can feel the Lord's support. I work twenty-five to thirty hours a week for Domino's Pizza, plus I'm taking six hours of school.

When I first came home from my mission, I did not want even to home teach although I've always loved it. A missionary comes home drained—physically, mentally. I just didn't want to be involved with anything when I got home. They made me a senior companion and I had three active families and one inactive family. It's hard to teach an inactive family. I'm spending a lot of time right now helping one of my families. She's had a lot of problems with her car. For the last three or four weeks, I've visited her about once or twice a week. Right now I'm the Webelos den leader for the ten- to eleven-year-olds. I love it. I can be with kids for an hour or two and then get rid of them. I like spending time with the boys. I'm also ward singles representative. We've had an ongoing stake family home evening here for all the singles. When I left for my mission we had a good home evening going, and then it fell apart. I started it back up after I came home.

Since I've been home I've given away only one Book of Mormon. Dad and I went out with the missionaries tonight and I was out with them last week. I'm finally able to do that. I was trying to convert a girl. We met about two months after my mission. Whenever I talked about my mission, she worried that I was going to go back. I explained that the church won't let me go back. I did not tell her that the church expects me to marry and set up a family because she might have taken the hint. I couldn't do that unless she was a member.

When I first started going out with her, there weren't too many hours of the day that I wasn't thinking about her. I went down to the temple just to see exactly how I stood. I wanted some reinforcement. The Celestial Room was almost empty. I love sitting there to meditate. A temple worker asked me to go up and do sealings. As I listened to the words I said to myself each time, "Yes, that's what I want." I had been praying that I would get a witness of some sort, and I got to kneel across the altar a few times and think about the significance of it. I feel strongly that I won't be married any other way. I would rather leave off a romance than get married outside the temple.

One night Kevin O'Day was telling me there was no way you should date a nonmember. He started dating a nonmember two weeks later. She was having the missionary discussions and was baptized. Still, I had to laugh because it had been only two weeks.

Scott Christensen, 25

Scott Christensen was a missionary in Korea from 1979 to 1981. A graduate of BYU, he became a member of the Elkton Ward in September when he began studying for a Ph.D. in chemical engineering.

I grew up in Orem, Utah. My father has been a professor of chemical engineering at BYU for as long as I've been around. It was my mother's influence that brought my father into the church. He was baptized a year or so before they were married in the temple. I think my father always wanted one of us four boys to go into chemical engineering. Each of us started out in chemical engineering, but I was the only one to stay in it. My dad's had the most influence on me. He's influenced me in my thinking, how I perceive other people, and also in my choice of a career. I did my master's degree work under him and took two or three classes from him.

Going on a mission was a major break in my plans. It was not a tradition in my family to go on a mission. My parents always told us they would help us if we wanted to serve a mission, but they did not attempt to influence our decision. My friends started going on missions so I started thinking about it. I decided that I needed to know for sure whether the church was true or not. I thought I ought to at least read the Book of Mormon so I could have some basis for a choice. Before, I'd always gotten stuck somewhere in 2 Nephi and given up. I read through the book in a short time and prayed with a desire to know that the Book of Mormon is true. I had to pray very hard several times, but I did get a very strong feeling that the Book of Mormon is true. After I had gained that deep conviction that the church was true, everything at church meetings seemed to be new. I listened a lot more closely, and all the doctrine seemed to be new and fresh and exciting. I was troubled that blacks were banned from the priesthood. Of course, that was all changed by President Kimball's revelation. I don't know what I would have done if that practice had still been in effect at the time I was thinking about going on a mission.

I was surprised at how different missionary life was from what I had imagined. I had pictured very hard-working missionaries knocking on doors hour after hour, totally committed to bringing people to the church. I had imagined the ideal missionary who never quarreled with his companion, never did anything wrong. In a mission like Korea the language is such a big factor. I think my first senior companion was still unsure of how to approach people and of what was the best method of finding people to teach. I sometimes felt that we weren't working hard enough and that caused some friction with both of my first two companions. Then I became a senior companion and I realized what they had gone through.

Door-to-door tracting was very unsuccessful in Korea. You ended up wasting a lot of time. We'd make a street board and set it up in front of a train station and try to talk to people about the church. If they'd come up and talk to us, we could hand out pamphlets with our phone number. We could give them a brief overview of the Joseph Smith story from the board. Then we tried to get appointments to visit them at home with their families.

Another very popular thing, which I never did like very much, was giving English classes. A lot of Koreans liked to be around Americans and liked to come to English classes but were not interested in the church, even though they'd talk with us about the church. We could meet with them ten, fifteen different times and go to their houses, but they'd never join. I felt if they came up and talked to us as a result of the street boards, they were at least a little bit interested in the church. It was hard to get people interested at all in the gospel. I've never seen a Buddhist converted; they were always either Christians or people who had no religion at all.

It was very exciting to have someone commit to completely turn his life around and become a better person through joining the church. Working so hard to try to get people interested made me that much more devoted to the church and to the gospel. It was frustrating when someone who believed what we said about Joseph Smith or who believed the Book of Mormon was a true book was not willing to change his life.

If I hadn't gone on a mission, I might have drifted further away from the church and perhaps become an inactive member. I think I'll put more emphasis on the church than my parents did. My parents could have encouraged us more in church-related matters, such as holding family home evening, family prayer, reading the scriptures together, encouraging us boys to think about going on missions. I was baptized at the age of eight. Becoming a deacon at twelve and a teacher at fourteen was just like graduating to a new class. On my mission, though, I had some experiences of giving blessings and saw some of the real strength and power in the priesthood. I felt close to the Lord and the real power of the Holy Ghost directing me in what to say.

I was bothered by Elder Boyd K. Packer's talk on how we shouldn't destroy people's testimonies by bringing up things that early church leaders might have done. Russell Nelson gave a talk at Brigham Young University that seemed to be saying not to bring up any history that might damage the reputation of an early church member. It might bring members to doubt that some of the miraculous events had happened. I think the church is strong enough to stand on its own. It doesn't need to change its history. It especially bothered me that he gave that talk at a university. A university should be a free and open environment. That BYU doesn't want a free and open environment was made obvious when they banned the *Seventh East Press*. I enjoyed the *Seventh East Press* because it was fresh and different. Nothing in it was obscene or needed to be banned. Even if I get upset by what Brother Nelson says at BYU or at how BYU is run or how the church is run or how the ward is run, I still know that the Book of Mormon is true, that the gospel is true.

Neil Owen, 29

Neil Owen joined his high school girlfriend's church in Seattle, Washington. As a missionary in Colorado, he met his wife, Terryl. They have been members of the Elkton Ward for two years and have two children, seven and four. He has held several positions in the Elkton Ward and is now Priests' Quorum adviser.

I didn't even know my high school girlfriend was a Mormon for the first two years she was my girlfriend. We got in trouble a couple of times, drinking. We had a bottle of wine in the back of the car. A policeman stopped us and took us to the police station. Her parents were devastated. I decided I ought to investigate her church because that was the only way we could still see each other. I joined a couple of weeks after finishing the discussions. I had some spiritual feelings, but I was joining mostly for her. I didn't know how to recognize those feelings, but now I know those feelings were testifying to me that it was true.

My parents were divorced and my father had moved back East and remarried. I used to spend summers with him. I didn't live with my mother in Seattle because we didn't get along well. I lived with a friend. There was no one to guide me in the decisions I should have made.

My girlfriend was going to BYU. I hadn't applied to any colleges. I was worried about her going to BYU. I went to talk to the bishop. I said, "I think I need to go on a mission." I was thinking, "This girl will never marry me unless I go on a mission." I had just turned eighteen and had a year to save the money. My dad found me a job as a laborer in Florida at one of the nuclear plants which paid nine or ten dollars an hour—pretty good for a kid just out of high school.

When the bishop's wife found out I was looking for my own place she said, "You can't spend money on rent and food. Come and live with us." Living with the bishop's family, I learned what it's all about.

I put in my papers to go on a mission two months before I turned nineteen. When I didn't hear from my girlfriend for two months, I started to get worried. We had made a pact that she would not write me a "Dear John" letter. We had been together for seven years, ever since junior high school. I called her and sure enough she'd been going out with some guy for three months. I said, "If I don't hear from you, I'll know that you're getting married to him. I'll be praying that you make the right decision."

The day I arrived in my first mission area, my girlfriend was getting married in the Salt Lake Temple to this other guy. I was thinking about that the whole six hours on the bus. Pretty great way to enter the mission field, right? I knew she was no longer a part of it. Was I doing this because it's true? A couple of months into my mission I knew why I was there. It wasn't for her.

I came back from that two years a completely different person. I learned more than most missionaries because I had had so little experience. I didn't even know that the Book of Mormon was about Christ's visit to America. I knew the Joseph Smith story, that's about it. I learned as much from the discussions as the people we taught. Then I began to learn from the Spirit as opposed to learning from books. My first companion was very letter-of-the-law. We didn't get along very well, but he was good for me because I needed to learn the gospel and learn what I was out there for.

That mission was the whole foundation of my life. Even when times have been bad, I've known that the church is true, that the gospel's true. All the things that happen are insignificant if you know that the gospel's true. The missionary who baptized me probably knew I was doing it for the girl. I wish I could tell him that I went on a mission and that fifty more people joined the church and two or three of them went on missions, that now I have two children, and about all the positions I've held. I'll bet he'd be shocked.

The day before I was to go home was my twenty-first birthday. The ward mission leader's wife made a cake and dinner, and her cousin Terry was there. As we left, the mission leader's wife gave me a card and two packages I wasn't supposed to open until I was released. I opened them as soon as we got to the apartment. One was a box of goodies for the trip home. The other was a book of two-for-the-price-of-one coupons for the Denver area. The next day, I left Terry a card and a coupon for a date with me and twenty bonus coupons for free kisses.

Within two weeks I was on my way back to Denver with everything I owned in my car. I had a date for that night, but I'd never talked to Terry much. All my clothes were two years old. I put on the nicest clothes I could dig out without looking like a missionary. We ended up going downtown to the planetarium. I knew I would marry her and it was hard not to tell her then. She used up all her coupons. We got engaged three days later and married six weeks after that.

I went into the air force, planning to go to school at night and become an officer. That didn't work out. I spent four years as a weather equipment technician. When I got out, I thought I could find a job pretty easily near Sacramento. I went without a job for six or nine months because I wanted to do what I liked.

My air force electronics experience helped me get my present job as a station mechanic at Hope Creek. We do repairs and calibrate and maintain all the equipment in the plant. I like the money and not too much else about it. I think it's dangerous. There aren't many jobs where you can make this much money with only a couple of years of education. When I worked for Bechtel I was the planning and scheduling engineer. I want to get back to the engineering side of the company.

The first thing we noticed about the Elkton Ward is that it has a lot of professional people. Our last ward was in a very poor area of Sacramento and a lot of the people were somewhat transient and lived in rented homes. I didn't feel accepted here or like it was an outgoing and friendly ward. Looking back on it, that might have been my own problem. The people here aren't much different from other Mormons. I'd just been through a heck of a time with my career and moving.

I've been Priests' Quorum adviser for five months. We have three active guys and three more who are not active. I guess I should be going out trying to get the inactives to come to church. The best thing about it is that I don't have to put any time into it because I'm so busy with my job. When I have to work on Sundays I know I don't have a class of twenty people waiting for a lesson. Last week I had just one boy. We talked and I got to know him a little better. I prepare my lesson on the way to church—just thinking about the topic or some experience I've had. I'll look in the book to get some ideas.

When we first got to California I was made Elders' Quorum secretary. Six months later I was Elders' Quorum president. I was twenty-three years old, and the quorum was bigger than Elkton's. I was on the high council for three months before we moved here. I was also stake Young Men's president. I hated leaving that calling, and I was mad at the Lord. I never have been in such an environment in my life as sitting at the big table with all these great men and praying with them. I was trying to find anything I could do to stay out in California. I was offered a job in California, but I would have had to work four nights of the week.

I went to the stake president and said, "I need a job. If I take the job here, I can't be on the high council because I'll have to work every Wednesday night. Since the Lord called me to be on the high council, that can't be the right job. The other job's in Delaware and I can't be on the high council if I move to Delaware." I wasn't too crazy about selling insurance but I would have, just to stay.

The stake president said, "You're going to have to decide what you want to do."

I said, "I have a job. It starts next Monday. I have to leave tomorrow morning. I feel like I'm deserting."

He said, "Do you think they have a church in Delaware?"

I said, "Yeah, they probably do."

"Well, what are you deserting? You just go out there and do your work, just like you're doing here."

That experience has affected the way I've approached my callings here. I was unbalanced. I was so valiant in my church work. When I was Elders' Quorum president some months I would home teach twelve or fifteen families myself. We tried to visit everybody, all the inactives. It wasn't like here. I could have gone to school free in California, but I was doing all this church work. I should have been getting the right training to prepare myself. When I got out of the air force I was nowhere. Being an Elders' Quorum president at twenty-three didn't help me support my family. I was a high councillor at twenty-six, without a decent job. I've figured these things out since I got here. Now my career is in a good position, but I'm not where I should be spiritually. I'm trying to get myself balanced again.

When I was unemployed I prayed continually that I would find a job, but I never did. I was paying my tithing; I was living the gospel as best I could. I was supposed to be blessed, and I wasn't getting blessed quickly enough. Coming here was exactly the right thing to do. My career is now on its feet. I have enough experience to go somewhere else. Whenever the time is right, I'll send out resumes to every utility company west of Utah. Somebody will grab me.

Daris Parsons, 33

Daris Parsons was a missionary in Thailand from 1975 to 1977. A native of California, he attended Ricks College in Idaho, then BYU, where he met his wife, Janean. They moved to Delaware in 1983 and are the parents of three daughters, ages five, four, and three. Daris works as a real estate paralegal and goes to school. He is a seventy and is the Deacons' Quorum adviser.

I went to Driggs, Idaho, to work on a farm before going to Ricks College. After the semester was over I moved back to California to play semipro baseball. I thought I was going to play baseball for a living. I was asked to come back to try out for the Salt Lake Angels, but I went on my mission to Thailand in November. When I decided to serve a mission, I felt I was finally putting down an anchor. I was twenty-three when I went on my mission, four years behind most people. My roommates had been to Brazil and France. Because of their influence all I could think about was a mission.

We didn't have much success in the mission because we were working without a Thai Book of Mormon. We used the English Book of Mormon and a couple of people got the spirit from the rough draft of the translation. It was frustrating not to have the results, but it has taught me that I'm not always going to see the results. I might in the end find out that I laid the groundwork.

I did all my preparation for life on my mission. I had a real battle with the devil. After my fourth month, I had told the mission president that I needed to come home. Just after that he made me a senior companion. I wasn't ready, but it was perfect. My parents apparently told the mission president, "He's never finished anything in his life. You can't let him come home now. He can't quit." He sent me up to Chem Rai next to the Burma border. Everyone wanted to go there because it is cool, not hot and muggy.

I was put with a guy who was also having trouble. I had told the mission president, "I'll accept it, but on the basis that I'll teach myself the discussions." I wanted to show off that I was pretty neat. "But," I said, "I don't think I'm going to be able to do it because I don't have a testimony." I went up there with that attitude. Then I started having a desire to know. I didn't recognize that desire, but I spent more time studying *Jesus the Christ* and *A Marvelous Work and a Wonder,* and I taught myself the discussions several times. I learned how to pray properly. A few weeks later I sent a letter to the president saying that my companion and I were not getting along because he wasn't letting us work enough. Within sixty days I had received a strong witness that what I was doing was right.

When I was a child, maybe because I didn't have a father to guide my thinking, I never planned anything. I didn't learn about planning until my mission. In my praying, searching to do what I thought was important, I learned about goals. I think that's why I was called to work as a zone leader. I dedicated most of my six months as a zone leader to showing the missionaries how to use goals to perform the work we were asked to do.

When I did not become a baseball player, I had nothing to shoot for. I was constantly jabbing at things to see what I wanted to do. I've worked in title insurance and real estate paralegal research for six years, off and on. My employer sent me to business college to learn accounting. I was a collections officer and then vice-president of a title company in Provo. I'm finally going back to school. It's going to be tedious, but at the end of three or four years it will be worth it.

It used to be difficult for me to understand that my family needs me. Because I did not have a dad, I grew up pretty much by myself. I've had to learn how to share myself. My church callings have many times kept me away from my family. My wife can put up with it because of the temperance she has learned from the callings I've had. I've always had to work more than forty-five to fifty hours a week, usually closer to seventy or seventy-five hours, with a church calling on top of that. I will not turn down a calling. If it's a call from my Father in Heaven, it was inspired for various reasons.

Every day I ask for help in being an instrument in the Lord's hands—to do some good. I try as hard as I can to be sincere. I've been successful in impressing on others that I truly believe in what I believe in. When I was in basic training I had a tremendous experience over a period of time. I would not go without my garments. Everybody told me that in the military you have to wear what they tell you to wear. I made a vow, but when I went in I started to get scared— "What a dummy I am trying to tell the U.S. Army what to do," forgetting, of course, nobody tells God what to do. I went ahead and kept the faith. As a result, I can't think of a day that at least one of those flight members didn't come to me and ask my advice about something. I became a squad leader and, not even a week later, a dorm chief. We baptized one guy before we left and several people were investigating the church.

I've become a great believer in tithing. Tithing has always been tough. I knew it was ideally necessary, but realistically I didn't think it was possible. One of the general authorities said in conference that there was not a commandment you couldn't live. I immediately thought of my mission president's wife saying, "If you don't get along with your companion, it's because you are looking at his faults and not for the strengths." I applied that to the commandments. Since then I've been 100 percent committed to tithing. A lot of people try to fudge a little bit—pay 10 percent of their net.

We went through financial hard times not too long ago. We had to exercise a great deal of faith to pay our tithing. I don't know how we got through that. I don't think I'm supposed to know, but I think I'm supposed to remember that it took faith.

Linda Hansen, 44

Linda and Robert Hansen are members of the Wilmington Ward but attend the Elkton Ward during the summer because their summer home in Chesapeake Isle is within the Elkton Ward boundaries. They make their community's private beach available to the Elkton Ward each summer for a beach party. Linda was baptized in Seattle, Washington, during her freshman year in college and transferred to BYU the following year. She interrupted her teaching career to serve a mission in Peru and later earned a doctorate in music education at Columbia University. She moved to Wilmington in 1976 after her marriage.

My father threatened to disown me when I joined the church. I tried to tell my mother I was getting baptized, but she said she wasn't feeling well and went into her bedroom and shut the door. At the end of the year I decided to transfer to BYU. My father said he wouldn't give me a penny if I went. I worked during the summer and earned six hundred dollars. I wouldn't even spend five cents for a pack of gum or an ice cream bar.

As I was beginning to pack up my things, my mother had a serious heart attack. The family said it was my fault and I should stay home. Even the bishop was a little nervous and thought perhaps I should stay home, but our family doctor said I should go. It was a very heartbreaking experience. I wasn't exactly the kind of person who fit in at BYU. I can remember many a lonely night looking out the window of my room at Whitney Hall wondering if my mother would live. The next year my parents came to BYU to look around. Then they did help me financially. Almost thirty years later, my mother is still living.

I taught music and English for two years in Seattle. Then I received a call to the Andes Mission in Lima, Peru. I had a great time there. The mission president loved "lady missionaries." I started out in Arequipa, Peru, with a girl I had known in the language training mission. We thought we'd get senior companions who knew the language, but we didn't.

When I got typhoid fever, the mission president called me to work in the mission home in Lima. I helped train Primary and Relief Society leaders. I also took over directing the El Coro Polyphonico Mormon. It sang on television and in various shows. I was in Lima for sixteen months. The mission covered Peru, Bolivia, Colombia, Ecuador, and Venezuela. Now there are many missions and stakes there.

The people were the greatest pleasure on my mission. I loved their deep humility and their implicit faith. We had some baptisms, but most of my mission was spent in organizational activity, choir directing, and teaching. Sometimes my companions resented all the music things I was doing. Of course while I was directing the choir, my companion had to sit and wait for me. The tremendous growth of the church has necessitated some decentralization of power and authority since then. On my mission the Mutual handbook had us teaching the foxtrot to the remnants of the Inca civilization. I think the leaders have had to come to grips with the worldwide church and adapt it to all people.

When I returned I was offered a job teaching French (after two years in South America) so I took a job as secretary in the school district. The next year I taught music, and at the end of that year I had an offer from a publishing company to be their music consultant for ten Western states. I went to graduate school at Teacher's College for three summers, going back to teach in California every year. I took a leave of absence to finish my master's degree. When they wouldn't give me a second year's leave, I resigned and began work on my doctorate.

One of the reasons Robert's parents opposed our marriage was because they said I'd be interested only in a career. Twenty, twenty-five years ago I saw young LDS women in Seattle sitting behind typewriters waiting for Mr. Right to come along. I decided then that wasn't for me. I was going to go to school and get ahead until I found someone that I would like to marry. I certainly would sacrifice anything for my family. I don't think it's been a big sacrifice to give up this career.

I have sixty recorder students every year at Ursuline Academy. This year I took over the high school chorus at St. Elizabeth's. I also teach preschool music classes at the YMCA. For the last seven years I have taught part-time at the University of Delaware.

I'd say 85 percent of the women in the church have some sort of income-producing job—whether it's full-time out of the home or working in the home teaching piano or making cutesy things to sell. The church can't say that women shouldn't work. They say to be prayerful about it, but the masses of the women in the church are going out to work. Unless a family has an income significantly above average or has family help, it can't buy a house. However, there are many who could sacrifice more and get by with less. Many people who bought houses within the last few years are paying a thousand dollars a month mortgage.

I have a difficult time with what I perceive as the church's discrimination against homosexuals. I've had so many friends from Stanford and New York and Bloomington who have gone through shock therapy treatment at BYU, have spent years talking with their bishops, have gone on missions, and who would give anything to have a happy LDS marriage, but are unable to. I know people who have tried so hard to do what is right, but cannot change their sexual orientation. The church so often picks up on that one study from the seventies that says it is caused by a domineering mother and a passive father, but nobody really knows. It bothers me that they punish homosexuality. Certainly, I believe in chastity no matter what one's orientation is, but the church can't seem to find the key to help these people.

We call our summer house our spiritual investment for the future. It's fairly obvious that we'll have to sell one house to pay for college and missions and weddings. Instead of putting the money in a bank, we felt that we could put it into property and have a lot of fun on that property while it's appreciating in value. Having two homes and two wards has been very interesting. When Robert and I thought about building our house, we wanted to make sure it would not diminish our commitment to the church. Last summer when we went down, Robert was released from his calling and has not been called to another. This summer, I was released from my calling. We're active all the time, but since our records aren't in the Elkton Ward, they don't feel they can utilize us on a regular basis, and the Wilmington Ward doesn't seem to need people who aren't there every Sunday.

We think the Elkton Ward is heaven. When Robert was stake Sunday school president and I was on the Stake Relief Society Board, we used to visit the Elkton Branch when it met in Holly Hall. We have tried over and over to put our finger on why we like it better than Wilmington. I don't think there could be a finer bishop in the church than Bishop Bushman, but the branch had a great spirit even before he came. The people are more down to earth, not the middle-class strivers who want to get bigger homes on the other side of town.

Robert Hansen, 44

Robert Hansen grew up in Wilmington where his father worked for the Du Pont company. He served in the Western States Mission from 1961 to 1963 and works for Du Pont as an accountant.

Both my parents graduated from BYU, and my grandfather was a bishop in Provo, but my father and his older brother found it hard to fit into the church. When my father came back East, he fell into the pattern of Uncle Reed's friends. On Sundays they played tennis or golf. My father got into making his own wine. I learned how a siphon works by helping him siphon the wine.

My mother's family was also very active in the church. I think she wanted to be active but wasn't able to overcome my father's influence. That they had not been married in the temple bothered my mother and her mother for many years. Although we went to Utah a number of times for family reunions, they didn't go to the temple until 1960 when I was nineteen years old.

Most of the people in the Wilmington Branch were Utahans who had come here to work for Du Pont. They met in someone's home for a while. Then they rented Orange Hall on Delaware Avenue. It's amazing that they struggled along as well as they did. Then they moved over to the Odd Fellows Hall. A few people joined the church. My mother and father were active in the Wilmington Branch in a way that I think was helpful to them. A lot of the other members of the branch were not very strong in the Gospel, either, so my parents weren't pushed out of the way. At one point my father was a counselor in the bishopric and he was later President Johnson's financial clerk. While I was on my mission my mother was the Philadelphia Stake Relief Society president.

There wasn't much of a youth program. There were three people my age. I guess we didn't know what we were missing. A lot of my friends were not members of the church. I went to their homes for parties and learned to see their points of view. There wasn't a church Scout troop so I went to the Presbyterian Boy Scout troop.

Several things came together at the same time for me. I went to the temple to be sealed to my parents and I was impressed by the importance of the temple. At the same time, I had been frustrated in trying to help my friends at the University of Delaware understand about the gospel. I realized it was time to do something about my feelings about the church.

When I was interviewed for my mission call, they asked if I had a preference for a foreign mission. I said, "Oh, yes, I'd like to go to Austria, Germany, or Switzerland," because I spoke German quite well. I'd completed my college language requirements, and I lived with a friend from Germany. I listened to the German news every night on my shortwave radio. When I got my mission call, I opened the letter and read it through. When my parents came home a few hours later I told them I got my call, but it didn't say where I was going. The very first sentence in the letter said I was called to the Western States Mission. Even though I had read the letter several times, it hadn't registered.

I loved having only one thing that had to be in my mind for two whole years. My only goal was serving the Lord through whatever means were available to me. It was exciting to put all my energy and all my thoughts into one thing. It also made me realize that I had a talent for organizing, which I hadn't had the chance to utilize before. I learned to get along with people in a close relationship. As I was an only child, trying to have close emotional ties to my companions helped prepare me for marriage. You might disagree or be angry at your companion for the things he does, but you can still love him and work together for a common goal.

When I went on my mission, I would not drive a car without seat belts because of an accident I had been in during my senior year of high school. The car was totally demolished and my father and I were both unconscious for a few minutes. I had ordered a set of shoulder-lap seat belts and put them into our next car. My first mission car did not have seat belts, and I felt naked after several years of wearing seat belts. I explained to the mission president why I felt as I did about seat belts and asked if I could put them in at my own expense.

He said, "No, absolutely not, you don't need seat belts." A month or two later one of my former companions who had become a zone leader showed me his car, which had seat belts. When I talked to the mission president about it again, he said that the zone leaders traveled more so they needed the belts. We went five hundred miles a week in my area. Not long after that a lady missionary, in fact a second cousin of mine, was thrown from her car when it skidded on the ice. She was left paralyzed, and immediately the word went out to all the missionaries to have seat belts put in their cars. I had a problem with that because I felt this missionary's injuries were preventable.

I'm inclined to judge the church by the lives that the members lead. All the different teachings combine to strengthen the family and the individual—to make the individual want to live the best possible life and to try to make the most of his talents and opportunities, not just for his own egotistical needs but for the benefit of others. Dramatic changes come into the lives of some of our adult converts. It's as if they were getting made over again.

A big goal is increasing our abilities as parents. We have two neat kids who are smart and lively and challenging. We're very concerned about leading them in the right paths. In many ways, being a parent makes you more godlike in a hurry. You learn a lot about patience and about leading people to water and not trying to make them drink, and why people do perverse things that will not do them good. Parenthood has made us a little more appreciative of the plan of salvation. Seeing how we can forgive our kids shows us how maybe our Heavenly Father can forgive us.

15 | The Empty Benches

On a good Sunday, the Elkton Ward Chapel, which can seat 250, is about three-quarters full. Out of the 283 adult members of the church who live in the Elkton Ward, 81 of the 126 men and 95 of the 157 women members of the Elkton Ward never attend. Active members expect a high level of commitment from themselves and each other. One member defined an "active member": "The bare minimum is to attend meetings and accept callings, magnify his calling, attend activities and functions and additional meetings, hold a temple recommend, pay tithing. The really active member tries to do additional things: have a garden, keep a journal and life history, 'friendship' his friends and neighbors, assist in missionary work, send his children on missions, plan to go on a mission with his spouse, do genealogy, support the Boy Scout program, pay fast offering and budget, hold family home evening, study the scriptures, exercise, be a good person, be willing to look after others and meet their needs, be willing to give his all to the kingdom, to partake of the sacrament worthily, accept the Atonement, repent continuously, truly love the Lord and each other, be worthy to receive personal revelation, take upon himself the name of Christ."

During leadership meetings, the Wilmington Stake presidency and other leaders exhort the ward priesthood leadership and Relief Society presidency to try to reactivate the ward members so all ward members can have the blessings of church activity. With far fewer home teachers and visiting teachers than inactive members, the Elkton Ward is unable to provide home teachers or visiting teachers to all the ward members. The more active members sometimes feel burdened by the large number of inactive members to be loved and served and advance various theories about the causes of inactivity: "they never had a true testimony," "they were offended," "they weren't committed enough." On the other hand, many active members have close relationships with one or more inactive families.

Lynda Hipps, 33

The first two years I lived in the Elkton Ward Lynda Hipps came to church every Sunday with her four children and, sometimes, her husband, John. She taught Sunday school and was the cooking chair for the Relief Society homemaking meetings.

When one of my sisters and her husband were stationed at Hill Air Force Base in Ogden, Utah, they went down to Salt Lake City, to Temple Square. They had signed a visitor's book, and the next thing we knew, they were becoming members of the church and my brother-in-law was going to be a priest. None of us understood what was going on. One day I walked out into the hall of my apartment building and there was a lady scrubbing the walls. She said, "You must think I'm crazy, but I just can't stand this dirt. My name is Anna and I'm a Mormon. Do you know what a Mormon is?"

I told her about my sister and asked her if she had anything I could read. She gave me a Book of Mormon. The next thing I knew, she wanted to send the missionaries over. I didn't want to offend her and didn't know how to say no, so I said yes. I found that instead of asking them questions to find the flaws, I was asking questions to find out why. I was getting answers that made sense to me and seemed to fit in with what I'd believed all along—especially the things about infant baptism.

My mother had been brought up with a favorite line, "Take it on faith, my child." My belief is that if you have a question, ask. That's one of the things I like about our church. Most of the time they have an answer, but if they don't, they'll tell you honestly they don't. The one problem I couldn't pry answers out of the missionaries about was evolution. I wondered how the anthropology department at BYU reconciled anthropology with their belief in the young age of the earth. The missionaries never did entirely answer that question. Enough of what they said made sense that I knew, almost from the beginning, that what they were teaching was right. It amazed me because I was a first-class agnostic. I wasn't even sure there was a god. If there was, he surely didn't want to be bothered with me.

My former church always discouraged us from reading anything that wasn't by someone of that faith. We laymen weren't even allowed to read the Bible—other than selected sections, primarily the gospels. I haven't found that here. No one has ever said to me, "You can't read that because it's not ours." I like that freedom of thought.

The concept of the eternal family is definitely tops on my list. Also, there's the idea that in order to be here, in a physical body, you had to make one right choice. Even though you don't remember it, you know you did something right and you kept your first estate. That gives me a confidence that I did something right somewhere.

There were some things that I wanted to straighten out before I would even consider being baptized. I said, "I will be baptized, but you have to give me time."

They kept saying, "Make a commitment." I'd made the commitment. I needed time to get my life in order. Another sister and one of my brothers also joined the church.

I find the idea that we can all be together very comforting. I'm not sure I entirely understand how it works in a situation like ours where John may never change. He's always saying, "I'm not a joiner." They tell you if you live righteously and worthily you don't have to worry about it. Suppose I manage to accomplish this and he doesn't? What if I don't want to give him up?

I would like to be able, as a married person, to go to the temple even though John can't or won't. My sister, when she was going through that new-convert fanatic stage, told me that if I divorced him I could go to the temple. Since single people, widows, and divorcees can go, I think it would be nice if there were some provision for us poor souls who don't want to wait until our husbands die. I would like to have a temple marriage. They say you learn so much at the temple, and I'm always interested in learning. There are so many things that I wonder about and would like to have more guidance on.

I had an awful lot of trouble dealing with the idea of the male being head of the household because I was definitely a women's lib person. Bishop Bushman helped me understand the way it's supposed to function: the husband as the head of the household has the priesthood, but he can't make unilateral decisions. He can't use his priesthood as a weapon.

At first I was terrified of Bishop Bushman. He was just such an awe-inspiring person. I thought him to be very austere, very hard to talk to, but the first time I talked to him it was almost as though I'd known him my entire life.

My first calling in the church was as the Relief Society mother education teacher. At the time I thought that I was the worst excuse going for a mother. How could I teach anybody anything? I was going through one of my impatient periods where I probably should have been going to school or working to keep my sanity. I enjoyed that calling very much. I only had it nine months. When they released me from that, they asked me to be cooking instructor. I told the bishop, "Okay, I'll give it a try, but I don't know anything about Mormon cooking."

He laughed and said, "What do you mean 'Mormon cooking?'"

I said, "Well, I've never made anything with wheat in my life." When I got off the telephone I was so depressed. I felt I was pretty good at mother education, but the miniclasses weren't as important. Another teacher asked me if I was going to the Relief Society teachers' meeting, and I didn't know anything about it. When she asked the Relief Society president, "How come Lynda didn't get an announcement," she said, "Oh, she's not a teacher."

I thought, "Gee, thanks." That was not only me, but anybody else who was involved in the homemaking meetings. They had told me that they didn't want to lose a "good teacher" so they were putting me in cooking. I thought, "Well? This is supposed to be inspired?" I prayed about it, but I never could feel good about it. I did have fun with some of it, but it just didn't do anything for me. I thought, "Well, it's my pride."

Then I was called to teach the fourteen- and fifteen-year-olds in Sunday school. They also asked me to give a sacrament meeting talk the day of my first Sunday school lesson. Homemaking meeting was coming up on Wednesday. I spent the week preparing the cooking lesson, cooking everything over and over again to make sure I could do it, and I had to make cookies for a Relief Society activity on Sunday night—the "Celestial Airlines." John had hardly seen me for two weeks and he said, "Something's got to go." I didn't think they were ever going to release me from cooking.

I loved the kids I had for Sunday school—Tom Young and Arvie Wrang and Angie Dean and Cindy McPherson. I was sorry to have to give it up, but when I began working every other Sunday, I had to drop it. They almost gave it back to me last January. They were going to get somebody to team teach with me, but they couldn't work it out. That was disappointing. I learned so much from the kids and I think most of them related pretty well to me.

I still work every other Sunday. If I'm not working on a Sunday, I sleep and clean and do all the things I'm not supposed to do. There isn't any other time to do them. My callings kept me going to church steadily. I was there almost all the time. It carried over onto what I expected of the kids. I'd read things and say, "Wow! This is interesting," and John's ears would perk up and he'd ask me what I was reading. I thought we were getting him close to it, then it just faded. Treena, Jody, and Michael all seem to be fairly spiritual. Treena won't let us forget to say a blessing. Michael is always asking me about Jesus. The kids always ask, "When are we going to have family home evening? When are we going to church?"

The Word of Wisdom is hard for me, especially in a house with a nonmember. I was a bartender for a while, but giving up alcohol has never been a problem. Cigarettes and coffee are hard to deal with. Sometimes I think every time I take a step forward I fall back five or six. It's funny because I never was much of a coffee drinker until they told me I couldn't have it. Even now, it's not coffee coffee that I drink—it's Swiss Mocha or Irish Mint. Technically it's coffee, but the flavor I'm after is not coffee.

I do wish we had the priesthood. I used to feel like a burden to other people when I had to call them. Our home teachers came by a couple of nights before Treena went into the hospital to have surgery on her ears. I didn't ask them to bless her because I thought, "This is a routine thing. Don't worry about it." The day she was admitted to the hospital in Philadelphia I got the feeling that I should have had her blessed. I called a number—the Mormon Hotline, I think they call it. The missionaries, of course, weren't there because they were out doing what missionaries do. Finally I talked to the chaplain at the Navy Hospital and he got in touch with his contacts, who in turn gave me numbers to call. I ended up speaking with a woman who was supposed to get in touch with her husband and call me back at the pay phone, but she never did.

The next day Treena didn't come back from her surgery. When the anesthesiologist walked in, I just froze. He said, "We've had some trouble with the anesthetic." Her heart became erratic, but they managed to correct it. I guess that was what was nagging at me.

I'd give anything to see the home teachers more often. Tom Robinson is the senior member of the team. He sees John quite a bit; I'm the one he never manages to cross paths with. His lessons always make me feel good. He'll answer any question and I can tell him anything I think. No matter how heretical it is, he doesn't fall over or have a heart attack.

I began working for Fashion Bug Clothes on August 9, 1983. I started in the Newark store, worked there until May. Then they transferred me to Elkton and promoted me. On August 1 I was transferred to Chestertown, Maryland, as an assistant manager and promoted to manager in September. I've just been transferred back to Elkton as a manager. I'm planning to stay in retail. I've managed to achieve each of my goals more quickly than I thought I would. I'm working toward being a supervisor now. The company has excellent benefits, excellent promotion, retirement. I like working to get my girls with potential promoted, getting them trained and ready to go on. The next step for me would be as an assistant to a supervisor who has nine stores. In time, I want to be a supervisor, myself.

Six days a week I'm totally involved in what's going on at work and one day a week I'm totally involved in what's going on at home. Working in Elkton is better because I see the kids and John. When I was commuting to Chestertown, I left at 10:00 in the morning for an afternoon shift and got home at 10:15 at night. For the day shift, I left at 8:00 and came home at 6:45. I was chronically exhausted and everything was pushed aside. I just got out of bed, went to work, and tried to achieve so that I could be transferred back. Now I have more time with the kids. Today I managed to get everything done early and I actually felt like a stay-at-home mother for a change.

I would like to get my children out of this particular neighborhood. I won't have them behave like street hoodlums. I want to get them out of this environment, to take them somewhere that has a very strong educational system.

I like getting into the different things the ward does. I've told them before,

"If you want me, be persistent and you'll get me. But if you can't get me one time and just forget it, then I never do anything and you never get what you want." I have to have that little bit of extra motivation. I've always managed to make time, I think, for everything they've ever asked me to do. I just wish that they would ask more often.

Bernard Callery, 56

Bernard and Betty Callery joined the church in Massachusetts in 1960 and moved to Delaware several years later. Their six children were brought up in the church. One son is an active member of the church in Utah, and their daughter Linda is active in the Elkton Ward.

I had read a lot of church history, history of the popes, the different religions. I studied all religions. I just became convinced that the church of God was not upon the world as such. I went to the point of asking one of the priests about a few things. He said, "Well, you don't need to bother with that. Take that on tradition, on my say so."

And I said, "Well, wait a minute now. I'd like to know. These things just don't jibe."

"Well, if you're going to start inquiring, asking questions you're not qualified to hear the answers to, you're going to commit a mortal sin."

I had some very strong doubts and I was trying to find the right answer. I considered Protestantism, but that was just a branch off the Catholic. I looked into the Jehovah's Witnesses. I read all their books. They've got some great history books, but they denied the Holy Ghost. One day some Mormon missionaries came to the door. "Hey, I'm curious, come in." As they spoke I applied it to what I knew.

The missionaries gave me the answers to the questions I had never been able to find answers for. I already believed the spirit of the law they taught me. I had some very difficult questions. They're simple now, but at the time it was difficult even to formulate the questions, to have enough intelligence even to know what was important to ask. Of all the churches in the world, the Catholic Church is the closest to the Mormon Church. The difference between them, basically, is the priesthood.

When I joined the church, things were very erratic in New England. The missionaries came in and went out so fast. You'd take four or five lessons, then they'd get a new group of missionaries. I had completed only four or five lessons. The church was supposed to take over, but there were only four or five members of the priesthood. They were all deacons or priests. The mission president was interested only in baptisms. He didn't want to be bothered with explaining things. He was finally released, then Salt Lake sent Henry Isaacson to take over the mission. He lives in Idaho, and I still receive postcards from him. He taught me a great deal.

We came down here from Massachusetts about nineteen, twenty years ago. At that time all the textile mills were moving out and the electronics and plastic industry hadn't yet moved in. You either worked in textiles or shoes. At the time they started importing all the textiles from Hong Kong and all the shoes from Taiwan. We had an opportunity to come here to work, so we did.

I always liked gadgets. I was always playing with toasters, fixing my mother's washing machine, taking clocks apart. Electronics just seemed to come naturally to me. It was an industry that I could cope with. It involved a great deal of sitting down, painstaking training. Because of having had polio, I wasn't able to stand to do heavy work so I knew I had to choose a field where I used more of my brains than brawn. The rest of my family eventually worked for General Motors up there. One of my brothers is a supervisor. In fact, they hired me to repair the electronic and pneumatic tools, but the union wouldn't let me work unless I went on the production line first, which I wasn't capable of doing.

When we were in the Wilmington Ward I was involved in the home teaching and we worked very hard to get some people who were inactive, nice people, to attend the Gold and Green Ball. The lady was reluctant because she hadn't been going to church, but we kept after them to go. It would be just a start, just to have them meet some of the people. At the dance a lady walked by us then stood nearby and said to another lady, "Funny that people who can't go to church can certainly get out for a social event, isn't it."

When they divided the ward, the people who I consider my friends were put into the Elkton Ward. There are very nice people in the Elkton Ward—and in the Wilmington Ward. I know many of them in the Wilmington Ward, but some of them have been in the church for a lot more generations than we have, and a lot of them are from out West. Believe me, it makes a difference. I'm not the only one who has this feeling. It has caused a lot of people I know to be inactive.

I always enjoyed home teaching. Call it a gift, call it what you want, but when I go into someone's house I can almost know what they're up against. In my own home, someone can walk in the door and I know what's on his mind. We enjoy the missionaries. We love to have them to dinner. We've actually helped them to handle people in the local area. They're strangers here and we have been able to tell them what type of people they're going to meet and how to answer the local questions.

I started working on genealogy in high school. I started asking questions of all my living relatives. Even then all I had was a bunch of birthdays and notes and little remarks. Then I found out that we had eight ancestors right off the Mayflower who had intermarried. That opened another door for me. We lived only sixty miles from Plymouth so I started collecting information there. Before you know it, I had a mess of unrelated information. I wanted to get everyone who was still alive. They were my best sources. Some of the names didn't mean anything to me, but I said, "Well, sooner or later they will."

Then Linda got hold of them. She said, "Dad, can I help with this? I love to write letters." Then Betty became intrigued by it, so we do it as a family project. We have relatives in Alaska, in Hawaii, in Australia, in New Zealand. We've got a big chain of relatives. We've been collecting books and histories of the different towns in New England. This genealogy is a missionary all through New England. Martha's Vineyard is almost entirely related to us. My relatives settled Massachusetts, fought the Revolution, the Civil War, every war of this country. Genealogy is a privilege, not a chore.

I grew up in a good family. It was just taken for granted we'd each live moral lives and do decent things. My mother and father set a great example. They lived what they believed. Breaking away from the Catholic Church and disappointing my folks was a very difficult thing to do. On her deathbed, my mother asked me if I would convert back. I said I would do anything in the world other than that. I said there was one thing she could do for me. She said, "What's that?"

I said, "Give me the family records and I promise you I'll do something better for you." So I got the records and had the work done for her.

My daughter Linda was about six months old when my father died of cancer. When she was about four years old, I was in a room with a glass door, lying on my stomach reading the daily paper. Linda was playing on the bed with me. There was a knock at the door, and I said "Linda, open the door, would you." She stood there and said, "Daddy, it's Grandpa."

I said, "Oh, yeah?" I began to feel my hair standing on end. I said, "Tell Grandpa to sit on the bed and read with you." I saw the bed go down beside me with all the weight, but I couldn't feel the weight. I said, "Ask Grandpa what it is we can do for him."

She said, "Daddy would like to know how we can help you, Grandpa." All of a sudden she said, "He's gone." She started looking around under the bed and said, "What does that mean?" I had not heard of the church yet.

I said, "Maybe he wants something done for him. I don't know what it is, Linda, but someday we're going to know and we're going to do it." That promise was kept.

I know the scriptures pretty well. I have a choice selection of books: *Mormon Doctrine,* Joseph Smith's translation of the Bible, *The Miracle of Forgiveness,* the basics of church history, priesthood manuals. If I ever did have any questions about the church, I looked them up and found the reason.

There's a great deal of peer pressure to do wrong. You will be singled out if you try to live a decent life. I've been singled out because I refuse to go watch pornographic movies on my lunch hour or go out in the yard and have a drink. I've had wires cut in my work. But what difference does it make? I've been told that I think I'm better than everyone else. I don't look at myself as being any better than them, but I have a standard to live up to, and I have the priesthood to live up to. I wouldn't dare to face the Lord with a polluted priesthood. Anyone who accepts the priesthood and doesn't live up to it, Whew!

I want always to keep the priesthood in my home and bring up my grandchildren to love and respect the Lord and always to be worthy of the priesthood. I want them to live decent, moral lives, hopefully participate in the church, and live so that they can appear before the Lord in such a manner that they'll be entitled to a celestial life.

I would like to go to the temple. The main thing Betty and I want to do before we pass to the next world is go to the temple. We want to be married for time and eternity. Frankly, I believe we're worthy.

E. J. Arnold, 62

E. J. Arnold was an active member of the New Castle Ward for twenty years and was a clerk to four bishops. His three children are grown, and his son-in-law is bishop of the Dover Ward. After living in Newark for twenty years, E. J. and his wife, Bonnie, bought land in Conowingo, Maryland, in the northwest corner of the Elkton Ward.

I was born in Toledo, Oklahoma. My father died three months before I was born. My grandmother was the "delivery man." She named me E. J. When I graduated from the eighth grade, they wanted to know my full name. I told them my grandmother named me with the initials from two uncles, Earl and James. They wrote "Earl James" on my diploma. Later, when I needed a birth certificate, my mother sent it in as a document of proof. My legal name became Earl James Arnold, but I keep telling people that's not my name.

My mother remarried when I was two years old. My stepdad worked in the coal banks. He was a fireman on a steam shovel that stripmined coke. We weren't rich, but we had plenty to eat and clothes to wear, and we had lots of relatives around. He worked from daylight till dark during the depression and was paid in sweet potatoes. Anyway you want to think of cooking them, my mother has prepared them. She even made a lot of sweet potato pie, and that's a lot like pumpkin pie. Pumpkin pie is not my favorite pie.

When I finished high school I went to work for Rita Pump Company, which was a Russian-owned company that manufactured deep oil well pumps. I enlisted in the air force in October of 1942. My job could have kept me out of the service because we were manufacturing some aircraft parts, but five of us enlisted together. I left my old '36 Pontiac sitting in front of the post office. When I got located somewhere, I wrote the folks, told them where it was, and asked them to get it. They sold the old thing before I got home because it was just going to rot. Two of us ended up in a troop carrier squad on the ground crew. We had good commanders and were highly democratic. We did pretty much what we wanted as long as we could get the planes in the air and stayed alive. I went to Brisbane, Australia, on the USS *Lurline*. From Brisbane to Port Moresby in New Guinea and then over the hump. From there we went to Beck Island and Okinawa. The next step would have been Japan, but the war ended. I was discharged in October 1945 in California where the folks had moved.

I went to Oklahoma for a visit and looked up the old kids. We all got together and we still had fun. When I got back to California and got a job, I sent for Bonnie. She came and stayed with the folks for a few days. We decided we might as well hitch it up, so we went to Reno as soon as I got a day off.

While I was in Oklahoma I had to buy another car to replace my dad's. I had a lifetime ahead of me, but they hadn't built up any savings or anything. I drove it back to California and gave it to my dad, but he let us use it. He was good enough to do that because he knew I couldn't afford to buy another one. We thought we'd take the short cut out of Martinez to Reno to get married. I was going through the hills, and it was crooked as a snake. We came back into a little town. I said, "Dadgum, this looks familiar."

She said, "It ought to, it's Martinez." I had my chance to back out but we turned around and kept on.

I went to work for Tidewater Associated Oil as a swamper. When Getty took over Tidewater in 1955, I was transferred to Delaware. By the time I retired in February, Texaco had taken over Getty.

When I started as a swamper I was assigned into operations where they take the crude oil, split it up, change the molecules to make gasoline or butane, propane, fuel oil, stove oil, diesel oil, and number six fuel oil. I moved along pretty fast. When I went to work they were going off the forty-eight-hour week and that created more jobs. I got into the bottom job. Many times it was just reading meters and oiling pumps. Then I advanced to watching towers and pressure gauges and control valves.

A good portion of my time in operations I spent on the cat cracker. It heated the catalyst up, mixed the oil with it, and it would crack the oil. The gases condensed into a big fractionated column, which was like a teakettle with lots of different trays in it. The gas and oil came off different spots—gasoline and naphthas, butane, propane, methane, and hydrogen. The cracker will run almost a thousand days. It costs millions of dollars to overhaul it, so they shut it down only when they have to.

For a couple of years they gave me a camera and told me to crawl through vessels and lines and take pictures. I was on my own just running around taking pictures all day. They took them to the inspection department. Sometimes they'd assign me to take pictures of a special spot. The lines were four feet in diameter and as slick as glass inside. I had to keep track where I was because

I knew somewhere that line dropped straight down. I came out here as a shift foreman. After eight years at the cat cracker here they sent me to Denmark. I was there four months. On the way back I took a quickie tour of London, part of England, Paris, and Berlin.

Don O'Day and I were both shift foremen. Then Don got a straight days job in personnel and employee relations but I stayed in operations for sixteen years. During those years I spent a lot of time in the NMC. Every time they overhauled the cat cracker, I'd go into the NMC as a supervisor. The maintenance company would go from one hundred to two thousand men. They needed a lot of people who were familiar with the jobs. I always got along well with the NMC. When they came into my unit I always treated them as guests. It paid off over the years because I could get things done. From 1979 until I retired I was the night superintendent, which is the top job an operator can get. I got along with both sides of the fence. The worst part was the public. After everybody went home at 4:30, we were the ones that everybody talked to about odor complaints or spills. There were people who always wanted to shut the refinery down, especially in Delaware City. That refinery had built that city up. One time I said, "Well, I kind of wish they'd bust them all down. I'd like to see how you run your automobile or how you have the electricity running in your house."

Bonnie helped me out a lot when they started moving women into the plant. Both Bonnie and Nantha are female chauvinists. A lot of the jobs are sitting and watching instruments, but if something goes wrong with those instruments it could mean the rest of somebody else's life if you aren't strong enough to get that valve to move. I think the feminists are wrong when they say women are equal when it comes to physical jobs. Mentally, they're just as good as men. I think they should get equal pay for equal jobs.

I joined the church in 1952. Bonnie joined the church first. I was in and out, listening to the lessons, and it sounded like a pretty good idea. We went through the series of lessons and it excited me. We went over to Berkeley or Oakland when they had an archaeologist from the church who had brought back tempered copper they had found in the ruins. He tied all this together with the Book of Mormon and I felt that it had to be right. I was kind of like Joseph Smith. There were just too many churches. They couldn't all be right. Here came physical proof which tied in with the Book of Mormon and made it very authentic. I don't hear much anymore about that, but tying in the stories from the Yucatan pyramids was one of the best weapons they had. The church's teachings are more clear than what I see other religions teaching. It seems less contradictory.

I've never regretted joining the church. I think our family's been better. I have two inactive kids for which I can blame myself. My shift work sapped the energy out of me and the church took a lot of time. I insisted that they go until they were fifteen or sixteen years old, then I let up on them. Bonnie never did.

She kept after them until they got out of the house. I hope I get active again and I'm hoping the kids do, too. I think it's a wonderful church. All the people in the church have treated me nice. I think I'm a little bit rebellious.

When they made a stake missionary out of me, it just didn't go right. I felt inadequate. Of course, working shift work, Sunday was a work day. Maybe I had the wrong attitude, but I always felt the family, the job, and then the church, third. When we came out here in 1956 we started going to the branch in Wilmington. I tried to teach a Sunday school class for the young kids. It didn't last very long. Those kids were smarter than I was, and they let me know it.

We did quite a bit of work on the Wilmington ward building. I enjoyed helping out on the building there. The members put up sheetrock and ceiling tile and paneling. The building program has changed since then. Now, a little area or little ward can build and not feel the total strain.

We went to the Wilmington Ward until we moved out here, but I believe they had split the ward by that time. I was ward financial clerk for quite a few years because I went through more than three bishops. First was Rulon Johnson, then Vern Rice. I was with Don O'Day and then Bishop Cross when we moved out here. I kind of quit. I haven't gone back to church since we moved. Maybe some of these days, I'll get back.

I have no problem with the church other than just that I was bored. I couldn't stay awake in the church. I do not want to get up and speak. I was the valedictorian of my eighth-grade class and I took that seriously. When I got up, I said the first portion of my speech backwards. The rest of it went right, but I was scared to death. I hear the scriptures, I read the scriptures, but I cannot quote them and I'm wasting my time. I don't have anything against the church or against religion. I think this world would be one terrible place to be in if we didn't have it. I know I've disappointed Bonnie a lot that I don't go.

I wouldn't want to make the Holy Ghost mad, and I think I do have a strong testimony of the truthfulness of the gospel. I have one little thought that bothers me. The church teaches eternal progression and there's going to be no let up. When we get up to heaven, we're still going to be pushing just like we do now. If I follow all the rules and don't do things like going to an automobile race or watching television on Sunday, I'll still have to push the things I want to do aside. I may learn enough and become wise enough that this stuff won't be important, but there's still that little worry.

I've done some home teaching. Sometimes those hours have been enjoyable, but most of the time I felt I was imposing on people's time. Of course, Bonnie and I are independent. It would be very seldom we'd ever call on a home teacher. They've gone to visit Bonnie in the hospital, which was very nice of them. The program is good. It's the only way the church can go into the homes. You get an insight by going into the house that you won't get at church. Maybe a family is hurting when they don't have to hurt, or doing without, and the home teachers can give them counsel or help. I hate to have somebody come to my house just because they have been told they have to get in their home teaching this month. That is the only bad part of the home teaching program.

I believe the Book of Mormon is true. The Bible's surviving all these centuries is a testimony of it, yet I would question some parts of the Bible if I were smart enough. I don't think it's infallible. I'm not sure the Book of Mormon is. It has had several changes over time and there have been changes in the Doctrine and Covenants. I'm not student enough to know whether those changes are significant. I don't believe either one of them to be infallible, but I do believe them to be the work of the Lord.

I enjoy Sundays now. I look forward to them as a day of rest because I don't work. "The seventh day, thou shall rest," but when I go to church I don't rest. I know I need to go to church meetings, but I don't want to get into that rat race because it makes me feel that I don't want Sunday to come around. I don't have an explanation unless it's that I'm lazy. I get tired. It's an hour you kill getting ready to go, getting in the car and driving to Elkton. Now Bonnie can drive across that bridge over to the Chesapeake Ward in about fifteen minutes because that's only twelve miles. I don't suppose that anybody in the church would hang Bonnie if she went over there. One thing I like about the church is you can drop in any ward and find a friend. You belong.

Our door is open. We like to keep it that way. We don't send out invitations, but people are always welcome here.

Patricia Sumner, 49

Patricia Sumner's most recent calling was teaching the nursery class for children aged eighteen months to three years, and she sang in the choir. A native of Pennsylvania, Patricia joined the church during her first marriage. Subsequently divorced, she raised her three older sons before marrying David Sumner in 1978. Her second son, Scott McAlees, worked in the Elkton Ward's Young Men's organization until he moved to Utah, where he was a full-time missionary from 1982 to 1984. Her fourth son, David, is five years old. Patricia works as a bottlewasher at the Texaco refinery in Delaware City.

My son Bryan is alive and well and has use of both his hands thanks to the church. We were in a bad automobile accident when he was a year and a half old. His arm was hanging by the outer skin. He wasn't expected to live. It took a lot of faith to know that it would turn out all right. Three days after the accident, thanks to the blessing he had, he was moving his fingers. He didn't need therapy. A lot of comments were made at the hospital about the blessing. The nurse who was in there when the blessing was given came running out with tears streaming down her face crying, "He's going to live! He's going to live." Thanks to the priesthood I've had a lot of miracles happen in my family. When

Dave, my husband, had his automobile accident he was given a blessing. He had to have sixty stitches all over his face, but you can hardly tell.

I was inactive in the church for a long time, but I never denied my feelings for the church. I reactivated one day because I decided I didn't like where I was going in life or where my kids were going to end up because of me. My life was not only bad for me; it was bad for my kids. I wanted better things for them. I gave up smoking because I didn't want my children to smoke. I had enjoyed it a lot because it was very sociable. I have three grown sons who have not messed with any of the stuff that a lot of kids do. I want that for David, too.

My testimony comes from when I decided I was going to change my life. After I did a lot of repenting for stupidity, I saw a bright light and I had a beautiful feeling. After that when I picked up a book the pages would just open to the answers to specific problems that I had. How can you help but be converted when things like that happen?

I had family home evening with my older kids; it came close to my having to tie them into their chairs. There was a lot of door slamming until they realized I wanted it. I finally discovered the only way we could have any kind of a civilized home evening was to read to them from the children's version of the Book of Mormon every Monday night. The kids loved it a lot. Then some good sister told me that wasn't the way to have family home evening. I felt real bad about that because the kids and I were finally making progress.

About a year after I went back to the church, a lovely woman in the church knew how badly I was doing financially. I had worked at the Dog House Pizza Shop for ten years. She talked to one of Bishop Don O'Day's counselors. The word passed on that I needed a decent job. Don O'Day got me an interview at Getty. I took the tests and was hired. He more or less said, "Now it's up to you. I got you the job. Now you are going to have to keep it." I've been there for eleven years. I'm a bottlewasher at Texaco—doing work that's just unheard of for a woman to do.

Needless to say, my first marriage was pretty bad. A life like that and a divorce are not fun, but it's different with Dave. I'm quite happy now. My biggest problems are me. I have difficulties with depression. I try to ride it out. That's the only way I can fight it. Dave is very patient with me when I'm moody. I made the right choice when I married Dave and had David. He's a good little guy. I think how great I've got it! A good man makes a big difference.

When we went out on strike I was home for three months. David was only a year old, and needless to say, he got very close to me. When the strike was over, he screamed all day at the sitter's for the whole week. By Thursday he had lost his voice. I was upset because I thought it was a sin to have him upset like that. The following Sunday I asked for a blessing for him. On Monday when I took him to Judy's, he only cried as long as it took for me to get out of sight. That was an impressive experience.

I was in the nursery for two years. I loved the little doll babies. They are just wonderful, just so full of love. They may fight you when they first come in, but they all eventually come around and like to be there. It's difficult before they settle down. Some of them get hysterical. Though I liked the nursery the best, I also liked teaching social relations in Relief Society. I learned a lot of things. I try to do my callings the best that I can. I cannot accept a calling that would require a lot of time. They wanted me to teach Primary, but there's no way I could do that when I work as hard as I do all week long.

They're doing a much better job in the nursery now. They have structured classes, which I just could not do. I'm glad the children have someone in there who has the time to put into a structured program. I did the best I could in the nursery and I don't feel bad about that. Working all week makes going to church on Sunday difficult for me. When I can get out to church, it seems to be a big uplift, but it is very difficult for me to get there.

I heard the angels sing at the last dedication of the Washington Temple. I really did. There couldn't have been that many voices in the temple at that time. I got out the first line and a half of "The Spirit of God like a Fire Is Burning" before the tears were streaming down my face and I couldn't sing another note. I was in a side room. The few people that were in there weren't enough for what we heard. That was a moving experience.

"O My Father" is the only hymn that mentions our Heavenly Mother. It's something that I have never heard anywhere else. The words are super: "For a wise and glorious purpose, Thou has placed me here on earth." It's a pretty good life in spite of all the trials and tribulations. The reason I can be contented and happy in my life is because I joined the church. That has given me direction that I didn't have before.

Ellen Lilley, 36

Ellen and William Lilley were among those who began meeting together at Cloyd Mullins's house in 1976. Both natives of Newark, Delaware, they were baptized in October 1973. When missionaries came to their door, Bill, who had had an LDS friend while serving as a medic in Vietnam, invited them back to hold discussions. The Lilleys decided to stop participating in the branch shortly before it became a ward.

My husband was convinced sooner than I that what the missionaries had to say was true. Finally, Elder Fenton said something that touched me. He asked us if we said prayers.

I said, "Well, yes, but not every day. I've always felt my little problems are not of that much importance. Heavenly Father has so many more important things, important people to look after." I felt I should only say a prayer when there was something big. I said thank-you prayers, for instance, when I saw something in nature that was beautiful. I was holding Robert who was just three or four months old. I usually had to rock him the whole time we were having the discussions.

Elder Fenton said to me, "You know how much you love that baby. I'm sure you're going to love all the children you have in the future just as much as this one. You're not going to love this one more than the others. Well, that's how our Heavenly Father loves you. Even though there are a lot of children, he doesn't love this one more than that one. He's interested in everything that happens to you—not just the extraordinary things—just as you and your husband are interested in everything that's going to happen to your son." That struck home. I think that convinced me that what they had to say was true.

Bill and I were two of the original group who met at Cloyd Mullins's home. It wasn't even the Elkton Branch yet. We had lived in Pleasant Hill, Maryland, when the idea was conceived. When they finally brought us all together we had moved here, right over the Delaware line. There were so few priesthood holders out that way that they asked us to help with the start of the sacrament meeting in Elkton.

Having been an only child, I was never around children. I find it still very hard to know how to deal with things. What's normal? What's beyond what I should put up with? That's what I enjoyed about Relief Society. I could get another opinion on all these homemaking things—or at least realize that I was not the only one with a problem. I guess I have a real need for what Relief Society has to offer. It's the only place I've found that I can get that.

I enjoyed being the chorister for Primary, too, because I like to sing. I was a Sunday school teacher, too. That helped me get my mind functioning again. At first I had to write down everything I wanted to say. Then, as time went on, I had to jot down only a word or two. I became more at ease in front of children. It helped me a lot because I am a quiet person. That little push was good for me, and the LDS people, as a whole, are very understanding because they know that their turn to stand up in front is coming. They're not too critical. Church callings showed me that I could do a lot of things.

There were a lot of times that I think it took away from time that I needed to put toward my family. My husband found that it was too much for him to do. A lot of negative feelings were generated. I think going to the consolidated schedule was for the better, but I did enjoy it when Relief Society was on a weekday. Getting everybody up, dressed, and out the door on Sunday was very hard. When we finally came home everybody was starved to death and fighting and fussing.

We've been inactive for four years now. The first two years we were inactive we lived the Word of Wisdom, but gradually we crept back into coffee and tea. When my husband was laid off, we had unemployment and he found a temporary job, but our income was a lot lower than it had been. We did have things stored, because of the teachings of having a year's supply, although it wasn't a full year's supply. It did help us at that time. We have slid from having family home evening, too, but that's another positive thing about the Mormon church—that little push to spend time with your kids doing something together.

I think the home teachers are wonderful. We have not been to church in four years and we still have a home teacher who comes. My visiting teachers get here a lot, too. They don't always make it, but I understand because I've been on the other end. I know how hard it is. It helps you get to know some of the other members. You might see them on Sunday morning, but actually being in their homes, you get a better idea of what they're like.

To be truthful, I never thought I would get married. It wasn't that I didn't want to, but I was always very quiet and I just felt I probably would never meet the right person. I thought I would just work. My mother had been a secretary. It seemed like a practical thing to do. I could learn how in high school and be prepared to go to work. I didn't have any big goal. I never was accustomed to using the word *goal*. I've been made aware of it through the Mormon church.

I wanted three children because I didn't have any brothers of sisters. My mother was the youngest of ten children. I saw a lot of caring and a lot of support for each other there. I felt three was all we could handle financially and physically. I enjoy being able to see my children grow and to see them change. I feel like I'm able to influence how they're growing—hopefully to raise them to be responsible and caring adults. It's lonely, I think. There's no one around, really, in our neighborhood. I have worked as a volunteer each year in the classroom of one of my children. I would like our whole family to be more interactive with other people.

There are a lot of things that I admire and think are great about the Mormon church and the Mormon religion. There are a lot of things that I think our society needs and that I need as an individual. I also think there are an awful lot of expectations that are hard. I wasn't used to the whole idea that you have to do all these things or you're not going to be sent to the celestial kingdom. Having come into the church at twenty-five and progressing from there, I feel it is insurmountable—to the point of feeling, "I'm never going to get there so why should I even try?" I do think there's a lot of love taught in the Mormon church. Besides the belief that God cares about each one of us, we were impressed by the concern of the people for each other.

Maybe I need to learn—not to shut out—but to postpone a lot of the things that we're required to do. I feel going to church should give an uplift so we can get through all the worldly confrontations of the next week. Sometimes, with the Mormon church I feel, personally anyway, a negative input. I feel like I'm being told, "Well, you should be doing this and this, too, and you're not." I guess I just have to learn to deal with it—just to put off some of it for now. Perhaps that's what we're supposed to do and I hadn't realized that until now.

Nancy Quinn, 28

Nancy Quinn stopped attending church when she was a teenager. She attended the University of Delaware and began an excavating business with her future husband, Howard. She began attending church again after two members of the ward knocked on her door. She is the mother of two children.

When Howard and I got into the excavating business full-time, I stopped going to college. I'll pick it up again when the kids are older. We're going to school Eric at home the way we're schooling Tabitha.

I used to drive a dump truck. I sanded job sites and whipped down dirt until the day before Tabitha was born. When this huge, pregnant person jumped out of the dump truck at the quarry, it made the men a little politer. I didn't have to wait in line as long for my stone. I thought I'd just get back in the trucks after Tabitha was born. I thought, "Gee a little baby's not going to be any problem. We'll bring a little playpen up to the job site and she can play under the tree." I expected to take a month off, then two months, then three. I never got back to the outdoor work again. I miss being outdoors.

We decided to school Tabitha ourselves because we want a better balance of religion and academics. It's very hard with our life-style to say after school, "Now we're going to sit down and read the Book of Mormon." Doing things with the children was getting left out because everyone's tired in the afternoon. Sometimes we're still out running with the business until five.

We weren't happy with the schools and thought she was doing better at home. We had trained her to be very positive and outgoing and to explore her environment. Kindergarten was kind of a letdown for her. My girlfriend teaches her children at home. I looked at her curriculum· and it had a nice blend of religion and academics. The academics are presented with the idea that God did create the world and his influence is in everything that we do and feel. I've since found out that the bookstore where I bought it sells anti-Mormon literature. I haven't decided what to do about that. Home schooling takes less time. We spend two and a half hours every morning having school, which includes the religion. If the day turns out hectic, we've still rounded everything off. She has her music classes and her swimming classes, too. There's a whole group in Newark of home-schooling kids. We take them on a field trip every month—Linvilla Orchards, the Franklin Museum, Baltimore's Inner Harbor. I want them to feel "I'm different. I'm okay. I'll do things my way."

That's my spinning wheel. You can see it's very modern in design. It's very well balanced so I can spin for two hours and not get tired. It just flows. That's my other occupation. I don't weave, as yet. I seem to have enough trouble finding time to spin. I knit and the first garment I made, a coat, took second place at the Maryland Sheep and Wool Festival. I took first place the next year. It's satisfying to take something from the animal to a finished product.

I've only been to two wards—the New London Ward in Connecticut and the Elkton Ward. I stopped going to church when I was thirteen. I was rather a handful for Mom and Dad. The few church activities I went to just seemed so Mickey Mouse. I considered kids who went to church as the goody-two-shoes of life. I didn't want to be like them. I guess I'm probably straighter now than most of the kids I thought were straight then. I started coming to church again two years ago.

Children make you so pure, so good. I had the guilts. "My word, my children are being raised without much formal religion." I did go looking for the church once. I thought it was the one in Wilmington, but I don't know if I would ever have had the nerve to go. It's hard to walk into a room full of such quiet people. It's real easy to walk into one of the more folksy revivalist churches because everybody is jumping up and down. A while ago Salt Lake sent out letters trying to collect all the loose people. My parents got mail in New Hampshire and they sent it down to me saying that the ward was trying to find me. Somehow it got down to Elkton. Rufus Lanier showed up on my doorstep one night. Howard had a good time. Rufus asked, "Does Nancy Zizka live here?"

Howard said, "Yeah, she lives here. We have two kids, and we're not married yet."

As I started coming back, I started reading, which is something I had never done when I was younger. I started in the Bible because that's the number one book. I haven't read the Book of Mormon through, but I read as often as I can. I've started picking up the Doctrine and Covenants and some of the books the missionaries bring by. The church has given me a more positive outlook. Things don't trouble me as much as they used to. I guess I've got more faith. Lately I've had to put it more into use. Before I worried about all the little details. Now I just do my best and then I don't worry about the rest. I was never worried when Howard had his heart attack because of the blessing he got at the hospital. It said that he was going to be fine. I took that at face value and said, "Great." It got me through two weeks of having the total workload—the outside work and the family work. I know God got me through that.

I'm hoping Howard will become more interested in the church. Since he's almost bought the ticket home three times, I would think his curiosity would be piqued. In all fairness to him, he does sit and read the Book of Mormon when he has the time. When he gets back on his sixteen-hour days, business becomes his total focal point. He's noncommittal now. If it's something I'd like to do, that's okay, but I shouldn't infringe on his time.

The church has become the one area in our lives where we don't see things in the same perspective. So, I don't push things like family home evening. I just try to see that he has quality time with Tabitha and Eric. Making it a formal thing right now would be pushing. I'd like him to say, "Come on, it's Monday night. Let's have it."

I don't understand a lot about the roles of men and women in the church. I understand the importance of the priesthood, I think, but I don't understand why it is only for men. When you read through the history of the Bible and other religious books, women get the dirt so badly, and the men who are supposed to have this great responsibility seem to totally disregard it. I don't understand why a man could be sealed to more than one woman but a woman can't be sealed to more than one man. Sometimes when I'm feeling good and getting along with all the sisters in the ward, I think, "Yeah, sisterhood's great. I could see it working out," but when it gets down to reality, I can't. I do enjoy visiting teaching. I do it every month, partly because I have a companion who likes to do it every month. I've been able to meet people and know them better. You can't carry on lengthy conversations or get to know people at church. I still don't feel like I'm involved, though. I don't have a calling. I volunteer if they need something, and I've helped in the nursery.

Rufus tried to get me last week. What a guilt trip! He offered me the fourteen-year-olds' class, the girls. I told him that I can't, with my work obligations and my family obligations. I don't have the time to sit down and prepare a meaningful lesson. I don't feel that I'm well enough informed. When I substituted in the five-year-old class, I had to ask them who's the president of the church. They were very happy to tell me, and they didn't hold it over me that I didn't know.

Rufus said, "That's okay. Primary or Relief Society will get you."

It takes me an hour every night to prepare Tabitha's schoolwork. We're doing three of her five subjects now. When she picks up social studies and language arts, that will be more prep time. Unless I deal something out, there's just no more spare time. Eric usually loses out because he's the smallest. All morning during school he has to play with his crayons and his trucks. He can come into the kitchen and we give him paper and things to do. He even gets to watch television once in a while, which is usually a big No.

Henry Tingey, 51

Henry Tingey has taught the gospel doctrine Sunday school class and is currently serving as Sunday school president in the Elkton Ward. A native of Logan, Utah, Henry joined the University of Delaware faculty in 1965, where he is now associate chair of the mathematics department. A statistician, he was educated at Utah State University and the University of Minnesota. The father of two grown daughters, he is the Sunday school president.

I grew up in Logan, Utah, well-steeped in Mormonism. My dad was chairman of the mathematics department at Utah State University. Dad farmed for many years throughout the war, dairy cows. Then in his retirement he surveyed the property and subdivided it. Where I used to have six acres to romp over, there are now nineteen houses. I helped him milk the cows, and I got 10 percent of the milk check—about four dollars a week. I learned my love of the outdoors and hunting from my father along with my love of mathematics and academics.

Out of 169 graduating seniors at Logan High School, 165 started college. Utah State had a very good undergraduate program, so I saw no reason to go to another school. A couple of quarters my father and I never talked to each other because I was in his class. I was appointed an instructor in my junior year. I taught algebra, but when my father became ill, that spring, I had to teach his calculus course.

I did not go on a mission. If I'd been called, of course, I'm sure I would have gone, but I was not. I was not ordained an elder until I was twenty-two, shortly before I was married. At the time I went in for my interview to get a temple recommend to be married, the bishop asked me if I wanted to go on a mission. I said, "Hey, I didn't come in here to be interviewed for a mission! I came in here because I'm getting married."

He said, "Well, I guess it's as appropriate to get married and bear children as it is to go on a mission and convert people."

My academic training is in bio-statistics, which is generally related to work in public health and medical research. The University of Delaware has neither. I'm fairly well trained in mathematics. Even in an environment without public health work or medical research, I've survived as a statistician. I teach courses in general statistics, a required course for business and economics majors, and graduate courses related to experimental design or analysis of variance.

I've been involved in a number of research activities that are a team effort. I was involved in, and I like to think fairly instrumental in, the development of the Trauma Center in Baltimore. The idea really belongs to Dr. R. A. Cowley from Layton, Utah, a good Mormon boy who was in the Korean Conflict and applied the MASH hospital concept to civilian medicine. I've worked on statistical analysis, handling data from patients who've been subjected to severe physiological shock and deciding how they could best be monitored and treated.

I also did a lot of work monitoring the Medicare/Medicaid system. We're currently involved in a ferreting out physician-condoned patient abusers. You wonder about someone who has 346 office visits in a given year. It's a different style of research than many academics think of, and it's been satisfying. As associate chairman of the department, I have administrative responsibilities. I have a great deal of satisfaction when I deliver a good lecture series or I teach a good year. Teaching is part of my immortality. Part of my energy goes out and attaches itself to everyone I teach.

I'm very impressed with what man has done in medicine. We have man standing on the threshold of being able to create life. That makes him a god. After all, we have been promised that, haven't we? We're certainly fertilizing human eggs outside of human beings. My religion tells me that "as God is, I may become," and that "I am as he once was."

From the time I was married until about five years ago I was totally inactive in the church except for one little episode in Aberdeen. When we went to Minnesota I tried to become active in the church. I can't figure out why things didn't click. All of a sudden I was not active. It's very easy to stay inactive. People are just like dogs. A dog does something wrong once and it knows how to do it very well. Brother Somers said one day, "Beulah and I, all our lives have gone to church. On Sunday morning, what are you going to do? You go to church because you've developed that habit." I had not been 100 percent for a number of years. When Mary and I were dating, we went to sacrament meeting as was the style, alternating between our wards, but the habit never came back. In three short months before I got to Minnesota I had fallen out of the habit.

At Aberdeen, a major on the post informed me of the branch activities, so I went to my favorite class, gospel doctrine. A friend of mine from Utah State was teaching the class. He passed the manual around and had people read from it. I went to the branch president and said, "This is not teaching." Of course, with that wonderful statement I got myself on the hook to teach gospel doctrine. I had a terrific time teaching *Jesus the Christ*. Sometimes I reached the group and sometimes I didn't. Many of the people were converts to the church and were not used to the scholarly approach.

When we moved here, there was the Wilmington Ward. I'm not like Brother Somers who was probably the first Mormon ever to come to the University of Delaware and was regularly exhibited by its president as, "This is Fred Somers; he's my Mormon." I was particularly impressed by the gospel doctrine class in the ward. There was free-wheeling open discussion. In an attempt to give the kids a chance to make a rational decision about religion, I proposed that everybody go to church with me. The deal I made with the kids was if they couldn't learn anything, we'd discuss it and I might release them from the bargain. I finally talked my wife into going because it was such a great gospel doctrine class. I'm extremely lucky when I do things like this. The day my wife came with me, we spent the whole class period debating who was smarter, Adam or Eve. She can still remember every word of that. That's the last time she's been inside a Mormon church.

Before I began coming to church again I had fallen under an influence that was dragging me not only away from the church, but away from a lot of other things, too. I realized that I had to decide whether what was happening to me externally was more powerful or whether I was more powerful. One June 2, 1981, shortly after I'd made the decision that things were going to change, I was going through a terrific conflict. About two o'clock in the morning I prayed, and at the end of the prayer I heard something. I don't think I hallucinated. A voice said, "Henry, everything's going to be all right." Ever since then, everything has been all right—at least with me. I haven't got my family back into the church, and that may never happen. At least the thing that had been working on me for a long period of time was mostly gone. When you drift that far away, you don't come back instantly.

Shortly after that, Bishop Bushman contacted me. I'd been contacted by Bishop O'Day a number of times, but Bishop Bushman had in mind some sort of job. When I explained my situation he probably changed his idea, but I became the gospel doctrine teacher. Of course, it was a great delight to me. I get a real bang out of studying the scriptures. Even at the depths of my despair there wasn't any question in my mind about the veracity of the gospel of Jesus Christ. I've never had a problem with the principles at all. I'm not going to let the Word of Wisdom drive me into a corner, and I'm not going to let people take the church away from me again. Looking back with that 20/20 hindsight I can tell myself that I'm a fool for what I did. My problems were not with the church but with people in the church. I had a hard time distinguishing between the church and the actions of people within the church. The backbiting and the hypocrisy drove me crazy in Logan. On Sunday I saw people in important positions in the church and on Monday, Tuesday, Wednesday, Thursday, Friday they were out there in the scrap with the rest of us. Their tactics were not exactly honorable, certainly not Christian. I'm making a judgment, which I'm not supposed to do, but that bothered me. That cost me my religion; twenty-five years of inactivity is a long time. When I came back this time I promised myself that people are not going to take it away from me again.

I think I would still be teaching gospel doctrine except that I offended somebody. I wish that sister had confronted me with the accusation of teaching false doctrine. I'm not sure we can understand the value of the truth of the scripture until we've compared it with a contortion of the scripture. I would have liked to have dealt with that head on rather than have somebody sneak around behind my back. It was probably easier for the bishop, who knew I would do what he told me to do, to move me into the background. Sunday school president is not a very visible job.

In coming back into activity, I asked the bishop that I not be given any explicit priesthood callings. You don't have to hold the priesthood to teach gospel doctrine, but you have to hold the priesthood to be the Sunday school president. I suppose it's strange to see somebody fifty-one years old who was born in the covenant and is still an elder. The high priest is an administrator, but that's not a responsibility that I'm looking for in the church. The priesthood, the exercise of God's power on earth, has been something I have used very little, and I hope judiciously and effectively. I certainly believe I have that power. The power of the priesthood is one cohesive force that I think I've had in my family relationships.

Everyone of us in the church has the Holy Ghost. For thirty-five years that kept me from stepping over boundaries that would have caused me to be excommunicated from the church. There are many people who go through my experience who don't make it. They lose their moral standards; they lose their judgment. I don't think I could have lasted much longer. I was losing the battle. The greatest contribution of the Mormon church to our society is the Holy Ghost in every one of its members.

During my period of inactivity, at least half the time, I had home teachers. One of the things that brought me back was a home teacher who had gone through much the same turmoil I'd gone through. We were from very different circumstances, but we'd been to the same place. He was masterful.

I used to sit in testimony meetings and listen to people say, "I know." I thought, "How do you know? How do you have any idea whether Jesus Christ was really God when he was on the earth 2,000 years ago? How can you know something that you can't witness? You can't even trust somebody to relate an eyewitness account very effectively." Once in a while I heard somebody say, "I believe." I could buy that. Being inactive in the church didn't mean I was inactive in studying the scriptures. I read the Book of Mormon and I studied a variety of commentaries. The promise at the end of the Book of Mormon is indeed true. If you study diligently and you pray, you come to know. It's something you can put into a reasonably logical structure. I've never had the science/religion problem. I can live with two compartments. I enjoy reading something, taking it apart, and putting it back together, and that's how I got my testimony. I probably have given my testimony in many different forms, but I never have stood up in a testimony meeting and given it.

16 | Pioneer Day

Thursday, July 24, was a bright, hot day—perfect for celebrating the arrival of the Mormon pioneers in the Salt Lake Valley. The Elkton Ward was commemorating the day with an activity for the Primary children. As I arrived at the church with my four Primary-age children and one toddler, Colleen Pierce, the Primary president, was posting signs saying Nauvoo and Kirtland on the front of the building. Stacey Pierce was pulling her sister Bonnie in a wagon that sported a cardboard cutout of a covered wagon.

We quickly made our way inside to the cool dimness of the Primary room. About thirty children were there by the time the Blazer Scout color guard—Aaron Robinson, Josh Crowe, Alan Taber, Matt Robison, and Randy Pierce—entered to perform the flag ceremony. The boys' uniforms were stiff and new.

While the mothers sat at the sidelines, in front of wagon cutouts, Deborah Johnston led the children in singing "Little Pioneer Children," "Busy Pioneer Children," "The Oxcart Song," and "The Handcart Song."

After the singing, Colleen Pierce had the children line up to go outside for a trek. She described the pioneers' exodus from Nauvoo while the children stood on the front steps of the chapel. Some of the Sunbeams rode in the two decorated wagons that Randy Pierce and some of the other boys struggled to keep upright. The pioneer trail led over to the little house where one door was labeled Council Bluffs and the other Cheyenne Pass.

Instead of proceeding on to Emigration Canyon, which was posted on the back door of the building, Colleen Pierce divided the children into two groups. The older children went to the lawn beside the parking lot where Thelma Roberts directed them in passing Lifesavers using toothpicks, carrying water in spoons, and peanuts on forks. Then they teamed up for three-legged races. On the lawn between the church and the little house, Debbie Roeder organized the younger children to play Duck, Duck, Goose. They were less successful at tossing water balloons; some of the smaller children were frightened.

Soon Colleen Pierce pulled a wagon with a huge kettle of water in it over to the back stairs and ladled out cups of water for each of the children. Then they went downstairs where the long tables had been set up. The children began to make covered wagons using small cardboard boxes, white paper, and pretzels for the wheels. Elizabeth Stone had made all forty little boxes out of lightweight cardboard. There were not quite enough boxes to go around so she quickly made three or four more. Teachers circulated around the tables admonishing the children not to eat the pretzels and helping them to assemble the wagons.

Virginia Lund then called the children over to the end of the large room and explained how butter is made. Each child received a small baby food jar containing a tablespoon or two of cream, which they shook to make butter. As we left, the children were given bags of popcorn to eat on the way home. Away we went—five children, four jars of butter, four covered wagons, and five bags of popcorn—driving the seven miles home in our air-conditioned station wagon.

Every ward I have lived in commemorates the trek of the Mormon pioneers. Special events such as picnics, camp outs, or pancake breakfasts are often held, and sacrament meetings during July feature hymns and speeches about the sacrifices and faith of the pioneers. The history of the LDS Church is part of its religious beliefs. The members of the Elkton Ward identify with the pioneer tradition in several ways.

First, some members of the ward are descendants of pioneers who crossed the plains with the Mormon covered wagon trains or handcart companies. Many of these members not only take pride in their church heritage but see themselves as modern pioneers or colonizers. Just as their ancestors established new settlements in the far reaches of the Mountain West, they have brought their religion and way of life to the East where members of the church are relatively scarce. Many of them have worked with other members of the church to establish a closely connected LDS community that includes not only the church organization but friendships and social and moral practices within the mostly non-Mormon communities in which they live. Fred Somers, Blane Parker, Lee Anderson, and Detta Watts are among the Elkton Ward members who have come East because of professional or other opportunities.

Because every ward in the church has the same organizational structure, members who move from ward to ward understand the purpose and mission of each of the ward organizations. New arrivals in the Elkton Ward are soon called to positions in the ward that give them well-defined roles to play in the congregation. The ward also benefits from the members' experience in other wards. Members who have held callings in other wards can draw upon their experiences as they fulfill their responsibilities in their new ward. Thus, ideas for programs and special events as well as for methods of carrying out defined tasks are transmitted informally from ward to ward. Grant and Jeanette Robison and Debora Ennis are among those who moved to the Elkton Ward during the Record Year.

New converts also sometimes identify with the pioneer heritage because they are not only helping to build up the church but because they also are leaving their old way of life and adopting a new one. Finding a role or niche in the ward is often more difficult for newly baptized members than for members moving in from other areas of the country. They are not familiar with the myriad organizations within the ward, nor have they had experience in working in such organizations. Receiving a calling signifies to new members that they are, indeed, full-fledged members of the church and helps initiate them into the community. Michael Wheeler and Georgette DiVirgilis joined the Elkton Ward as new converts in May and June.

Elizabeth Stone, 19

Elizabeth Stone, second counselor in the Primary presidency, has been a member of the Elkton Branch since its earliest beginnings in Cloyd Mullins's living room. She has two children, seventeen months and three months old.

I was married at seventeen in my parents' house. I intended to go to college before I got married. As soon as the kiddies are old enough and my husband, David, gets out of school, I'll go back. I feel that I'm lacking in education. Sometimes I feel bad I'm not bringing money into the house because David works hard. When Matthew was born David was working two jobs and going to school full-time. Suzie was born this spring. I want David to get settled in his job and get his degree.

When I get up in the middle of the night, I realize I work hard, too. I think it's very important for mothers to stay home with their children while they're little, but I don't like feeling that I'm not contributing financially. I like staying home because I feel close to the children. It's fascinating to watch them do new things. Matthew learns a new word every day.

I like being with the children in Primary and I feel I'm contributing something to the ward by teaching other people's children. It's neat to see them get excited when they realize they learned something they didn't know before. It is a lot of work and it's hard to explain to David why I have to go to meetings so much. Actually, he is very good about it. He hasn't given me a hard time about getting the kids blessed in our church. Considering that his parents raised him as a very strong Catholic, I was surprised that he didn't go against me. Once in a while I have to go out at night when I could be home with him.

I enjoy attending church now. Before I got married I was just there. I had to go every Sunday. When I moved out, I could decide whether or not I wanted to go. I finally decided that I wanted to go. Seminary also helped; the Ridges are important people to me and I admire them. They strengthened my testimony.

My family is similar to my parents' family in that David isn't a member and my father isn't a member. When I was growing up it was hard to be good on the Sabbath because of my dad. My mom wanted us to keep the day holy while Dad wanted us to do other things. I like to treat it as a day of rest. It's David's only day off. We just visit our parents on Sunday. As the children get older, I want them to appreciate the Sabbath day.

The Word of Wisdom has been a big help. In high school it was hard to say no when everybody was going out drinking on the weekends. Having something more to stand by than just what my parents said made a big difference. In our school, at least one senior was killed every year for the past ten years—it was all related to alcohol and drugs.

The emphasis that the church puts on families means a lot to me. Eternal life and baptism for the dead are the most important things. It's good to know that if my father passes on, or my grandmother on my dad's side, we can get baptized for them. If they don't believe the gospel in this life, I feel they will after they pass away. I always admired my mother for being so strong in the church when my dad wasn't supporting her in it.

I want my children to go to college and get married in the temple, be faithful to the church all their lives. I hope Matthew will go on a mission. It sounds kind of funny, they're so little, but that's what I want for them.

G. Fred Somers, 71

G. Fred Somers, a plant physiologist, joined the faculty of the University of Delaware in 1951. As one of the first members of the church in Newark, he has held many church positions in the Wilmington Branch and Stake. He is director of the stake's genealogy library, which has branches in Wilmington, Salisbury, and Dover. He and his wife, Beulah, are the parents of three sons.

I was raised in East Garland, Utah. I was the eldest with three brothers and a sister. In those days, six-day weeks were common on the farm. Saturday was the day for baths. In the summer we just went swimming in the canal. Quite frankly, our expectations were not much beyond living until the next day. My life has surpassed what I might have ever have tried to imagine. My parents always said we were going to college so that we would have opportunities that they did not have. Even though Father died when I was still in high school, two of us got doctorates, one got a master's.

I went away to college in Logan, Utah, when I was seventeen, two years after the October stock market crash. The youth just older than me went into agriculture or into the nearby businesses. We were in the forefront of a flight from that. We used education as an avenue of escape from being peasants. We had only small pieces of land to farm. I would have enjoyed being a farmer, but I didn't have the capital. Almost all my classmates, both from grade school and high school, moved away from their home villages. Many of them went to California or other distant places. The six of us who graduated from Utah Agricultural College in botany in 1935 were in graduate school at Cornell at the same time.

While I was an undergraduate I was given an opportunity to do research in the field that became my field of major interest—plant science, actually plant pathology. My junior year I was given my own project. My senior year I had one undergraduate under my supervision. This not only provided some income but was invaluable experience in solving problems and in management. I've been doing active research for over fifty years. I had a difficult time choosing between botany and chemistry and ended up with a combination of both. For a long time I was better known as a biochemist than as a botanist.

In 1936 I was fortunate enough to get a Rhodes Scholarship to Oxford where I got a B.A. in the Honours School and a research degree called a B.Sc. Getting that scholarship changed everything. It opened up the world. After I received my doctor's degree, Beulah and I recognized that we could no longer think in terms of a particular community. Our opportunities were now nationwide, worldwide. Our modus operandi has been to make the most of them, not in a crass, materialistic way, but in a whole life way. We have a son in Hawaii, a son in Mexico, and one in Ohio. We go to Hawaii and Mexico at least once a year. We went to the Middle East in March. We will take advantage of opportunities like that as they come along. We hope that our finances and our health continue to let us do that.

My scholarship didn't permit me to be married. The day after I got my last stipend in 1939, Beulah and I were married. Then I went to Cornell for a Ph.D. I was on the faculty at Cornell University for ten years and for seven of those years was simultaneously employed by the U.S. Department of Agriculture. At the University of Delaware I was at the Agricultural Experimental Station and later held a named professorship. In 1958–59 we spent a year in the Philippines, which gave us a chance to travel around the world. You don't know your own country until you have lived in another one. The one weakness in my education was that the training was all intellectual and technical. There was no training for management. I spent almost twenty years in management. I was associate director of the experimental station, associate dean, department chairman. I have research still to be analyzed and published. We're finding retirement is not a time of leisure. It's a time of choices.

When we came to Delaware in 1951 there were very few church members in this community. I was the only one on the faculty. We have tried to let people know that Mormons are good, dependable people who can do things. When our oldest son was born I decided that young people should have Scouting, so I volunteered as a Scout leader, an association that continued for twenty or twenty-five years both in New York and in Delaware. I was also on the Newark

Recreation Association Board and the County Parks and Recreation Commission. The university frequently called on me to chair commissions of one kind or another. I'm now on a university committee that is trying to develop a plan to help youngsters develop more leadership. I also served on state committees. I represented Governor Boggs in developing plans for the use of atomic energy. We feel that as citizens we owe something to society.

I was called to manage the stake genealogical library nearly four years ago though I had never even used a genealogical library. It has been an interesting challenge; I've had a chance to work with a lot of good people. It's disheartening that so few of our members use the admirable facilities we have. The church has put a tremendous amount of money into developing the facilities. One of the brightest spots is our auxiliary library in Dover. A couple of years ago Salt Lake said we could set up an auxiliary library. I advised the stake to take advantage of that. We didn't read the word *auxiliary* very carefully (the church allowed just one microfiche reader). We ordered three microfiche readers and three microfilm readers. The auxiliary library in Dover has about as many patrons a month as Wilmington, but the bulk of theirs are *members*.

I just wrote a biography of my father based on memory. It's ten typewritten pages. Maybe that's too short, but perhaps something like that gets to the essence of the matter. His mother stayed in Australia for several years after Father came to the United States, and the letters she wrote to him have been bound in a book. It's interesting, but it would be a chore to read them if it weren't my own father and grandmother.

For a long time Beulah and I have said that we'll accept any church calling, but only one. The calling I've enjoyed most was teaching the gospel doctrine class. I liked the intellectual challenge. I enjoyed presenting the material, and it forced me to do background studying. When I was on the high council I disliked sitting on courts. I don't like having to be judgmental. I don't feel we do enough subsequently to rehabilitate the so-called sinner.

The opportunities that the church gives us change us if we try to magnify those opportunities. Learning to speak before an audience, to lead a discussion, or organize activities provide us with growth and development that many people don't have. That's one reason many church members have succeeded in management and leadership.

Since I've been in a position to do so, I've always asked that Beulah and I be called to the same organization. We were both in the stake Sunday school. We couldn't have both been on the high council. Maybe someday we could, but I don't think we'll ever come to that. Part of the time I was on the high council she made visits as a stake leader at the same time as I was making visits. At our age, we depend on each other. I don't think we should be asked to serve in disjoint activities. Quite properly the church's emphasis is on young people and young families. Two groups, maybe three groups, are by and large ignored.

They are the senior citizens, the single adults, and the divorced people. Except for Sister Roberts, who is about our age, we are old enough to be the parents or the grandparents of practically everybody in the Elkton Ward.

Frankly, I don't find our church meetings very stimulating. Maybe it's because we've been here so long. Rarely do I find challenging ideas or ideas challengingly presented. I recognize that youngsters have to learn to speak and to grow and develop, but very seldom do we hear anything new. Occasionally, someone will present a new idea or present it in a new light, but it's fishing in a pretty fished-out pond.

Doug Taber loaned me *An Approach to the Book of Mormon* by Hugh Nibley. It's a much more intellectual, substantial, and more interesting account than our Sunday school lessons. The lessons strike me as being aimed primarily at people who are younger, less educated, and less experienced in the church. They don't deal intellectually with the concepts and challenges that could be issues for the church. I know that many of our church leaders face up to these issues. We've had giants in the past—for example, Talmage and Widtsoe. When a more intellectual approach is attempted in the wards, the more traditional members complain that it's not orthodox, and we tend to lose those stimulating teachers. A Doctrine and Covenants course could benefit from the kind of approach that Claudia or Bishop Bushman would be able to bring to it as historians.

When we lived in Ithaca, the priesthood manual provoked me so much that I decided to correct it. The things it said about the history of the church in the area of New York where we were living were in error. I organized visits to some of the nearby historical sites and wrote a guide to them.

There's beginning to be some understanding of the historical perspective of the early church. A lot of the myths and misunderstandings that have become a part of our church traditions are being reexamined. That reexamination strengthens my confidence in the church, although many people seem to be afraid of it. The Sunday school teacher has a real problem because he is told to teach only what's in the manual. He can use other resources, but can't bring them into the class. I think I understand why the church puts these restraints on the teachers. After World War II the general authorities went back into the German wards and found there had been some drift away from church teachings. We have to have some central direction, particularly now that the church is so big and so widely scattered, but I'm not sure it has to be at such a juvenile level. I recognize there are people who probably are not ready for this reexamination. On the other hand, if it's presented properly, it shouldn't hurt them. It should strengthen them. Look at our ward. I don't think there's any adult who isn't a high school graduate. Many of them are college graduates. We're not a bunch of dummies.

I nearly always read the scripture assignment for the Sunday school lesson and I reflect over it. So much scriptural writing is couched in such broad terms that I'm afraid we read too many specifics into it. For example, we're told these are the last days before Christ comes. Paul was saying the same thing centuries ago. The last days will take care of themselves. If I've lived as I should, fine. If I haven't, then I will pay the price. Some people worry and fuss so much about this sort of thing. The scriptures tell about the degrees of glory, but we're just beginning to understand something of our own universe. The celestial kingdom is incomprehensible. I don't worry about it.

The Book of Mormon is difficult for me to understand. I have some sociological problems with it. My experience has been that societies do not turn from all saints to all sinners in such short time spans as the Book of Mormon recounts. Many of the teachings in it are very valuable: "There must be opposition in all things," for instance.

Where does that leave me? The same as I am with respect to a lot of things, with an open mind. So many people stand up in church and say, "I know." There are very few things in this life I know for sure. In science you never assume you have the final word on anything. Later information may not undo it, but it will reinterpret and extend it further. My testimony is that following these teachings has proven to be beneficial. I have seen humble people grow to giants by participating in the church.

The church now, in many ways, is not the church I knew as a youngster. The big difference is its world outlook. It is now administered by regions and areas. The membership will soon be more non–English speaking than English speaking. When we were in the Philippines there were no organized church activities at all. Now there are several stakes. Contributing to welfare aid for Ethiopia recently was an interesting change. In the past, welfare has been for our church members.

There has been a rather artificial structuring of our attitudes in the church. When our son was at the University of Utah he lived off-campus after his freshman year. A Sunday school class in the student ward he attended as a freshman turned him on, but when they found out he didn't live on campus they told him he could not attend church there. He had to attend his ward of residence, where he knew nobody. He became inactive. They were more concerned about the technicality of where he lived than they were about him.

Our parents were simple folk who had not experienced much of the world. Their beliefs were inevitably influenced by their experiences. We adhere to the general principles of the church as our parents did, but our understanding of what those may mean is colored by our experiences. In my very orthodox country ward in Utah they were convinced that the only good people in the world were Mormons. One of the reasons we were so good was that we had the Word of Wisdom. When I traveled to England with a party of Rhodes Scholars, I noticed that almost all of them drank quite a bit of liquor and they were every bit as good as I was intellectually. Many of them were brighter. I think the Word of Wisdom is an excellent guide, but we should not make the interpretation that it alone makes us superior.

The concept that God once was as we are and we might become as Gods is very humbling. If we're to become as Gods, think of what we must accomplish—not just keeping our noses clean, but putting something in our minds.

We've seen in our short life span some fantastic things. When I was a mature adult, we thought that there was something magic about any machine that could exceed the speed of sound. Now, we can see live broadcasts from Salt Lake City and from the moon. We now know far more about the matter around us, both inanimate and animate. My high school teacher said, "Someday, maybe some of you will know what enzymes are." I have written books about them. It's bewildering to think of all the things I would like to know and how little time I have to learn them.

Lee Anderson, 41

Lee Anderson has taught natural resource economics in the College of Marine Studies at the University of Delaware since 1974. A native of Salt Lake City, he was educated at BYU and the University of Washington. He and his wife, Sheila, are the parents of two children.

My great-great-grandmother came across the plains with a handcart. My grandfather met his wife in Norway on his mission. I was reading my great-great-grandmother's journal the other night. She described the problems of pulling the stuff across the icy streams in the middle of the winter. Her first husband died coming across the plains in the handcart company. It was a tough life. During my sabbatical we visited a lot of relatives in Norway. It's been fun to trace things back and know the extent of the family—my cousins. I appreciate my lineage both in the church and out of it. The family in Norway are not members. My grandmother never went back to Norway.

My family was not super religious. My father always had a job, such as Sunday school president, and he was on the high council later in life. My mother still goes to church. Still, the atmosphere around the home was casual. I was good friends with the stake president's son. It seemed that every time he walked out the door to play baseball with the guys, his mother, Sister Romney, would say, "Now, remember you're a representative of Zion." I never got that at home. I think my parents felt more strongly about it than I do.

The bishop used to come into the Deacons' Quorum and say, "How many of you are going on a mission?" Everyone raised his hand. I never did.

I was in student government at BYU, and during graduate school I did engage in some marches, war protesting during the Vietnam War, and collecting money for the war on poverty.

Sheila and I were married August 20, 1966, in the Oakland Temple. We went immediately to Seattle for four years of graduate school. I worked with Professor Crutchfield at the University of Washington, which sent me in the direction of fisheries' management.

One of the most satisfying aspects of my work is that it involves a lot of travel. I've been to India, Hong Kong, New Zealand, Australia, Japan, and Portugal. I've been to Rome for FAO a number of times. Sheila and I lived in Norway for six months. I work hard, but sometimes my vacations are these trips. Sheila was able to go with me to Hong Kong and New Zealand. We spent two months driving around Europe three years ago.

I don't mind at all working with students who make an effort to learn, but this afternoon I gave an example straight out of the text. I said, "What's the answer?" Not one of the students had read the text for the day. I said, "Look, this is depressing to me." None of them defended themselves and said they had read it. I don't think all students are that way, but I'd just as soon be doing my research instead of wasting time with students who do not care.

For the church, I teach the teacher development class in Sunday school. Two weeks ago only one person out of eight showed up, so we just canceled the class. I guess I take it too seriously. A number of the students are doing their assignments, but some of them merely glance over it on the way to church. I'm feeling a little dejected and not devoting the energy to it that I could. Maybe it's a vicious circle. The bishopric pulled one of the students out and gave him a teaching job before the course was over. If it's so important that the students are going to make a commitment, it seems the ward administration could leave them in there.

I'm not your basic straight-arrow Mormon. I don't attend sacrament meeting. I don't keep the Word of Wisdom. I was in the Elders' Quorum presidency in Seattle in the student ward. I was asked to do it in Miami, but when I went to the first meeting and realized some of the jobs they wanted me to do, I was forced to come to grips with my view of my religion. I told them I couldn't take the job.

I'm a sixth-generation Mormon, but I am like the Jew who eats pork and shellfish but was out on the docks helping load Israeli boats during the six-day war. I may not go home teaching, but I try to go out and help somebody. I have a bond to the people, but I can't say that the church is the ruling force in my life as I know it is for most of my colleagues at church. I can respect that and know it's genuine, but it's not me.

I'm not a hypocrite. I didn't bless either of my children. I had Bishop O'Day, a very fine man, bless Bronwyn, and I had a friend bless Pearce. I did baptize Bronwyn, but Bishop Bushman confirmed her. I haven't always felt this way about the priesthood. When I was in graduate school we would go out and administer to people. I would not do that now.

At the University of Washington I enjoyed the student ward because a lot of people thought the same way I did. Once when the Romney boy I knew in high school gave the standard answers in a priesthood discussion, the teacher came back at him with "Why, why, why, and why?" That was the way we looked at things in that ward. I enjoyed the intellectual stimulation. Some of these guys knew the scriptures far better than I did, but at the same time could ask questions. I don't enjoy priesthood meeting as much now although Tony Peer gives a good lesson. I have been going so long that I have a little brain switch that I turn off. When I listen I click into some questions. I can always throw out questions that seem to make other people in the quorum nervous—"Is he saying that just for shock value?" I'm really not, although I can see that people might think that.

In Seattle, there was a rumor that they were going to mix the university people among the other wards. They thought a hotbed of radicalism might develop. Once, a high councillor was talking about the church and the blacks in Sunday school class and said, "I want you to know that the church is doing the job. A black woman wanted to join the church, and some of the ward members didn't want her, but we solved the problem. We baptized her when no one else was around and she now meets with the bishop once a week." Everybody in our ward was appalled that he was saying this was a good solution to the problem. He was shocked that anyone would question it, and he was shocked by the vehemence with which people said, "We won't accept that line of thinking." It was right after that the rumors began.

I don't think the ward was radical. A lot of those folks were very orthodox. I was very happy when the revelation came that the priesthood was for *all* males. It made it a lot easier for me to accept the church's teachings, though I think a lot of members had to come to grips with it. When we lived in Miami I heard a lot of comments from the pulpit that were downright racist. Now there's no excuse for that sort of thing. The former policy gave people an excuse to think of blacks as second-class citizens. I thought some of the church's explanations were mealy mouthed: "If you join our church you'll get the priesthood in the hereafter and you'll still be better off" is a pretty hard thing to sell to somebody who has been deprived of his rights here on the earth.

Maybe other things will change. The church is a flexible organization. I once did some research on this for a conference at BYU on Mormons in economics. I love the way the church has changed with respect to circumstances. At the time when the United States government took over all the church's property, Mormons burned an American flag as part of the July 24 celebration in protest of the American government. Brigham Young said from the pulpit, "Don't buy from Gentile producers." If I remember correctly, he used words like *vipers*. Now the priesthood handbook says not to engage in bazaars or other activities in direct conflict with the merchants in the area—Gentile or not.

If the church wants to take a stand on an issue of the day, it should allow for individual ideas to be expressed. I certainly would have no qualms about the president of the church's saying, "This is how I feel." It would carry weight because of his position, but I don't think the church should say, "You should vote this way." Once you cross the line, how far do you go? The church made a stand on the ERA, on the MX missile. The liquor laws in Utah probably foster alcoholism: buy a bottle rather than a drink. If you believe in direct revelation, then you have to say, "Yes, thus saith the Lord." I just cringe if you start that kind of thing. When the Lord says everything, the individual becomes nothing. It's a very harsh criticism, but I think there's not much difference between the true believer in Mormonism and the true believer in communism. I reject both views for the reason that there's the possibility that the leader could be wrong.

I believe that "man is that he might have joy." Why do we have a distribution of resources such that there are people starving to death in Ethiopia? Why do we have government structures we can't do anything about? I have friends of many different nationalities. Their citizenship doesn't make any difference in the way I associate with them. I would like to see government policies, church policies, give options to individuals. I'm not letting them define *happy*.

When I was a kid and relatively gung-ho on the church, a teacher gave the example "Look at all these people who stop off at the bar and have a drink with their friends before going home" in a disdainful way. At that time I didn't drink, but I can remember thinking, "I'm not so sure that's so bad. Maybe he gets a considerable amount of enjoyment tossing back a couple with his chums as long as his kids aren't starving to death." Everybody doesn't have to think the way we do to be happy.

Things that I have no control over are difficult for me. My son Pearce has had two accidents. He had his right index finger cut off while Sheila and I were in another room. We were visiting friends and Pearce stuck his finger right in the chain of an exercise bicycle. It was a terrible feeling. I don't feel guilty, but I'd have given anything to help my child. We're so vulnerable. Just two weeks ago Pearce was riding his bike and I was following on mine. He hit a parked car and knocked out his permanent bottom teeth. I didn't even warn him because I thought he was going to dodge. The dentist said, "It's a long shot, let's go look for the teeth." There were both the teeth on the street. He told me to put them under my tongue. We ran about three red lights and he put them back in. I was physically sick for two days afterwards. The most difficult things are those that happen to your children. I'm not reckless with my children, but some things I just cannot control.

Blane Parker, 38

Blane Parker has moved from the West to Delaware, where his wife's parents live, twice. He came the first time to teach school and the second, in 1982, to

work in construction. He and his wife, Robyn, have three children, thirteen, nine,
and six years old, and Blane is a counselor in the Elders' Quorum presidency.

I grew up in Paris, Idaho, a little town in the southeastern part of Idaho, by
Bear Lake. It was settled by Charles Rich. My great-great-grandfathers on both
sides migrated from England to be with the church and settled in Idaho. My
younger son, Craig, makes the fifth generation in my family that has been born
in the covenant. My grandfather was Ezra Taft Benson's Sunday school teacher
for about three years.

My father worked in construction. I started working with him when I was
about six and have learned all that he had to teach. My mother's father was a
farmer designer for International Harvester. He ran prototype machinery for a
year and told them how to update it. I first worked away from home after the
eighth grade, for three months for the state of Idaho. We worked for a dollar a
day and our room and board. I worked summers away from home from then
on. I took six years to get through BYU and I worked for the Forest Service in
the summers. Saturday, now, is a day to play. I've made my mind up that I'm
not going to work any more overtime.

Robyn and I were married in the home of Robyn's friend in Salt Lake City.
My uncle was a bishop, so he married us. After Robyn and I were married we
moved to Buhl, Idaho, for about a year. We moved out to Delaware where I
taught, then we went back to Idaho. Dad and I were in business together until
the interest rates went way up and we folded. All of our children were born in
the Twin Falls hospital. Each time we moved back to Idaho, we had another one.

When I was training to be a teacher, I figured I wouldn't be able to spend all
of ten thousand dollars a year. I taught wood shop, metal shop, drafting, and
art. In the summers I worked construction and made more money in one week
than I made in two weeks teaching school. The first year I taught we had a district strike. There were a lot of politics in that. They jerked our credentials and
played a lot of games with us. In what would have been my third year of teaching, the desegregation suit was in the courts and there was a statewide teachers'
strike. I wasn't willing to strike again because of the politics that were involved.
In construction when we struck, we got something or we didn't strike. There
was only one other way I knew to make a lot of money relatively quickly, and
that was to go back into the union. Since then we've had a string of good times.
I can drive from coast to coast and my kids can say, "There's the building you
built" or "There's the dam you built" or "There's the powerhouse you built."
We're working now to get enough money to buy the gas station that Robyn's
parents own.

My kids don't know what hard times are. They've had a fairly easy life because we've moved to the work rather than waiting for work to come to us. I

moved here three years ago because I was unemployed in Washington State. As long as work lasts, I'm staying right here.

Right now there is a deterioration in quality and craftsmanship because of the decline in personal pride and because everything comes down to an accounting procedure. That takes all the pride out of your workmanship because you have to justify every move in dollars and cents. Before, no matter what it took, you got it right. Now it's "Hurry up. Let's collect our money and go on to the next one." Construction as we know it today is going to be dead. We'll still have to build buildings, but it's going to be more competitive. People are going to be paid for the amount they produce instead of for the quality of it. The people I work with here have a different mind-set than I'm used to. I'm just too trusting, too honest, and too open. I have a hard time accepting a lot of things that happen here.

My co-workers either want to fight with a Mormon or else they want to find out more about it. In the last few years, I've felt like we can stand on our own with anybody. Before, I was intimidated by religious discussions. Now it doesn't worry me. They can accept it or they cannot. In the last few years I've found a lot more people who are more tolerant of our ideas and beliefs. It's amazingly easy to argue with those who aren't and confuse them.

I'm fairly sure that modern-day revelation is quite different from the beliefs of most churches. Even though most active members of other churches admit they receive answers to prayer, the concept of modern-day revelation staggers them.

If you're going to have a position, you've got to be able to justify it. You can't just take the words of other men; you have to get into the scriptures and find it. Because my family was fairly well enlightened in the gospel, anything that's troublesome to most people was explained to me when I was four or five. There's very little that wasn't discussed. When everybody was concerned about the blacks and the priesthood, I knew my grandfather's scriptures, from his mission in 1906, documented that the blacks would receive the priesthood. There are always points of controversy. I teach the Elders' Quorum about every third or fourth week, and I know where I can get a rise in a hurry. If you want to stir a controversy, you say certain things to certain people. Then you can sit back and take the rest of the day off.

What I was taught as a child is the basis of my testimony. After several years of trying to disprove the teachings of the gospel and not being able to, I convinced myself that it's true.

I've been a counselor in the Elders' Quorum for about a year and a half. We have had two social activities that have been fairly satisfying. When you get the quorum to pull together, that's pretty good. The day-to-day operations of the Elders' Quorum generally aren't too satisfying. You could find a lot to complain about with the elders. Sometimes I think it weakens your testimony when life runs along smoothly and you don't have to depend on the powers of the priesthood. You don't have to call on the angels. The most enjoyable calling I ever had was teaching the seven-year-olds in Sunday school. It was when I was just coming back into the church. They learned; I learned.

I've seen some changes in emphasis in the church. Even though everybody says we're a church of change, we don't change that much. I have noticed over the last few years that people are less committed to the church, more self-centered. If this doesn't change, the character of the church is going to be lost. A lot of people in the Elkton Ward think that it's unique, but the conditions that exist here exist in most other wards.

In some ways the church has led to a deterioration of my family life. At one time we trusted too much in the idea that if we were busy doing the Lord's work, everything at home would be taken care of. We had a pretty rude awakening about six or eight months ago. I take care of work, then the family, and then the church. If my job's running seven days a week, I work seven days a week. If you can't support your family, you can't do anything. I'm sure that without the church our last five years wouldn't have gone as smoothly as they have. We've made some fairly lucrative moves since I folded my business tent. We were about three steps from bankruptcy, driving two ten-year-old vehicles, and living in a house that we didn't know how to make the payments on. Then we went to Washington and pulled ourselves out of the hole. Before we slipped back in, we came out here. I gave up fishing; I gave up hunting; I gave up skiing; I gave up living in the West and my four-wheel drive. I don't think I've made that many tremendous sacrifices. None of those are things I can't have back.

Detta Watts, 71

Detta Watts moved to Delaware in 1963 when her second husband retired from the service. Born in Utah, she spent her teenage years in California where she married and had a son. As a young widow she worked in medical research during World War II. After moving to Delaware, she attended the Wilmington Ward and then the Dover Ward before being assigned to the Elkton Branch.

I was born in the church. My second husband was born in Delaware, and I met him in California. We traveled throughout the United States and Europe during his military service before we retired here, twenty-one years ago. When my membership was first moved from Dover to Elkton, I wrote to Bishop Barrett and asked him if I couldn't continue going to Dover because I was known there. After I had attended several times in Elkton, I met him one day in the Dover Air Force Base hospital and said, "Do you remember the letter I wrote to you? Please erase that," because I liked Elkton very much.

I lived in American Fork, Utah, until I was about ten. My father was an explosives engineer for the Union Pacific Railroad. We moved to Nevada while he helped construct the tunnels for the trains. I had seven brothers—four are living—and one sister. My mother is now ninety-seven. She is a polygamist's child. My grandfather had three wives. After the Manifesto in 1890, he went to Canada rather than discard any of his wives.

Saturdays were happy days because I could spend them with my brothers and sister. I used to go skating and cycling with them. I still have my skates that I used for competition. Until I was about forty-two I used to skate frequently. My brothers taught me to ride motorcycles and to fly.

I thought I was going to be a model because I had a nicely proportioned figure though I was never pretty. I wanted to know how to walk properly so that someone behind me wouldn't say, "Well, look at that awkward person." I took a modeling course, which wasn't expensive because the manufacturers paid my way. I modeled shoes in the department stores around Los Angeles and Pasadena. I could keep the shoes and the suits that were made for me. The opportunity of learning how to walk and how to hold myself was of value all throughout my life.

I went to beauty school so I could become a cosmetologist and work my way through school. I went to Pasadena Junior College and Glendale Junior College. When it was convenient, I went to the University of Southern California.

I married at eighteen and I still went to school. We were so devoted to each other. We could sit in the same room all evening reading. We could just look at each other, exchange a glance, and that was enough. When my son was four years old my husband was killed in a longshoreman's strike. The only thing I regret is that I didn't remarry earlier and have a family. When I was young I said I was going to have one child and give her all the advantages that I didn't get. Looking back, I see I deprived my son of all the advantages of having brothers and sisters. I wish that I had had more children.

After the probationary time in nursing school, three or four of us were very disillusioned. We figured that if we had to work that hard, we wanted some of the glory, so we transferred to pre-med. About that time the preparations for World War II began, and I was shoved aside and ended up in pharmacology. My son stayed with my mother while I did my traveling.

I went to Dallas, Texas, and worked for Armour Laboratories. They were trying to combine bovine blood and the serum and make an acceptable serum for the boys in the service. They were never able to combine it successfully. We processed the blood that the Red Cross collected in the Southeast. In 1951 I became a crystal oscillator maker. I was assigned to Honolulu, and I attended the Waikiki Ward.

One thing that strengthened my testimony was the first time I attended church there. I had heard there was a church about two blocks from where I was living. A big strapping Hawaiian greeted me at the door. I think he said welcome in Hawaiian. There was not a blond in the house. They were singing "Come, Come, Ye Saints" in Hawaiian. I thought, "Here are these people who are singing 'Come, Come, Ye Saints' and believing all the things that I do about our church, how can I have any doubt about the truthfulness of the gospel?" They had Samoan-, Japanese-, Hawaiian-, and English-speaking classes.

I met my husband Liston when he and his friend stood up to give me and my sister a seat on the bus. We became acquainted in the interval between Riverside and Los Angeles and exchanged addresses. We corresponded for about fifteen years. He would go to Europe and I would go to Hawaii. He went to Korea and I went to Fort Worth. Finally, he wrote and said, "If you are still interested in getting married, let me know. I'll send you a ticket." He met me in Philadelphia and we went to Elkton the following day and got married. I thought it would be so easy to convert my husband to the church, but he can't accept some of the things. I miss a lot by not being able to go to the temple.

If my mother said to Liston, "Please be baptized for my sake, so that my daughter can go with me to the temple and get her endowments," he would go immediately and be baptized, but I can't force him. At the time my mother and father took all the boys and girls and were sealed in the temple, I was in the hospital. I am the only one in the family who is not sealed. I have many people praying with me that my husband will join. Some people have been successful in getting their husbands converted. Sister Whitney is a good friend of mine, and she's in the same circumstances that I am. Her husband has not joined yet.

When I was in California for two years I wanted to go to the temple to get my endowments. I even had a letter from my husband giving his permission. I was interviewed by several people including Howard Hunter, one of the church's Twelve Apostles, who was a friend of my family. As familiar and close as we were, he refused to give me a recommend. I am very disheartened about that, and I was rather bitter for a good long while. I have faith that my son will do my work for me after I leave this earth.

My son is a doctor and lives in California, but I don't solicit his services because he's a pathologist. He's fifty-one. I think he's reached his goal. He has a lovely family and is very happy.

When Liston and I lived in upstate New York I got pneumonia, which lasted all summer. From that time on I have had bronchial difficulties. Eventually, they removed my pleura and in 1965 my right lung. I have broken my ankle, foot, and legs several times, and my depth perception is marred. I have difficulty standing and walking, but I can sit and I can drive. I don't know whether the trouble I have with my legs or the medicine I take accounts for it, but I have gained a lot of weight. It is very humiliating and uncomfortable.

Wilson Davis in Dover has given me blessings on several occasions. He came to visit me once when I had had the flu. I asked for a blessing and the next morning I got up as if I had never been ill. This is why I have so much faith in him and his wife. The missionaries have also given me blessings. Before I had my first operation in Chelsea, Massachusetts, the missionaries came and gave me a blessing that felt as though someone was pouring warm water from the top of my head. It spread over my body. I knew that I was receiving the Holy Ghost.

My home teacher, Frank Crowe, is a very interesting fellow. I've asked if Frank could please visit us because when he comes, my husband makes sure that he's home. Liston enjoys hearing Frank discuss things, and Frank can get across more to my husband than anyone else has been able to. It is difficult not having the priesthood in my home. I told Brother Crowe that if I had any problems, he would be my priest, the head of my household, because my husband does look up to him and he is my ward teacher. My husband has enjoyed books like *The Mormon Country* and *Faith of Our Pioneer Fathers* because he likes history. He has said, "If I joined any church it would be the Mormon church, but there are certain things that I can't accept. Until I can, I'm not joining."

In three years my mother will be one hundred years old. I hope to visit her frequently between now and then. I would like to see her become one hundred. I would like to learn to pray sincerely to accomplish the things I am praying for, such as the conversion of my husband and for my own health and peace.

Jeanette Robison, 33

Jeanette Robison and her family moved to Newark from Greenville, South Carolina, in March. Within a month of her arrival Jeanette, mother of five boys ages four months to ten years, was asked to be in charge of the Relief Society's Sisterhood Quilt, which would be hung in the Relief Society room of the new building. The women who had served as Relief Society presidents in the Elkton Branch or Ward, and a few others, were asked to cross-stitch replicas of the Nauvoo monuments— women in prayer, teaching, playing with their children—for the quilt. Jeanette was also called to teach a Primary class of ten-year-old boys.

I still feel like I'm visiting here. I haven't found my niche. A few weeks after we moved to Greenville, I was called into the stake Young Women's presidency. Of course that got me into things quickly. I know the Blazer boys very well, but I don't have any close friendships with the women.

I'm a sixth-generation Mormon on my mother's side. My mother wasn't as strong as she could have been if she'd had the proper priesthood leadership. Whenever there was a problem we went to the bishop or to our home teacher. I hope my children are growing up in a different atmosphere than I did.

When my parents were divorced, my mother went to work as a receptionist for a man who later became our bishop. He was our home teacher and would say, "How are things going, Varla? I hope, okay," at the office. He didn't come to home teach us, but we knew that if we needed him, he was available. After she remarried, she went back to work at an animal hospital. I went to work there when I was sixteen.

I've always been a member of a choir, whether in church or in school. When I was in Mutual, our ward went to Salt Lake and participated in a four-thousand-voice choir. We all wore pastels; we looked like a box of mints. We sang everything from "Up, Up, and Away" to church music. At the end, as people were filing out and the orchestra was leaving, someone in the alto section started to sing "The Spirit of God like a Fire Is Burning." It spread throughout the choir and the audience. Tears were streaming down our cheeks. I feel that's how it was when the little children were encircled by fire in 3 Nephi.

I was not the kind of person who planned a lot. I dreamed a lot. When they had us write out our goals in Mutual, I always wrote that I wanted to get married in the temple and have a family. I always wanted to be a lady—refined— and to be the hub of a happy home.

I went to college, but I didn't have the drive to get my degree. After a semester at Brigham Young I ran out of money and decided that I wanted to go on a mission when I turned twenty-one. Three weeks later I met my husband. We got married two days after my twenty-first birthday. Grant's father and mother were both married twice and so were mine. We always closed our dates with prayer. We prayed and we fasted and we discussed and we did not get married until we had a special witness that it was right for us. That was one of the most sacred events in my life. I have never doubted it was right for us to be married. I know a lot of women who are continually reevaluating their marriages—trying to decide if this is the year of the divorce or if they can stay together for the children.

At the time I met my husband, I was working as a sales girl at Castleton's College Shop and did the display windows. When we decided to get married, I knew we couldn't live on my $1.60 an hour so I went to work at J.C. Penney's and worked there until just before Matt was born.

We moved to Texas two weeks after Adam was born. The first year of Adam's life was so busy because Matt was still very demanding. Grant was called as Elders' Quorum president right away. He was twenty-six at the time and the ward had a lot of people who did not like having a twenty-six-year-old come in and become Elders' Quorum president. I had three miscarriages between Adam and Aaron. Aaron was born eight months and twenty days after we moved to Raleigh, North Carolina. We had two children born in Utah Valley Hospital, one born in Raleigh, and two born in South Carolina. I've got the hang of it now. Moving around is difficult, but we always have the church. I know this will be home. We want to make the best of it.

I'm content to be at home with my family. I would be even if I didn't have a family because I enjoy having the freedom that a job would take away from me, but sometimes I come away from Relief Society wondering how valuable I am, really. I wonder what will I have when my kids leave? What have I done with what my Heavenly Father has given me? In class we present ourselves as very together people, yet at home we lose it all.

The last month or so has literally been hell for me. My husband worked eighty-five hours last week and my five little boys were at each other's throats and I've been at their throats. I have had some hurtful struggles the last year that have culminated in this move. Not having a close friend in the church to share it with has been tough. I've had spiritual struggles before but I've had friends I could go to; we've been able to commiserate and offer each other an opportunity to change. I haven't felt that here because I'm new. When we first moved here, several sisters came over and were helpful. I appreciate that friendship, but at the same time I'm very hesitant to call and say, "I've got a problem." I'm too proud. I think we all are, don't you? We're not as involved in each other's lives as we used to be before the church changed to the consolidated schedule. When we were together two, three, and four times a week, we couldn't help but have each other more in mind.

I would like to go back to college, but obviously this is not the time. The education I've gotten in the church has served me very well. I have learned a lot that I have used in dealing with my children and in my own personal growth. After Matt was born I was called to be in charge of the Relief Society's Christmas miniclasses. I thought, "How in the world can I do that? I'm holding this baby twenty-four hours a day!" I had to do it because I'd been asked to. It taught me how to do two things at once. In Greenville I was put in charge of the ward's booth for the Holiday Fair one year. We wanted some painted items, so some of us took a tole-painting class. I found I was good at it. The instructor invited me to put some things in her store. I started doing a lot of folk-art painting, and eventually bought a jigsaw so I could cut my own pieces.

I felt the most spiritually inclined when I was in the stake Young Women's presidency. As we met twice a month and talked about who should be called to positions, we got so we were trying to find out what we could do to help Heavenly Father's daughters. When you work with someone in the church, you get to know her in ways you wouldn't know a casual friend.

One Sunday I was supposed to go to a certain branch conference. Leaving the children was a hardship, but I decided to go. It was a struggling branch. The branch's Young Women's president had been active for only a year. When we met together at the close of the conference to discuss the individual girls, the statistics, and any problems, Sister Blackwell became flustered and said, "I'm not supposed to tell anyone, but what do you do when you've got a real severe problem?" One of the girls of a very active family had confided in the her that day that she was pregnant and was scheduled for an abortion the following week. Sister Blackwell didn't know what the church's teaching was. She had been inclined to counsel the girl to go ahead with the abortion to avoid problems with the family. I talked to the counselor in the stake presidency and the three of us met with the branch president. I got home very late that day. The next week I got a call saying the girl had not had the abortion and that things were going to be all right. If I hadn't been there, she would have had an abortion, which would have been the biggest mistake she had made up to that time in her life. That was a very humbling experience.

Our family is more strict on the Sabbath day than many Latter-day Saint families are. The children don't play outside. I try to stay in a dress or at least a nice robe. If I wear pants, I'm more inclined to vacuum. The meetings are a marathon. I struggle with the kids through breakfast; we get out to the car but someone's forgotten something or David messes his diaper at the last minute. I sit in church, if I'm lucky, through the sacrament, go out to the car, nurse David long enough to leave him with his daddy while I teach Primary. Then I nurse David again during Relief Society. We have a roast or something in the oven for dinner. I put the little guys down for a nap, listen to the other kids squabble and complain about what they can't do. We either play Seek or read scriptures. We try to do what we're supposed to do, but it's tough.

Paying tithing is not difficult. There have been other contributions that were more difficult. In Greenville, the bishop asked for a thousand dollars to build a new chapel. That was all we had in the bank. We were living on our food storage. We gave it to the bishop and we were blessed. We didn't have a thousand-dollar windfall the next day, but we were saying, "Okay, Heavenly Father, we're willing to make the sacrifice for you."

I need to show to my neighbors what a positive thing the church is in my life, so that it becomes something that they're curious about. I have seen members of the church who exemplified it as such a burden that nobody else would want to be a part of it. I don't feel Mormons are the only good people. Some people are more in tune with their Father in heaven than I am because their personal worthiness is greater. After all, the Lord loves us all. The idea of eternal progression and becoming like God is very offensive to some of my friends. My closest friend is a woman who moved with us from Raleigh and from Greenville. We've been able to shore each other up quite a bit. I think she believes more like a Mormon than she knows. They had a baby who died within hours of birth. The child was baptized in the hospital, but once that had happened, she could no longer believe that an unbaptized child would not go back to Heavenly Father.

As members of the church we feel that we need to multiply and replenish the earth. How far we're supposed to multiply is my question. I don't know how I could possibly manage to have five children, but I do. How many will I end up with? I don't feel terribly adequate as a mother. I feel like they're missing out on having a happier mother, but I'm always rushing around changing a diaper or nursing a baby or stopping a quarrel. Sometimes I wonder if God expects me to have baby after baby or does he expect us to use our free agency and our intelligence to decide for ourselves? We have read the church's statement on birth control so many times that it is dog-eared. When I pray about not having more children the answer is that it is up to my Heavenly Father. I don't feel that I can use birth control, but when I die is he going to say, "You dummy"? If I have more, I guess I'll manage somehow.

Child-bearing and mothering and being a wife—those things which are so necessary—are put down by the feminist movement. I feel like people don't think I'm an adventuresome person because I stay home and take care of my children. I get that at church, too, sometimes. Did you hear the comment that was made on Sunday? One woman said, "Well, why don't we take these women who are sitting home with their own children and have them babysit each other's children and do something productive with them?"

The church's principles have always come from the Lord, but we do have a lot more women who are without husbands, who are working outside the home, and who have needs that need to be met in a different way. I've become more defensive. I'm aware that I need to be prepared to go into the work force if I should need to. That's on my list of things to do, but right now, I've got a baby to nurse. I have goals that my husband and I are working on—building our relationship, attending the temple more often, becoming closer to the Lord.

Grant Robison, 36

Grant Robison, a manufacturing engineer, was transferred to Delaware when the Du Pont company purchased from Exxon the division for which he worked. He has been Elders' Quorum president in two different wards and was called to be the secretary of the Elkton Ward's Elders' Quorum.

I went to Australia on my mission. When I went in for my mission interview, I told the bishop that my grandfather and my uncle had gone to Australia. I met a woman there who remembered my grandfather. My mission was extremely traumatic. Having to go up to somebody's house and talk to them about, of all subjects, religion was a nightmare. I got so I could sit down with a person I didn't know and carry on a conversation without having any obvious symptoms. I just can't stand to feel that I'm inflicting what I think on somebody else. I don't mind discussing religion with people, but I'm very wary of doing anything that might convince someone of something that he doesn't want to be convinced of. I saw a lot of people baptized who had no idea of what the church was about.

One time my companions and I made a slide show in which we poked fun at the missionary experience. I think I wrote the script. We started a guy out as a greenie and had pictures of him at the first door. My pet peeve in the discussions was the segment that went, "What do you think the name of the church should be, Mr. Brown?"

The answer is supposed to be, "It should be called the Church of Jesus Christ."

The missionary discussion says, "That's right, it is. It's called the Church of Jesus Christ of Latter-day Saints."

We had the missionary say, "That's right, it's the Church of Jesus Christ of Latter-day Saints. It's almost the same." We just showed the slides to each other to vent our frustrations.

When I got off my mission, I'd never been on a date. Back at BYU I ended up living with some people who were expert in dealing with women. One fellow in particular could go up to any girl or any apartment and begin a conversation. He would notice, on his way to school, a girl or some girls in an apartment. He would walk up there after school, knock on the door, and end up being invited for dinner. For some reason, on occasion, he took me with him when he did this. It was a real eye-opener for me.

I noticed Jeanette at church one Sunday, and that afternoon I did as I had learned. Just as I got to her apartment, a group of people were going in, so I went in and looked around. I found her in the kitchen making popcorn. I had a little sports car at the time, so I asked her if she would like to go for a ride up the canyon. I'm not sure I even told her my name. While we were up the canyon we ran into the fellow that I worked for. He and his wife invited us to their house for something to eat. It developed from there.

In my own family, including uncles and aunts, there had been a lot of marital difficulties. It was not worth getting married to have that. As I started dating and being around women at church and family home evening groups, I could tell which women had set ideas that you couldn't change for anything and which ones were high-strung. I was looking for somebody who was even-keeled, even-tempered, and rational, who would discuss a problem without slamming doors.

Love is just not a rational thing. When people fall in love they feel that means you can live together. I was looking for somebody who I knew I could live with. I was attracted to Jeanette first because I thought she would make a good wife, and I fell in love with her. My initial perception was true; she is very easy to live with. It's a very calm, even relationship. For example, when I was working so much, I got very distant from home and a barrier built up between us. She was having to do everything. One evening we just sat down and talked about it and both of us felt a lot better afterwards.

Having a concept of being married for time and eternity affects my behavior toward my wife and children. It helps us not get excited over the problems that are trivial in comparison with eternity. It must be unnerving to go about all the arduous tasks of developing a relationship and feeling close to somebody just to know that it's all over once you die.

I think the feminist movement has misled women into saying that men's values are the right values, and they're not. I can't see the number of women in the workplace as being good for families and children. Children don't learn the gospel in day-care centers. The church used to say that the woman's place was in the home, but they can't say that now or they'll offend more than half the women in the church. It's still a value I would have in my house. If I didn't have to work at a paying job, I wouldn't be. I'd be doing something else. When I look at people who go to work just to have something to do, I say to myself, "What kind of a person is this? This is a person who cannot in and of themselves do something meaningful." There are plenty of other things to be done with life if you can afford to do it. I'm hoping that I'll be able to have Jeanette in a position where she can afford to do some of those things.

Most of my callings in the last ten years have been in the ward leadership. Attending PEC and bishopric meetings has given me a feel for how a ward is operated and the philosophy of the ward leadership. I've seen bishops operate in completely opposite modes with different philosophies. I'm starting to pick up a few things about the Elkton Ward. The Easter egg project seems to be a good ward project. On the other hand, the problems with the wood project here are pretty typical. Many wards, particularly on the East Coast, seem to have lots of inactive members. It's practically impossible to home teach all of them. I've been interested in Bishop Bushman's method of handling that by making a letter contact once a year and an actual visit once a year.

Every ward we've lived in until now has had a program in which every male member was supposed to go out at least once a month with the missionaries. I never could figure out where it came from because I've never read about it in any church publications. The program took more of my time than anything else. If someone backed out, I had to be ready on a moment's notice to go myself or to find somebody else who could drop everything and go. There doesn't seem to be an active exchange program here. I don't want to suggest it.

The first time I was an Elders' Quorum president I wasn't prepared to handle the people who always complained but never contributed. The second time I was Elders' Quorum president I was a little smarter in how I dealt with people. I gave people tasks related to their complaints and explained in pretty understandable terms what I thought about people who complain and don't contribute. I think I learned how to do that very tactfully. People feel that the bishop is supposed to be perfect and the Elders' Quorum president is supposed to be semiperfect. I explained to them if they were called to be the president, they'd still be the same guy. They'd just have to do the best they could.

I've been thinking about how I can open up so I can empathize with people and be the kind of person that they would like to have come to their house. It takes a long-term relationship, but I haven't ever been a long-term home teacher. I don't think I come across as somebody on whom people would like to lay their burdens—unless they know me. People who know me don't mind confiding in me. It happens all the time at work.

I learned early on in Texas that pushing people to go home teaching is not successful. If I said, "If you're going to have a problem with your home teaching this month, let me know early so I can help you with it or we can get somebody else to help because the people need to be visited this month," we could get the people visited without the home teacher feeling bad about it. If he felt my concern was that the people needed to be visited, he might be a little more motivated to do it the next time.

Our bishop in Texas stressed home teaching in an effective way. In bishopric and PEC meetings he went right around the room and asked his first and second counselors, the clerk, the executive secretary, the Elders' Quorum president, the High Priests' Group leader, the seventies' group leader, "Have you done your home teaching?" If you hadn't done it, he'd commit you to do it. You knew you had to get it done or you were going to have to admit in front of all the other guys that you hadn't. I felt I had a personal commitment to get it done. If the men in that room did their home teaching, it was a long ways toward getting all the home teaching done. It was easier for the Elders' Quorum president to commit his elders when they knew he'd done his.

Being secretary in the Elders' Quorum is basically what you make of it. There are the minimal tasks of taking the roll and working up the statistics for home teaching and attendance. There are quorums where you can't get the secretary to do it, so the president has to do it. A lot of other things can enter in if you're willing to do a little more. I haven't been able to do as much as I would like in the church because last month we worked thirty days straight. The peak week was ninety-eight hours.

When we first moved in I told the bishop that one of the real frustrations I had in my other callings was when work prevented me from carrying them out in a way I could feel good about. A lot of times at 4:00 I don't know if I'll be leaving at 4:30 or if I'm going to be there until 10:00. When you're gluing things together, if something doesn't go right, you can't just stop and pick it up the next morning. If you're in charge of a ward work project and suddenly find out you can't be there, then what are you going to do? I guess they decided to try me out in the secretary position. I've been able to work out my schedule so I could take roll at priesthood meeting before going to work.

The first time I administered to somebody was when I was a missionary. I have never shirked from a priesthood obligation because I didn't feel like I was worthy. If I happen to use the priesthood unworthily, I'm probably going to have to take some lumps for it at Judgment Day. If I don't feel I've been doing everything that I ought to, I just tell Heavenly Father that I've got some problems, but I also have duties to perform and he's just going to have to help me with my weaknesses. When you're an Elders' Quorum president, people are always asking you to give somebody a blessing.

I've never given a blessing where anything miraculous happened. Heavenly Father has made us so that our bodies are going to heal us of most of the things people ask to be healed of. When I give a blessing, I'll bless the person that his body will work properly so that he'll be healed. When you're dealing with a situation where a person is seriously injured or has a serious disease then that's a different story. Once I gave a blessing to a woman who had been in a coma for a long time. I felt she was going to die. I was not only giving a blessing to a person in a coma, but there was her husband who was not a member of the church and who, undoubtedly, had feelings about it. I felt I ought to bless her that she and her family would be able to move on to a position of peace and comfort. The tenor of it was that she would be relieved of that problem by dying. The husband seemed to understand. I had more feelings about that blessing than any other. When I set people apart or give blessings to my children, I know that I'm interacting with a power that is beyond me. I just don't get all emotional over it. I've seen the priesthood work in my life, with our children.

It seems to me that if you pick any two opposing Christian philosophies, the Mormon church cuts down the middle between them. For example, what happens to people who die without being baptized? Some churches say if you're not baptized, you go to hell. Others say you don't have to be baptized. We go right down the middle: you have to be baptized, but there's a way to take care of people who died without being baptized.

I personally enjoy Sunday. I like the hustle and bustle of getting ready for church. Everybody's kind of in a rush and you get excited. Jeanette doesn't like it. She's a nervous wreck by the time we get in the car. I kind of enjoy the last-minute making sure everybody's ready—even having to change a diaper. Sometimes I go home teaching on Sunday, but I look forward to Sundays when I can just stay home. Lately the kids have enjoyed putting on plays from the scriptures. They loved acting out Nephi and his brothers going back to get the brass plates.

I've heard people say they don't like the hymn "Praise to the Man" because they don't think we ought to elevate the prophets. I think it expresses how we ought to feel about Joseph Smith. Joseph Smith and certain other prophets were great people who struggled against tremendous odds. Joseph Smith and Brigham Young were flamboyant and shot from the hip. They didn't mind telling people exactly the way they felt about things. What they did was tremendous. We now have the kind of prophets that we should have. They're very conservative and they are making the church something that is more acceptable from the outside. The church is trying to grow and to develop influence. Today's prophets wouldn't have been any good at trying to do what Brigham Young did.

Debora Ennis, 31

When Debora and Wayne Ennis moved to Newark, they were, in a sense, coming home to New Castle County, where Wayne grew up. They returned to Delaware so that Wayne could go into business with his brother. Debora grew up in Mississippi, Greece, and Florida, among other places. The mother of three children, six, five, and a newborn, she is first counselor in the stake Primary presidency.

About a year and a half after Wayne and I were married I started going to church—the Baptist church. Wayne went to the LDS church. I finally consented to the missionaries' coming over, but about half an hour before they were supposed to come, I said, "Call them and tell them not to come." When they finally did come, I knew the church was true after the first lesson. Everything made perfect sense. It answered all my questions.

I had asked my pastor one day if it could help me in any way to be baptized again. I was twenty years old and I didn't feel right about a lot of things. He said, "Baptism is just a symbol. Baptism itself is not the important thing."

I used to wonder, "How can I know if things are right between me and the Lord?" When I joined the LDS church I learned you only need to be baptized once, but you can regain the purity you had at the time of your baptism through the sacrament.

The church has had tremendous impact on my life. I know how to teach my children that we are going to be together forever. It's very comforting to know that and to have the answers—not feel like I'm floundering. I know how to answer the children's questions about death, what we're like after we die. The church has made me understand why we're here and what we're doing.

When I first joined the church the home teachers used to ask, "Do you have family home evening? Do you say your prayers? Do you do this? Do you do that?" I resented it very much. I felt they had no right to come in and ask me anything about my personal life. They came once a month and asked those questions and never did anything else. The only positive experience I've had with a home teacher was when one of them helped me get my car out of the ice once when Wayne was gone.

It was the same with visiting teaching. They used to ask, "How many hours of compassionate work did you do this month?" I would never tell them because that would be self-serving. I've had some very good experiences visiting teaching, visiting women who needed someone to talk to.

It was hard for me to keep coming to church at times when we were trying to have children because people said very unkind things—"Don't you want children?" "What's wrong with you?" Then they would sit around and talk about, which I've done myself, their birthing experiences. This seems like a silly thing to be a test of faith. I come to church because I believe in the gospel. I know the church is true.

When Wayne got out of the air force, it was very difficult for me. Having been raised in the military, married into the military, and having moved all my life, I never had to make any attachments that I had to be accountable for in the long run. It was, "It was nice to know you. Bye-bye"—new surroundings, new everything. I thought I would be bored to death staying in one place. It hasn't been that bad.

I like being home with my children. I enjoy having conversations with them. I like to play with them and help them. I like to go to their schools. I get more enjoyment out of staying home than I do getting no-thank-yous from a boss.

My last job was collecting past-due medical bills for a group of two hundred doctors. I talked with the patients and helped them figure out a way to pay. I used to go up on the wards to see the patients. A lot of times they just wanted someone to talk to, even a bill collector. I enjoyed that contact with the people. The most difficult thing was leaving my children at somebody else's home. I always left them with LDS women, but I didn't know what was going on or how it was going to affect them. Children are pretty resilient, but it was difficult not to have any control over what they did.

In some respects the women's movement has been good. I know what it feels like to be treated like you have no brain. I've had bosses and other men treat me like, "Hey, hon." I'm not their hon. I want to do my job. I wasn't hired to get their coffee or to pick up their wives' birthday presents at the store.

I was called to the stake Primary here two weeks after I was called to work in the ward Primary. I served in the same position in New York for a year and a half. I love visiting the wards and seeing the Primaries. It is very satisfying to see that they are doing things correctly.

Being Primary chorister or Sunday school chorister are the most enjoyable callings I've had because there's instant reward when the children respond. Everything about being Relief Society president is difficult. I can't think of any time that I did not feel pressure under that calling. I don't think anyone should hold that calling for more than a year. The hardest was being on call twenty-four hours a day. I was in a blizzard one time coming home from a funeral. I didn't even pick up my son because my car died. I had to carry my eight-month-old baby home in the blowing snow. When I walked in the door I had three phone calls right after the other, all three different problems.

Being Relief Society president made me much more compassionate, much more understanding, much more willing to help when something came up. I began to realize that there are a lot of things that we don't know about and it's just best to keep your mouth shut and not to pass judgment. There's a lot going on in people's lives and in the church that even Relief Society presidents don't know about. Bishops don't know about them. Only the people themselves know about them. You can't judge anybody.

Michael Wheeler, 30

Michael Wheeler was baptized in the spring of 1985. He is a physical education teacher and a recreation leader at the YMCA and and the Girls' Club of Delaware. He was born in Indiana and moved to Delaware when he was nine. Several months after being baptized he was called to teach the Valiant class in Primary.

The missionaries started teaching me in November or December of 1984 and I was baptized in May. I was looking for a church with more discipline. At the LDS Church there might be people who don't like other people, but the bottom line is we all have to follow the same rules. It's not just our ward, but all the wards throughout the church.

The church sought me out. The missionaries kept coming back even though I was kind of turning them away. I went to the ward meetings and met the people. Everything in the lessons made so much sense. It was easy to fit in because I already believed in a lot of the commandments. The church has had a very tremendous impact on me. It's taken up a lot of my life. It has justified my life more than anything else, and it has answered a lot of questions, a lot of feelings that I didn't have any answers for. I thought the Word of Wisdom was great. I did a little drinking, I guess, going out to bars with friends. That wasn't too tough to cut out. The trick is going into a bar and asking for a soda.

I work for the Girls' Club of Delaware and part time for the YMCA. I'm a certified lifeguard and swim instructor, so I teach swimming and I teach other kids to become lifeguards. I teach a basketball class in Newark, too. I've thought about moving up into administration where I'd set up programs that other people would teach. Once when I was teaching basketball, I could actually see this little kid getting better. I got a real big kick out of that. I guess that's what has kept me in teaching. It's nice to see the kids I work with learn something new and be able to do it again. A lot of times they have a lot of problems; they come from broken families and from the lower income areas. The tough thing is seeing kids treat each other poorly—calling each other names.

My church activities have also been very satisfying. Going there on Sundays is almost like going home. There just seems to be some security there. Teaching Primary—talking with the kids, getting them to be good—is very satisfying. It's satisfying to give the kids a chance to express some of their feelings. Keeping them happy or feeling like I can talk to them person to person is satisfying. I don't get that all the time. Since I haven't been in the church long, I'm still learning a lot. I've given two talks now. The first talk was short, but it was a start. The next talk, at the missionary fireside, was better.

I haven't been a home teacher that long, and I'm learning. I've been switched to another partner. With my first partner our schedules were off. I work in the evenings and it didn't seem like we could get together. I wanted to home teach and we just couldn't work it out. Now it looks like it's going to work out well because we both want to do it on weekends. The families I have now live further away and, other than one family, they're all inactive.

The more involved I am in the church, the more I can learn. I get impatient sometimes because I have a lot to catch up on. The missionaries were always asking me, "Have you been called to something yet?" It was driving me crazy because I wanted to do more than just go to church. It took time for the Lord to influence someone to decide where I was going to serve.

I can only tell my friends a little bit about the church at a time because I don't want to get up on my soapbox and start preaching. When I joined the church my sister said, "You're not going to become strange now and start preaching to us, are you?"

I said, "No, I'll be the same, rotten guy, the same old person." Then, "I guess I will."

I told my parents, "Well, if you don't join the church now, you will later. I'll take care of you, after you're gone."

My mom says, "Don't do that for me." At first she was upset about it. I talked with my father and then he talked with her and straightened it out. I have to be careful when I start talking about some of the church's beliefs. Sometimes when I've talked about the church I've gotten a little carried away, but I try to think about it ahead of time. I pray about how I want to talk to people, what I might say on different subjects. In the beginning when people asked me questions about what the church believes, I had to say, "I don't know." A lot of times if I believed something, they thought the church believed it. I have to separate those things. I've had a lot of questions and I've turned to the scriptures. It's not easy because you can't just open it up and get your answers, but I've gotten some answers by scripture study.

I'm not sure if it's a doctrine or practice of the church, but I have a little trouble with the inequality of men and women. Maybe individuals within the church interpret things to say the man is a little higher up than the woman. Everything I've heard in classes is that it's supposed to be a pretty equal deal in the family. There are church positions for women. Sometimes I think women could hold the other positions and there wouldn't be anything wrong with men holding some of the positions that the women do. It would have to come through revelation to the prophet. I see that as a possible change for the future.

I'm trying now to find out more about my family. Genealogy is a great thing to do as a new member. I had thought about it before but I didn't have any reason to do it. That's another great thing about the church, there's a very good reason for anything it asks you to do. I'm just getting started, but it's obviously important to do temple work for people who have passed away and haven't had the same opportunities we've had.

When I first joined, I thought tithing was going to be tough, but it hasn't been. It seems when things get tight and I get a little worried, a little extra money comes along. I can make a little adjustment here and there and still make some impact on the bills. After I was baptized I didn't know how to pay tithing. When I went in and had an interview with the bishop to receive the Aaronic priesthood, I said, "Yes, I want to pay tithing. I don't have any problem with that. Should I pay for all the time since I've been baptized?"

He said, "Start right now. Start today and pay a full tithe, 10 percent." I've been doing it since, with no problem.

When I received the Aaronic priesthood, I had a deep feeling of the Spirit. It's commanded in the Bible that we hold the priesthood. It's an honor. I would like to hold the Melchizedek priesthood because I want to do those duties.

I've realized that Satan causes all harm on the earth. I had always thought, "How can all these bad things happen if God's supposed to be so loving?" I used not to believe in Satan. I think I was starting to think that God has a good side and a bad side. When I found out that there is a Satan out here on the earth, that made a lot of sense. We get the opportunity to learn good and bad. That's the only way we're going to be educated down here on earth and build the great spirits that we need to have to live with our Heavenly Father.

Everything that we do in the church makes a lot of sense. It may not have fit into societies of the past. Some of the things people did in the Old Testament were okay back then, but they wouldn't be accepted today. At first it bothered me that we have meetings instead of a church service and that everything's set up like a corporation. That's the way our society is. It makes sense to set things up like that.

I would like to be involved in the church almost every day of the week, maybe not doing church work, but with the members every day. Being a member of the Church of Jesus Christ has been a big blessing. I'm just looking forward to doing more in the church.

Georgette DiVirgilis, 37

Georgette DiVirgilis, who lives in Elkton, was baptized in June, and her thirteen-year-old daughter was baptized later. A single mother, she has been attending classes to learn bookkeeping. Her first calling in the church was as an assistant nursery leader.

We've been attending church at the Elkton Ward since Mother's Day. My friend, Grace McCleary, sent the missionaries over to the house. When she joined the church, I told her that I wanted to see her pamphlets. Reading through her pamphlets, I said, "Well, this looks like it could be the church that I would like to join." She let me glance through her Book of Mormon, and I said, "This definitely sounds like the church I would like." After I read the pamphlets, I sat down and prayed about it. I asked the Lord if it was the true church, and I got a peaceful feeling that it was. I was baptized on the ninth of June.

It has given me a lot of peace. I didn't know where to turn when I needed help. I can talk to Bishop Bushman and he will help me. It's given me some peace about Pearl. If I need help I know I can call someone. I don't know if it's the church or the Elkton area, but I've never been to a church where the people are so friendly.

Until we started going to this church we didn't do anything on Sunday mornings but sleep late. Now we enjoy going to church. I'm enjoying the classes that I'm in. It's helping me to understand. When I used to ask questions as a little girl, I'd always get, "You don't need to know about that. Let us worry about it. We will do your thinking for you." This church answers questions that I've always asked. Since I joined the church, I've started going back to school. I feel more at peace now than I ever have in my life. I haven't sacrificed anything for the church—yet. I have one slight problem with the Word of Wisdom—my coffee and tea. I am cutting down. I was up to ten cups of coffee a day, and I'm down to about one and a half. If I'm not going to school I can go two or three days without a cup of coffee.

When I told somebody that I was going to join this church, she said, "They don't believe in Christ."

I said, "You're not talking about the same church that I've gone to."

Everybody said, "Don't get mixed up with them. They believe in more than one marriage." Everybody I know is married to only one person. I had trouble at first accepting Joseph Smith. The more I thought about it, I realized I had no reason to be upset. He is a modern-day prophet. I guess people had trouble accepting Moses, too.

I have one brother and, more or less, seven sisters. My father was never married to my mother, but he raised us. I hated school, but it was a release from the house. I had what you would call a wicked stepmother. I had a very hard childhood. My sister and I looked like twins and my parents dressed us as twins. I would dress like her at the house, sneak my clothes out of the house, go to the bathroom at school, and change. When they found out about it, I got the beating of my life. I guess we dressed like that until we were in high school.

When I was growing up, the only thing I ever wanted was to be a wife and a mother and stay home and take care of the house. I have found out that education is so important. Motherhood and taking care of your home are important jobs, but I think every woman should have a career behind her. I'd like to talk to the teenagers graduating now and tell them that the world is not rosy-easy, peaches and cream. My husband was in the service.

If I could do it over again, I would cut out the last eighteen years—or go back eighteen years. I would definitely have my daughter. She is a blessing to me, but I would have had the education that I needed so that I could have a decent job. It's hard right now just to buy her a pair of shoes for gym and books and clothes for school.

I stayed home with Pearl as much as I could. I would take a job off and on, but I always got guilty feelings. The only job I could find was three till eleven or eleven at night until seven in the morning. If I worked the eleven to seven I was too tired to be with her. The three to eleven gave me the guilty feeling of not being with her in her vulnerable years. I wouldn't have just any baby-sitter. I had my own day-care center for a year and a half. I loved it. I had eleven children. I love babies, but after my day-care center experience, it was five or six years before I even wanted to hold another baby. A lot of times I was on social services. That's why I think the education is important. It was hard to try to make ends meet when I had no money coming except for what the social services gave me.

I was talking to the woman at the state unemployment office about how I wanted to find a job but I had nothing that would qualify me for anything but minimum wage. She asked me if I would be interested in a bookkeeping class. I thought, "Bookkeeping is math! Math is my worst subject." I said, "It sounds like it would be fun. It wouldn't hurt to try." After the first day of class I knew I had my work cut out for me. Toward the middle I started enjoying it. I would like to further my education—not just in the bookkeeping area but stretch into something else. My biggest goal is to get a decent job and take care of my daughter financially.

17 | Eileen Johnston Speaks in Sacrament Meeting

The talk Eileen Johnston gave in sacrament meeting on Sunday, August 24, created such a stir in the Elkton Ward that one of my friends who had been out of town that day called me to find out what Eileen had said. "Of course," she said, "since she's a recent convert, anything she says will be all right."

Eileen had begun by expressing her concerns about raising her infant daughter, Marie. "Women have never had such rich opportunities for good health, personal growth, education, and development of their talents. Never before has there been such wonderful opportunity for eternal progression in the mortal lifetime. On the other hand, women today face greater challenges to their virtue than ever before in the history of our church. The path to salvation has never been so slippery; the siren calls to leave the path have never been so sweet. How will Marie find her place as a righteous Latter-day Saint woman in our larger society? I am certain that if she is prayerful, Heavenly Father will help her find her way. How can I as a mother help her learn those things she'll need to meet life's temporal and spiritual challenges?"

Stating that she was drawing upon the counsel of President Gordon B. Hinckley, first counselor to President Kimball, as well as an article from the July issue of the *Ensign,* the official church magazine, Eileen quoted statistics indicating that many women in the church will have to work to support themselves and their families and that most women who are employed work at low-paying occupations.

She continued, "Sadly, I am afraid many of our young women are not achieving their potential. I believe there are several reasons for this. When I graduated from dental school I was one of 6 women in a class of 150 students. It seems that as the requirements for mathematics or mechanical ability for a profession increase, the number of women in that field decreases, and as the requirements for mathematical or mechanical ability increase for a certain career, the amount of monetary reward increases. Looking back on my education there are several areas that hindered my progress.

"The first and foremost hindrance was *math*. My parents knew I was woefully behind in math but felt that since I wasn't going to need it, why bother? Another hindrance to my education, one that is common to many women, was getting a late start on a career path. I have known so many women who worked at jobs they hated, hoping that a knight in shining armor would rescue them from their dreary fates. When it finally occurs to them, if ever, that there are no knights in shining armor, they are off to a late start.

"Two summers ago my son Neil took a computer course for children. Of the thirty students, only one was a girl. Neil was thirteen. At such a young age, are girls already being tracked into those lowest paying jobs?

"I'd like to propose a question to the young women. What would you do with the rest of your life if tonight the Angel Moroni stood at the foot of your bed and said, 'Young woman, you will never marry in this temporal life?' Remember that for 3 percent of all Mormon women this is so. What would you do? What education would you strive for? How would you serve your family, friends, and community? How would you serve the Lord? Chances are these are the very things that will cause you to cross the path of a very compatible eternal mate. Chances are these are the very skills that would enrich your marriage and be a blessing in the lives of your children."

Eileen Johnston, 38

Eileen Johnston, a native of Philadelphia, has lived in the Elkton Ward for two and a half years, where she has taught the Laurel Class (sixteen- to eighteen-year-old girls) and Relief Society classes. She and her husband, David Obzansky, were baptized in 1982, and have two children, ages twenty months and five months.

I went to nursing school because my parents wanted me to have a profession that I could fall back on. I wanted to quit, but they convinced me to finish the three-year program. It was brutally hard. We used to work nine days in a row. Many times we were in charge of whole wards. At eighteen, just one year into nursing school, I was put in charge of the obstetrical unit. During my shift we had several admissions, several deliveries, a miscarriage, and a person who hemorrhaged. I was the only nurse for twenty people without even an aide to help me. It was not unusual to have such a thing happen.

By the end of nursing school I was determined to escape. Later that year I read Betty Friedan's book, which convinced me even more that I should abandon nursing. I realized there is no reason why women couldn't be engineers or chemists. I felt as if I had been cheated by society and my family out of an education.

I went to night school and worked as a nurse during the day. When my first husband, David Smith, finished his education I started going to Villanova full time. I was twenty-four and had a one-year-old infant. We didn't have a penny to our names, but I got a package of grants and loans together. My education was very costly in terms of my home life. By the time I graduated I was divorced, and my son Neil went to live with his father.

I took the pre-med and some engineering courses. I was accepted at all the dental schools I applied to. I chose dentistry because there are no politics involved in the care I give. It doesn't depend on whether there are enough nurses available or if it's a weekend or Christmas. It depends on my skill at that minute.

David Obzansky began graduate school at Ohio State about six months before I finished dental school. My son Neil lived with us from the end of his third grade to the beginning of fifth. Now he just spends summers with us because his father has moved to California.

When I graduated from dental school, the economy was terrible. Even if I worked every hour of the week, I could not make enough money to pay back my school loans. I was advised by two attorneys, two accountants, and one financial adviser to go bankrupt, but I didn't. I just paid as much as I could. David paid one loan off, and the government came through with a program to extend the payments over twenty years instead of ten.

I thought I was a failure. I was laid off from three jobs in one year. One dentist had a stroke; another sold his practice and was prosecuted for moral turpitude; the third was a dental chain that almost went under. I read positive-thinking books. Each of these books stressed that a religious philosophy was helpful in maintaining a positive outlook. I began to think about putting some kind of religious structure into my life. Maybe Heavenly Father was making it so horrible for me that I would have to make some changes in my life.

I wasn't particularly interested in our getting married, but if we did, I wanted us to become involved either in a community group or a church. I had observed that couples who had strong community ties seemed to have the strongest marriages. We went back to the Catholic church, and it was very much as I had remembered it. Then we sat down and talked about the Unitarian Church, the Methodist Church, the Society of Friends, and even, briefly, the Jewish religion.

The Sunday I went to the Mormon church, David wouldn't come with me. He said I had tried so many crazy organizations. There was a terrible ice storm. I lost my way several times, and I arrived in the middle of the service. A man from Brazil who had been in the States a few years was speaking. He said a prophet is someone who knows the past and can perceive the future and can tell you that bad things will happen to you if you do certain things. I remember having such a feeling come over me! I said to myself, "This is no reason to get emotional. This feeling is just not reasonable." I did not realize at the time that it was the Holy Spirit that was speaking to me. I went home and I told my husband that the Mormons seemed to be normal people and they were very friendly. We were baptized six months later.

At first, I couldn't see any point or reason in some of the practices of the church. For instance, in the young men wasting two years of their life to go on missions. It wasn't until much later that I came to a testimony of the missions. In many points of the church, I came to a testimony later. "For once," I said, "I am not going to be critical."

The church makes sense; philosophically, intellectually, it comes together. I have come to a testimony of Jesus Christ that was very hard for me to accept. I have learned that there is a God in heaven and that he listens to my prayers and he's given me answers. So many things wouldn't have happened unless God were listening to me. For example, when I was trying to sell my practice, I began to doubt the expertise of my consultant, and I wanted to be released from our contract. I prayed and fasted about it before our appointment. I wanted a clean break without any legal difficulties. I prayed that I would say the right thing and be tactful, that the Holy Ghost would inspire me with the gift of tongues. When I went in, I found that the man had completely forgotten about our meeting and had gone to a banquet. Heavenly Father's answer was that the man had forgotten about this contract and I would not have any difficulty with him. I never heard from him again.

David and I have been together almost ten years. I thought I was happy before, but our family now is truly a little bit of heaven on earth. I have seen things happen in this family that could only be described as miracles. One night Chris had a very bad cold and cried and cried. Finally, past midnight, I said, "David, could we give him a blessing?" We gave him the blessing and he fell asleep in our arms and slept the whole night. Having a family has been a tremendous joy to me. I would have traded every degree, every diploma, every honor I ever got for a family. I felt I had missed my opportunity and I was very distressed.

I never had to worry about cash flow after I started paying tithing. The Ohio State Welfare would withhold repayment money for three or four months, sometimes six months or a year. I could not pay my staff. I couldn't pay myself. After I joined the church I never had to worry about paying a laboratory fee or paying my rent. I always had enough money. There would be ten cents in my checkbook, but everything was paid.

When we joined the church, Neil felt it was another "crazy Mommy" scheme and that we would force him to go to this awful church, which we did. The first summer, in Ohio, he was miserable. He didn't have as much self-control as the other Mormon children did. He used to wiggle all over the pew—eleven years old! The second year, I told him we were strangers in this area, and this was an opportunity to meet people and make friends. I also told him that whether or not he came to a testimony of the church was his responsibility. I think I used the right approach. He got very involved in the New Testament and even read it out loud to me in the car. He asked me questions about what it meant. At the end of the summer he asked if missionaries could visit him in California.

He joined the church in the spring of 1984. His father went to church with him for a full year, but hasn't joined the church. Neil is very active in the youth group, goes to seminary, reads the scriptures, keeps a journal, and everything. I hope he will maintain his testimony, but even if he does not, it will get him through a very difficult teenage period.

My first calling in the Elkton Ward was Laurel adviser. I felt terrifically unsuccessful. The young women gave me no feedback at all. They just sat there, stoney-faced. Sometimes they wrote notes to each other. Another difficult thing was that I had a very hard time remembering when all the meetings were. You would think a successful businesswoman should be able to keep this straight. I could never keep the YMMIA straight from the BYC. The different camps during the summer—some were for boys, some for boys and girls, some just for older girls. I was constantly surprised. About three weeks into being Laurel adviser (I'd been a member of the church for six months), I was given the project of decorating an enormous gymnasium for the Rose Prom, which would be attended by all the young people of the stake and their families.

In one respect I've never seen such active, liberated women as in the church. I've never been to any other church where women spoke equally with the men. I think it is good that the men have a separate priesthood and the women aren't permitted to participate in it. That must sound strange because I am a feminist. The Catholics have a professional clergy who do all the sermons and the women take care of all the details. For a baptism, a confirmation, a first Holy Communion the women organize the feast. They get everybody to and from church on time. They organize the prayers. The priest does the ceremony, and there is absolutely no role for the husband. The men are out on the front stoop drinking beer while the women run the show. Maybe in the future (revelations do come) women will participate in the priesthood, but I don't think it would be wise at this time. Look how the women run Relief Society. Can you imagine if they ran the church? The men would be totally out of a job.

If I had been a Mormon, I feel there is no reason why my first marriage couldn't have been very successful. Both of us were just doing everything wrong. My focus was on getting A's in all my courses and getting into dental school. I'm doing it differently this time. We bought this house in Elkton because it was zoned for business. I can have my business in my home and be close to the family while I'm working part-time. We'd like to have more children. I would like to work a busy twenty-hour week. I'd like to build the denture portion of my practice. I'm going to pray and think about how I can do that.

Barbara Bowes, 41

Barbara Bowes grew up in Philadelphia and joined the church when she was twenty-one. A mother of two children, she also works part-time and is a full-time student working toward a degree in elementary education.

No matter how bad it gets at times, going back to school has been the best thing that could happen to me. I've learned so much. I feel better about myself. Our kids know that no matter what they do, they're going to get more education than high school—whether it's vocational training or college.

I wanted to quit when I got into student teaching. Every day I quit. The first week was disastrous. The next week, after two days, I said, "This is it. This is why I was in school all this time. Heavenly Father had me going to school for this."

Strange things have happened. When I was seriously thinking about going back to school, I didn't know what I wanted to do. I'd started looking down the years and thinking, "Is this all it's ever going to be?" One day my new Avon lady knocked at the door, sat down, and proceeded to tell me that she was graduating in three months with an elementary teaching credential. I said, "That's something I always wanted to do." I've paid for all my own education.

Even on Saturdays I have to work and I have to clean house and study. The bishop understands that I can't do anything in the church right now, so I don't have any problem. Our family home evenings aren't the kind where we sit down and have a lesson, but we do manage to do something together during the week. It's not on Monday nights because of my school.

The most satisfying callings I had were in the Mutual. I was stake camp director. I enjoyed working with the young women, but I think the church does not treat the young women fairly. Even my husband agrees with me on this. There are so many programs available for the boys that are not for the girls. If the boys want to go to Florida with the Boy Scout troop, they raise the money and go. Do the girls do that kind of thing? I had to go to battle once for the girls to play a basketball tournament. If I were still in that type of calling, I'd like to have more freedom to do what I wanted to do. The problems weren't with the rules of the church in some cases, but it was how people interpreted them. In Girl Scouts I could pretty much do what I wanted, when I wanted, but when the girls in the church wanted to do the same kinds of things, we were just walking up against a brick wall.

My daughter and I have talked about the church's not encouraging girls to go on missions. The girls are expected to get married and have families. They say, "It's nice if you go to college. You're better educated so you can raise intelligent children." I think the church should encourage young women to have careers, to become educated, and to go on missions. They shouldn't make them wait until they are twenty-one. By then they're married and don't want to go on missions.

Women's liberation has been important to me—to a point. I'm not out there marching, but the thought that "I can be in charge of my own life, I can do what I can do" has changed my life. Growing up, I had a zero opinion of myself. I was never allowed to have any opinions of my own. That's pretty much the way my husband kept it for a lot of years. He felt I shouldn't think anything other than what he thought. We had a terrible time when I decided it was time to start standing up for myself, start thinking my own thoughts, and doing what I wanted to do. I've raised my children to be individuals and not to be afraid of anything. If they want to go skydiving, I think they're crazy, but they can do it. You'd have to know how I grew up to see why this means so much to me. In some respects the feminist movement has been bad because it has caused a lot of split-up families, a lot of confusion. We're going from one way of living to something that, eventually, I think will be good. Right now we're in a lot of turmoil.

The church used to teach that women had to be in the home. Edna Young has worked almost as long as I've known her. We used to go to Relief Society meetings where they talked down about women who worked. Sometimes I saw Edna get tears in her eyes. She had no choice about working and it was rough on her, but she stayed in the church. Now most women in the church work, whether they work at home baby-sitting or whether they work outside the home. The church is becoming more realistic.

When my husband was excommunicated, he didn't run away from the church. He missed only the very first Sunday because he was angry and hurt. Probably the best thing they did was to ask my husband to help with the Boy Scouts. He went to church every Sunday from then on. His coming to church helped the family stay together. I admire him for having been willing to face everybody and to do whatever they told him to. They ran him through the wringer for three years before he was baptized again. They'd say, "We've decided you also need to do this." No matter how he felt about it, he did it.

I have a testimony about visiting teaching, although there have been more years when nobody's shown up than when I've had one. After my husband was excommunicated, nobody called me. Nobody talked to me; it was as if I didn't exist. Connie O'Day, my visiting teacher, knocked on the door. All she said was, "I thought you might like to have somebody to talk to. If you want to talk to me, I'm here. If you don't feel like talking, then I'll just leave." I asked her in, I sat down, and I started talking. She was what a visiting teacher should be.

For a space of time we had no priesthood in the home. As much as I argue with my husband, I would not want it out of our home again. The fact that he holds the priesthood authority means a great deal in my life. I've asked him to give me a blessing at times.

Most of my life prayer has been the thing that's gotten me through. I firmly, absolutely believe in the power of prayer. Most of the times my prayers haven't been answered the way I wanted, but they've been answered. When my husband was excommunicated I prayed because I was ready to quit. I expected to get the answer that it was okay to leave him. I'd been praying in our bedroom and I walked out into the hall. As I was standing between my daughter's room and the bathroom, I heard just as clearly as if someone was standing behind me, "Give him a break." I thought, "But I don't want to give him a break." I didn't want to do what I was being told, but I did—not graciously. I see now why I was given that answer.

Marriage has been a hard struggle for both of us. In the past year he's had a real rough time at home with the children. I think he's been willing to do everything he could to improve that relationship. I'd like to see that we continue to grow closer as we've been doing the last couple of months. My going to school has been hard on the family. I've given up a lot of things I've wanted to do, but I hope it will pay off.

❀   ❀   ❀

That women in the Elkton Ward find their role in the family, the church, and society problematical is apparent in the struggles of the Relief Society leadership to make Relief Society relevant to the lives of each of the women of the ward. Until 1980 when the consolidated schedule was adopted churchwide, Relief Society was held on a weekday morning and attended by women who did not work outside the home; although beginning in 1970 most wards held second session Relief Societies for working women on Sunday mornings or a weekday evening. With the consolidated schedule in force only some women, those who do not teach Primary or Young Women classes, are able to attend the weekly Relief Society sessions. The Relief Society holds monthly homemaking meetings on a weeknight, social events, and other special events in an attempt to involve all the women of the ward in at least some of its activities.

Terryl Owen, the Relief Society leadership trainer, devoted several months to planning and preparing for a lightly attended leadership conference held on January 12, and she also spent many weeks preparing for the Wilmington Stake's Celebration of Sisterhood held on April 27 at the Dover Ward. The day-long event was preceded not only by hours of rehearsal and decorating but by competitive walks and runs in most of the wards. All women in the Wilmington Stake were invited to send in favorite spiritual quotations for a booklet that was given to them at the celebration.

Janice Kapp Perry, a composer of LDS popular music, was the featured guest. After the opening song and prayer, everyone sang two songs they had practiced in Relief Society meetings—"Things of Eternity" and "As Sisters in Zion." Janice Perry related that she had begun writing music only eight years ago.

Up to that time she had been devoted to sports, but her musical talent had blossomed after she had experienced some of life's vicissitudes: the death of an infant son and the loss of the use of her left hand, which prevents her from playing the piano. She said that since music can intensify emotions, women should guard themselves and their children against the popular music of today.

Then the lights went out. Against a background of Janice Perry's easy-to-listen-to music, a tape-recorded narrative described the experiences of life—children, family, death, loneliness, separation. Each experience was illustrated by a live tableau and followed by one of her songs. After three deaths in one half hour, women all over the chapel were sniffling and blowing their noses. The program was especially poignant because the narrator's three-year-old daughter had died in an accident just the week before. In fact, many of the actors and singers were replacements for members of that family. The stake Relief Society president had said at the beginning of the program that Satan had tried very hard to keep the celebration from happening, but that the chair had, in her faith, assured her that it would be all right.

After the drama, the women went to the first of their four assigned workshops. Mine included slides of someone's trip to China, a workshop on genealogical research, a craft class, and a slide show by an amateur astronomer.

Lunch was served in the cultural hall, where the walls were covered with a display of quilts. A tape recording described the displays set up around the room and on the stage. The display on the stage, the handiwork of Terryl Owen, was a multimedia exhibit—artifacts, slides, and tape-recorded narration—of the celebration's theme, "Things of Eternity."

Although some of the women from the Elkton Ward attended these two conferences, most did not despite the many hours that had been devoted to organizing and preparing the workshops, displays, decorations, and refreshments.

Terryl Owen, 35

Terryl Owen grew up in Bountiful, Utah, served a mission to Brazil, and was just ten credits short of graduating from BYU when she married her husband, Neil. The mother of two children, she moved to Newark in the spring of 1983. Her artistic and organizational skills were quickly pressed into service in the Elkton Ward.

My father died in February 1956 of a heart attack two months after his baptism. I remember my dad going to church with us for years before he was baptized. I've always believed he was called away as a mission. My mom was thirty-three, had two children, and was six months pregnant. When he died, Mom sold the house and moved to Utah. Two years after Dad died, my mom took out her endowments and my dad was sealed to us by proxy in the temple.

After my mom remarried, it was hard for her to be active. She was Sunday school secretary for years, but she never went other times.

From the time I was sixteen, my bishop asked me every year at tithing settlement, "Are you going to go on a mission? If you want to go, don't worry about finances." The year I was twenty he said, "How would you feel if you got a mission call?"

I said, "Well, I don't know how I'd feel, but I wouldn't turn it down.

He said, "That's good because I never knew anybody who turned down a mission call whose life turned out right for them." By the time I was twenty-one I had been working full-time for a year and saving my money. I thought I would buy a car. I didn't know what to do with my life. One day I grabbed my patriarchal blessing and went to see the bishop.

When I came home, my mom said, "Where have you been? What have you been doing?" When I told her she got quiet for a long time. Finally she said, "I got out your patriarchal blessing and I know that this is the right thing for you to do."

When she found out that the bishop had asked twenty people in the ward each to give five dollars a month for my mission, she got upset. She said, "I never accept charity and now all these people are going to be sending you money. I can't ever show my face in church again." She told the stake president, "Nobody ever asked me if I wanted to help." I had quite a bit of money saved, so I didn't require much help.

I told the Lord I'd go anyplace, but Belgium or France would be best. I was called to Brazil. There were some problems with the way my mission president treated the missionaries. At zone conferences he had the elders raise their arms to the square and say they were each going to baptize forty people. He offered rewards—like trips to Rio, dinners at restaurants, even Popsicles. The sisters were treated like gold. The elders knew we were valuable to them. We could open up areas where they hadn't been able to go. Some of the district leaders, though, did lead the sisters to believe that they were romantically involved with them in order to get the sisters to perform.

We met a man named Vincente, who was a concierge. The first time we taught him was a glorious experience. He knew the church was true. He wanted it. We had to say, "You can't be baptized" because of his lineage. He told us his ancestors were Norwegian, so we asked if we could visit his mother. She was black! We told him that if he wanted to to be baptized he had to go through a two-week waiting period. After that if he still wanted to take the lessons, we'd arrange something. He showed up at church every Sunday. He begged us to give him the lessons. From the time he was baptized, he was a missionary. He gave us as many as thirty referrals a week. After I came home, he went on two one-year work missions. When the revelation came he was given the priesthood and immediately went on a proselytizing mission.

I just knew that the blacks would get the priesthood sometime. We were baptizing so many people. We could tell within minutes if someone was ready or not. When I left the mission we were baptizing six hundred people a month. Not all of those remained active. Some of the elders were just pushing them in. The Doctrine and Covenants says, "The field is white all ready to harvest." All we had to do down there was harvest. I trusted that the Lord would take care of the priesthood.

After my mission, I moved down to Provo. I got a job cooking for an apartment of fellows. That was the one meal a day that I ate and they also paid me. Finally I got a permanent job as a unit dose technician in a hospital pharmacy. I worked there five years, two years full-time, then part-time while I went to school. I finally decided to major in Portuguese because I could get the credits and it was easy for me.

I had great faith that things would happen the way they were supposed to. I became engaged, but after I broke up with my fiance, no one asked me out for two years. Things began to go wrong at work. A young pharmacist there, who had a little boy and a beautiful wife, came up to me one day and said, "There's something I want to talk to you about." When he put his arms around me, I thought he was going to reprimand me in a very gentle manner. He said, "I have feelings for you that—" I ran out of there as fast as I could. By the time I got home I was hysterical, thinking, "What did I do to deserve this?" He apologized to me, but it was very difficult to work with him. I couldn't get single men to ask me out, but married men, married in the temple, had no compunctions about what they suggested. My self-image was so low; I felt I must have "I want to get married" printed on my forehead.

I had one semester left of school when I went to Denver to visit my aunt, supposedly for the summer. I thought, "I'll get a job, and I might not come back unless I'm married." I was so sick of BYU.

I'd been at my cousin's house half an hour when the missionaries came to talk to her husband, who was the ward mission leader. One of those missionaries was Neil. When he started asking my cousin about me, I thought, "Well, that's no big deal. I'm flattered, but so what?" He had two months left on his mission. In the meantime I dated a lot of guys. Some were customers at the bank where I worked who ended up telling me that they were "still married, by the way." I dated a gym teacher, who wanted me to be the mother of his four teenage children. Another fellow took me to lunch and interviewed me right down the list of qualifications his future wife had to meet.

Neil had plans to go to Ricks College. He had a grant, a place to live. Two weeks before he was to go home, he asked my cousin if I was interested enough in him to go out with him if he came back. I said, "Okay, tell him I'll go out with him when he gets off his mission. He can come back." He canceled all his plans to go to Ricks, and I stopped dating. On our second date he asked me to marry him and we set a date for six weeks later.

We tried to get jobs and housing and things set up for BYU. It didn't work out. Neil joined the air force so we could start our family and still be self-sufficient. His last air force assignment was in California. We loved California and we wanted to stay there, but we didn't want to take the chance of being transferred. My husband had great faith that he would get a job, but he didn't. We were unemployed in California for a year. He did some odd jobs, and we always had enough money to make our house payment, but we never had any more than that.

He finally called his dad and said, "You don't know how bad it is. I've got to have work." He jumped in the car the next day, had the interview, and started work. When he had enough money, he came back and moved us out. When the first person that walked into our house bought it, it seemed like, "Okay, I guess we're supposed to go."

I don't have any problems with church programs or doctrines. The thing I have a problem with is my relationship with the Savior and knowing how he works in my life. I always thought he had a great deal to do with our lives because he loved us so much. I thought he cared if we moved to Illinois or cared if we moved to Utah or cared if we moved to Delaware. People tell me, "Well, I fasted and prayed to know whether we should put a new radiator in the car." Really? If it doesn't matter to the Lord whether we live in Delaware, three thousand miles away from my folks and my husband's mom, then what does matter?

Things were pretty good for two or three years after we married. I thought, "Well, the Lord's leaving me alone now. I had my trials before I was married." Now I think I've got them all over again. I learned how to sacrifice. I learned how to work. Why do I have to do it again?

After my mission I thought the only thing I wanted was to be married and have a family. It turned out that I'm not content to stay home all the time. I work for Delaware Trust as a relief teller. I love my children, but if we're around each other too much, I just don't have enough patience to keep an even keel. Even when I haven't had a job, I've made my church callings like a part-time job. I've spent four hours a day on them. I thrive on going to meetings. I work better if I have a time frame to work in. If I have an open-ended time frame, I'm not very effective. I think, "We can read that story later," but if I know I'm going to work the next day, then we read the story now.

Being Relief Society leadership trainer is frustrating because I can invite, but if nobody comes, I can't train anybody. I feel I have a lot to offer because of my experiences—not that I'm a great leader, but I have a talent for telling people how to do things. I don't know whether it's my fault they aren't coming or whether they just won't come anyway. I love my callings and I do everything to fulfill them to the best of my ability. It's been hard for Neil to have me throw myself so much into callings. The house is a mess for a week, meals aren't fixed on time, the children are left with sitters. Neil recently said, "I've realized that you're not going to be standing at the cottage gate waving me off to work. You like doing this church work." It's hard for me to accept that Neil doesn't do his church callings the way I do mine. I hope that the church is awakening to the fact that men's priesthood callings aren't the only callings. Sometimes the forward momentum of the church isn't because of the priesthood. It's because of the work women do.

In the Elkton Ward it's a struggle to get anything accomplished. Someone whom I asked to help with this leadership conference turned me down saying, "I'm not getting any reward out of this. I don't see any good coming from it." I think that attitude's contagious. I find myself thinking, "I can't get anybody to give a seminar so why should I do this?" Then I thought, "If I don't do it, who will? So I'll do it."

Elena Larsen, 43

Elena Larsen, who glories in being a homemaker, questioned the need for women's conferences. Elena grew up in Idaho, but has spent most of her adult life in the East. The mother of five children, ages six to twenty-one, she has lived in the Elkton Ward since June 1984 and is the ward historian.

We moved here with the idea of returning to Utah as soon as we could. When we moved to Orem, Utah, we had expected to be there for the rest of our lives. I want to go right back where we were. We were ten minutes from BYU and a five-minute walk from the church and the stake center. All our doctors and dentists were five minutes away. I had a number of cousins in town, and we were good friends. Most of Wayne's nieces and nephews were going to BYU. We had them over for dinner once a week. I could go over to BYU to swim, to the genealogical library, to plays, to night classes.

We tried so hard to stay there, but by the time we moved I was convinced that the Lord wanted us to move back here. His definition of what was good was certainly different from mine. You never know until you are tested how you will respond. I thought doing the Lord's will was not going to X-rated movies and keeping the Sabbath day holy. I was happy to do the Lord's will in those things, but when he wanted me to move, I didn't want to. I wrestled with that for a long time. I've tried to forgive the Lord for doing this to me. This past year has been one of the hardest years of my life. I think I'm through most of it. Driving around in this little corner of Pennsylvania saved me in the beginning. The drive over to Bonita Cherry's to go visiting teaching is indescribable. As soon as one flower is over, the next one is in bloom. These farms are so well kept, it looks like a park.

The times I've known that my prayers were answered are very important to me. As a teenager I prayed about something that had bothered me so much

I was crying. Before the prayer was even over, a tangible peace started at one end of my body and went to the other. Sometimes I've been perplexed because something insignificant will be answered immediately. Then I'll pray for something that's important and I don't see the answer. I don't understand how prayer works exactly. I've had to listen very carefully for answers.

I never graduated from college because I could never decide. I started out in art at BYU. I did well in watercolor, but when I did very poorly in basic drawing, I changed to human development and family relations. I didn't want to go into home economics because I didn't want to take chemistry. I had never had to study very hard in high school, and I didn't know how. I was having a lot of fun and thought, "When I go back to school and decide what I'm going to major in, I'll settle down."

My brother, a professional artist, got me started in oil painting. Then I got interested in crafty things. In my goldleafing period I practically did the entire house, everything but the refrigerator. Most recently I've been doing flower arranging and grapevine wreaths. I do what looks good to me. That's another reason I had trouble in school. When my teachers told me I had to do things differently, I was in trouble. My mother is one of ten girls, all very strong, very dedicated, very creative women. I always expected to be a homemaker and raise a family. It wasn't until just recently that I decided to stop feeling guilty that we've had to work on our marriage. I decided to start feeling pleased that we've been married for twenty-two years and we intend to remain that way.

The best part about being a housewife is that I can choose what I do, when I do it, how I do it, if I do it.

I think it's a harder world to raise a family in than when I was younger. I was somewhat protected and sheltered on the farm in Idaho. I have a battle with the media right now because the kids are so exposed to it. I'd rather not have a radio in the house. We do monitor television very closely. Sometimes they watch when we're not aware of it—baby-sitting or at a friend's house. My sister sent me tapes of the BYU devotionals that I can watch on the VCR. That's the media at its very best.

In high school I was active in church and did everything there was to do— road shows, speech festivals, dance festivals, music festivals. My parents were supportive but they let me decide what I wanted to do almost entirely on my own, which surprises me. I'm not willing to let my children do the same. Raising children requires an enormous amount of faith.

We've moved often. Moving has been even harder than having others move away because there's always some continuity in a place even though people are moving in and out. It's hard for me to make new friends because it takes so much time. Because I'm overly sensitive I find relationships difficult, even when they are established.

Raising my own children is very satisfying. I can see how I am becoming like my mother. I'd rather my kids became like me than the day-care worker. It's very satisfying to be with my children and to know what's going on inside their heads—as much as they'll let me in. I feel very challenged to be aware of teaching moments.

I enjoy children most when they're Ross and Tina's age. Once they get to be Shanan's age, fourteen, they think we're trying to stop them from doing everything in the world they want to do. I didn't think I was going to live through Tara's high school years. I was amazed when she turned out to be a nice person. Even with younger children, in some ways, you're just trying to impose your will on theirs—everything from toilet training to wiping their noses to table manners. I haven't given up anything I wanted to do to have a family. Being with them and teaching them is what I wanted to do. Sometimes I want to do it the devil's way and force things instead of letting them choose.

I used to have trouble with the concept of free agency because I felt we had no choice but to do the right thing. If we didn't choose the right thing we had to take terrible consequences. What kind of choice is that? That doesn't bother me anymore. Freedom comes from having knowledge and knowing that you do take consequences.

When someone was talking about writing in her children's journals every day, Sister Bushman said, "Sometimes there can be too much record keeping." That was a new thought to me. I like keeping a journal and I encourage my children to. I used to insist that they do it every single day. Kirk hated it. Once he drew an X across the page and tore through about four pages. I finally quit fighting with him about that. He won. Last year he wrote home and said, "Guess what, Mom, I'm writing in my journal every single day."

My first aspiration for my children is that they will have strong testimonies of the gospel, that they will marry in the temple and raise children with strong testimonies. When that doesn't happen, there is built-in heartbreak. Since Heavenly Father lost a third of his right off the top, he certainly must understand. I don't know how he handles it.

I've done most of my volunteer work within the family organizations. I edit two newsletters and I edited a family history book five years ago. I had no idea of what I was getting into. One organization is the descendants of my mother's parents, a thousand of us. My aunts and uncles are still alive and interested. I picked up the family newsletter and made it grow again. I also do the newsletter for my parents and their children. There are fifty-four of us. Genealogy was a lot easier in Utah. All I had to do was go up to the BYU library. Here, I have to drive to Wilmington just to order the film.

I haven't ever wanted to work in the Young Women's program, but I would like to be involved here because I see so much work that needs to be done. As I see Shanan's needs, I think, "Ah ha, this is a place where I'd like the ward to meet this need." I'd like to see the Young Women's program succeed and grow.

We have such a good group of Beehives. I hope they will stay active all the way through. I want to do anything I can to support that effort.

It's hard to run all the youth programs here because of the distances, but they're even more essential. It's so hard to work a Salt Lake program. I think the church's efforts to adapt the programs would be even more beneficial if more leaders came out here to live for a while. The other day I was talking about how wonderful the seminary materials are—the music and the filmstrips. Bonita Cherry said, "But they don't apply. My kids don't come from model LDS families. They are coming from broken homes." I was disappointed to hear that the church is still coming out with materials like that. I told her the only thing she could do with them was to say, "When you have your own family, you can work toward that."

I'd like to influence the kids in the ward to go out to BYU or to Ricks. I'd like the children of convert families to have the experience of being where the church is the majority, where it's wonderful to be a member of the church. BYU is an incredibly idealistic, unreal world, but it's fun. They seem to go to BYU from the two Wilmington wards, but not from Elkton.

Women's liberation is possible because of hot running water and electricity. Women don't die of overwork at thirty-five. There were legitimate reasons for women to be unhappy with their lives, but I don't think any good that has come out of the movement is worth the harm that has come from it. The family has deteriorated because of mothers working. I find myself getting hot under the collar about working women. I think women should work if the Spirit tells them they should, but I don't think they should say that everyone should. Personal revelation is sometimes different from the generalizations we hear from the pulpit. It bothers me when members generalize what should be individual. I don't understand how active members can simply rebel against church counsel. I don't like having to feel defensive about following it. I would hate to go to work. It's a good thing to be prepared, to have an education and skills. I enjoy my freedom as a homemaker much more than I would any money that I could bring in. I'm concerned whether my children will be willing to do without things to stay home and raise their children. Will other people raise my grandchildren? I wish there were more members speaking in support of the church's counsel, not so many defending the opposite.

The feminist movement has made the church develop programs specifically for women. I resent all of that. Apparently Celebration of Sisterhood was a wonderful thing, but I think we have enough to do without having to go to special women's meetings. I don't need them to feel good about my lot in life. I think they've been started because of pressure to address the needs of women. I don't have to be convinced; I don't have to be catered to. Maybe these are revealed programs but to me they look like reactions to the women's movement.

Julie Ridge, 34

Julie Ridge became president of the Relief Society when Deborah Johnston was released in October. Julie fits her Relief Society work into her already full life as a mother of five children and provider of day care in her home. A native of Magna, Utah, she attended BYU until she married her husband, Douglas. They moved to Delaware in 1972 with a six-month-old daughter. Since then, they have added four boys, including a set of twins, to their family.

Magna's not a very big town. The elementary school was directly across the street; next to it was the public library; next to that was the junior high school. The high school was through the block. Our ward consisted of two streets. My mother's parents lived directly in back of us. My father's parents lived a mile away. My mother and two grandmothers had very powerful testimonies of the gospel. Because I loved them and I knew they loved me, anything they felt so strongly about was obviously right. I was very active in the church. I got all five of my individual awards and I never cut class or did anything that could be construed as even mildly dishonest. My bishop once told me I had an overactive conscience.

I chose to go to BYU because my two sisters loved it there, and I thought I would. Living away from home, accepting responsibility for myself, my finances, and my studies was quite an awesome thing. Superimposing dating and, even more important, not dating, and learning to live with roommates made it even more of an education. I lost my scholarship my freshman year. I did a lot of hard growing up in my first two years there.

I found a lot of the elaborate social and dating games that people played there repulsive. BYU has a large number of returned missionaries who are blatantly shopping for a wife. I felt like a piece of merchandise instead of a human being. There were a lot of young men whom I would have liked to be friends with, but if you sat by the same returned missionary twice at Mutual he felt you had designs on him. I was friends with young men who were "safe." I got to be good friends with guys who were eight inches shorter than me.

The summer after my sophomore year, I went to Hawaii with two of my friends to find jobs. When I told my folks I needed to come back because we couldn't find jobs, my mother told me that her cousin, Julie Oakley, was about to undergo her third major cancer surgery. She and my mother had been raised more like sisters than cousins. Her husband was bishop of the East Pasadena Ward and they had three adopted children. At my mother's suggestion, I flew to Los Angeles on the first Sunday in June. The ward and stake had a special fast for her followed by a ward family prayer, and she came through the surgery with flying colors. My parents left me there to help with the children and the shopping, cooking, and laundry. Julie had always been a beloved heroine of mine. Spending the summer with her was a pleasure and joy.

I met my husband, Doug, at the young adult family home evening in the Pasadena Ward. He hadn't shaved or cut his hair for a year. He was wearing purple bell bottoms and a crepe shirt with mother of pearl buttons that he had bought at Laguna Beach. The only free seat was next to me. The young man giving the lesson asked him what would be the greatest source of problems in the church in the near future. Doug said he thought it would be the Negro and the priesthood question. When the teacher asked why, Doug said, "Because we're wrong."

My back just arched like a cat. I jumped at him with all four feet. I didn't know what I was talking about, but that had never stopped me before. Someone had told me that he went to Cal Tech, and I wasn't impressed. I thought Cal Tech was like Utah Tech, a trade school. Later I found out he had graduated from Harvard cum laude. By then it was too late. We became engaged at Christmas. I finished the first semester of my junior year in February and we were married in the Salt Lake Temple in March during his spring vacation. I enjoyed going to school, but wasn't highly motivated to get a degree in any particular field. Doug's asking me to marry him gave my life a new focus.

Doug was an RA at Cal Tech, so I moved into the dormitory with him. It was the first time I had any close association with people who were not members of the church. They would talk to me about everything under the sun. They always respected my point of view, but they were exploring all sorts of intellectual and moral mores—from drugs to homosexuality. They were trying to compete in a very intellectual society and trying to adjust socially. There were a large number who were suicidal. We lived together, ate together, talked together, and had fun together.

The next year, Cal Tech became coeducational, and women moved into the dorms. The sexual activity that went on was a shock to me. I felt pity and sorrow for the young women and young men who seemed to be so morally adrift. I began to see the principles of the gospel, which I had always taken for granted, juxtaposed against the lives of kids who were floundering. I began to realize how differently I perceived things, that I am truly a product of the Mormon culture.

In Utah you are bounded by your ward boundaries. I think it's nice to have large geographical boundaries. I don't feel hemmed in emotionally or spiritually or geographically here. I'm grateful for the people I've met, the ideas that I've been exposed to, and the experiences that aren't available in Utah.

The biography of Emma Smith that has just come out has been unsettling to me. I'm disappointed by how both Emma and Joseph treated each other when they were trying to implement polygamy in their lives and in the early church.

I'm curious about how my great-great-grandmother coped with polygamy in her life. I've been very unused to having anything uncomplimentary said about the leaders of the church, particularly about the prophet, Joseph. I felt angry. How dare he be human? How dare he do anything less than perfectly? He had no right to sin! Didn't he know how it would affect us all? Regardless of what happened with polygamy I do believe that Joseph Smith is a prophet of God and that he did restore the gospel in its fullness to the earth. I am more willing now to let him be a man with human frailties.

The Elkton Ward members are willing to support one another, to substitute for one another. The unique character of the Elkton Ward comes largely from Bishop Bushman. The way he magnifies his priesthood and interacts with women influences the other priesthood holders of the ward. There are probably more men in the ward who are like Bishop Bushman than there are in other wards. He brings out those similar tendencies in them, and those who don't have those tendencies tend to downplay their authoritarianism.

I accepted authoritarianism when I was growing up. The husband was the undisputed and unquestioned leader of the home. The woman's role was to support and take counsel. My father was probably on the liberal end of the spectrum in Magna. He respected my mother's talents and abilities and always supported what she wanted to do. I didn't, though, ever need any more justification for doing something than that my dad wanted it that way. He didn't waste time or feel an obligation to explain himself. As I have worked with various bishoprics and priesthood leaders, I have become aware of differences in the ways different men perceive women and in how they administer their priesthood.

People within the church have had to take notice of women and reevaluate their feelings about women in society and in the church. I have become more self-aware and have a greater sense of my value. It has made Douglas put his money where his mouth is. He says it's important for women to develop themselves fully and to have the support they need to do that. In reality, his priorities take first priority. I also think the women's movement has divided women into camps with very bitter feelings toward each other. I think there's enough to face without having to fight each other.

Since Emily was born, I have felt very strongly that being a mother is what I want to do. I couldn't know my children as I do if I didn't spend the time with them. I feel there are a lot of children who know they take second place to their mother's careers. I've never been able to put this into words until I heard the bishop say that one of the negative things that has come out of the women's movement is the devaluation of children.

I come from a family of women who have meticulously kept homes and beautifully dressed children. They aren't gourmet cooks, but they know how to make something special out of nothing. Organizing and keeping up a house is a never-ending battle for me. I've been married for fourteen years, and I still haven't settled into the housekeeping side of it.

I wish our family were better at observing the Sabbath day. It would be much better if I prepared more thoroughly for it. Sunday is an exhausting day. Doug is ward clerk and leaves at 6:30 to attend bishopric meeting. I have to arrive at church between 8:15 and 8:30 every Sunday to attend PEC meetings, welfare meetings, or ward correlation meeting. Getting the family up and launched out the door by 8:00 is a challenge. We're seldom home before 1:30. In between every meeting there are many people to see, much business to be accomplished.

Doug was just made a full professor, and he's reaching the top of his earning power. We have four boys looking forward to missions. My father has said to me, "You should take advantage of the educational opportunities at the University of Delaware. If you want your sons to go on missions and be educated, then very likely you'll be called upon to help financially." That's probably right, but I still struggle with the idea of whether or not to have another child. Part of me very much wants to, but another part sees that as not very practical. I love having children. It's sad to think that part of my life might be ended. While reading the Doctrine and Covenants this year, I've been struck by the instances where the Lord said, "It mattereth not to me. Do what seemeth good to you." Perhaps we should do what seems good to us. I think every married couple in the church agonizes about the number of children that they have, unless it's just taken completely out of their hands.

Last fall when Bishop Bushman called me to be Relief Society president, I immediately had a strong impression that the calling was from the Lord. As I was thinking about who to have as counselors, Lynne Whitney's name came to my mind very forcibly. I felt that June McVicker should stay on as homemaking counselor and that Clara Burke should stay as secretary.

When Bishop Bushman set me apart the following Sunday there were three things in the blessing that touched me. He blessed me with the keys, the authority, to carry out my calling and promised me that my tongue would be loosed to teach and counsel the women of the Elkton Ward. Second, he promised that as I magnified my calling as Relief Society president, my earthly mission would unfold unto me. When I received my patriarchal blessing I was told that I was given a special mission in this life and that my life will not be cut short until my mission has been completed. I never could find in my patriarchal blessing a clue as to what this mission might be. What Bishop Bushman said was an answer to a great prayer and puzzlement in my life. Third, he blessed me that my home would continue to function well and that my children would grow in faith and testimony.

Visiting teaching is the bane of my existence! With members in three states, we have to pay long-distance charges to talk to each other and travel many miles to get to each other. Since I was called, I've reorganized the routes in the Newark area. I've prepared and given three visiting teaching seminars. About a dozen visiting teachers have attended so far. I was discouraged, but those who have attended have given very positive feedback. We've also made a room available where visiting teachers can visit sisters who attend on Sunday but who are impossible to see during the week. I've called several new supervisors who need to be trained. The districts need to be reorganized so that the reporting system can be more effective. I'm making up a little three-by-five looseleaf booklet so that the visiting teaching records will be at my fingertips. Each page will have the name of one sister, her visiting teachers, and how many times she has been visited in the past year.

The most challenging aspect of being Relief Society president has been the people who call upon the church welfare system for help. Filling out orders for the bishop's storehouse for them has made me very grateful. If we were ever in difficulties we could turn to our families. I feel great sympathy for these people who often feel very alone. They are greatly humbled by having to come ask for help from the church. Many of them have problems in every aspect of their lives. They come from dreadful family situations; they have no means of support; they have horrible personal problems. Some people are chronically this way. I often feel that they are accepting only the material aspect of what the church has to offer and ignoring all the emotional support and spiritual help that is available. There are even cases where I feel that they are manipulating the situation in order to take advantage of the church.

In our last presidency meeting we were talking about some of these incidents. My counselor, June, said, "Well, you never know what is going to make a difference in their lives. For some people it won't ever make a difference, but you never know when somebody is going to change."

I'm grateful that I don't have the priesthood or the responsibility of deciding what happens to these people. I'm very happy to do whatever is delegated to me. I don't like being in a position where I have to evaluate other people.

The church has served as a lifeline to me in living far away from home. Many times friendships have dovetailed with callings in the church. Sometimes I've given time not to the calling but to the friendship that has come out of it. The relationship that has developed between me and my counselors is very satisfying. Bishop Bushman is entirely supportive of the things that I feel inspired to do. I also like the women in the ward, as a group and individually.

I have wanted to reach those sisters in our ward who are having troubles either because they are not married or because their husbands are not members. Lynne's lesson in December talked about the challenges and problems that women face in those situations. I was sorry that more of the sisters who could have been comforted and blessed weren't there. We have been concerned about involving the young single women in Relief Society.

I feel that we have had a lot to offer on homemaking meeting night, and I've been a little disappointed that attendance has not been better. There always seems to be a major conflict or else inclement weather on those nights. On January 12 we had a women's leadership conference that had been planned when Debbie Johnston was the president. Terri Owen had the whole conference organized to the nth degree. We had trouble getting enough people to help put it on, so it meant a great deal of work for Terri. She was able to find some sisters—the same ones who always seem to be supportive—to help her.

I wish that more of the sisters would take advantage of Relief Society activities, but I understand the demands made on women today. I hope that I'll be able to keep a good perspective on it. When I was in the presidency several years ago, I became very upset with some of the sisters. I felt that they had no excuse to sit home when the presidency was going to great efforts to make Relief Society a pertinent force in their lives. The stake president reminded me that that was not the right attitude. We need to love and understand the sisters and make an effort to produce worthwhile things for them to participate in.

18 | The Weddings

Though eight people were married during the Record Year, none of them were married in the Elkton Ward Chapel. By the end of the summer Kevin O'Day and Lisa Welch, David Shepherd and Judith Downey, Scott Christensen and Deborah Hickenlooper, and Robert McPherson and Rachel Porter had married. Scott Christensen and Deborah Hickenlooper were married in Valley Forge, Pennsylvania. David Shepherd and Judith Downey were married in the Washington, D.C., Temple and Rachel Porter and Robert McPherson in the Manti, Utah, Temple. One of the requirements for marriage in the temple is that both the bride and the groom had been active members of the church for at least one year. Since Lisa O'Day had been baptized in January, she and Kevin were married by Richard Bushman at her parents' home near Baltimore. Though temple marriages are always looked forward to, Bishop Bushman remarked that it was fortunate, in a way, that they had decided not to postpone their wedding until they could be married in the temple. By being married on the lawn of Lisa's parents home, with both families and friends as witnesses, Lisa and Kevin avoided excluding her parents from the ceremony.

Kevin O'Day, 29

Kevin O'Day grew up in the New Castle Ward, where his father was bishop during Kevin's teenage years. Following several years in California, Kevin moved to the Elkton Ward in 1984.

Originally, I was looking for a house in the Wilmington West Ward because I have a lot of friends there. When the agent took me to see this house, I knew it was the house I wanted. It was just beyond the Wilmington West Ward boundary. Purchasing this home required a sizable down payment because I assumed the mortgage. I was short quite a bit. I asked the Lord for confirmation that this was the house for me. Somehow, all the money came in. I had to take out all the cash I had in my business, but within three or four months I had it back in the business again. I know I was blessed. I was supposed to have this house because I was supposed to be in the Elkton Ward.

My first calling in the ward was to teach the member missionary class. I felt a very strong impression that there would be explosive growth in the Elkton Ward. I think tremendous missionary work is going to take place. When I found out later that the stake center will be built in this area, it just confirmed my feeling.

I had the impression that I would meet my wife in the Elkton Ward. I tried to make sure that I got to know all the girls in the ward and dated each of them at least once. I became discouraged and decided that maybe I had lost the blessing that had been promised in my patriarchal blessing, of having "the friendship and love of one of the great daughters of Zion." The Sunday that I felt the most discouraged was the Sunday that Lisa showed up at church.

I was adopted when I was not quite four years old. My mother was raised a Mormon. My father joined the church some time after my sister was born. We were in the Wilmington Ward, then the New Castle Ward where my dad was bishop for four years. I was a very difficult child to raise. As a child I always wanted to go do things with my father. My father was so busy in his church callings that I didn't get to do too much. I hope I don't repeat that mistake with my own children. I work Monday through Thursday. By then I've put in sixty or so hours.

I was one to accept a challenge. I went out for all the awards. The stake had an extra-miler award, which I earned as a deacon. Three or four years I had 100 percent attendance at early morning seminary, and at least one or two years I had 100 percent at all my meetings. I remember visiting another ward with my dad when he was on the high council. I was sicker than a dog. He said, "Kevin, if you don't go, you won't get your 100 percent award." I went. I made up my mind that I was going to be an Eagle Scout.

I didn't follow all the rules at BYU. I let my hair grow long and I wore blue jeans on campus. The Elders' Quorum there had discussions about what to do with me. I drove my first roommate crazy. He was a very nice guy. I couldn't stand him. He was there on a scholarship, and I stayed up all night and slept during the day. The following semester I got another roommate, a returned missionary who was trying to reform me. I told him it wouldn't work.

Of course, I always planned to go on a mission. On my mission, my rebelliousness kind of caught up with me. I was going to do what the Lord expected of me, but I was going to do it Kevin O'Day's way. The Paris, France, Mission is one of the most difficult. When I went there, the average number of converts per missionary was one-half convert per year. When I left, it was up to two per year. In Rouen we rode our bikes down the hill, did street contacting in the city, and rode back up the hill to lunch. After lunch, we rode back down to the city, back up again for dinner, then back down for our evening appointments, which were not in the city but way out in the boonies. It took an hour or an hour and a half just to get to the appointments. Half the time the people wouldn't be there.

Five weeks later when my new companion got transferred in, I had made up my mind I wouldn't go down anymore. We had all these names that had been collected from street contacting. He argued, "Kevin, some of these names are going to be golden contacts. We don't know which ones, so we are obligated to go out and see them." I argued that we wouldn't be able to see as many people because of the time spent riding all the way out there. He prevailed because he was senior companion, but I refused to go anywhere. Finally I prevailed on him to go see if there were people living on top of the hill. We got permission from the zone leaders. We rode our bikes through the countryside. All of a sudden we came to an area where there were apartment buildings as far as you could see. There was a university there. Our mission president had told us to go for the young fathers. We found a gold mine because there were young fathers everywhere in the university town.

We soon had appointments to teach in the day and the evening, twenty-five or thirty a week up there on the hill. One of our converts later became branch president and then district president. My companion was able to go home at the peak of his mission. It was the peak of my mission, but I had to stay for another eight months. I was never able to accomplish the same thing again.

When I came back, I had some testimony problems that actually began toward the end of my mission. I was delving into a lot of the mysteries. I would warn anyone against doing that. One of the reasons I married wrong is I didn't have enough spirit to realize I was going in the wrong direction. That marriage was very trying. I found out that she did not marry me because she loved me, but because of what she thought I could provide for her. I wanted to go to the temple and have our marriage sealed, and she didn't want to go. I realized if I stayed in that marriage I would become totally inactive in the church. I had stopped paying my tithing.

You're supposed to meet your wife at BYU and live happily ever after. I was living in unapproved BYU housing, so that was the first mistake. Some of the students referred to the apartment house as Sodom and Gomorrah, but it wasn't that bad. She lived two apartments down from me, and my roommate was dating her. I wish I had never taken the challenge of dating her. We were married in February 1980, and I left her on Memorial Day weekend, 1982.

I made a commitment to serve the Lord when I left that marriage, and I've held to that commitment. I realized that unless I relied totally on the Lord there was no way I could survive. I questioned whether I had done everything wrong with my life—not just the marriage, but my career and everything. The Lord helped me every step of the way with my decisions. I had a lot of repenting to do. Step by step, by reading the scriptures daily and praying, I came out of it. Now things are very good.

Since my patriarchal blessing said something about going into business, I thought I was supposed to major in business. I thought of changing from business to psychology, yet I didn't think I could make money as a psychologist. I worked for a financial planning company and a mortgage company. I quit school to the chagrin of my parents. Then I got my securities license and became a stockbroker. I went to the College of Financial Planning to become a certified financial planner. Now I have my own insurance agency, my own investment business, and my own financial planning company. I believe the Lord has led me.

I get a great deal of satisfaction out of being able to help people with their financial situations. Having someone have enough confidence in me to take my advice is probably my most satisfying reward. I have had to apply the principles that I learned on my mission because a lot of my work involves convincing people to do things. I always strive to put the interest of my clients before my own. Eventually, I hope not to work more than one or two evenings a week so I would have more time to be home and serve in church callings.

My main ambition is to be able to provide for a family. It's very difficult now, with taxes as high as they are, to do things the way the plan was set up. A family is so expensive from birth through college, mission, and marriage. I believe if I put my faith in the Lord, that if he wants to bless me with six children, I will be able to provide for them financially. My goal is to become financially self-sufficient. As long as you're working for someone else you will never have financial security. Even if we have a depression, I will have clients because there will be people who are profiting. I'll talk to them. I have found by paying my tithing at the beginning of the month, the Lord does open up the windows of heaven. I wish I could quote it exactly, but he's basically saying, "Try me, and I'll show you."

I was recently called to be Teachers' Quorum adviser and Varsity Scout coach. I'm also supposed to be first counselor in the Young Men's presidency. I'm still waiting for them to call an assistant for the things I cannot do. To give 100 percent to this calling, I would have to give up one night a week. That would affect my income, and I can't do that.

My greatest concern is what kind of future there will be for my children—not so much economic as the values of society. The schools have changed so much from when I went. The problem is not the schools; it's the erosion of values in the home.

The feminist movement has confused women's minds to where they don't understand themselves. My first wife was too busy wanting to be a man; she didn't understand the importance of being a woman. A lot of women in the church don't understand it. It's a good thing my mother isn't hearing this because she wouldn't keep her peace too well, but I believe that the movement is of the devil. This is what's assaulting the family. When just husbands worked and wives stayed home there were no taxes, or very little. In reality my wife will have to help me in my business. She won't *have* to, but it will free me up to double my income and keep me from having to hire a secretary. I can't say that it is wrong for women to work, but working should not take them away from their most important responsibilities—being a mother and a wife. I think a husband should help at home especially if he's expecting his wife to pitch in and help him. I feel very fortunate to have met Lisa because her values are right in line with what the church teaches. You don't find a lot of women like her today. It's like finding a precious gem.

❀   ❀   ❀

On July 27, Robert and Colleen Pierce and Linda and Anthony Peer drove ninety miles to the Washington, D.C., Temple for the wedding of David Shepherd and Judith Downey. They met David and Judith in one of the temple's sealing rooms. Judith was dressed in her white lace wedding gown and David wore white temple clothing. Since neither David's nor Judith's family belonged to the church, their friends were their only attendants. As David and Judith knelt on opposite sides of the altar, the officiator married them for time and eternity, contingent upon their faithfulness to the covenants they had made in the temple. After the ceremony, he asked them to look into the mirrors placed on opposite sides of the altar. There, they saw themselves reflected endlessly— just like eternity.

David Shepherd, 29

David Shepherd moved to Newark in 1976 from Chesapeake City, Maryland, and was baptized in the Elkton Ward in September 1982. His former wife, Dawn, and her best friend, Cheryl Downward, were baptized at the same time.

Before the missionaries tracted us out, my first wife, Dawn, and I were both searching for something. Especially me. Cheryl Downward was living here because her car wouldn't run. We had another person here that I had met at K-Mart. She didn't have a place to live so Dawn and I were letting her stay here.

Linda was an atheist. She just saw no good in the world and she didn't believe in the Bible or God or anything. We always used to get in lively discussions. She would hit me with some good arguments about where the Bible contradicts itself in places and about how can the different religions all be right? At that time three of us in the house believed in God and the Bible and one person didn't. It was always a heated debate. At times it seemed Linda was so strong in her argument that your soul was injured after talking to her.

We were having discussions with the Jehovah's Witnesses plus I was reading everything I could to prove to Linda that God did exist. Then the Mormon missionaries knocked on the door with a message about Christ in America. For about two weeks I had been noticing two guys riding bikes, dressed sharp; then they knocked on the door. I said, "Sure, come on in." I thought, "This is going to be good." I had always wondered why Christ taught the gospel only to Jerusalem. What about the rest of the world? We went through all the discussions. There was so much to learn and so much made sense. After the fourth or fifth discussion Dawn and I knew that the church was true, but we didn't know how Cheryl and Linda felt. It turned out that Cheryl felt the same way. Linda broke down crying and said that it was what she had been looking for all her life. It built my testimony. It turned an atheist into . . . She believed in God and believed that there was still hope for her.

Cheryl and Dawn and I were all baptized in 1982. It turned out that Linda couldn't be baptized. She went back out to Washington State and was baptized there. Linda was very interested in the premortal existence. She wanted to know if there were male and female spirits there. Her big question was "What if there was a mistake when you came into this world?" She finally told us what had happened. She was a man and she had had the operation to become a woman. She always felt that she should be a woman. She was in Vietnam. I think that's what messed her mind up. She said in Vietnam there was no respect for life. She couldn't see how God could allow all this to exist. She didn't feel right about all the killing she had done.

I don't want Judy to think I still love Dawn, but I couldn't figure out how my wife could just leave me when we were both members of the church. Nobody came over—other than Bob Pierce, my home teacher. There was no program to get us back together. I don't think a couple in our church should go through a divorce or separation without first going to the bishop.

At times I've wanted to stand up in fast and testimony meeting and say, "If there's anybody out there who is having problems in their marriage, go to the bishop. At least give the bishop a chance to call the husband or wife in and say, 'Hey, do you know there's something wrong with your family?'" If you accept the gospel, you know the bishop is a judge in Israel. If Judy and I had a problem, I hope she would go to the bishop if she felt she couldn't talk to me about it—even if the bishop had to come over here and say, "Hey, Dave, your wife's leaving you if you don't straighten up. So straighten up."

It's a great responsibility and a great privilege to be an elder. I gave my first blessing just this past week. Matt Burke called me about 8:30 last Thursday night and asked if I was doing anything. Of course I went right over. I talked to them for a while about the problem. I had prayed for guidance before I went. Matt anointed his wife with the oil, then I sealed the blessing. Hearing about it is one thing, but when you act in the name of Jesus Christ, with his authority— I was overwhelmed by it. I've got this authority from when Bob Pierce conferred the Melchizedek priesthood on me. He gave me his line of authority all the way back to Joseph Smith.

I don't think most of the elders in the church feel the power that men can have to call on Heavenly Father and have him heal and comfort people through them. A lot of elders don't exercise that authority because they don't feel comfortable with it. We need to realize that though we're not perfect, we still have that priesthood. If the elders exercised the priesthood and had the faith in it that they should, I think we would see miracles performed. With some people it's there. Bob Pierce knows the power of the priesthood. Before he gives somebody a blessing, he prays, and he knows through faith that Heavenly Father is going to heal that person.

I think home teaching is probably the most important calling any individual will ever have. From the time we first joined the church to when our marriage split up, we were home taught once—the month before Dawn left. I was appalled when I found out that the ward only did 33 percent home teaching and 27 percent visiting teaching. Distance is a problem, but home teaching is the backbone of the church. As soon as we start doing it the way we should, the church is going to grow a great deal. When Bob Pierce and I go home teaching we run into cases where families might have dropped out of the church if it weren't for their home teachers. There are inactive families who have come back to church and have even borne their testimonies because of home teaching. We always try to prepare a good lesson—not just something from the *Ensign*. Sometimes we make different lessons for the different families, depending on their situations. I'll study the scriptures for hours to find certain scriptures—for example, where it talks about animals having spirits. When our families have a particular problem, I'll pray for inspiration and go through the scriptures until I find the particular scriptures that relate to their problems.

One family was bothered because the church doesn't make a big deal out of Easter or other holidays. That's one reason they're inactive now. Another reason is that the day they got their endowments and were sealed in the temple, it was too rushed and they didn't understand it. Another family heard some gossip one Sunday at church that wasn't true. They took it personally and that affected their church attendance. When a family is telling you about these things— they're crying and it's a big emotional thing—you've got to study the scriptures together to strengthen their testimonies. If one of my families went through a divorce or left the church, I'd feel responsible.

When Dawn left I prayed for an answer as to why this happened. I had a dream, which I wrote down, that I would meet a beautiful woman with flaming red hair. We would get married in the temple and have many children. Though, in my dream, things weren't real smooth, through our faith we worked them out. We were prosperous and happy and I went on to perform various church callings. It wasn't too long after that I met Judy. Receiving my endowments, marrying Judy in the temple set my life on the course that it should be.

I admire Judy's integrity and her honesty. We can talk about anything. On our second date she showed me her patriarchal blessing. That touched me. Not too long after that she gave me her journal and said I could read it. We have an open, honest relationship. We can talk about anything. She supports me. If I have to go home teaching, it's fine with her. She sees the big picture: the blessings you receive and the people you help outweigh the night or two that might be taken up.

My callings in the church have not been that tough. Sometimes new members are given too many callings. They put me in the Primary. I would have loved to have been upstairs associating with the adults. I haven't had a calling that takes a lot of time. Talking to other men, I've learned that people have a lot of guilt because they can't do the wood project and canning projects and home teaching. They can't find the time to do it and be with the family. I think you can, if you plan your time. Bob Pierce finds time to do it all. The bishop is another one who is great in time management.

I feel privileged that I've done some work for the dead in the temple. I guess we were proxies for thirty-five or forty marriages in an hour or so. It was routine in the worldly sense, but on a spiritual level I tried to feel the great joy that those people had when their families were joined together for all time and eternity. If we could have removed the veil and seen what was taking place we would have seen the tears of joy and happiness. Temple work is the one place where mortal men and women can for a split second part the veil. In that split second of doing someone else's endowment the door between the living and the spirit world opens.

I have great aspirations. I look forward to having children—camping with them, playing baseball, soccer, taking them to games, Scout outings, being able to baptize my own children, bless my children, watch them grow. I think it will make my life meaningful. I want my children to go on missions. I want them to get a good education. I want to be able to support and raise a Mormon family the way it should be done.

I always wanted to have a business of my own. I went to the Commercial Electronics Institute planning to get an associate's degree, work some, then get a degree in electrical engineering, but I found that I'm not a nuts and bolts type of person. I like working with people more than I like working with machines. Selling burglar alarms, you have to deal on a one to one basis—go door to door, set up appointments, make presentations, make sales. I like all that and I also like the bigger aspects of business—accounting, financing, Wall Street, mergers. The most satisfying thing is making a sale. When I don't make a sale, but I know the people wanted it, it is very disappointing. Before I did this I worked on the Chrysler assembly line. I didn't like the monotony, the boredom. If I had it to do over, I would not have worked at Chrysler. I would have gone into sales sooner.

I would like to pattern my life after someone like Bill Marriott. Probably everybody wants to be a great businessman. It's not so much the money he's made or the big business or the contributions he's made to the church. In his position he can help a lot of people. I want to be able to help poor children, raise a successful family, and be a beacon of light. When other people saw my success and drew near to me, I would be able to let them know that my belief in God and in the scriptures have given me what I have. I know we aren't supposed to ask for callings, but I would love to be a mission president. To be able to do that, you would have to be in a good financial position.

Judith Shepherd, 27

Judith Shepherd joined the church as a teenager in California. She came to Delaware in 1984 to work as a nanny.

When I was in the eighth grade, my best friend and I liked the Osmonds. I was impressed by what I read about family home evening and eternal marriage in the fan magazines. The next year my best friend's piano teacher invited us to an open house at the church. We made an appointment with the missionaries that night and we were baptized in April. I was on the verge of getting into a lot of trouble. I was experimenting with smoking and drinking and on the verge of getting involved with drugs. I have had a direct blessing from living the Word of Wisdom because I have not had asthma since I was baptized.

My parents respected the church for keeping me out of trouble. They knew I wouldn't be running off with some weird guy for the night or getting drunk. They'd give me rides every now and then to church things, but I had to go to the bishop's counselor and ask for a job to earn money for my first year of seminary. My parents made me promise not to try to convert them when I asked for permission to be baptized.

My junior year in high school I was busy with so many different things. I was taking the teacher development course and I had practices for the dance festival every week, plus I was teaching Primary and going to Mutual. I'd dash in and out. I hardly ever ate dinner. I was MIA Maid president and then Laurel president. I loved all the girls in my class and worked hard to get the inactive girls activated.

My MIA advisers were my confidantes. They were like second mothers and gave me the advice and help that I needed. I saw the way the families I baby-sat for lived the gospel—not only at church but in their homes. Watching the way the children solved disputes, hearing them say, "Is that the way Jesus would want us to do it?" had a very profound impact on me. That's the way I want to raise our family.

The day after high school graduation I started a job as a secretary for a real estate agency, and I went to a junior college for about three months. I went to

Utah when I was nineteen. I wanted to go up to BYU, and I wanted to be where there were more single LDS young adults to associate with. I felt I needed to be there for some reason.

After a couple of years in Utah, I went on my mission. Ever since I joined the church I had wanted to go on a mission. I had planned to put it off for another three or four years, but all of a sudden Heavenly Father said, "I want you to go now." I served in the Connecticut Hartford Mission but I was never in Connecticut. I was in Albany, New York, for thirteen months. I served the last four months in Agawam, Massachusetts. Sometimes it was so cold we couldn't go outside to go tracting. People wouldn't open their doors and let the cold air in, so we'd tract by phone. "Hello, I'm Sister Downey from the Church of Jesus Christ of Latter-day Saints. Have you heard . . ." I had the hardest time picking up that phone. It wasn't that I didn't want to teach the gospel, but I've never wanted to interrupt people with a phone call.

When I came back I worked at Utah Valley Hospital as a central processing technician. I learned to clean, prepare, sterilize, and distribute almost anything reusable in the hospital. The Lord put me in the right place at the right time to get that job and I became very interested in all that they were doing. In June 1984, I decided I wanted a change of scenery. I applied for a position as a nanny because I'd always liked children. Most nannies are between eighteen and twenty-one, but the agency had received a call just the day before from a man in Wilmington who wanted someone a little bit older to take care of his kids who were twelve and thirteen. I prayed about it, and felt good about it, so I decided to come out here.

Things here didn't turn out quite as I had expected. I almost left before Christmas, but we talked and smoothed things out. Then Mr. Knox was nice enough to send me out to San Francisco for a week at Christmas. When I came back I went to a New Year's Eve party at the home of one of the single adults. There was a man there whom I didn't know. We watched each other for the first half of the evening. When we happened to be alone together in the dining room, I introduced myself and David introduced himself. We stuck together the rest of the evening, and he took my phone number and said he was going to call.

He called five weeks later, February 8. He said he'd been busy trying to get his business started up again, but I found out the real reason later. He was scared to death because he knew . . . Two years before I met Dave, I saw in a dream the man that I was going to marry. When he picked me up for our first date, I recognized him as that man. He later told me that he had had a dream the year before about marrying a red-headed woman from the West. He took me out to dinner that Saturday night and then called on Tuesday night to invite me to a family dinner because his uncle was visiting from Florida. After dinner we went to Friendly's together. He kept looking at me and saying, "Oh boy, I'm in trouble." He poured out his heart to me. I said, "Well, I feel the same way." We felt the Spirit there with us and felt that the Lord had guided us to be together.

We didn't decide to get married that night. The next night was his birthday, but he had to go home teaching. I wish I'd had him for a home teacher, all these years. Valentine's night we exchanged cards. He had roommates and I couldn't have any privacy at the Knoxes' house, so we went for a drive. I had brought along my journal and my patriarchal blessing for him to read. We talked quite a bit and he said, "Well, what do you think we should do?"

I looked at him and said, "Well, we ought to get married."

He said, "I know that, but when?"

"Mr. Knox said I can be free at the end of school." I told him that I'd always dreamed of being proposed to on a clear starlit night with a full moon on the beach.

He drove me down to the canal and took me out on a pier down the street from his parents' house. I had never seen the stars brighter. He looked at me and he said, "Judy Downey, will you marry me?" We were married on July 27, 1985, in the Washington, D.C., Temple. It definitely took faith getting engaged to David because I had always said I would not marry anyone unless I had known him for at least two years before we got engaged. When you decide to marry in the temple, it's an eternal decision. I have faith that things will work out for the best because we're meant to be together. The dream I had about meeting the man I was to marry was an answer to a prayer. I had just had a relationship turn sour because the man was deceiving me. I was deeply hurt and I asked one of the most fervent prayers of my entire life.

I want to be a friend to our children. I want them to learn to live the gospel, to serve missions, to serve in the church, to have strong spiritual foundations, to choose as their life's vocation whatever their talents are best suited for. I want to find out what their individual talents are and encourage them in those. Boy, do I want to study! I want to study up on early childhood education because I want to be a good, sensitive, informed mother. I want to be able to give my children as much stimulation as they need.

Recently, I've had to deal with being so far away from my family. I started feeling guilty about having moved so far away. As much as I miss my family, I have always felt I should follow the guidance of the Lord, which is how I came to be out here. My dad was found to have cancer earlier this year and passed away three weeks ago. Not being able to go see him was hard on me. I had written to my mom, but apparently she didn't get the letter because they have to drive twenty-five miles to get the mail. She was upset at me for not writing. My younger sister called me because she didn't think I was taking Dad's illness seriously. I reassured my sister that I know this is where God wants me to be. What his reasons are for keeping me here and why I was not able to go see Dad before he passed away, I don't know. I'm afraid my mom might be mad at me.

Knowing I will see my dad again makes it so much easier. When my dad passed away, I just asked Heavenly Father, "Please help him learn the gospel." Next year I want to go to the temple and have David do the work for my dad.

*   *   *

Saturday, August 31, we attended Robert and Rachel McPherson's wedding reception at the Wilmington Stake Center. Rachel had spent the year working as a nanny in Philadelphia. She and Robert had met at a regional Young Adult activity, became engaged in the spring, and were married in the Manti Temple.

At the back of the hall was a long table with plates of sandwiches and nuts, fruit, and a peach-colored punch in a fountain punch bowl. We ate a little, a bit self-consciously because the next day was fast Sunday and we wondered if we were eating too late in the evening. We spoke with Rob and Rachel, and then as we talked with other guests, Rob ascended the stage and announced the beginning of the program. One of their friends from Philadelphia announced that he would sing "The Lord's Prayer" because it embodied all the qualities necessary for a successful marriage. After singing, the young man, functioning as a disk jockey, announced that Robert and Rachel would dance two dances alone, after which everybody was invited to join in. Later the couple managed to survive the ritual eating of the cake, though Rachel ended up with cake all over her nose, chin, and hands. As we participated in the revelry we realized that this was a fitting end to the Record Year.

Epilogue

Many changes have occurred in the Elkton Ward since the close of the Record Year. A number of members have moved into the ward, and others have moved away. Some members have become inactive and stopped attending church; other members have become active again. Significant demographic changes in Delaware and Maryland have led to explosive growth and to changes in the identity of the ward.

In addition to the institutional changes which have occurred in the Elkton Ward since the close of the Record Year, a number of changes have occurred in the personal lives of the members. Eileen Johnston, Debora Ennis, Elizabeth Stone, Terryl Owen, and Diana Noren had babies during the Record Year. Janean Parsons's baby was born in October 1985. Colleen Pierce, Lisa O'Day, Deborah Johnston, and Eileen Johnston had babies in 1986. Debora Ennis, Judith Shepherd, and Julie Ridge had babies in 1987. Lisa O'Day, Jeanette Robison, Judith Shepherd, Joey Robinson, and Deborah Johnston also had babies in 1988.

Cheryl Downward was married in the Washington Temple in May 1986 to Nelson Sebright, a newly commissioned graduate of West Point whom she had met at a singles activity in Philadelphia the previous December. Tom Young, Jr., was married December 20, 1987, in the Wilmington ward chapel to his high school sweetheart, Sandy Cherkofsky. Michael Wheeler married Monique Van Dam on March 18, 1988, in the Washington Temple. Philip Parkinson returned to New Zealand after his mission and married there four years later.

Angela Martinez and Denise Lanier graduated from the University of Delaware. Angela married and moved to the Washington, D.C., area; Denise moved to California. Dianna Cannon served a mission in Spain and graduated from the University of Utah before beginning law school there. Scott Christensen moved to West Virginia after completing his Ph.D. Serge Bushman transferred to Columbia University after coming home from his mission and was married in 1990.

Although no members of the Elkton Ward died during the Record Year, there were three deaths in the twenty months that followed. Abigail Taber, age 5, died in August 1986 of leukemia; Bonnie Arnold, 65, died of a heart attack in February 1987; and David Russell Shepherd, 6 weeks, died on Easter Sunday 1987 of a congenital heart defect. More recently, Craig Morris died in 1988, Detta Watts in 1989, and Blane Parker and Roy Queenan in 1991.

In writing about the Elkton Ward during one year's time, I had hoped to create a candid snapshot of a Latter-day Saint ward. The task proved to be more difficult than I had anticipated because the subject of the photo simply would not hold still. A few of the changes occurred as converts were baptized and as members moved into or from the ward. I began to appreciate the degree of interconnectedness within the ward as I began trying to organize the chapters of the book. Frequently, the calling a person described when interviewed was not the calling he or she held when it was time to appear in the book. The change in the bishopric that occurred in October resulted in a new Relief Society presidency, ward mission leader, Young Men's presidency, Cub Scout leader, Primary chorister, and Blazer leader, as well as changes in teachers in several organizations. Changing the Young Women's presidency in December led to a change in the Primary presidency, among other changes.

Members of the Elkton Ward, and of the LDS Church, are accustomed to living and functioning in the middle of this kind of domino effect; it is a rare Sunday that does not involve one or more release or call to a new position. By the Record Year the Elkton Ward had grown large enough that members did not have to fill three or four callings apiece, but not so large that there was a pool of unemployed members who could fill vacancies. There are two practices that contribute to this situation. First of all, members are not called to positions for a predetermined term of office, but indefinitely, that is, until they are needed in another organization. Second, although the Elkton Ward enjoyed explosive growth after 1985, it was divided and subdivided in order to keep from having more active members than available callings.

After the close of the Record Year, the Elkton Ward grew rapidly. Attendance at sacrament meeting between September 1, 1985, and September 1, 1986, grew from an average of 180 to 240 per Sunday. The chapel became so crowded that one Sunday when I returned after taking my youngest child out of the meeting I found a stranger sitting in my place. Most of this growth was the result of an influx of members from other areas. The first wave was of members from other wards in the Wilmington Stake who bought homes in the new developments that were erected south of Newark. During this year ten families, fifty-two individuals, moved to the Elkton Ward from other wards in the stake. Four Elkton Ward families, the Peers, Owens, Quinns, and Bezerras, and Scott Christensen moved to other wards within the stake soon after the close of the Record Year.

The ward also grew as church members moved to booming New Castle County from other parts of the country. Corporate transfers and new faculty members at the University of Delaware accounted for some of these, but others came independently in search of better economic opportunities or to live nearer to their families. Nine families, forty-eight individuals, were moved to Delaware by Du Pont, Hercules, American Stores, Texaco, and other companies. Three faculty members and five graduate students came to the university. People moved from the Elkton Ward for similar reasons, but in much smaller numbers. The Adams and Hipps families were transferred; John and Diana Noren finished school and moved to North Carolina; Kelly Hindley and Diana Cannon returned home; Robert and Rachel McPherson went to Ricks College; and the Lund family moved to upstate New York to enter a family business. By the end of 1991 the Pierce family had moved to Florida as had Karel Vander-Heyden. Richard and Claudia Bushman had moved to New York City, and Anne Mace and her husband had moved to Hagerstown, Maryland.

As the Elkton Ward grew, every available space was utilized for classrooms. A few Primary and Sunday school classes were divided, but the Sunbeam class of three-year-olds grew to nineteen because no more classrooms were available. Many of the incoming families had teenage children, and some of the youth classes tripled in size. The Newark early morning seminary class for high school students, which had shrunk to one student during the Record Year, had twelve members in 1986 and was divided into two large classes by 1987. At church the deacons began meeting in the basement of the little house and the high priests took over the chapel while the elders went to a smaller room. In the summer of 1987 it became necessary to find more seating for sacrament meeting. The partitions between the choir loft and the chapel were removed each week for sacrament meeting and replaced for Sunday school.

On January 26, 1986, five months after the close of the Record Year, Richard Bushman was released and Douglass Taber was sustained as bishop of the Elkton Ward. Gary Johnston, who had been one of Bishop Bushman's counselors, and Greg Bramwell, who had moved into the ward four months earlier, were called as counselors in the bishopric.

One of Bishop Taber's first official acts was to read in sacrament meeting a letter he had received from the First Presidency of the church. It stated that the policy that kept Anne Mace, Detta Watts, and other women from going to the temple had been changed. The former policy had allowed men, but not women, who were married to nonmembers of the church to receive their temple endowments. The new policy stated that men or women who were married to nonmembers could be endowed, provided that their spouses freely consented to it. Anne Mace, Detta Watts, and Lynne Whitney went to the temple and received their endowments.

With the growth in membership, the ward leaders decided that the funds needed for ward budget and the stake building fund assessment could be provided by members' budget donations. During 1986 and 1987 there were no fund-raising projects; the Easter egg project, priesthood wood-cutting project, and Relief Society dinners were abandoned. During 1989 and 1990 the general church leadership changed the way in which ward expenses were to be paid for. Members were asked to take turns cleaning the meetinghouses, and each ward received an allowance from general church funds to pay for other ward expenses. That is, wards were no longer allowed to raise funds for the ward budget. This cut the funds available to many wards, raised them for others, but had little impact on the level of spending in the Elkton Ward.

The growth in membership and the construction of a new church building in Newark, Delaware, led to the dispersion of the Elkton Ward members among four units, two wards and two branches. On January 10, 1988, the stake president, Vernon Rice, visited the Elkton Ward and announced that the portion of the ward south of the Chesapeake and Delaware Canal would be joined with the north part of the Dover Ward to create the Smyrna Branch. He read the names of seventy-five Elkton Ward members whose memberships would be transferred to the Smyrna Branch. It was the first time since the beginning of the Elkton Branch that the boundaries had been reduced. The Crowe, McVicker, and Pierce families as well as six families who had moved into the Townsend area during the previous two years would provide a nucleus for the new branch. Kenneth McVicker was named as branch president, and the Smyrna Branch began meeting the following Sunday in the Smyrna High School. Attendance at the branch's sacrament meeting grew from seventy-five to ninety-four by the end of its first month. The Smyrna Branch continued to meet in the high school until a meetinghouse was completed in June 1991.

Land for a new building for the Elkton Ward was purchased in late 1986 in the southwestern corner of Newark, Delaware. Construction of a standard Cody Plan stake center, with room for three wards and stake offices, began in July 1988. On November 12, 1989, stake conference was held in the new stake center, and the Elkton Ward began meeting in its new quarters. On November 26, the name of the ward was changed to the Newark Ward. The building in Elkton was put up for sale.

On March 4, 1990, at a joint meeting of the Newark and Wilmington West wards, a third ward was formed—the Christiana Ward. The Burke, Callery, Harding, Lanier, Parker, Robinson, and Wheeler families, Gene Dean, Imogene Meekins, and Thelma Roberts were among those who became members of this ward, and Thomas Robinson was called as a counselor to its new bishop. On the same day Douglass Taber was released as bishop of the Newark Ward and James Melby, who had moved to Delaware from Utah in 1987, was called as bishop. The Christiana Ward held its meetings in the morning and the Newark Ward used the building in the afternoon.

On November 29, 1991, the Newark Ward was again divided when the Rising Sun Branch was organized. The new branch's boundaries include all of Cecil

County north of the Chesapeake and Delaware Canal and west of the town of Elkton. It meets in the Cecil Community College in North East, Maryland. Lynne Whitney, Carol Beatty, and Elizabeth Stone and their children, Henry Tingey, Sharon Mlodoch, and the Shepherd and Stroup families were included in the new branch. During the meeting at which the branch was created, President Vernon Rice asked members of the new branch presidency to bear their testimonies. He also asked Lynne Whitney, who had been a founding member of the sacrament meeting group that met in Cloyd Mullins's living room and had continued as a mainstay of the branch and ward to speak. She left her place from behind the organ, walked to the pulpit, and began, "I have often said that everyone should have the experience of living in a branch at least once. I'm fortunate that I get to do it twice." Lynne became the first Relief Society president of the Rising Sun Branch and visited all the women of the branch during the University of Delaware's Christmas break.

The practice of keeping wards small by dividing them has several effects on the Mormon community. Members who have developed close relationships as a result of working together in church organizations frequently find themselves working closely with other members in new organizations. Although members often develop a strong sense of personal identification with their callings, those callings may be changed at any time. Functioning in the organization of the church thus requires the members to subjugate their loyalty to a particular calling or organization to loyalty to the ward or branch. Similarly, loyalty to the particular ward or branch is less important than loyalty to the church as a whole.

Serving in a variety of callings gives members a breadth of experience. A woman might be presiding over the Relief Society one month and teaching children to sing the next. Because positions may be vacant for a period of time, members who have a calling are often asked to substitute in unfilled callings for a short time. Not only does this help members become more competent at a variety of tasks but it fosters a higher degree of cooperation among the various ward organizations.

While the feelings of loyalty and cooperation fostered by keeping wards small probably benefit the ward, this practice requires the bishopric to spend a great deal of its time and energy in trying to keep the organizations staffed. Some teenagers stop attending when a well-liked teacher is called to a new position or lose their momentum in Scouts or other goal-setting programs.

The Record Year project was well received by the members of the Elkton Ward. Members were glad to share their stories and have them recorded. Those who conducted interviews or who transcribed interviews felt that we became emotionally and spiritually closer to other members of the ward as a result. Probably because of its experience as a small branch on the fringes of the Wilmington Stake, the Elkton Ward had a strong sense of identity as a community prior to the start of the Record Year. It is difficult to say whether the experience of the Record Year changed the ward. In some respects, the Record Year was just one of many activities, like the Easter egg project, in which ward members worked together. It did seem to enhance the feelings of identity and pride as a special ward that already existed.

On a personal level, participating in the Record Year brought me into an intimate relationship with almost every member of the ward. As it turned out, the events that followed the Record Year would probably have had a similar result. My husband's calling as bishop brought us into the center of ward life. The many acts of service the ward members performed for our family before and after the death of our daughter in 1986 also strengthened our ties to the other members.

Glossary

Aaronic priesthood. The division of priesthood that has the responsibility for
ordinances such as baptism and the sacrament. The offices in this priesthood are deacon, teacher, priest, and bishop.

Administer to the sick. A priesthood ordinance in two parts for the healing and
comfort of the sick. The recipient's head is first anointed with a few drops
of consecrated olive oil. The blessing is sealed by the laying on of hands,
and the elder gives words of comfort as he feels inspired to do so.

Adversary. Satan or the devil.

Apostle. An office in the Melchizedek priesthood with the responsibilities of
governing the church as a whole and of serving as witnesses of Jesus
Christ. The Quorum of Twelve Apostles selects and ordains the president
of the church from among their number.

Baptism for the dead. Latter-day Saint doctrine teaches that everyone who lived
to the age of eight must be baptized. The ordinance is performed by proxy
in the temple for deceased persons who were not baptized.

Beehive. Member of the class for twelve- and thirteen-year-old girls in the Young
Women's organization

Bishop. The presiding authority of a ward. The office of bishop is the highest
office in the Aaronic priesthood and must be held either by a direct de-
scendent of Aaron or by a high priest in the Melchizedek priesthood. Once
a man has been ordained a bishop he continues to hold that priesthood
office although his term as bishop of a ward lasts for a limited number
of years.

Bishopric. The bishop and his two counselors.

Bishop's storehouse. A cannery and warehouse that provides food and other
commodities to members in need. Distribution is authorized by the bishop
and Relief Society president of the ward.

Blazer. Primary class for eleven-year-old boys. It combines religious lessons on
Sunday with Boy Scout activities, which are held during the week.

Book of Mormon. A book of scripture recorded on golden plates by some of the ancient inhabitants of the Americas and translated "by the gift and power of God" by Joseph Smith.

Born in the covenant. Children born to parents who were married or sealed in the temple are said to born in the covenant and are automatically sealed to their parents.

Branch. A small congregation that does not have enough members to be a ward. The presiding officer is a branch president.

BYU. Brigham Young University is the church-owned university in Provo, Utah.

Calling. A position of responsibility in the church organization. Members are called or asked by the bishop or stake president to accept callings in the church.

Celestial kingdom. The highest of the three degrees of glory is known as the celestial kingdom. Those who will inhabit it will live in the presence of God and Jesus Christ.

Chorister. Person who directs the singing in a church meeting.

Confirmation. Melchizedek priesthood ordinance performed immediately after baptism by the laying on of hands. Members are confirmed as members of the church and commanded to receive the Holy Ghost.

Consolidated schedule. A schedule adopted churchwide in 1980. Sacrament meeting, Sunday school, and priesthood meeting, as well as meetings that formerly were held during the week, such as Relief Society, Primary, and Young Women's classes, take place during one three-hour block of time each Sunday.

Cultural hall. A large hall in most LDS buildings that includes a basketball court and a stage for plays or shows. The Elkton Ward does not have a cultural hall, but ward members often refer to the basement room in which the Primary meets and where ward dinners and activities are held as the cultural hall.

Deacon. An office in the Aaronic priesthood.

Degrees of glory. Belief that after the resurrection and judgment individuals will be assigned to one of three degrees of glory: celestial, terrestrial, or telestial.

Doctrine and Covenants. A book of scripture comprised of revelations, most received by Joseph Smith, containing instructions for organizing the Church of Jesus Christ of Latter-day Saints, instructions to individuals, and explanations of doctrines of the church.

Elder. Office in the Melchizedek priesthood. Men must be ordained elders to serve as missionaries, marry in the temple, and give priesthood blessings, such as confirmation, blessing babies, or administering to the sick.

Endowment. Temple ordinance in which members receive instruction and make covenants. It is performed by proxy for deceased individuals.

Ensign. Official church magazine.

Ephraim. Son of Joseph of Egypt who received the birthright from his grandfather Jacob or Israel. The church teaches that the mission of the house of Ephraim is to prepare the earth for the Second Coming of Christ.

Eternal marriage. The belief that marriage will continue throughout eternity for couples who are sealed in the temple and keep the commandments throughout their lives.

Eternal progression. Belief that the purpose of life is to become like God and that progression toward this end continues after death.

Excommunication. Procedure by which membership in the church is revoked. This may occur as a result of action by a bishop's court or a high council court. Reasons for an action of excommunication include apostasy, adultery, particularly when the member was married in the temple or is a church leader, embezzlement of church funds, or conviction of a felony.

Family home evening. Weekly meeting that is supposed to be held by each family. The meetings often include a lesson, a family activity, or a family business meeting.

Fast offering. A contribution made on the first Sunday of each month by members that equals at least the value of two meals. Fast offering funds are used by the bishop to help needy members of the ward.

Follow the brethren. Follow the advice of the general church authorities.

Food storage. Members are encouraged to store enough food to sustain their family for one year. They are also encouraged to store clothing and, if possible, fuel.

Foreordained. Belief that a particular responsiblity to be fulfilled during mortal life was given to an individual during the preexistence.

Free agency. Belief that humans have the power to choose between good and evil and that God cannot abrogate that right.

Friend. Official church magazine for children.

Garments or temple garments. Undergarments worn by members of the church who have been endowed in the temple. The garments serve as an everyday reminder of the teachings of the temple and the covenants made there.

General authorities. Includes the president of the church and his two counselors, the twelve members of the Quorum of the Twelve Apostles, members of the First Quorum of Seventy, and the presiding bishopric. These men have responsibility for governing the church as a whole.

Golden couple or golden contact. Missionary slang for individuals who seem likely to be converted to the church and become strong members.

Golden questions. Questions members are encouraged to ask in order to find people who would be willing to be taught by the missionaries. They are "What do you know about the Mormon church?" and "Would you like to know more?"

Gospel. The teachings and covenants of the church. Joseph Smith is said to have "restored the gospel" to the earth.

Gospel doctrine class. The Sunday school class for adult members of the church.

High council. Governing body of a stake composed of twelve high priests who live within the stake.

High priest. Office in the Melchizedek priesthood. The responsibility of this office is to preside over wards or stakes. The bishop and his two counselors, members of the high council, and the stake president and his two counselors are high priests.

Hill Cumorah pageant. Pageant held annually at the Hill Cumorah near Palmyra, New York, which dramatizes events and the message of the Book of Mormon. Joseph Smith was shown by the Angel Moroni where the plates were buried in the Hill Cumorah.

Homemaking meeting. Activity held once a month by the Relief Society during which women share homemaking skills and socialize.

Home teaching. Program in which each household is visited once a month by two men, one of whom holds the Melchizedek priesthood.

Inactive. Member who does not attend church.

Iron rod. In the Book of Mormon the prophets Lehi and Nephi saw a vision in which holding to the iron rod, interpreted as the word of God, prevented people from being deceived by the temptations of the world and the devil.

Lamanite. One of two main groups of people in the Book of Mormon. Native Americans are believed to be the descendents of the Lamanites.

Laurel. Member of the class for sixteen- and seventeen-year-old girls in the Young Women's organization.

Magnify your calling. Taken to mean that people called to a position in the church should work as hard as they can and accomplish as much as possible in that calling.

Melchizedek priesthood. One of two divisions of the church's priesthood. Offices in this priesthood include elder, seventy, high priest, and apostle. A man must be ordained to this priesthood in order to serve a mission, go to the temple, confer the Holy Ghost, or bestow a priesthood blessing.

Mia Maid. Member of the class for fourteen- and fifteen-year-old girls in the Young Women's organization.

Mission. The period of time, two years for men and eighteen months for women, during which an individual devotes all his or her time to church service. Most missionaries are called to proselytyze, but some serve as health or social welfare missionaries in underdeveloped countries.

Mission field. An area where missionaries are sent to preach the gospel. It formerly referred to areas outside of Utah where there were relatively few members of the church, but missionaries are now sent to Utah from other areas of the church.

Mission president. Called for a term of three years to preside over missionary work in any of the church's missions.

Mormon. The ancient American prophet who compiled most of the Book of Mormon on the golden plates.

Moroni, also the Angel Moroni. The son of Mormon, Moroni was the last Book of Mormon prophet to write on the golden plates and, as a resurrected being, he delivered them to Joseph Smith.

Mutual. Short for Mutual Improvement Association (also known as MIA). This activity program held on weeknights for twelve- to eighteen-year-olds formerly included lessons as well as social, sports, and cultural activities. It now refers to only the week-night activities since class meetings are held on Sundays as part of the consolidated schedule.

New Era. Official church magazine for teenagers.

Ordination. Men are ordained to offices in the priesthood, such as deacon, teacher, priest, elder, seventy, high priest, or bishop by the laying on of hands.

Part-member family. A family in which either the husband or wife is not a member of the church.

Patriarch. A priesthood office that involves giving blessings of inspiration to church members. Also refers to the father's role as patriarch or spiritual leader of the family.

Patriarchal blessing. Blessing given to a member of the church by a patriarch. This blessing reveals to which of the twelve tribes of Israel the individual belongs and may give counsel and advice about the purpose of his or her life.

Pearl of Great Price. One of the four books of scripture. It contains portions of scriptures written by Moses and Abraham as restored by Joseph Smith, Joseph Smith's account of his calling as a prophet, and an inspired revision made by Joseph Smith of part of the Book of Matthew.

PEC. Priesthood Executive Committee, which meets weekly to discuss the needs of the ward. The committee includes the bishopric as well as the leaders of each of the Melchizedek priesthood quorums and the Young Men's president.

Plan of salvation. Summary description of Latter-day Saint beliefs about preexistence, purpose of mortal life, and opportunity for exaltation and eternal life with God after death.

Polygamy, or plural marriage. Former church practice of allowing men to marry two or more wives. Today, polygamy or sympathy with polygamists is grounds for excommunication from the church.

Preexistence. Belief that individuals lived with God prior to birth.

Priest. An office in the Aaronic priesthood.

Priesthood. The governing authority of the church. Males may be ordained to the Aaronic priesthood at the age of twelve. Adult men may be ordained to the Melchizedek priesthood.

Priesthood blessing. A blessing given by the laying on of hands by someone ordained to the Melchizedek priesthood. Such blessings include giving a name and a blessing to babies (christening), confirmation, setting apart for callings, administration to the sick, and blessings for comfort and counsel.

Priesthood revelation. Refers to the revelation received by church president Spencer W. Kimball in 1978 that all men could be ordained to the priesthood, depending only on their personal worthiness. The former church policy had barred individuals of African descent from being ordained to the priesthood or receiving the ordinances of the temple.

Primary. The organization for children aged three through eleven. Provides a weekly meeting and occasional activities.

Prophet. One who speaks for God. Members believe that the president of the church is a prophet who was called of God to lead the church.

Quorum. All those who are ordained to a particular office in the ward, e.g., Deacons' Quorum, Elders' Quorum.

Relief Society. Women's organization organized March 17, 1842, by Joseph Smith after "the manner of the priesthood." The Relief Society carries out the visiting teaching program and organizes women to give service to families in need. The Relief Society program includes educational, social, and welfare activities.

Sacrament. Ordinance in which church members partake of bread and water in remembrance of the Atonement of Jesus Christ.

Sacrament meeting. The weekly worship service. It includes the sacrament service, in which members partake of bread and water in remembrance of Jesus Christ.

Sealing. Ordinance by which covenants, such as marriage, are made binding in heaven as well as on Earth. Couples can be sealed in a temple at the time of marriage or later. Children whose parents were not originally married in the temple can be sealed to their parents after the parents are sealed to each other. The ordinance is also performed for deceased persons by proxies.

Seminary. Religion class for high school students. When possible this is held daily in the morning before school. When travel makes this impossible, students may do the seminary lessons at home and attend class once a week. The course of study includes one year's study each of the Old Testament, the New Testament, the Book of Mormon, and the Doctrine and Covenants and church history.

Set apart. A priesthood blessing given to individuals who have been called to serve in positions in the church. The blessing authorizes them to act in the calling and usually contains words of counsel.

Seventy. Office in the Melchizedek priesthood. The particular responsibility of seventies is missionary work. Missionaries who serve in the stake are usually seventies.

Single Adults. Group that organizes social and other activities for members of the church who are not married.

Smith, Joseph. The founder and first president of the church.

Stake. An ecclesiastical and administrative unit of the church comprised of a several wards and branches, usually between six and twelve. The presiding officer of the stake is a stake president.

Sustain. Members of the church are asked to ratify decisions made by the ward bishopric or stake presidency by raising their hands to show that they will support those decisions. These decisions include the appointing of other members to positions of responsibility and decisions about church finances.

Teacher. An office in the Aaronic priesthood.

Temple. Building where the highest ordinances of the Melchizedek priesthood are performed. These include marriage for time and eternity and the sealing of children to parents for eternity. These ordinances and baptisms are also performed for deceased persons by proxy in the temples. Members must have a temple recommend in order to enter the temple.

Temple marriage. Marriages performed in a temple for time and eternity.

Temple recommend. Issued by the bishop and also signed by the stake president or one of his counselors, the recommend allows members to enter any of the temples. Before receiving a recommend, members must affirm that they pay tithing, observe the Word of Wisdom, and keep the other commandments of the church.

Testimony. Statement of conviction that a teaching or doctrine of the church is true or statement that an individual has received a witness from the Holy Ghost that a teaching or doctrine is true.

Tithing. Members are expected to pay 10 percent of their gross income to the church as tithing. The money is sent by the bishop to church headquarters in Salt Lake City. Most tithing funds are used to build church meetinghouses throughout the world.

Tracting. Missionary activity in which missionaries knock on the doors of homes and try to interest people in learning about the church.

Visiting teaching. Program in which each female member of the church is visited once a month by one or two other women.

Ward. A congregation of usually four hundred to eight hundred members. The membership of a ward is determined by geographic boundaries. The presiding officer of a ward is a bishop.

Welfare plan. System of church welfare. Commodities are stored in a system of bishop's storehouses to be distributed to members in need of food. Many stakes own farms or other production facilities, such as canneries, where the commodities are produced or processed. Church members are discouraged from accepting government welfare.

Word of Wisdom. Found in section 89 of the Doctrine and Covenants, this revelation to Joseph Smith advises church members to abstain from alcohol, tobacco, and "hot drinks," meaning coffee and tea. It also advises them to eat meat sparingly. Observance of the Word of Wisdom was later accepted as a commandment by church members.

Young, Brigham. After the death of Joseph Smith, Brigham Young led the church first as president of the Quorum of Twelve Apostles, then as president of the church.

Young Men. The organization for boys aged twelve to seventeen that supervises midweek activities for boys. The presidency of the Young Men's organization often serve as advisers to the Deacons', Teachers', and Priests' quorums.

Young Women. The organization for girls aged twelve to seventeen provides weekly lessons on Sundays, midweek activities, sports, and camping programs.

Zion. The city that was taken up into heaven because of the righteousness of the people. The church teaches that Zion will be established in the last days and that one of the missions of the church is to develop a righteous people who will build Zion.

Index

Note: Oral histories are identified by page numbers in boldface.